WES PENRE PRODL

Synthetic Super Intelligence and the Transmutation of Humankind

A Roadmap to the Singularity and Beyond

By Wes Penre

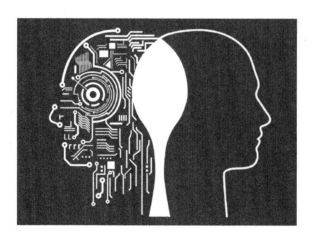

A critical study guide in Artificial Intelligence and the Singularity Movement.

i

Synthetic Super Intelligence and the Transmutation of Humankind
A Roadmap to the Singularity and Beyond

[First edition, July 2016]

Acknowledgements

I would like to thank a number of people who have assisted me in different ways while I've been researching and writing this book.

First, I want to thank my family for the love and patience they have showed me when I spent these early morning hours, and sometimes many hours on the weekends, researching and writing. Without their support I would not have been able to finish this book.

A person I want to thank in particular is writer, researcher, radio host, and musician, Robert Stanley (http://unicusmagazine.com), who has been a real trooper. Throughout the entire researching and writing process, he has tirelessly sent me great links to websites, and many of them I have used as references in this book. Robert and I have also shared information and ideas with each other, something that has been both stimulating and helpful. He has been a true inspiration throughout the process.

In addition, I want to thank three persons who have assisted me over the years by sending me relevant websites and videos on the subjects of this specific book and the *Wes Penre Papers*. They have also provided me with important information on other matters of interest. Thus, I want to thank, in no specific order, Sabreena Topham, Gina Laudy, and Carol Cassis—a big hug to all the three of you.

I can't possibly mention every person who has contributed over the years—you are too many to mention, but you know who you are. Rest assured that I am very grateful for your willingness to assist. Helping others is the true nature of humankind, and many people have showed, with great passion and compassion that this is true.

Last but not the least, I want to thank Professor Bob Stannard, who has spent endless hours editing chapter after chapter of this book, as well as having edited much of my previous work.

--Wes Penre, July 25, 2016

Contents

Prologue:
Is Artificial Intelligence a Concern?

DIFFERENT TERMS USED IN THIS BOOK

B EFORE WE BEGIN THE REAL discussions, it's a good idea to get a general concept of what we will be discussing in this e-book.

First, I need to explain who is behind Artificial Intelligence. You are probably checking this book out because you have read about this subject somewhere else and are curious to know more or because you already know a thing or two about it and you're curious to see if there might be something more to learn from this book. You might also belong to a third category of readers: those who are familiar with my previous material. If you are in this third category, you will have no problems with the terms and the topics I'll be discussing here.

If you are fairly new to this, you might not know that Artificial Intelligence (AI) has extraterrestrial origins. This needs to be discussed in detail and understood or it will be impossible to comprehend the *real* objectives behind the AI Movement. In addition, and preferably before you read this book, I would suggest that you review my earlier work, *The Wes Penre Papers—The Multiverse Series* (WPP), if you haven't done so already, because that series of papers discussed, at length, the extraterrestrial concerns we are facing here on Earth. In the WPP, I named the most prominent and controlling group of ETs the *Alien Invader Force (AIF)*;[1] a group

---

[1] For more information about the AIF, see "The Wes Penre Papers—the Multiverse Series," "The Fourth Level of Learning" through "The Fifth Level of Learning." This is an alien group that invaded Earth about 450,000

that can be directly compared with Lucifer and the *Fallen Angels* of the Bible and those of the Urantia Book. In this book, we will discuss the AIF and the problems it causes.

To avoid confusion, I'd like to list the terms that I will use for humans and ETs working together behind the scenes *against* our freedom and our sovereignty as spiritual beings. By listing these terms here, you can go back to see who is whom and what is what, when needed. However, after some further reading, it will soon become quite obvious. All these terms will always begin with a capital letter, except for the term in Number 4 below.

These are the terms I will use:

1) **ETs who Run the Show:** The *Alien Invader Force (AIF)*; the *Overlords*; the *Cosmic Outlaws*; the *Outlaws*, the *gods (with a small "g")*, the *Fallen Angels,* and the *Warlords.* Their cosmic military force I will call *Lucifer's Legions.* I sometimes also refer to them as the *Anunnaki* because this is the most common name for this ET group for those who have read Zecharia Sitchin and similar works by other authors and researchers.

2) **ET/Human Hybrids of the First Generation—the Power *Above* the Rothschild's , the Rockefellers, and the Bush's, etc.:** The *Administrators (for the gods)*; the *Controllers,* and the *Emissaries (of the gods).*

3) **The International Bankers, CEOs of Industry and Trade, and top Politicians (e.g. the Rothschild's, the Rockefellers, the Bush's, etc.:** The *Minions* (*note:* spelled with a capital "M"). These people are often as human as you and I, but could be ET hybrids as well.

4) **Regular Corrupt Politicians and Others "Not in the Know" or "Partially in the Know:"** the minions (*note:* spelled with a small "m"); puppets. These people are almost always human. Even some heads of the CIA fall into this category, being kept totally in the dark about the real agendas.

Interestingly enough, the word *controllers* includes both the

---

years ago and created hybrids out of an existing human race in order to use them as slaves. We are still under this alien control.

word "con," which means "to swindle [a victim] by first winning his or her confidence; dupe,"[2] and the word *troll*, which could denote someone who *infiltrates*—a typical example is so-called *trolls* infiltrating forums and comment sections on the Internet.

The Emissaries have managed to misinform and disinform us on a number of different subjects, and the truth is often more or less the opposite from what we've learned in grade school, college, and universities. This makes it hard to let go of old programming, beliefs, and paradigms that we are holding onto, and often we are not even consciously aware that we are holding onto old beliefs that don't serve us well. The test is to let go of them all, one by one, until we shed them almost automatically, such as peeling an onion, and our real, free-thinking self comes to the surface. When we reach this state, we become quite difficult to manipulate.

HOW REFERENCES ARE USED IN THIS BOOK

THE MAJORITY OF REFERENCES in this book come directly from mainstream media or from the horse's mouth. What can't be backed up by existing sources will be my own speculations, conclusions, and knowledge that I might have gained from anonymous sources. As far as my anonymous sources are concerned, they need to be protected, but when I use them on occasions where the information can't be solidly backed up, you can make your own decisions, or use the information as food for thought. The majority of information that I've received from anonymous sources not only fits into the picture but also can usually be backed up by checking ancient documents and cuneiform, which I did in the WPP. Hence, for those who want more solid references on certain issues that are not clearly referenced here, I also want to refer back to the WPP and ancient texts.

Interestingly enough, the existing sources and references are mainly from 2015-2016. This shows how rapidly the AI Movement has progressed over a short time period![3] It will be obvious even for

---

[1] "The Free Dictionary by Farley," http://www.thefreedictionary.com/con
[3] This Prologue was written in January 2016.

the skeptic that the first part of the Machine Kingdom is already here, *and we are living in the midst of it!*

The problem with using mainstream media on the Internet as references is that after a while, some of the online newspapers and news broadcasts take their information off the Internet, or after a few weeks they just make the first few paragraphs of their articles available online. If the reader wants to know more, he or she needs to subscribe. If you find such articles or videos in the footnotes or in the reference section at the end of the book, you can do a simple Google search *on the same title as the original article in the footnote or reference section*, and there will be a good chance that someone else has copied the article to a website, where it then can be studied.

HOW TO USE DISCERNMENT

BECAUSE OF THE WEALTH OF DATA and information flooding the Internet, it can be extremely difficult to discern truth from fiction. What is definitely true, however, is that we can't use only our intellect, believing that this is enough. At times, even more important than the left-brain intellect is *intuition* and what I sometimes call *inner discernment*. When evaluating data and information, most people only use their logical/analytical mind and forget that they need to add intuition and body reactions into the equation. Only if we do all of this and become good at it and sensitive enough to it can we more easily discern good information from disinformation. The disinformation campaigns these days are so cleverly done that using our intellect is definitely not enough. This is why some highly intelligent people still can't see beyond what's in front of their eyes—they evaluate data *only* from a physical perspective; if it can't be proven with the five senses, it's not valid. These people miss out on the entire metaphysical spectrum.

However, as a rule of thumb, be critical of everything you hear and read from mainstream society and media. Then be even more critical of anyone who is *exposing* mainstream society and media. Always look for potential hidden agendas, such as gaining trust amongst alternative researchers and truth-seekers, only to later add disinformation to the soup. Finally, be most critical of yourself and do not believe something because you want to believe. Look for motives in everything. When these criteria are met, there might be some new insights to gain.

There is nothing wrong with gathering information from mainstream media, but we need to be able to use discernment and always look for hidden motives, messages, and manipulation—it's almost always there, if we really look. We can also, as I have done in this book, use mainstream media to *expose* the media. Always be aware, however, that mainstream media is never independent and in public service; they are *always* running someone else's errands, and much of the news we hear is encoded and only understood to its full extent by Insiders. These Insiders are often using media to communicate hidden messages.

WHAT IS INTUITION?

SOME SCHOOLS OF THOUGHT teach that you are a soul/spirit in a body, and that's all there is to it. The soul, supposedly, is the part of you who thinks, solves problems, and is in charge of things in your own universe. After you're dead, the soul moves on, and only the body succumbs. Because the body is mortal, it's not of any greater significance—at least this is what we are taught.

To believe this is a mistake, however. Your body is phenomenal in more than a few ways. You can talk to your body, you can think to, and with, your body, and you can give your body compliments and love. If you do so, you're going to have a wonderful relationship with it, and you and your body will work together to learn about new things and to raise your vibrations into higher states of consciousness. Look yourself in the mirror and, regardless what your body looks like according to the norm, tell it that you love it and that it is a wonderful companion. If you've never done this before and continue doing this for a while, your body will not only become healthier, but it will also connect with you on an emotional level. There's also going to be a telepathic communication between the two of you (if you train yourself to be sensitive and open enough to recognize it).

This is going to help you in your discernment when it comes to deciding what is real and what is not; you will be able to better distinguish between what will work for you in the long run and what will not. For example, if you read something that sounds as if it could be true, and then you read something else on the same subject that is very different from the former but also sounds true, you'll probably get confused. Someone is apparently seeding disinformation or is misinformed, or perhaps both sources are. Therefore, how can you discern what is what, when in theory both pieces of information could potentially be true? This is when you consult your body. You can use the following formula; *think, feel, and act*. First, you are evidently going to *think* about what you're reading, watching, and hearing. The feeling part has to do with the body, which is also a connection with your *inner self*; a gateway to the different inner dimensions. In the WPP, I called these dimensions the *VOID* or the *KHAA*.[4] When you turn inward, you will discover where the real Multiverse is located. The society calls a person who does this *introverted* and often considers this to be a weakness or even brands it *escapism*. However, many turn inward because they feel that this is a more natural state of existence than having to follow the strict norms; most of them having in common that we are not supposed to look inside, but instead focus on what is outside, i.e. in the *physical realm*.

The body is like an intermediary between your spiritual world and the third dimensional (3-D) personality. If you acknowledge your body as something more than a piece of meat and bones, you will get a response when you ask or tell it something. Sometimes you might get an instant reaction from your body, and other times it will take a while; you just need to be patient. Often, it will take some practice to build a good relationship with your body, but once it is established, it will be very rewarding.

Your body is also your antenna to other dimensions. It filters what comes in, and when a good relationship is established, after you've learned to trust your body instead of fearing it, it will give

---

[4] The word KHAA is an Orion term, denoting an "outbreath." In the Orion version of the creation of this universe, the Creatrix—the Great Dragon—is said to have breathed out in order to create the Universe.

you good information.

The more we pay attention to our inner selves, the faster we will be able to break down the prison walls and let our *fire*[5] free. In the spiritual world, our bodies are part of the ticket to get there, contrary to what many claim.

You can, by now, probably see how important the body is for us in order to connect with the Spirit Universe whence we came from.

In summary, love your body unconditionally and start listening to it—it's cleverer than you and I with our egos getting in the way. You can't reach above a certain state of consciousness on this planet unless you use the psychic abilities that exist inside of you; inside your body. "Go inside for answers" is an excellent idiom.[6]

FIRE, AVATAR, AND OUR PLACE IN THE UNIVERSE

ALTHOUGH THERE ARE BEINGS living on planets throughout the Universe, this is not always the norm; many beings live in what we call space or in the stars (hence *star beings*). The KHAA is teaming with life, and beings living there are creating their reality by using the formula, *thought-imagination-manifestation*—in that order. When we're in our natural state, things manifest instantly (think "Q" in Star Trek; he could create anything by using this formula—one could say he was *creating something out of nothing*).

When we are free from manipulation, we will see the Universe as it really is, whereas we are manipulated into only perceiving 4% of it, and even that 4% is compromised. The communication between star beings is done by exchanging thoughts. This means

---

[5] *Fire* in this case refers to the "Real Self," which is different from how we are used to perceiving the *soul*. We will discuss the fire more extensively in this book, but you can also learn much more about the fire in "The Wes Penre Papers—The Multiverse Series." For the sake of convenience, occasionally I might use fire and soul interchangeably.

[6] In order to learn more about that the physical body is *one* with the spirit and the mind—being part of the Spiritual Universe (the KHAA) rather than the physical universe, and that there was no separation before the AIF came, please read the following very important sections of The WPP, the Fourth Level of Learning: http://wespenre.com/4/paper16-ongoing-battle-between-spiritual-and-material-realms-what-is-matter-and-what-is-spirit.htm#vi.i, and http://wespenre.com/4/paper16-ongoing-battle-between-spiritual-and-material-realms-what-is-matter-and-what-is-spirit.htm#vi.i.

that everything that's manifested and shared by others will be observable and can be experienced by us, too; once we are free from our boundaries and we *decide* to see it. It's up to each being to block and unblock frequencies—we humans do this all the time without being aware of what we're doing (albeit we are more often unblocking than we are blocking under current circumstances).

During the creation of our Milky Way galaxy, stars were created to form the galaxy. Stars are known to have their own consciousness, and a galaxy would function as the *mass consciousness* of the stars contained within it. The stars/suns give birth to souls/star beings—thus the term *fire*—which is a large group of *fires* gathering together to create a composite of fires, which we call the *soul*. The soul can then split itself in even smaller groups of fires, which can be "sent out" in the Universe to explore and learn on behalf of the Creatrix—the feminine force of the Universe. These splinters are the *minds* of the soul, but they are all connected and share experiences with each other throughout the different dimensions. All these experiences are then absorbed by the soul (some schools of thought call this the *Oversoul*, by the way, which can be confusing), who, in turn, adds to the learning experiences of the Creatrix.

The group of fires that make up the *mind* make up an *etheric body*, which we have many names for; one such name being the *spiritual body*, which is the body that leaves the physical body when the physical body expires. In the WPP, I call this spiritual body the *avatar*. The avatar can shapeshift into anything on a spiritual level by rearranging the fires at will if the fires (mind) that form the avatar wish to do so. We humans usually form our avatar after the shape of the physical body we currently possess, and we also reshape our physical body to a certain extent to mirror how we feel "inside." After death of the physical body, the avatar usually keeps the shape and form from the last incarnation, although some minds shape their avatars to look the way they did when their physical body was in its prime rather than when it was old and sick—mainly to impress on other avatars or to feel better about themselves in general.

Before the soul was created, we were pure consciousness, being *One* with the Universal consciousness—the *Divine Feminine*, as I call it in the WPP. Being born from *star dust* made us individually aware, and from there we could create minds by splitting our soul fires and go out and create. A number of avatars can be created from the same composite of fires (the soul). Thus, the soul can be in many places at the same time. As in a hologram, each fire contains a picture of the whole.

This is how star beings operate, and this is how we humans have the potential to operate as well. Our problem, however, is not that we can't split our fires (we actually are split already), but when a small group of fires (minds) are getting disconnected from our fire composite (the soul), the new unit (mind/body or fires/avatar) is being manipulated into incarnating into another space/time here on Earth, different from where a previous unit is located. Add amnesia to this, and one unit no longer knows about the other, separated as they are in space and time. Thus, each of us lives several lifetimes simultaneously on Earth. Then augment death as well with yet another incarnation following upon that, and you will have the human condition. Each of us is unaware of our other-selves, living in other times and places on the planet. These other-selves have had totally different experiences than you have had, and therefore they have developed different personae. You wouldn't even recognize your other-selves as being parts of you even if you met them.

This is how spirit/mind/body work in coordination with each other—all three being part of the same spiritual structure. In summary, the composite of fires is the *soul*, who gathers experiences from the fragments or fire splinters that the soul is sending out; similar to how we usually perceive the Sun sending out different beams of light in all directions; the Sun being the soul in this allegory and the beams being the soul splinters. The small fires, grouping together, become one *mind*, and the shape that this group of fires makes up becomes the *avatar*—the *spiritual body*. Thus, one soul can have a number of different minds (fire splinters) living different lives.

Each person is a splinter of his or her soul, and depending on how many splinters of that soul were trapped by En.ki (a.k.a. Lucifer) long ago, the same number of minds are not "retrievable" by the soul so long as they're trapped here. All these minds, including other souls' minds, together become the *human soul group*, although it could just as well be called the *human mind group*. These minds are captured in this 3-D reality until they are able to release themselves. There is a way to do this, fortunately, and I will bring that up in the end part of this book.

This might be an entirely new concept to most readers and might seem difficult to grasp at first, and if so, a second and third review of this section is advisable, until this important model is totally grasped. Once it "clicks," it should create an "aha" moment.

Because time technically does not exist, every present moment has to be recreated constantly on a level of existence that some quantum physicists call the *subquantum*. Unlike here on Earth, where the illusion of time creates a linear timeline concept, it's different for other star beings. They too can create a chain of events that might seem linear while they are happening, but when an event is over, it's a present time memory, happening in parallel with any new event that's occurring—we locate ourselves where we have our focus. The past and the future, however, can always be recreated in the present by a soul who can focus enough to do so. In a way, animals are much better at this than humans are; animals are more in the present, where it's the moment that counts. They are not as stuck in linear time as we are. Hence, we can see a dog recreating the same excitement every time mom or dad comes home, as if it was the first time it happened.

THE RAPID EXPANSION OF THE AI MOVEMENT

IN THE WPP I GAVE SOME predictions of what is going to happen in the near future concerning the *Machine Kingdom*, i.e. the new world of Artificial Intelligence (AI). Unfortunately, a majority of these predictions have already been fulfilled since I finished the papers in April-May of 2015, and there are now open discussions about Artificial Intelligence all over the media. The Controllers want us to get used to the idea that AI is the new reality for mankind. In the WPP, I wrote that in the very near future, people will have sex with robots instead of having sex with human partners because with robots people can drop the responsibility part that goes with having sex with a human. Robots have no demands or feelings. I wrote that people will even marry their robots (more about that later in this book). Little did I know at the time that I was writing about something that would be discussed in the open just a few months later.

The last part of 2015 was the time when a wide exposure of the Artificial Intelligence agenda was being made in the media. The idea is to prepare people for what is to come. In the first few chapters of this book we will put Dr. Raymond Kurzweil under scrutiny. He has been a spokesman for Artificial Intelligence since he was a teenager, and he is now in his sixties; he has held innumerous lectures, possibly been giving just as many interviews, and written a number of books on the subject, overtly discussing all the details about the plans for a *united humanity* in what he calls the *Singularity*. His most detailed and bestselling book is his latest, *The Singularity is Near*, which was released in 2005. In one of his video presentations he says, and I quote him directly from one of his video monologues,

> The term, Singularity, is a metaphor borrowed from physics. Physics dictates that in a [sic] the gravity of a black hole, which also increases exponentially as it is approached, there is a threshold distance away from the center, the Event Horizon, past which nothing can return.[7]

As if this doesn't sound eerie enough, he further says that the goal of Artificial Intelligence is the Singularity, and he expands on this term by saying that it means, in layman's term that, by 2045, we will have cloned the human brain into its smallest details.[8] This brain template will then be used as an artificial computer system that will connect all other human brains on this planet (including yours and mine, if he gets his way). From there, we will all be as *one* mind in many bodies (which by the way will become part machine and part biological), centrally controlled from this *Super Brain*. Kurzweil is quick to add that we all will have our own personality intact, but we will also be telepathically connected in this global, electronic network.

---

[7] "Ray Kurzweil: The Coming Singularity," (scroll down until you get to the video).
[8] *Ibid.*

After that (and this will be stunning for the readers of the WPP, as it is mentioned there over and over), the intention is to let this new cyborg hybrid race travel out in space. Although Kurzweil says that he does not believe that there are any aliens out there, he for some reason uses the word "conquer" in this context; he says that the new human hybrids will go out and "conquer space." Note that in his circles, the choice of words is crucial, and it's very rare that mistakes are made by this level of Insiders. The word *conquer* is most certainly consciously chosen in order to hide the real agenda in plain sight. The cyborg human conquering space is exactly what I wrote about in the WPP.

Those who don't want to mentally face this subject might call it impossible, or they will call it science-fiction, although it's evidently anything but. Some might even say that this is Kurzweil's delusional agenda, which has nothing to do with the real world. This is incorrect. Kurzweil is, as mentioned above, only one spokesman of many on this subject (as we will see). Moreover, mainstream media, in all their different formats, are all over this right now, and the topic is being openly discussed; we can even see it happening around us. Kurzweil writes in *The Singularity is Near* that they can't do this without our consent, so they need to inform us about both the advantages and disadvantages (which he admits exist) for humanity to make an informed decision. Hence, he welcomes an open discussion on the subject. This, however, is a contradiction to what is actually being played out. Kurzweil is playing the role of a scientist of great integrity, who only wants to inform us so we can make a balanced decision, but in the next breath *he boasts about how quickly this whole scientific movement is progressing.* Why do they let the movement progress if people haven't yet made up their minds about it yet? If he wants our consent, shouldn't it all be kept on hold until everybody is informed and have made a democratic decision? No, they don't care (and besides, we don't live in a democracy); it's just a dog-and-pony show, and they think we won't notice that we basically have no vote on the matter.

In fact, our silence is our consent; we let it happen, and therefore, we indirectly agree to the agenda.

We humans are responsible for our own evolution and should

xii

be left alone while evolving and not be interfered with by other star races. However, we all know how it is here on Earth; if we create a law, the intelligent criminal finds ways to bypass the law and sometimes get away with it. This can be exemplified by looking back at the Old West (and the same thing would apply today). If someone was on trial for a serious crime, such as murder, and the same defendant made sure the witness or witnesses to the crime were killed, there would be nobody who could testify against him or her, and the case would be dismissed. This happened quite often back then. When there were no eyewitnesses left to the murder, nothing could be proven, and the criminals were acquitted, although it was commonly understood that they were guilty.

In a similar way, the Law of Free Will can be bypassed by cosmic criminals, such as the Alien Invader Force (AIF). They don't need us to say "yes, we want what you offer us;" all they need is our indirect consent.

There are three basic ways to react to a crime; one can either openly participate in it, fully aware of what one is doing; one can indirectly participate by not objecting or by being blissfully or conveniently ignorant about the crime; or one can openly speak up against it, or silently decide not to participate.

In humanity's case, the second way is most common. It has gone so far that most people are not even aware of that they are manipulated into an agreement with the criminals. Still, the effect would be the same; we are adjusting to whatever the Administrators and the AIF are manipulating us into. The Cosmic Outlaws and their Emissaries are well aware of this but continue to proceed with their agenda anyway, knowing they will get our indirect consent on a continuing basis because the game is rigged. On the other hand, they have already informed us—again indirectly—by creating all these new movies about AI and killer robots. Thus far, very few people have protested, thinking it is all science-fiction because it's presented as such. However, indirectly the Minions have properly informed us about the danger of AI, and for all they care; we gave our consent by not protesting against their propaganda in any large numbers. Those who protest are just "conspiracy nuts" anyway. This is how it is being done. Their defense before a higher Galactic

Court would be for them to say, "No one can seriously propose that we didn't warn them," speaking in terms of humanity.

THE NAZIS AND AI

A S MENTIONED EARLIER IN THIS prologue, 2015 was the year of AI exposure of great magnitude in the mainstream media. Dr. Ray Kurzweil's books have been out for decades now, but the general public hasn't paid too much attention to them, being one thing too many to deal with, and TV Reality Shows have been more important for most people than learning about what the Controllers have planned for us. Hence, the population has had little knowledge about what is really coming down the pike, although it's been revealed to us for many years in one form or another. Of course, Kurzweil and his ilk knew this would happen, and it's been part of the plan to let us know what they are planning, without having us interfering.

However, not until this year has the media got a go-ahead by those in charge to expose the plans in public on Internet sites, such as CNN, ABC, NBC, and other channels with a large number of international viewers. Online newspapers around the world are also bringing this up on a large scale, as we shall see. Also, most of us have noticed that there is a huge increase in Hollywood movies on this theme. None of this is by chance, of course, and they are eager to prepare us for the future; they do not want any shock reactions, but want to introduce this successively. After all, the plan is to have most of the Machine Kingdom established by 2045. People who are young today will still be alive when the time comes. Ray Kurzweil makes a good case when he says that this goal *is* attainable. Those who will not live to see the Singularity might have children and grandchildren who will experience this upcoming event. Finally, those who don't have any children and therefore think this does not apply to them are incorrect. Much of it is happening right now, before our eyes, and the majority of people don't notice. This is how powerful the propaganda is, and it works in at least two ways: it manipulates us into accepting the Singularity by making it interesting and exciting, and it shows us the agenda in plain sight, so we can't say we weren't told beforehand.

Some might wonder how the ones in control know so much about us and how we think, but it's actually quite obvious if we know our history. The intense research into the human mind began on a large scale during World War II when Nazi scientists, such as Dr. Josef Mengele, looked into the human psyche and the human brain on deeper levels. These criminal scientists experimented on twins, war prisoners, Jews, Gypsies, and other, for them, unwanted minorities, and the experiments were often unimaginably cruel. They started compartmentalizing the brain by using trauma-based mind control. They could then program these traumatized parts of the brain with new personalities that could be triggered by words, certain hand signals, a phone call, or otherwise. This research was then brought to America after the war in something called *Project Paperclip*.[9] Nazi scientists were smuggled to the U.S. to start working for what was later to become the CIA, NSA, FBI, NASA, and other key organizations within and above U.S. Government levels. The experiments on the human brain and mind then became known in the U.S. as *MK-ULTRA* (MK stands for *Mind Kontrolle*, where Kontrolle is the German word for "control." The CIA cryptonym *MK* probably originates from the joint efforts between the U.S. and Germany to create a totally mind-controlled, easy-to-manage population).

However, this is not the only reason they started researching the depth of the brain and the mind; it had everything to do with AI and the Singularity. I want to make it totally clear; what people call the *New World Order* and the *One World Government* is nothing but the Singularity; i.e. the goal to create a super brain that will control all other brains (and minds) on this planet. Other branches of MK-ULTRA were later established, such as the infamous *Project Monarch*[10] and more. All these branches of mind control had one thing in common, which was to learn everything about the human brain and mind in order to later create the Super Brain Computer (SBC), which is a term for a super-controlled collective consciousness.

---

[9] https://en.wikipedia.org/wiki/Operation_Paperclip
[10] http://www.outpost-of-freedom.com/operatio.htm

The astute reader might now wonder why the Overlords would need to study the human brain when, after all, *they* were the ones who manipulated our DNA in the first place. Wouldn't they already know how it works? Yes, they knew how the human brain worked when they created it many millennia ago, but human consciousness constantly changes the neuro pathways in the brain by creating new neuro-pathways as we learn new things, and the pathways in the brain get rearranged into new patterns to adapt to new versions of reality. For the Overlords, it's not just a matter of cloning the human brain; it also has to be compatible with the human soul, the way the soul is interacting with the brain *in present time*; not in some distant past. The mass consciousness is not vibrating within the exact same frequency band as it did when Homo sapiens were first created. Nevertheless, the complete cloning of the brain I suspect was achieved already decades ago. The only job left is to convince the majority of mankind that what is to come is "good for us." This is where puppets such as Ray Kurzweil come into the picture; Kurzweil sees himself as a *visionary*.

Fig x-1: *Lineup of 104 rocket scientists of Operation Paperclip at Ft. Bliss.* **Wernher von Braun,** *the famous NASA rocket scientist, involved in developing the Apollo Project, stands in the first row, seventh person from the right. These scientists, in conjunction with other researchers/scientists, such as the child torturer* **Dr. Josef Mengele** *(standing, face half covered, in the middle of the second row, having raven-dark hair), were smuggled out of Nazi Germany to the U.S. after WW II—some of them thus avoiding prosecution in the Nuremburg Tribunal for crimes against humanity, and if convicted they would have been executed. A number of these war criminals were now getting leading positions in the American Government and in various Black Budget projects, living long lives under U.S. Government protection. Many of these people operated from secret bases in Argentina, which up to this date*

is a haven for Nazis and war criminals. Pope Francis, the current Pope, being the first Jesuit in that position, was born in Argentina.[11] *(Photo: Wikipedia).*

Other ways in which we have been tricked are the Internet and other electronic devices, such as smartphones and Plasma TVs, which all have spy devices embedded in them, so that certain organizations can spy on the viewer even when the device is off. TV, in fact, was a forerunner to the computer and the Internet. The *letter agencies* and the Overlords wanted to observe human behavior and which choices we are most likely to make in any given situation. The motto was: *one TV in every home.* That turned into a similar motto a few decades later; *the goal is at least one PC in every home.*[12] Then the Internet came down upon us. Most people think this was an enormous achievement; so much more could be studied and learned so much quicker. The Administrators and the AIF don't care what you put out on the Internet or what you learn from there, as long as you don't step on the toes of their most current secret programs that they don't want to be exposed for any given reason. As long as you don't do that, you're relatively safe to say whatever you want on the Net without any serious retribution. After all, the Internet is there to study human behavior in present time and to monitor and store all data we so voluntarily put out on the Net.

The Internet was released as the *World Wide Web* from having been a military network, *before* it was implemented for the public. Virtually everything is tested in the military before we get to see it. The Internet is, on a grander scale, an attempt to understand human unpredictability and to determine how to get people on the same page. I would imagine that the Controllers have asked themselves; how much do the humans know? How much do they care about important issues, and how much do they care about trivial things? How social are they? How alike are they in all their uniqueness? The AIF wants these questions answered. Some of these beings are quite psychic and can read the mass consciousness without machines, but the Internet was still important because they wanted to see how easily we are distracted from a focus point. The fact that humans are

[11] https://en.wikipedia.org/wiki/Pope_Francis
[12] Freely quoted from Microsoft's founder, Bill Gates.

easily distracted becomes embarrassingly apparent in the different discussion forums, where someone starts a topic of relevance and others comment on it. By so-called *trolling*, the letter agencies then make comments on the forum thread that have nothing to do with the original subject, and almost immediately people's attention goes from the focal point to the distraction; thus, the discussion of the original topic is lost. This is specifically true when the *troll* begins to insult one or more people responding to a thread; people become easily reactive and divert from the topic in order to defend themselves. Others then fill in to defend the person who is attacked.

Those in charge must have learned much about us from the Internet over the years. We are telling the entire world about ourselves and our intimate thoughts on Facebook, Twitter, Google+, in other social media, and on personal websites and blogs. The Controllers couldn't be more pleased. *We are helping them to create our own destruction as a human species by falling right into their hands!*

The smartphones are even worse than computers. At least people know that they are exposing themselves on the Internet, but many who use smartphones think that it's relatively private when it's anything but. Just as with the Internet, every keystroke is traceable. As if this wasn't enough, people are bringing their smartphones with them wherever they go, text from them continuously, and browse the highly monitored Internet. Landlines have become almost obsolete, and when did you see a phone booth last? Now the agencies can collect information on almost everybody twenty-four hours a day, seven days a week. Wi-Fi makes it possible to spy on people through the phone even when it is turned off. George Orwell's classic book, *1984*, is since long surpassed in many ways. We don't have big cameras set up by the Government in our houses and apartments, but instead we have much more sophisticated surveillance systems via the Internet and the *smart products*. I wrote about *Smart Cities* in the WPP (another thing that mainstream media began to discuss in the open after the papers were released), but why do you think they name them Smart Cities? If *smart* stands for control and surveillance, you have the answer right there; they are cities where surveillance of their citizens is going on day and night. We are almost there already. Via satellites, any

xviii

person walking down the street—even in the big cities—can be zoomed in on, and Big Brother will know exactly where you are, where you're going, with whom you're talking, and what you're doing. It's a piece of cake.

It is obvious to me that the Overlords, who are the equivalent to the old Sumerian gods, are already here in great numbers. I also believe that Lord En.ki is back already as well; and of course, his son Marduk, the "Lord of this World," has been here for centuries, after he supposedly had left the planet for a while before then. It is soon time for En.ki to regain his leading position here on Earth, but the question is whether Marduk will let him; more about this later.

What the AIF is waiting for is the Singularity, i.e. when the biological human body is fully integrated with the machine, and the Super Brain Computer (SBC) is in an operating mode. CERN in Switzerland is playing a role in accomplishing this goal as we will discuss in this book.

DISCLOSURE OF THE ET PHENOMENON

FOR LONG, MANY PEOPLE IN the UFO community have anticipated that there will soon be a disclosure of the ET presence on our planet. It is believed, generally speaking, that the governments of the world (with the U.S. government being the forerunner) will come clean on the subject.

I believe this is naïve thinking; the governments have too much to lose because of all the crimes that must be revealed in the same breath. The spokespersons for Disclosure emphasize that we need to give the criminals in the Government amnesty because for certain individuals in power who believe they have much more to lose than to gain from a disclosure; a drastic thing such as disclosure would otherwise be out of the question. Many people would probably agree to give them amnesty in exchange for disclosure, but when everything is said and done, there would be so many angry people who would go berserk when they figure out that they have been deceived and lied to through their entire lives, and how children have been tortured under the umbrella of "National Security." A large number of citizens would probably make use of the weapons that are normally locked into their gun cabinets, and people would go out and buy ropes to hang the criminals with. This is exactly what those in the government fear will happen. Also, those in power would lose their wealth when alternative technologies would be exposed; technologies that have been suppressed for decades—all in the name of greed and power. One such technology would be free energy to everybody on the planet.

The fact is that none of the above is the *real* reason why a full disclosure will not happen. The real reason is because it's not up to the Government to decide when or if a disclosure will take place—it's up to the Overlords who control the Government and the rest of the world. Those familiar with my previous work know quite well that the Overlords only want partial incremental disclosure, which will probably eventually culminate in their appearance before us. However, even when the gods reappear in the open, we will not be told the truth about them—only the cover story.

The cover story, and a part of the partial disclosure, is the propaganda about the good ETs, who want to make contact. The cover story tells us there are *only* good ETs in Earth's vicinity at this time; the bad ETs have all left our planet and our solar system, or so it is claimed. This is promoted by different UFO researchers and is, of course, a very dangerous message, and taking into consideration that these spokespersons reach millions of people, they have a huge responsibility not to be gullible or to give information *they guarantee is true* when it's actually not. Some of the spokespersons are just that—gullible—and just parrot more prominent spokespersons who seem to intentionally give the wrong information, and these spokespersons might not at all be who people think they are. Some of them might be on the Military Industrial Complex (MIC) and the Intelligence Community payroll.

Convincing us that the ETs who want to make themselves known are all benevolent and that we should embrace all of them without discernment is what disclosure, or partial disclosure, involves. Of course, free energy and other benefits that come with partial disclosure are on the Overlords' agenda anyway—it's all needed for the Singularity to take effect. What these Disclosure and Free Energy Projects won't say, or don't know in certain cases perhaps, is that *when it's commonly believed that these "grass root projects" are gaining results, it's not because of their genuine involvement of freeing mankind; it's because such a "disclosure" was already planned by the AIF.* I think this is quite obvious. We humans are easily duped because that's how it's always been and always will be so long as the Overlords are in charge.

This book will build up to a quite disturbing "climax," and this information is not for everybody, but it is for those who are brave enough to confront the ultimate purpose with AI and the Singularity.

However, we will start out lightly by getting familiar with one of the AI Movement's greatest spokespersons—Dr. Raymond Kurzweil.

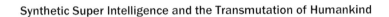

PART 1: The Singularity Movement

Chapter 1:
Dr. Ray Kurzweil—A Short Introduction

WHO IS RAY KURZWEIL?

RAYMOND KURZWEIL IS STILL relatively unknown to the great majority of people. Since his mid-teens, he has been on a passionate mission to develop Artificial Intelligence (AI), but his ideas actually started already in his earlier childhood.

In 1953, at the age of five, he decided that he wanted to become an inventor. At the age of seven or eight, he built a robotic puppet theater and robotic games. When he was twelve years old, at a time when computers were rare and not in the public domain, he took a great interest in them and built computer devices and statistical programs. Although his father, being a musician and a conductor and his mother being a visual artist, the family often discussed technology at home, further inspiring the young Ray to later in life become a brilliant inventor and computer scientist. He invented the charge-coupled flatbed scanner, the first print-to-screen reading machine for the blind, and he also developed the first text-to-speech synthesizer, named *Kurzweil K250*, which was able to simulate the sound from instruments, such as the grand piano.[13] These are just a handful of inventions he's completed over the years.

In 1999, he received the *National Medal of Technology and Innovation* from President Bill Clinton at the White House, and in 2001, he received the *Lemelton-MIT Prize*; the largest prize in the world for innovation,[14] making him $500,000 richer. He is also the author of seven books, of which *The Singularity is Near* (2005)[15] is the latest. It became a *New York Times* best seller and is the book that I frequently will refer to because it is his

---

[13] http://www.kurzweilai.net/ray-kurzweil-biography
[14] https://en.wikipedia.org/wiki/Ray_Kurzweil
[15] http://www.singularity.com/

most recent book, making it relatively up to date concerning his vision of the near future.

The predictions Kurzweil has made thus far have been eerily correct. In fact, he is said to have a 30-year track record of accurate predictions,[16] [17] and many of his ideas and visions can be read on his websites: http://kurzweilAI.net and http://singularity.com/. He is claiming that *Kurzweil.AI.net* has three million new readers every year. However, it's not very difficult to be prophetic when the agenda is already planned out in great detail.

Also mentioned on the same website is his appointment as a *Director of Engineering* at Google in 2012, "heading up a team developing machine intelligence and natural language understanding."[18] I will show later in this book how important Google is for the development and the promotion of AI, and now, with Kurzweil joining its team, we've already seen great progress in Google's own contribution toward the end goal— Kurzweil's Singularity.

I found this little section about Kurzweil on Wikipedia quite interesting (my emphasis),

> "For the past several decades, Kurzweil's most effective and common approach to doing creative work has been conducted *during his lucid dreamlike state which immediately precedes his awakening state. He claims to have constructed inventions, solved difficult problems, such as algorithmic, business strategy, organizational, and interpersonal problems, and written speeches in this state.*"[19]

This quote speaks volumes. We discussed in the WPP how different entities work on people in dream state. Some do this to help people increase their awareness, but the Overlords do it mostly to support their own puppets in order to make sure that they get the tools they need. It is quite apparent that interdimensional beings who are supporting Kurzweil's mission also are assisting him in his dreams.

---

[16] http://www.kurzweilai.net/ray-kurzweil-biography
[17] http://singularityhub.com/2015/01/26/ray-kurzweils-mind-boggling-predictions-for-the-next-25-years/
[18] http://www.kurzweilai.net/ray-kurzweil-biography
[19] https://en.wikipedia.org/wiki/Ray_Kurzweil#Creative_approach

BILL GATES ON AI AND THE SINGULARITY

KURZWEIL, DESPITE HIS IMPRESSIVE records, is merely a puppet for those who work on AI behind the scenes. Although one of the most promoted front persons for the Movement, he is not the only one. The majority of CEOs of the mega corporations have some part in the development of the Singularity. This is obvious because, as we learned throughout the WPP, the Overlords own the big international companies and industries that were set up on their initiative in the first place. Not all those CEOs are public spokespersons for the Movement, although I'm sure many of them attend meetings, held behind locked doors, on this subject.

One CEO, who is out there in the forefront and sometimes in Kurzweil's company, is Microsoft's Bill Gates, which shouldn't come as a big surprise to anybody. Albeit, Gates sometimes plays the role of a fence-sitter on the subject of AI and the Singularity and has even openly spoken against the Singularity (instead he wants less intelligent robots),[20] he has also held many lectures on his own on these subjects, and those lectures have mainly, up to a certain point, been in favor of the AI Movement. He had this to say in an interview at *Evolutionnews.org*:

> Gates was asked: "How much of an existential threat do you think machine superintelligence will be?"
>
> He admitted: "I am in the camp that is concerned about super intelligence." He took a somewhat more measured stance than Hawking, but sees AI as a real concern.
>
> "First the machines will do a lot of jobs for us and not be super intelligent. That should be positive if we manage it well. A few decades after that though the intelligence is strong enough to be a concern.
>
> "I agree with Elon Musk and some others on this and don't understand why some people are not concerned," he wrote in the thread.[21]

---

[20] http://www.evolutionnews.org/2015/02/bill_gates_join093191.html
[21] http://www.techradar.com/news/world-of-tech/scared-of-robots-bill-gates-voices-concern-about-the-future-of-ai-1282712

Fig 1-2: Ray Kurzweil (left), here with Bill Gates (right) [kurzweiai.net].

Kurzweil, in his latest book, emphasizes the importance of looking at both the pros and cons of the Singularity in order to form a public opinion, and Bill Gates plays an important role in this. These people know that in the end, the movement *for* the Singularity will prevail, regardless of the opportunity to have an open debate. Even if some everyday people would be invited on television or in mass media video panel discussions, it will probably, by most people, just be looked upon as another form of entertainment, and they will most probably be designed and set up to look that way. The few who will be allowed to raise their voices in the media against the Singularity will not be able to prove that this is the actual public opinion on this subject. Even if it were, only a handful people would speak up, and from the Controllers' point of view, these naysayers don't represent the majority, and business can continue as usual. However, by being so relatively open about their agenda, these Emissaries can, with good confidence, say afterwards that they did make efforts to inform the public, but not many took heed and voiced their opinion.

VACCINATIONS, CHEMTRAILS AND NANOBOTS

I AM PERSONALLY AGAINST vaccinations, including flu shots because I understand that many of the various vaccines not only contain poison, but also contain so-called *nanobots*—extremely small artificial particles the size of blood cells, inserted in certain vaccines and prescription drugs. Once inserted, the nanobots will forever run through our bloodstream.[22] Yes, you read that correctly; there is allegedly no way to remove these particles once they are there. Thus, Big Brother has most of us covered already, but just to make sure nothing is left to chance, nanobots have supposedly also been put in chemtrails, which means that most people around the globe are breathing them in.[23] These nanobots work as "antennas" that can receive commands remotely, are self-replicating, and will be used both to transmit and receive information (something we will discuss later). However, the purpose is to have nanobots replacing our immune system and to reverse aging.[24] Interestingly, Bill Gates is advocating *for* vaccines and health care *in an effort to reduce the population!*[25] These are his own words, and they sound like a contradiction, perhaps, but not in Bill Gates' world.

The first two years of a child's life, he or she gets *more than twenty vaccinations!* This is outrageous, and even if the vaccines would *not* contain any harmful products (which they do), they would still bypass and deplete the child's immune system, making him or her more prone to serious illnesses. The immune system, in many cases, then would continue being depleted throughout adulthood—particularly when we, as adults, get even more vaccinations. We build our immune system in early childhood, and if we have that process tampered with, the immune system in adulthood will not be fully developed.

INSIDERS WITH OPPOSING OPINIONS

B ILL GATES' ACTIONS, IN GENERAL, do not show that he is pro-humanity on the Singularity subject, in spite of what he tells us. Population control via vaccination is part of the Overlords' agenda.

In the video mentioned above, Bill Gates is discussing Global Warming as being caused by environmental issues, although this

---

[22] Raymond Kurzweil, *The Singularity is Near*, Chapter Five, p. 183ff.
[23] From various Pleiadian lectures.
[24] "The Singularity is Near," (e-book version), pp. 36, 39, 197.
[25] https://www.youtube.com/watch?v=gROhNaJoGzI (I suggest you watch the full 3 ½ minutes of this video, but if time is an issue, fast forward to 2 minutes into the video for the relevant reference).

phenomenon is happening in the entire solar system because the Sun is in a cycle when it's getting warmer.[26] The environmental Global Warming effect (which is minimal) is nonetheless important for the Controllers to over-emphasize because it justifies many of the actions they need to take in order for the Singularity to take effect; population control being only one of them. Bill Gates' role here is obviously to push the environmental Global Warming Agenda together with other people in high positions in the societal structure, such as former Vice President Al Gore.

Kurzweil and Gates are two examples of people who are part of the same agenda, although their messages at times seem opposed to each other. Things are not always the way they seem, and celebrities and others, who have the ability to influence the masses and are allegedly propagating against the AI agenda, are often just told to do so *as part of the agenda*; they are just expendable puppets to the Controllers and better do what they're instructed to do. Although more and more people doubt Bill Gates' intentions in general, he is also looked upon by others as the little man who made it big, and this is a part of the American dream; a concept deeply rooted into the psyche of the average American. People have a tendency to admire those who succeed in life from having started with two empty hands. Historically, many people also like when public figures take *their* side (whether it's in an honest effort or not), and unfortunately, they give their power away, believing that these celebrities will solve the problem for the rest of us.

Of course, that will never happen. We are our own saviors, and if we don't make up our minds where we stand on these issues, we will inevitably end up exactly where the Overlords want us—in the Singularity.

---

[26] "The Solar System is Heating Up," http://www.livescience.com/1349-sun-blamed-warming-earth-worlds.html

Chapter 2:
Nanotechnology

BUILDING MACHINES AND ROBOTS FROM INSIDE OUT

NANO MEANS A BILLIONTH of something. The term *nanotechnology* could therefore, theoretically, refer to anything within technology where we work with particles a billionth of something; we are talking about particles on an atom level. In this book, however, we are more specific when we use the term nanotechnology. We are here discussing nanotechnology in terms of building humanlike machines from the atom level and up. Not only that, scientists working in this field are instructed to replicate biological humans as closely as possible when working with this technology. Then, there are other definitions of nanotechnology in addition to the above. Let's examine two well-respected dictionaries, and we'll begin with Merriam-Webster,

Simple Definition of Nanotechnology:

− the science of working with atoms and molecules to build devices (such as robots) that are extremely small.

Full Definition of Nanotechnology:

− the science of manipulating materials on an atomic or molecular scale especially to build microscopic devices (as robots)[27]

Now, let us take a look at the Cambridge Free English Dictionary definitions and compare,

---

[27] http://www.merriam-webster.com/dictionary/nanotechnology

— the science of making extremely small devices the size of atoms and molecules an area of science that deals with developing and producing extremely small tools and machines by controlling the arrangement of separate atoms[28]

Not only is this technology used to build robots on the macro level; it's also used to build robots directly on the nano level—*robots that are a billionth in size compared with anything we can see on the macro level!* Now we are talking about nanobots again: particles on a cellular level that are already put in our bloodstream.

The idea of being able to maneuver things, atom by atom, first became public in 1959 when scientist Richard Feynman said, "the principles of physics, as far as I can see, do not speak against the possibility of maneuvering things atom by atom."[29] He won the Nobel Prize in 1965. Feynman's work then inspired scientists to expand on his work with the purpose of actually achieving what Feynman suggested was possible. Now, more than fifty years later, we can say with 100% certainty that Feynman was correct: science has to a large degree achieved that goal.

However, I want to alert the reader that it's all a dog-and-pony show because this technology is millions or perhaps even billions of years old and extraterrestrial in its origin. The exponential technological development we have experienced over the last 150 years does not originate from the minds of some brilliant scientists who came up with ideas out of nowhere; the technology was given to them in dream state or directly by the AIF. Some scientists have probably been more aware than others that they have had outside sources helping them to come up with their most brilliant inventions. Nikola Tesla, the ingenious scientist in the early twentieth century, who developed free energy and invented things that could have been very useful to mankind if he hadn't been stopped by the Controllers, admitted openly that he had help from extraterrestrials.[30]

The entire idea of nanotechnology is to have the atomic building block self-replicate. This is being experimented on and has, to some

---

[28] http://dictionary.cambridge.org/us/dictionary/english/nanotechnology
[29] "There's Plenty of Room at the Bottom," a talk by Richard Feynman (awarded the Nobel Prize in Physics in 1965) at an annual meeting of the American Physical Society given on December 29, 1959. Reprinted in "Miniaturization", edited by H. D. Gilbert (Reinhold, New York, 1961) pages 282-296.
[30] http://www.ancient-code.com/the-extraterrestrial-messages-of-nikola-tesla/

degree, already been accomplished. Not all of it is out in public yet; they don't want to reveal everything at once because every revelation must be followed by an action, and if the world isn't ready for the action, certain revelations have to wait. The multi-billion AI Industry knows this all too well, and IBM—a giant in developing AI—agrees wholeheartedly. IBM states that new technology usually rather comes in short steps than giant leaps, and this is for many reasons.[31]

Because of self-replication capabilities, nanotechnology in the long term will be cheap. Scientists who have followed Feynman's line of thinking know that everything from the smallest particle up to the largest robot can, with atoms artificially put in the right sequence, self-replicate. This certainly sounds as science-fiction to many, but later in this book, we will see that our media are already exposing this near future possibility. J. Storrs Hall[32] explains in more detail how this works. I know it's a little technical, but I want to show how mRNA (messenger RNA), transferring the information from the DNA/genes in living organisms to specify certain gene expressions, is required in order to achieve this goal of self-replication:

> Ribosomes[33] manufacture all the proteins used in all living things on this planet. A typical ribosome is relatively small (a few thousand cubic nanometers) and is capable of building almost any protein by stringing together amino acids (the building blocks of proteins) in a precise linear sequence. To do this, the ribosome has a means of grasping a specific amino acid (more precisely, it has a means of selectively grasping a specific transfer RNA, which in turn is chemically bonded by a specific enzyme to a specific amino acid), of grasping the growing polypeptide, and of causing the specific amino acid to react with and be added to the end of the polypeptide[9].

> The instructions that the ribosome follows in building a protein are provided by mRNA (messenger RNA). This is a polymer formed from the four bases adenine, cytosine, guanine, and uracil. A sequence of several

---

[31] New York Times, Feb. 28, 2016, "The Promise of Artificial Intelligence Unfolds in Small Steps"
[32] http://www.bibliotecapleyades.net/ciencia/secret_projects/nanotech.htm
[33] The ribosome ... is a complex molecular machine found within all living cells, that serves as the site of biological protein synthesis (translation). Ribosomes link amino acids together in the order specified by messenger RNA (mRNA) molecules. Ribosomes consist of two major components: the small ribosomal subunit, which reads the RNA, and the large subunit, which joins amino acids to form a polypeptide chain. Each subunit is composed of one or more ribosomal RNA (rRNA) molecules and a variety of proteins. The ribosomes and associated molecules are also known as the translational apparatus. [Wikipedia]

hundred to a few thousand such bases codes for a specific protein. The ribosome "reads" this "control tape" sequentially, and acts on the directions it provides.

[...]

The assembler[34] requires a detailed sequence of control signals, just as the ribosome requires mRNA to control its actions. Such detailed control signals can be provided by a computer.

In other words, the technology is already here to have machines—both on the nano level and macro level—self-replicating. This is a very important step toward the Singularity.

The above is of course a very simplistic way of defining nanotechnology because it's so much more complicated than this, but I am trying to be as non-technical as possible. Those who want to learn more on a scientific level can find many good scientific references on the Internet.

Now that we have covered the basics, it's time to see what mainstream media are telling us about nanotechnology and its progress in the scientific community.

NANOTECHNOLOGY IN THE MEDIA

IN A REPORT FROM RT (Russia Today) at the beginning of 2015, in an article titled *Enter the Matrix*, two scientists were interviewed, explaining what allegedly are the latest results from their research into how hair-thin fiber optic cables—each thin cable having seven different channels and functions—can be inserted into the brain and interact with the neurological system in humans.[35] The application of this, claims a female scientist, is to, for example, cure neurological diseases, such as Alzheimer's. By inserting fiber cables into the brain and have

---

[34] [The assembler is a] device having a submicroscopic robotic arm under computer control. It will be capable of holding and positioning reactive compounds in order to control the precise location at which chemical reactions take place. This general approach should allow the construction of large atomically precise objects by a sequence of precisely controlled chemical reactions, building objects molecule by molecule. If designed to do so, assemblers will be able to build copies of themselves, that is, to replicate. [http://www.bibliotecapleyades.net/ciencia/secret_projects/project207.htm]
[35] https://www.youtube.com/watch?v=7S9rRqn49fw

those interact with the neurological pathways, it will be possible either to cure Alzheimer's, or, at the least, make such persons much more functional.

This sounds as if it is a good idea, but the reporter is clever and asks some good questions. The first thing that came to his mind, apparently, was the similarities to *The Matrix Series*, where cables were inserted into peoples' brains, upon which they could experience a virtual reality where anything is possible—even to bypass the laws of physics, as we know them from modern science. He asks the scientist if this technique can be used for mind-control. The scientist laughs it off and says that the technique they are developing is too simplistic to be used for mind control, *but in the future we will probably be able to do it!* Is she implying that science is going in that direction? If it was a slip of the tongue or not is difficult to say, but either way, she is acknowledging that in the future we will have the ability to mind control people with nanotechnology.

The main reason I am bringing up this particular report is because it was released in the early part of 2015, and in comparison to what would be exposed just about five to six months later in mainstream media, this report was quite premature, although not insignificant.

As a side note; I don't know who was starting to use the word *Matrix* as a term for the physical universe, when the word actually means "Mother," as in the Creatrix of the Universe. *Ma* stands for *Mother* and *trix* can perhaps easiest be explained as a female suffix, as in Creatrix. *Matrix* has now become such a common term for En.ki's physical universe that everybody has adopted it.

NANOTECHNOLOGY AND FERTILITY

I N A SEPARATE CHAPTER, WE ARE GOING to delve deeper into how the media are promoting nanotechnology and AI to the public with the purpose to give us the impression that this technology can benefit us in major ways. Nonetheless, I want to give the reader some examples of how nanotechnology already now is going to be used in the medical field to enhance our standard of living. They make it all sound good, and indeed, some of this technology will have beneficial effects on people who suffer and in other ways have issues they want to resolve, such as infertility. Much of this information will appeal to people who either have the conditions themselves or know somebody else who does.

Because of different factors, such as chemicals, GMO food, chemtrails, and radiation from nuclear "accidents," secret testing of nuclear weapons, poisoning of the planet, and other secret projects that the Administrators and their minions in the Military Industrial Complex (MIC) are conducting on the planet and on mankind, fertility in both men and women has been affected. Couples who wish to have children sometimes spend a fortune trying everything possible in the medical field in order for the woman to become pregnant. At times it works, other times it does not. Fewer and fewer people can have children of their own; men's sperms are becoming useless in more and more cases, and women in their most fertile age can't make the sperm stick to the egg, or they have miscarriages.

We are told that research has been done in this field, and people are holding their breath, hoping a breakthrough is on the horizon. Lo and behold! In spite of many skeptics' pessimistic predictions that something revolutionary will develop anytime soon in this field, a breakthrough may now be just around the corner; at least, if the infertility is on the male's end. If the woman is fertile, but the man has slow-swimming sperms (which is the most common reason for infertility [see article excerpt below]), what may be *one* solution is now presented in the media. *The Daily Mail* published an article from January 13, 2006 that read,

Microscopic machines propel slow swimming sperm toward the egg

...One of five men have been diagnosed with slow swimmers, which makes low sperm motility a leading cause of infertility.

Artificial insemination and reproduction technologies are options, but the average success rate is under 30 percent.

In order to beat the odds, a group of researchers are developing spermbots, which could act as a motor that pushes the sperm towards the egg.

Researchers from the Institute for Integrative Nanosciences at IFW Dresden used a tiny magnet, made of titanium and nickel, to create the metal helices.

The coil is just big enough to wrap around the tail of the sperm and mimics a microscopicmotor by propelling the sperm to the egg with the use of a rotating magnetic field.

After the sperm makes contact with an egg, it wiggles itself inside and out of the spermbot.

Researchers have reported success during testing, as the spermbots have shown they can be directed to slide one the sperm's tail and travel to the egg in a petri dish.

Even though the devices are in early stages, researchers have noted they 'are not overly harmful to sperm'.

But ultimately further testing has to be done to determine how safe they are for human subjects and how effective it will be for patients.

During this process, a women's [sic] eggs are removed from her ovaries with a needled [sic], then fertilized in a petri dish and then transferred back to the uterus or a surrogate's a few days later.[36]

My point with this is not to show the current success rate, despite many people's excitement about this, but to expose where science in general is heading these days, which is toward robotic solutions to human problems. Nanotechnology is the cornerstone of what will become the Singularity in about thirty years, if Kurzweil's prediction is correct. Kurzweil claims that the Singularity will be accomplished by 2045.

In the meantime, they have to put hope in the general population for the future of this generation and the next. People in general want a world without disease, with vitality and a long life (some would even vote for immortality, if possible). I know this, the reader knows this, and of course, the Overlords know this. An imperative part of the propaganda machine is to convince people that science has the answers to their problems.

Although spokespersons for the AI Movement (Kurzweil being my example of choice out of many other spokespersons) suggest a balanced discussion, fear of death and long-term painful diseases will make many people blind to the negative side of the Singularity and embrace an eternal, vital life in the physical plane to avoid death and not being sure what is going to happen afterward—if anything. The Controllers want the

---

[36] Daily Mail, January 13, 2016: "SPERMBOTS could battle infertility: Microscopic machines propel slow swimming sperm toward the egg"

population to believe that the Utopia that has almost forever been the Holy Grail of the oppressed masses will now come true. To make people believe that we are about to achieve health and eternal life, a huge propaganda machine needs to be set up, while the real planning is taking place in secret, behind locked doors. Besides promoting a solution that people want, they also have to make things worse in the world in order to win over the fence-sitters. This is one of the reasons why authorities create severe environmental issues, mind-controlled people to do school and mall shootings in random places, instigate wars and viral diseases, create cancer or enhance cancer risk, in addition to taking other undesirable and fearmongering actions. The general population has a difficult time grasping how the government they think they have voted in can commit such destructive and insane acts, when these acts are obviously putting the entire future of mankind in jeopardy. Most people, however, just wonder about these issues in silence, or briefly discuss them with family and friends. Then it stops there. When people mention it to others, the fear mechanism is triggered in the others, and a snowball effect sometimes takes place. This is, of course, part of the plan. The goal with a propaganda program is typically to create fear, but after the initial fearmongering , they want *us* to do the main job, which is to spread the fear amongst each other; it works better than a fast-spreading virus.

When enough fear and chaos has been purposely perpetrated, it's time to come up with the solution, which in the long term is the Singularity.

Many readers have probably heard of the following formula, applied on the masses by the Controllers, but I'll repeat it here because it's so important to understand; it works on us like a charm. The formula looks like this: *problem-reaction-solution*. The authorities (the Emissaries) create a *problem* that people don't know was purposely created by them (e.g. the environmental issues mentioned above); then there is a *reaction* from the public that the authorities must do something about it. Finally, the authorities come up with the *solution* to the problem that they themselves initiated. The solution is always a further push toward the Global Agenda—a step in the progress that would have been hard to accomplish if the fear button in the population hadn't been pushed first. This formula is brilliant because it has more than one application. By demanding that the government or some other authority solves the problem, we also give our power away, which makes them stronger and us weaker; they draw energy/life force from the rest of us, which is the definition of vampirism.

For those who want to read more extensively about nanotechnology and the agenda from a scientific viewpoint, just to know how they think, there is a great 400-page summary in something titled *The NBIC Report* (which stands for *Nanotechnology, Biotechnology, Information Technology and Cognitive Science*). It comes out of the Netherland and is a compilation of many authors writing on these subjects and was written in 2003. It can be downloaded in PDF at the following web address, http://www.wtec.org/ConvergingTechnologies/Report/NBIC_report.pdf

Chapter 3:
Transhumanism

INTRODUCTION TO TRANSHUMANISM AND THE SINGULARITY

THE TWO CONCEPTS, Transhumanism and the Singularity, are sometimes intertwined, but in this book, I will look at Transhumanism as a bridge toward the Singularity. The term "Transhumanism," simply put, means "transformation of humanism into something else," which in this case is the Singularity. In this chapter, I provide examples of how the bridge is being created.

I want to begin this chapter by showing something quite disturbing. In order to understand the background to the following, I want to direct the reader's attention to a quote from a report called *Human Performance*, written by E. Williams for *The MITRE Corporation* in 2008.[37] This is a non-profit company, sponsored by the federal government, and it works in symbiosis with defense and intelligence, aviation, civil systems, homeland security, the judiciary, healthcare, and cybersecurity. The entire report is therefore a quite revealing exposé of the future AI agenda. Here is an excerpt:

> Invasive interfaces involve direct surgical connections to the nervous system, to allow sensing of neural signals, input of sensory stimuli, or to regulate neural activity. In the case of invasive interfaces, the parallelism of output or inputs is limited by the limited knowledge of the nature of the neural network and by the complexity of making multiple connections surgically. In both cases, significant improvements are possible for medically impaired subjects. However, the ultimate performance now achievable with such interventions falls far below average normal human

---

[37] http://www.mitre.org/

performance.[38]

This was in 2008, though. Today, it seems as if science has unblocked the barriers, and a device has been successfully implanted in a young man, who says he is greatly enhanced by this implant. This person is being used in an AI experiment, most probably against his knowledge.

I mean no offense to this young man, who says he benefits from this implant, but I want to look at it from a bigger perspective. The device put into the back of the artist Neil Harbisson's brain is being justified by declaring that it helps him cope with a condition he was born with: total color blindness. Since birth Neil has been living in a grayscale world, and although this device does not give him back the ability to see colors, it helps him *hear* colors: a synthetic synesthesia. CNN is telling us that he is actually the *first certified cyborg!*[39] Look at the following two pictures:

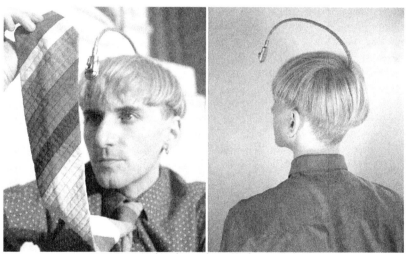

Fig3-1: Neil Harbisson, the world's first certified cyborg.

We can all understand that Neil wants to experience color the same

---

[38] *Human Performance*, [2008], p. 63 op. cit. [http://www.bibliotecapleyades.net/archivos_pdf/human-performance.pdf]

[39] http://www.cnn.com/2014/09/02/tech/innovation/cyborg-neil-harbisson-implant-antenna/

way that you and I do. Neil, being an artist, makes it even more understandable that he wants to be able to experience colors, but what he doesn't realize is that he is being used in a rather cruel way by scientists, who by using a prospect in need can manipulate him into having such a device implanted. It's getting even more extreme when we read Neil's own comments:

> It just feels like touching an extension of my body. It feels like a new body part, like a nose or a finger.[40]

I don't want to invalidate him in case this is how he really feels, but to me it sounds as if he is finding a way to justify this device implant so he can feel better about it.

In January 2016, CNN reporter Madeleine Stix wrote the following on CNN's website,

> Cyborgism, of which Harbisson is one of the foremost pioneers, is a slowly growing trend. The development of Google Glass has brought more attention to the concept of wearing technology for extended periods of time. Magnetic implants that allow individuals to feel the attraction of magnetic fields, like microwaves or power cord transformers, have become a popular piece of equipment among self-described "bio-hackers." And more recently, a Canadian filmmaker developed and implanted his own kind of eyeborg, a prosthetic eye embedded with a video camera.[41]

You are going to see very soon that these things are being more and more common, although much more sophisticated implants will replace these clumsy, inconvenient devices.

However, it doesn't end here. Neil Harbisson is also being used (without fully comprehending what he is getting involved in) as a propagandist for cyborgism. He is holding lectures on the subject, and he promotes it passionately:

> It will become normal to have tech inside our bodies or have it implanted. I think it just needs time.[42]

---

[40] *Ibid. op. cit.*
[41] Madeleine Stix for CNN, Jan, 7, 2016, http://www.cnn.com/2014/09/02/tech/innovation/cyborg-neil-harbisson-implant-antenna/
[42] *Ibid. op. cit.*

Also, we need to remember that some young people today were born to willingly experience the Machine Kingdom, exactly as I described it in The Wes Penre Papers—The Multiverse Series (WPP); these young people came here with the intention to dig deeply into technology already in their childhood and to be part of the new cyborg society—they are the children who are here to experience immortality. Some of these children are brilliant, by the age of two or three, at maneuvering electronic devices, such as smartphones and computers, with ease. This is not a coincidence. Souls from ancient Atlantis are now reincarnating to our time in large numbers—they are the so-called "technology geeks."

For those who want to hear Neil speak and see how he copes, there are several YouTube videos where he talks about his implant. See, https://www.youtube.com/results?search_query=neil+harbisson.

Here is more on the importance of what's going on. It's also from the Human Performance Report [my emphasis]:

> Although the present technical capabilities are not impressive, one can consider the potential that an adversary might use invasive interfaces in military applications. *An extreme example would be remote guidance or control of a human being.*[43]

The report doesn't suggest that the remote control of a human being *should* be done, but just by mentioning this potential in this context shows that this is absolutely possible, and if it's possible, it will be done! Still, people are willingly going to take implants, often to be able to experience something the average person can't, or just to be cool. It's not a pretty world when George Orwell's *1984* almost seems like a kindergarten book.

In another report called *Frontier Missions: Peacespace Dominance* that was presented to the *Air Force 2025* back in 1996 by the Department of Defense:

> While this is a reasonable portability rationale for the use of [a] chip, some may wonder, "Why not use special sunglasses or helmets?" The answer is simple. An implanted microscopic chip does not require security measures to verify whether the right person is connected to the IIC, whereas a room, helmet, or sunglasses requires additional time-consuming access control mechanisms to verify an individual's identity and level of control within the Cyber Situation.[44]

---

[43] *Human Performance*, [2008], p. 70 op. cit.

This is an older report, but the intention to totally control us was there already. Ray Kurzweil may assure us as much as he wants that the movement he is part of is benevolent, but the evidence points to a different agenda altogether. Overwhelming evidence is going to be presented in this book to an extent that I doubt no one who is reading it in its entirety will doubt the real intention behind the Movement.

Microchips *have* been used, *are* used, and *will* be used in the near future, but in general, more sophisticated ways of controlling our brains and minds will be developed. Brainwaves from the future Super Brain Computer (SBC) will ultimately put the population under surveillance and control.

Moreover, the same 1996 report explains how humans will accept the plan to control the mind, and even liken it to a video game experience:

> The civilian populace will likely accept implanted microscopic chips that allow military members to defend vital national interests.[45]

> It is an electronic interface for individual nerve cells to communicate with a computer. This human-machine linkage will. . . enhance human capability in many ways. If artificial eyes can convert video to nerve signals, won't it be possible to use the same technique to superimpose computer-generated information in front of one's field of view?...

> This capability will have extraordinary commercial applications from medical advances. These advances will help restore patients with damaged neural, audio, and visual systems as well as enable individuals to achieve the "ultimate virtual reality trip".[46]

In the last paragraph, we can see the parallel to Neil Harbisson's case, perhaps with the "ultimate virtual reality trip" excluded.

An interesting aspect of these reports is that they are both non-classified and are in public domain. They want us to read them and think they are taking an approach that this is a benevolent process. The above quotes show that there is an underlying agenda here that they want to hide in plain sight.

---

[44] *Frontier Missions: Peacespace Dominance, p. 35, op. cit.*
(http://www.bibliotecapleyades.net/archivos_pdf/2025_volume3.pdf)
[45] *Ibid. op. cit. p. 36.*
[46] *Ibid. op. cit. p. 25.*

PATENTED MIND CONTROL TECHNIQUE

S OMETHING REALLY INTERESTING to look into is patents. When spending time researching them, astonishing patents can be found on the U.S. Government Internet patent site. The following is just one example among many. I urge the reader to go through the patent site to find more; they will be there.

The following patent, which I will choose excerpts from, is Patent no. 6,011,991, dated January 4, 2000. In the abstract section, it says,

> A system and method for enabling human beings to communicate by way of their monitored brain activity. The brain activity of an individual is monitored and transmitted to a remote location (e.g. by satellite).
>
> At the remote location, the monitored brain activity is compared with pre-recorded normalized brain activity curves, waveforms, or patterns to determine if a match or substantial match is found.
>
> If such a match is found, then the computer at the remote location determines that the individual was attempting to communicate the word, phrase, or thought corresponding to the matched stored normalized signal.[47]

Here we have evidence that the MIC and the rest of the 3-letter agencies had the abilities already in 2000 to monitor our brain frequencies. However, here is more from the same patent,

> It is another objective of this invention to provide a system capable of identifying particular nodes in an individual's brain, the firings of which affect characteristics such as appetite, hunger, thirst, communication skills (e.g. which nodes are utilized to communicate certain words such as 'yes', 'no', or phrases such as 'I don't know', 'I'm not sure', or numbers such as 'one', 'two', 'ten', 'one hundred' and the like, thought processes, depression, and the like).
>
> When such nodes are identified, they may be specifically monitored by one or more sensors to analyze behavior or communication or words, phrases, or thoughts.
>
> In other embodiments, devices mounted to the person (e.g. underneath the

---

[47] Excerpt from brainwave monitoring U.S. Pat. no. 6,011,991, January 4, 2000, http://patft.uspto.gov/netacgi/nph-Parser?Sect1=PTO1&Sect2=HITOFF&d=PALL&p=1&u=/netahtml/PTO/srchnum.htm&r=1&f=G&l=50&s1=6011991.PN.+Ao00000.PN.&OS=PN/6011991+OR+PN/Ao00000&RS=PN/6011991+OR+PN/Ao00000

scalp) may be energized in a predetermined manner or sequence to remotely cause particular identified brain node(s) to be fired in order to cause a predetermined feeling or reaction in the individual, such as lack of hunger, lack of depression, lack of thirst, lack of aggression, lack of Alzheimer's disease effects, or the like.[48]

It becomes evident that the MIC, and others, are using technology to monitor and then control our brainwave patterns, i.e. our thoughts and behavior. In line with what we've discussed in previous chapters, we can see how this patent fits into the agenda of building the SBC that can *monitor and control our brain waves!*[49] There is really no way to dispute what is said in this patent (and as mentioned above, there is more of a similar sort). It is crucial that the AI agenda is exposed for what it is, before it's too late, because we're running out of time. We need to stop listening to talking heads on the news and AI prophets, such as Ray Kurzweil. There is nothing benevolent in this movement, and Kurzweil is lying when he's writing and saying that the Singularity is a natural step in our evolution, and that we will, because of the Singularity, take a super-leap in intelligence and unity as a new kind of human—super-enhanced that becomes immortal through technology.

However, at the same time, they are actually dividing us by taking control of our thoughts and our minds; thus being able to decide what the mass consciousness should think and experience. Therefore, regardless of how we look at it, it's the end of both individuality and unity. Instead, we are getting a unified hive mentality and a hive community that is manipulated from the top. I am aware that the enthusiasts disagree with this; they are saying that the purpose is to strengthen the individual in a unified society. This sounds like a great utopia coming true, but let us rewind and take a look at history.

THE BREAKDOWN OF THE FAMILY UNIT

THE FAMILY UNIT HAS BEEN a threat to the Cosmic Outlaws

---

[48] *Ibid. op. cit.* (Further reference: *NWO Frequency Weapon Controlling Your Mind! Patented Evidence & Link to Mark of Beast,* https://www.youtube.com/watch?v=NoEl4R7MR0Y [video length: 24 min.])
[49] See also researcher Lisa Haven's video called, *NWO Frequency Weapon Controlling Your Mind!* https://www.youtube.com/watch?v=NoEl4R7MR0Y for some sobering info.

for centuries because it creates a strong bond between people. In the middle ages, the family unit was kept under control by having people live in poverty, filth, and starvation, while the rich were wallowing in money, luxury, and delicious food. Families stuck together but had little time to do anything, except trying to cope with a situation where they lived from day to day struggling to survive.

With the Industrial Revolution and the new technological era, things changed. Regular people eventually received higher education, in order to be able to understand and work with technology and the society that emerged from it. Also, the living standard slowly increased in the Western World, and real poverty became rarer. The backside of this, viewed from the Outlaws' perspective, was that the family unit also became stronger and healthier. People had more time to talk about things of concern, and it became harder for the manipulators to control families. The Controllers had no idea what was happening behind locked doors. Consequently, something had to be done.

One of the ideas was to introduce television. The goal became *one TV in every home*. This was the *fourth* of many future steps to seduce the population with nonsense, so that they, instead of sitting around the table discussing subjects that could challenge the status quo, would be distracted and separated by watching TV (the first step to distract people was *silent movies*, the second step was *radio* and the third step was *movies that included audio*). As a result, people who did not go to the theater or listen to the radio could bring the theater into their own homes. By distracting people, often with nonsense programs, such as dubious western movies that distorted the actual history of the Wild West, TV series, subtle propaganda films, and biased and controlled news programs, they could more easily dumb down both the individual and the family unit.

This worked like a charm for many years (and still does to an extent), but the AIF still felt threatened. Therefore, they wanted to create an experiment to see how solid their manipulation and mind control of the masses really was. Hence, they created the counter-culture movement, which originated at the *Tavistock Institute* in the U.K.[50] The Vietnam War had started, and now the Controllers and their Minions thought it might be a good idea to target the kids. Hence, the *hippie movement* was created. It

---

[50] See, John Coleman, "CONSPIRATORS' HIERARCHY: THE COMMITTEE OF 300"

all started with Elvis Presley, who was succeeded by The Beatles and The Rolling Stones, upon whom a large number of other pop and rock groups, as well as individual singers and songwriters, followed. The entire purpose with pop and rock music was (and still is) to manipulate the teenagers.[51] Part of the agenda, in the 1960s, was to alienate the children from their families, by indoctrinating them and introducing them to drugs. *Woodstock* and other huge rock concerts had one major purpose—to drug down the hippie generation. At Woodstock, drugs were used openly, and the police were instructed not to intervene.

What a stunningly great number of the musicians of the hippie generation had in common was that they were children of high ranking military families. Many of these young musicians had been subjected to trauma-based mind control and had developed multiple personalities. Jim Morrison of *The Doors* is just one of many examples.[52]

Charles Manson, another mind-controlled puppet, together with his equally mind-controlled gang of fanatic murderers, put a nail in the coffin of the hippie movement, and from then on society became more violent and unstable, while heavy metal bands, such as Alice Cooper and Black Sabbath with their tuned down guitar music, being examples of forerunners of music groups who are spreading music with dark and often violent messages. These new bands now became the role models for a new generation. Alice Cooper (his real name is Vincent Furnier) said in an interview that he and his band were those who actually put the final nail in the coffin of the hippie movement. Most hippies were now in their late twenties or early thirties, and some of them succumbed to drugs while others cut their hair, married and got a job.

The Tavistock/Woodstock experiment had been successful, and the previous stability of the family unit began to show some serious instability, after having lost almost an entire generation to war, rock music, drugs, and promiscuous sex. Nonetheless, something more had to be done to once and for all break families apart, and the Rockefeller Foundation was put in charge to accomplish this.

---

[51] Ibid.
[52] I advise you to read the entire series of excellent and very well researched articles written by the late David McGowan, "Inside The LC: The Strange but Mostly True Story of Laurel Canyon and the Birth of the Hippie Generation." Click on the link, which will take you to Part 1.

They came up with a brilliant solution that also looked humane and fair on the surface, but its real purpose was to split the "dangerous" family unit and to more or less pull it up by its roots. The Rockefellers instigated and sponsored the *Women's Liberation Movement (Women's Lib)* in the early 1970s. They planted some mind-controlled charismatic women on the stage, and these puppets were proponents for women to have equal rights to men. This, of course, was a new concept in this male-dominate world and could have been a good thing, if it wasn't for the real purpose behind the movement. The idea was that women should have an equal right to fulltime jobs as men and to have equal opportunities to advance within the societal structure.

This agenda was a success! Women entered the job market in much larger numbers than ever before, and they now had their own careers to think about. Then, of course, they also wanted to marry and have children. This became a problem to a certain degree because how would they be able to combine their careers with raising children?

The answer was simple: Daycare! These Daycare Centers took care of (and raised) the children, while both their parents were busy working long hours. Also, society now had the opportunity to indoctrinate the children at an early age by taking charge of their early "education" (read *indoctrination*). Now, finally, the family unit was split up. The societal structure the Rockefeller Foundation created and sponsored has now become the norm. Before Women's Lib, parents usually raised children who were happy and who, because their childhood was peaceful, had a stable ground on which they could go out and face the world as young adults. This was entirely based on the father who could support his entire family with his income, while the mother could be a stay-at-home mom, taking care of the children and working around the house. This is the best environment for children to grow up in. This became next to impossible after the breakdown of the family unit. Suddenly, the father (in general) couldn't financially support his family anymore, when inflation made commodities much more expensive and income did not increase to match this upsurge in costs. Hence, regardless whether the mother wanted to work or not, she was forced to, in order to be able to contribute to the overall finances of the family.

In summary, the Administrators and the Overlords do *not* want us to unify on a spiritual level by our own means: a process that otherwise happens quite automatically when two or more people are able to connect on a deeper level, such as within solid and stable families. Since time immemorial, the Outlaws have worked hard to keep us separated from each other on a spiritual level. Today, it is worse than ever; both parents work, the children are brought up by strangers, when what they actually need are their real parents, who can give them solid guidelines on how to behave as children and how to best succeed as adults. Instead, the children are being purposely indoctrinated by society from a very early age. Then, when the real parents pick up their children from Daycare after work, they are usually so exhausted after a stressful work day that they have little energy left to take care of their children's needs. What this creates are unstable children with anxiety, depression, and low self-esteem. When these children grow up, they are easily further manipulated by society, and they often become obedient workers for the system. It's utterly important to have a stable and loving childhood to fall back upon, when challenges in life are getting the best of us.

Note also that I don't imply that women should be exempted from having a career if they want to, but I think the setup of the original family unit is the ideal. Moreover, I think it's important that a couple contemplate this important issue with the above in mind, before they dedicate themselves mindlessly to a very stressful job market, leaving the main responsibility of childcare to others, who have no connection to the family. I know it's hard to manage on one person's wages these days, but we don't need fancy houses, expensive cars, and increasing credit card debt in order to have a good life; less can sometimes be sufficient to survive and maintain a healthy work/life balance.

It's important for the Overlords to program us from our early childhood because that will format our way of thinking later in life. Instead, if sound and intuitive parents educate their children from the beginning, by giving them their love and their time, great moral and ethical values, and teach them how to survive on their own, but also teach them how to problem solve, to help out at home in order for them to learn how to function in a family, and have them learn different skills—based on the parents' experience and common sense—the children will become much more stable as adults. They will also be capable of critical thinking, rather than being subjected to the indoctrination given in Daycare Centers and elsewhere, which only creates obedient slaves. Of course, there is always a chance that the parents are flawed and will teach their children destructive behaviors that they are passing forward from *their* parents, or they might abuse their children in different ways, but in general, the old way of raising children creates more capable and compassionate individuals.

Separation makes people unhappy; we are a social species, and the Controllers know this, of course. It's imperative for the Controllers to separate us in order to unite us. The unification that the Controllers *want* is unification through technology, and to make that happen they must make humanity feel that it is in need of change. If a need for change is not created, no one wants to change. Having a sound family unit in place, few people would like the changes proposed by those in charge. However, after having separated us from each other and made us overstressed and unhappy, we are crying out for a change that offers protection and guidance. It's the Controllers' formula all over again, *problem-reaction-solution*.

Transhumanism is a way to further tighten the ropes around our necks, while presenting it as something positive by pointing out key things that are desirable to people, such as immortality, because most people are afraid to die. They are afraid of the unknown, and they don't want to leave their loved ones behind. With the Singularity in place, that won't happen; or deaths will at least be very rare and far between.

People get what they want (unity) and the Overlords get what *they* want (synthetic/artificial unity, created with technology). Then the new trap closes around people, who are turning into immortal cyborgs who can't escape. They are stuck with rejuvenating artificial bodies that never die or deteriorate because everything in their bodies can be replaced and eventually be self-healing; it's just a matter of reorganizing the manufactured cells/nanobots in the body, and new limbs and organs can easily heal, or rather self-rejuvenate. People will be stuck for an eternity, figuratively speaking, in cyborg bodies, in service to, and as part of, Lucifer's Legions. If this is not threating to us, I don't know what is. It is the same as the definition of "nightmare" or "Hell" to me. Fortunately, there is a "soulution", which I will come to later.

THE UNITED NATIONS' ROLE IN TRANSHUMANISM

ONLY BY LOOKING AT THE NAME, *United Nations*, it's easy to see that at least one of the goals for this organization is to unify all countries in the world into becoming one single Nation under "God;" a *One World Government*. This is not a secret; the UN freely admits to this. More specifically, they are the linking and negotiating body between countries, in order to unite them—they are the intermediary. However, what they don't tell us, but is known to many who work there,[53] is that they are also involved in preparing for the *Second Coming*; a religious leader who will sit upon the World Throne.[54] The UN supports the AI movement, as well.

THE SECOND COMING FROM A NEW PERSPECTIVE

BEFORE WE MOVE ON, I WANT TO MAKE A CORRECTION. In the WPP I argued that the returning Messiah would be an AIF leader, who will take on that role of becoming the World Leader. Aside from the fact that evidence of this was discussed in the WPP, it is also supported by a number of channeled entities, such as the *Ashtar Command*, the entities behind the *Great White Brotherhood*. This is going back to the *Theosophical Society* from the 19th century, founded by Madame Helena Blavatsky. She was channeling what she called *Ascended Masters*, and their message had everything to do with the Ashtar Command descending to Earth to help save us from ourselves.

Alice Bailey, one of Mdm. Blavatsky's successors, continued to spread her mentor's teachings, even more extensively emphasizing the Messianic message. She had deep ties to the United Nations[55] through something she called *Lucis Trust*, which is still part of the United Nations. The term "Lucis Trust" is actually a play on *Lucifer's Trust* and *Lucifer Publishing Company*, something that was discussed in detail in the WPP.[56] In the 1980s, a man who supposedly possessed unnatural powers, was a frequent visitor in the United Nations Building, and even met regularly

---

[53] See the Wes Penre Paper, The Fifth Level of Learning, Paper #14: "The End of Kali Yuga; When the World Religions Become as One, Section VI. Maitreya—the World Leader. Bogus or the Real Thing?"
[54] Ibid.
[55] See, http://wespenre.com/5/paper14-the-end-of-kali-yuga--when-the-world-religions-become-as-one.htm#6 for more info. on the new Messiah, here called *Maitreya*.
[56] See, "The Wes Penre Papers—The Multiverse Series," The Fifth Level of Learning, p. 604ff.

with U.S. Presidents, such as George H.W. Bush. He is believed by many officials in the United Nations to be the new Messiah (as a matter of fact, many who hold positions in the U.N. are Theosophists, i.e. they follow Mdm. Blavatsky's doctrines, while many others are Fundamental Christians and/or Born Again Christians and thus believe in the Second Coming).[57]

I wrote in my papers that the Second Coming would most likely be En.ki. This might or might not be the case, but I could have made a mistake when I concluded that. If we ponder the triad of Osiris, Isis, and Horus from old Egyptian mythology, Osiris is the equivalent to En.ki; Isis is his niece, being Prince En.lil's (Ninurta's) daughter and Horus is Marduk, En.ki's and Isis' son. Horus became the Messiah figure of his time, and there are similar Messiah scenarios earlier and later on in history. The savior figure who is most renowned in the Western World is, of course, Jesus Christ or Jeshua Ben Josef (there are other versions of this name). I also attached En.ki to Jesus; this is most likely false. The Jesus figure was most likely Marduk and not En.ki. The Messiah must be, as earlier mythology and history suggest, *the son and not the father.* Therefore, the future Messiah should be Marduk returning as Christ, not En.ki (if we go on what was written in the New Testament); thus, the correction. The "divine" figure different religions are waiting for, from what I can see, is Marduk. The Anti-Christ, seen from one perspective, is you and I and everybody else who does not support or believe in the Christ, i.e. Marduk, as our savior.

Then, what role does his father, En.ki, play in all this? Isn't he supposed to come back and rule in the upcoming Age of Aquarius? Isn't he the *water carrier* in the old Sumerian texts, whose sign is Aquarius, the water sign? Yes, he is! Lord Marduk is already here and has been here, on and off, for millennia. As much as he is Satan and the *Lord of this World*, he is also the Christ—something I'm sure Christians don't want to hear or believe. However, now it's soon time for Marduk's new glorious days, in which he can rule mankind openly. His father has already returned from what I have concluded, and albeit the Age of Aquarius is En.ki's sign, he will most possibly not rule openly—he is still playing the father role. En.ki will be the one pulling the strings in the background—if Marduk lets him.

---

[57] See, "The Wes Penre Papers—The Multiverse Series," The Fifth Level of Learning, p. 589ff.

En.ki's and Marduk's roles in the AI movement will be further discussed in an upcoming chapter.

POPULATION CONTROL AND TRANSHUMANISM

AT THE TIME OF THIS WRITING, there are more than seven billion people on this planet, and the Western governments are not willing to pay the cost to feed all the people who are sick and starving in the Third World countries. Also, seven billion individuals are far more than it's possible to control; the Singularity goal would probably have to be postponed to another time if all these people had to be kept in the fold, but the Administrators are receiving pressure from the Overlords to have the Singularity in place approximately by 2045.

The best, and perhaps only way, to accomplish this is to reduce the population drastically; some researchers say that the goal is to reduce the world population to 500 million people, and others have suggested that the reduction will be even more drastic. In Chapter 8, we will discuss what is being done to accomplish a population reduction, and it's not a matter of dropping bombs over our cities to kill us off (although this happens, as well); it's more sophisticated than that. By poisoning our food with GMO, destroying our environment, spraying chemtrails, giving people vaccines, giving us poisonous "medications", and so on, they weaken our immune system, and even make us infertile. We also get prone to heart diseases, diabetes, cancer, and other potentially fatal illnesses that will both control population growth and reduce the number of people in the next generation. There are many other measures taken as well; many of them are unknown to the general public, and also to those of us who are working on exposing the agenda. More details will most certainly emerge in the near future by those digging into the population reduction issue. The above measures are only the tip of the iceberg; those behind the scenes have it well planned out, and they hope to accomplish this in quite a covert way, so that people in general won't notice. Besides, very few people think that their Government would do all this to them.

Then, when the population is reduced to a more manageable number, the next preset target, leading to the Singularity, can be set into motion.

Part of the agenda is to purposely make people sick and dysfunctional. When people don't feel well, and very little seems to be done about it, it's convenient to introduce AI and the Singularity as a solution. Once again, it will be emphasized that with the Singularity in place, there will be no more death and diseases—in fact, this is what Dr. Kurzweil was discussing in his books.

After the Singularity, the population, by then heavily infested with Artificial Intelligence in the form of nanobots, can be increased to a new, desired number. Lucifer's Legions need human cyborg soldiers (so-called *super soldiers*) to assist them in their quest, and they probably need more than half a million soldiers, one would think. Eventually, the Outlaws might want to create a massive military base, covering most of Planet Earth. Hence, in order to have total control over population growth, the puppet scientists are well on their way to making robots that are capable of reproducing. This is not science-fiction. It is being exposed in mainstream media, which we will look into in a future chapter. Then, I can imagine, when the AIF decides that they have just the right number of cyborgs, controlled by a Super Brain Computer (SBC), they can stop the cyborg bodies from being able to reproduce. No one will probably protest because a little change in the "chemistry" of the SBC will affect and transform the neurological pathways in the world population, and everybody will think that whatever idea the Overlords come up with is brilliant. Also, by controlling our neurological system via nanobots (antennas), they can easily manipulate us into thinking that *we* came up with the idea ourselves. When the population ceiling is reached, very few new souls will probably be able to incarnate in this 3-D reality (who would want to incarnate under these circumstances, anyway?).

Now I would like to show you an interesting dialogue on the subject of life and death, quoted from Ray Kurzweil's website,

> Questioner: *If people stop dying, isn't that going to lead to overpopulation?*
>
> Ray Kurzweil: A common mistake that people make when considering the future is to envision a major change to today's world, such as radical life extension, as if nothing else were going to change. The GNR revolutions will result in other transformations that address this issue. For example, nanotechnology will enable us to create virtually any physical product from information and very inexpensive raw materials, leading to radical wealth creation. We'll have the means to meet the material needs of any

conceivable size population of biological humans. Nanotechnology will also provide the means of cleaning up environmental damage from earlier stages of industrialization.[58]

Kurzweil is absolutely right; there *is* technology that can clean up our environment. The oceans that have been destroyed by litter and oil, the atmosphere, the forests and cities, radiation, and virtually everything else can be cleaned up. It's not human technology that can do this, but ET technology in the hands of humans. The Controllers and the Minions rely on this, and therefore they believe that they can create any disaster they want because it's reversible.

According to Kurzweil, in the above excerpt, no population reduction is needed. We can create offspring around the planet more or less unhindered, he claims—even as biological beings—and will still have enough resources to spread them out equally to everybody.

This, of course, contradicts Bill Gates' agenda to reduce the population with vaccines and by other means, but that's just how the game is played; Gates is pretending to sit on the fence because that's what he's supposed to do. He represents the indecisive population that can see both the pros and cons of the AI Movement and the Singularity.

In perspective; what are we actually dealing with? Are we dealing with designed population control or won't there be any population control at all? We need to understand that there are agendas within agendas within agendas and that the AIF's (Alien Invading Force's) propaganda is full of oxymorons and doublespeak, but population control is already being implemented. The overall population is still growing, but the next generation will be less in numbers because of all the anti-fertility programs that are being run in the background.

---

[58] http://singularity.com/qanda.html
[59] http://www.wingmakers.com/

How Transhumanism will Affect the Human Soul Group

JAMES MAHU OF THE WINGMAKERS[59] made a very distinct statement in the essay, *The Fifth Interview of Dr. Neruda*, where Dr. Neruda says,

> Technology will evolve from external-impersonal, to external-personal, to integrated-personal, to internal-personal. Transhumanism is the last phase, and it is the phase that the elite are moving to.[60]

This is the agenda in two sentences. The Administrators are indeed merging technology with biology and are then transforming technology to become internal and part of the personal; the inner self. These cyborg bodies will become just as natural to people as our current biological bodies; the technology is going to be impeccable in that sense.

Nothing will be released to the public without first having been tested in the military; soldiers are the guinea pigs for all major projects, as they have always been. If you sign up for the military, they own you; once you put your signature on the line you become military property and you need to follow orders. You cease being treated as a sovereign human being and can be legally experimented on. This is obvious even to those who have never been in the military when we look at how war veterans with PTSD are mistreated, if treated at all. The great majority of homeless males are veterans. Some of them are so compartmentalized that they only have vague memories from their military service. Their trauma does not always develop in war situations; it can also come from cruel experiments. When the experiments are over, the victim is given amnesia and will not remember anything, until perhaps several decades later, when horrific memory flashes surface.

Once the tests have passed the military criteria, it's time to release the new technology to the public. Although the technology has been there all the time within the Luciferian Empire, not all of it has been tested satisfactorily on humans.

Before and after the Singularity, robots and humans will be living side by side, as we already are. However, there's going to be much more of that in the *very* near future. I know that many readers are quite concerned

---

[60] The WingMakers, *The Fifth Interview of Dr. Neruda*, p. 25, op. cit.

about the robots taking over the job market, and that's a valid concern. Robots *will* take over most of the job market, and they are successively doing so already now, as we will see. This, too, is part of the plan to instigate more fear in humanity. The machines are cost-effective, and therefore, the industries feel justified having humans replaced. Humans need restbreaks and lunchbreaks, which is time consuming and costly for corporations. Also, humans make errors and are slow, in comparison to their robotic partners, and people get sick, need time off, need sleep, have a family life, private time, a forty hour workweek, vacations, and often expect free weekends. They also need to be paid. A robot can work twenty hours of the day with few needs, besides occasional repairs and tune-ups. However, this is only temporary because self-repairing robots are now being tested on the market.

Of course, there needs to be some kind of equilibrium in the world of business. If most of the population is unemployed, they can't feed the corporations with money to buy their products, so the constant money flow will stop, and everything will crash.

The Administrators have thought of that, too. The robots, with their artificial intelligence, will not totally take over the market; there will still be workers, although they will be forced to work more and more, side-by-side with robots. However, the fear of having a totally robot-controlled market is a part of the initiation into the AI agenda. When Kurzweil was asked about robots taking over the job market, he admitted that this might be a problem in the beginning, but as soon as the world is under serious reconstruction to serve the Singularity, there will be work for everybody. In the meantime, to hold us over, we might need Government aid, he says. Well, with all the current and future financial crises, this does not seem feasible, but then again, the Administrators are busy working on crashing the world economy so they can create a new form of world currency that will supposedly work in the post Singularity world. Whatever happens in this regard, I sense tough times ahead.

Fig 3-2: Eric Schmidt, former Google CEO.

The big corporations are important players when it comes to making the Singularity a reality. They are also blatantly telling us about their agenda in the media. No one can say they didn't warn us. A typical example of this type of arrogant behavior is Google's former CEO, Eric Schmidt. Google is one of a number of mammoth corporations that is in partnership with the government. In a two-minute YouTube video that the reader can watch here, https://www.youtube.com/watch?v=MYA8xfyzEYk, he reveals that Google is currently gathering all the information it can on each individual on the planet who is using Google's search engine. He adds that a person does not have to type something in; the company still knows what we're doing. He is also quick to add that it is done with our permission, of course.

As I've mentioned previously, it's very important that they have our consent; even if we are not aware that we are giving it and what we are giving our consent to. Well, in this interview Schmidt gives it all away. Not only does he tell us that Google is learning everything about our habits. It's also been publically announced that Google has been caught and fined for hacking the passwords of its users.

Fig 3-3: Google hacking passwords from Google users.

As if this wasn't enough, Schmidt gladly gives away another secret. The interviewer gets into the subject of implanting our brain, and the CEO laughs and says that there is something he calls "the creepy line" that Google is not crossing; therefore, he wouldn't consider implants, *at least not until they have the technology to do so!*[61] That's quite an amazing statement, in my opinion. He can't commit to not having plans to implanting people because he would be lying on record. By adding this disclaimer, he thinks that he has protected himself. I advise you to listen to him at the above link. The Controllers are getting much more arrogant about their agendas now.

These days, the Controllers don't mind being much more open with their plans. It is part of the *partial disclosure* I wrote about earlier. These people know that even if a certain number of people get the message and understand the agenda behind it, most will still remain in denial, afraid to

---

[61] "Don't be evil" is Google's motto, whether the reader believes it or not, https://en.wikipedia.org/wiki/Don%27t_be_evil

take action, because if they do, their lives might change, and their current material status will be threatened. At the time of this writing, the YouTube video with Eric Schmidt has more than 24,000 visitors, not including all those who actually saw the interview on television, and life still goes on as usual. The arrogant Administrators and their Minions have very little to fear from the general public at this time, and they know it. The only real threat against them would be a mass awakening. One way to counteract such an awakening would be to increase their level of manipulation, in order to keep the lid on as tight as possible until the Singularity takes care of the control issue once and for all. Also, with the afterlife recycling center making sure that deceased humans are properly "taken care of," they don't believe that anyone can really escape or do any real harm to them.

SMART CITIES AND THE VENUS PROJECT

WHAT WILL THE FUTURE, post Singularity cities, look like? At this point, do we have a clue? Yes, we do have a clue because this is already in the planning, and as is the norm for the moment, the Controllers keep us informed, if we only know where to look and how to interpret the information that we are given.

One of the prospects out there, showing how they might want to set up these cities, is the *Venus Project*.[62] The following is a brief summary of what this project allegedly stands for (my emphasis in *italic*),

What is the Venus Project?

WRITTEN BY DARIUS MORAVCIK

Very briefly, The Venus Project is an organization that proposes a feasible plan of action for social change, a holistic global socio-economic system called *a Resource Based Economy* that works towards a peaceful and sustainable *global civilization.* It outlines an alternative to strive towards where human rights are not only paper proclamations but also way of life. The Venus Project presents a vision not of what the future will be, but what it can be if we apply what we already know in order to achieve a sustainable *new world civilization.* It calls for a straightforward redesign of our culture in which the age-old problems of war, poverty, hunger, debt,

---

[62] https://www.tvpmagazine.com/2015/04/the-venus-project-technologies

and unnecessary human suffering are viewed not only as unavoidable, but as totally unacceptable. Anything less will result in a continuation of the same catalog of problems found in today's world. The Venus Project presents an alternative vision for a *sustainable world civilization unlike any political, economic or social system that has gone before*. It envisions a time in the near future when *money, politics, self and national interest have been phased out*. Although this vision may seem idealistic, it is based upon years of study and experimental research. *It spans the gamut from education, transportation, clean sources of energy to total city systems.*[63]

The way this is written, it probably sounds pretty good to many people, but contemplating what we've learned thus far, the Venus Project fits right into the Agenda. This project has attracted significant media attention since it started, and I have little doubt that the architect, who designed this project, is working on behalf of the Administrators and the Overlords. There is a reason why I believe this to be the case, and I will show you soon. The visionary and the architect of the Venus Project is Jacque Fresco, who had his 100th birthday on March 13, 2016.

Fresco argued that it would be too costly to remodel the old cities we already have, so instead they want to build something entirely new and futuristic to emphasize the new beginning of this new world civilization.

The Venus Project is a model of a *Smart City*; something I also wrote about in the WPP. Ideally having a new monetary system in place (the Venus Project website refers to *Resource Based Economy*), the entire project seems like a utopia come true. However, the resources must come from somewhere in order to be able to build Smart Cities around the world. The solution is, according to this project, a One World Governance of a One World Economy, where all parts of the world contribute to pay for these Smart Cities; e.g. if a certain country needs a Smart City, the entire world will contribute financially to build it. Countries will probably still exist, but they may become more as provinces in a global *Super State*.

---

[63] https://www.thevenusproject.com/tvphistoryevent/what-is-the-venus-project

Fig 3-4: Smart City of Venus Project design. (Source: The Venus Project). It looks very similar to certain drawings of an ancient city from Atlantis.

These Smart Cities, as the plans go, will be populated with a new human species that are cyborgs—half human and half machine and infested with AI. The remaining fully biological humans, who refuse to be part of the Singularity, can't live in these cities by default—they will be *outcasts*. Life in those cities will be so different from life outside the cities that based on our human standards of ethics and morals, you and I would find ourselves in a nightmare if we lived in them, side by side with a great number of super-intelligent hive-minded cyborgs. We wouldn't be able to intellectually function there. The goal is to make cyborgs a billion times more intelligent than the most intelligent human who has ever lived (more about this later). There is no place for biological humans in this synthetic environment.

The Venus Project is heavily sugar-coating its vision; particularly mentioning George Orwell's *1984* and the *Terminator* movies as fearful propaganda, but the Venus Project is, on the other hand, promoting what it calls a *Cybernetic Government*, where everything is computerized and highly technological. Remember, this is the foundation for the cyborg society, and it's planned in a manner that will be more or less self-sufficient, overseen by a highly advanced computer network.

We have all seen the science-fiction movies, usually set far out in the future, and having futuristic city models. The new Smart Cities will look very similar to the ones we're already used to seeing in these kind of movies; we have been well-prepared and programmed, so that nothing seems to stand out as being entirely new; instead people will have an inner recognition when they see pictures of those Smart Cities, and they will have an epiphany, where they might say, "Ah, I've seen similar cities before. They were in (so and so) movie!" The architecture will already be familiar to the population in general.

Moreover, the Venus Project suggests that people in desert areas will be living underground. There will even be cities in the sea; something that's also presented by the Venus Project, and it shows pictures of these cities on their website, https://www.tvpmagazine.com/2015/04/the-venus-project-technologies).

The presentation of the Venus Project is, in my opinion, also a test of how well we can use our discernment. Many of those who go through the Venus Project's website look at all these futuristic pictures, absorb the same vision as those in charge of the project, and might find it rather exciting and attractive. However, if we look behind the curtain, we find the Wizard of Oz lurking and manipulating.

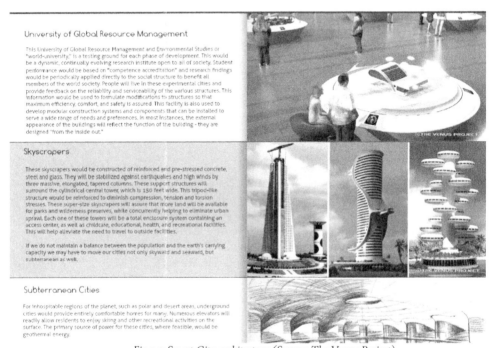

Fig 3-5: Smart City architecture (Source: The Venus Project).

The Venus Project is the brain-child of Jacque Fresco, who is sharing his vision with the world. However, can we say for sure whether this a unique project by a true visionary, or whether it's something that is originating from intelligent, manipulative beings not-from-here? A little research might give the answer (my emphasis),

> In the "sustainable new world civilization," Fresco notes in an online video that *"there will be no families."* Plus, *"children are a pain in the [rear end]" anyway, he said.* Overpopulation and global warming, among other things, "threaten each of us," the organization claims on its website.

> [The Venus Project] calls for a straightforward redesign of our culture," the site notes in its frequently-asked-questions section. "It envisions a time in the near future when money, politics, self- and national-interest have been phased out." To solve the problems, *"we must declare Earth and all of its resources the common heritage of all of the world's people,"* it concludes, echoing the terminology of internationalists the world over, especially those at the United Nations, about how to redistribute the world's wealth in areas such as the law of the sea, outer space law, environmental law, human rights, and humanitarian law.[64]

Fig 3-6: Jacque Fresco, Founder of the Venus Project.

By simply excluding children from the equation, Fresco is taking population reduction and the splitting of the family unit to a new level. Everybody understands that humanity can't survive without children, so a super-controlled cyborg society would be the only other option. After all, Fresco does mention the term *Cybernetic Government*, as I revealed earlier.

Also, Fresco is not shy to express his views, which are not short of hinting at a totalitarian society on a global level (again, my emphasis in *italics.* Fresco's statements here are quite stunning and remarkable).

---

[64] http://www.thenewamerican.com/world-news/north-america/item/10634-zeitgeist-and-the-venus-project

At his lecture in Sweden, in response to a question from this correspondent about what would guide production in the absence of prices, Fresco said it again, referring to the act of thinking as a privilege. *"If you give everybody a right to their own opinion, you damage society,"* he claimed. In the interview with The New American, he emphasized the point yet again. *"Giving everybody a right to their own opinion is dangerous,"* he said, adding that in the future, people could access all sorts of information, but not opinions.[65]

It should be sufficient to end the Venus Project discussion here because there is little doubt whose errand Fresco is running. There is much more to say about this project, but the reason I am bringing it up at all is because it's a typical example of how we need to use our intuition and discernment. Something that is presented as exciting and benevolent on the surface might have a much darker side to it, and it's up to us to become *clever* enough (I don't want to use the word *smart* here for obvious reasons) to see through this on a regular basis—indeed, it's crucial for our survival as a human species and as free-thinking spirits. This becomes even more important when we read that the Venus Project is getting a very positive response from people who have listened to Fresco's lectures, as well as others who have come in contact with his ideas. It is on its way to potentially becoming a grassroots movement. This is rather discouraging because with a positive response to such an obviously dangerous project, we notice how the human tendency to filter out what we don't want to hear is something the Controllers are well aware of and are playing on when Fresco boldly is revealing the entire Overlord agenda in public—here is the truth in plain sight, and people are getting positively excited over their own extinction.

FROM TRANSHUMANISM TO THE SINGULARITY

AS I WROTE EARLIER, Transhumanism can be seen as the process necessary to achieve what scientists call the Singularity. In fact, we are in the middle of the Transhumanism process right now.

Thus far, we haven't discussed in depth how the establishment is

---

[65] *Ibid.*

going to create this bridge, but we will. However, it's too much for one chapter, so I'm going to break it down, after I have presented the basics of the Artificial Intelligence idea.

CHEMTRAILS AND NANOBOTS

THERE ARE MANY SMALL AND BIG STEPS THAT NEED TO BE TAKEN in order for the agenda to progress. One important step is to make certain that we all have nanobots in our blood stream. Unfortunatley, it seems that everyone who's been subjected to chemtrails has them in their system[66]—including me. The city, in which I live, is being heavily sprayed on a regular basis. There is not much we can do to avoid this; after all, we need to breathe, and when we do, we are likely to breathe them in.

I know this might come as a big shock to people, and many will doubt that it's true. This is understandable, but the Controllers will see to it that everybody on the planet gets these nanobots in their blood, one way or another, and the proof of this is coming from the horse's mouth, which I will show the reader in the next chapter. After all, if you were to decide how to best infest as many people as possible with these nanobots, without their knowledge, wouldn't it be a good idea to include them in chemtrails? Also, as I wrote in the Prologue, nanobots are supposedly embedded in many medications.[67] It's been suggested[68] that it all started with pain medications (opiates), such as Vicodin/Norco, Oxycodone/Percocet, MS Contin (long acting morphine), and OxyContin (long acting Oxycodone/Percocet). Since then, it's allegedly been added to most medications on the market.

What effect will these nanobots have on the individual? Are we now doomed to turn into machines? At the moment, nothing drastic will happen, and what will occur in the near future depends on the individual and the person's level of consciousness, i.e. vibration. Those, who are totally ignorant, will respond exactly the way the Controllers anticipate, and the nanobots will, when activated, with time, replace the human immune system. The nanobots contain artificial intelligence on the nano-level that will respond to outside stimuli. The idea is that by replacing the

---

[66] Pleiadian lecture, Spring 2015
[67] Miscellaneous Pleiadian lectures
[68] *Ibid.*

human immune system, diseases can be cured remotely, by stimulating the bots in a desired way, in order to cure an illness.

This potentially paves the road to immortality, induced by technology, the ultimate question would be, why do we want immortality in the physical world when we all are entirely spiritual and could have full access to the eternal spiritual realm instead? No one needs technology to live forever; we are all immortal by default. When we realize this to the fullest, we no longer have any doubt that we are in a prison, and our sentence, in spite of the fact that we didn't commit any crime, is to live in it for an eternity, in service to the prison guards and their Masters.

Nanobots work in such a way that once we have them activated, those in control can stimulate any of these nanobots in the entire population simultaneously, or each individual can be stimulated in isolation without affecting those around them; all in the name of health, security and immortality, of course.

However, what we are not being told is that the Controllers can change our personalities remotely, as well, by manipulating the nanobots any way they want. In an instant, they will be able to program us all at once, and no one will protest because protests will not be an option when we're connected to the SBC. Exactly the same way it's done with robots, cyborgs can be reprogrammed, too, until they respond in accordance to the overall unified system. Many researchers have exposed how the Controllers are using *Extra Low Frequency* (ELF) to affect the human mind, and this has been done for quite a while. It is one way to keep us within the frequency band that is our mental and physical prison.

Fortunately, there are ways to avoid the profoundly negative implications of this nanotechnology, which is something we will discuss in   the   last   chapter.

Chapter 4:
Ray Kurzweil's Singularity

RAY KURZWEIL MONOLOGUE

AS MENTIONED EARLIER, Raymond Kurzweil coined the term *the Singularity*—a metaphor he said he had borrowed from physics. He further says that, "physics dictates that in the gravity of a black hole, which also increases exponentially as it is approached, there is a threshold distance away from the center, the Event Horizon, past which nothing can return."[69]

In this chapter, we are going to delve into the Singularity concept, and we are mostly going to use sources that come from either its spokesperson, Dr. Kurzweil, or the mainstream media. It is very sobering information, and Kurzweil is convincing in the sense that he gives the impression that he believes his vision is in humankind's best interest. If it were only the vision of one person, I would never have had a reason to write this book, but he shares his vision with the Administrators and, ultimately, the Alien Invader Force. In addition, mainstream media is all over it, and anybody, who is willing to do so, can see his vision unfolding all around us. It is up for debate how much Kurzweil knows about the ET connection. It may very well be that he is speaking the truth the way he sees it, when he says that AI is "not an alien invasion from Mars with machines coming to invade us..."[70] As a propagandist for the movement, he doesn't need to know the whole picture, and it's desirable for the Controllers that he doesn't. Anybody who is not *in the need to know* is going to be filled in about the ET situation.

---

[69] http://bigthink.com/100-biggest-ideas/the-singularity-of-ray-kurzweil
[70] http://bigthink.com/videos/ray-kurzweil-explains-the-coming-singularity

Kurzweil, who is also the co-founder and the *Chancellor* of the *Singularity University* and *Director of Engineering* at Google, said the following in a video monologue some years ago (my emphasis where indicated),

> By 2020 we will have technology that will simulate the human brain but we still have to find out the methods. Many measures of IT double in every 11 months or so—it goes fast. These technologies will be a million times more powerful in 20 years from now. And the speed of exponential growth is itself speeding up so in 25 years the technologies will be a billion times more powerful.
>
> We have already seen the incredible speed since the 1960s. Cellphones today are a million times cheaper and a thousand times more powerful. That's a billion-fold increase.
>
> In 2029 [and he's been quite consistent with this, he says (my parenthesis)] we will have completed the reverse engineering of the human brain. We have already reverse engineered several regions of the brain. By 2029 we will have the "software" that can simulate the human brain. Computers at that time will be far more capable than the human brain. Then we can make machines that can be like humans. Machines are already superior to us.
>
> It's not an alien invasion from Mars with machines coming to invade us; it's coming from within our civilization, and the whole point is to extend our reach [out in the universe]. SINGULARITY is not just that point when we achieve (combine) human intelligence and machine. Machines will be able to improve their own software design. 2045 we will have expanded the human intelligence with machines a billion fold. THAT will be SINGULARITY.[71]

It definitely does not sound as if he or the Controllers will go back on this for anything, regardless of public opinion. Speaking of public opinion, Kurzweil often, in his speeches, can't emphasize enough how important it is that they get input from the public in order to get a "balanced debate," as he usually puts it. We can hang our hats on the idea that he and his cohorts are thoroughly monitoring the Internet for public opinions on the Singularity.

---

[71] http://bigthink.com/videos/ray-kurzweil-explains-the-coming-singularity Op. cit. This is also on YouTube: https://www.youtube.com/watch?v=1uIzSiuCOcE

To contribute to the "balanced debate" and to sound credible, Kurzweil also mentions the downsides and dangers of AI. For example, in his book, *The Singularity is Near*, he writes about the downsides and dangers of *genetics nanotechnology robotics* (GNR), and I paraphrase:

1) Abuse of biotechnology in the military can potentially be an issue. The same technology that will empower us, e.g. by curing cancer and heart disease, can also become a potential danger to us if this technology gets into the wrong hands.

2) A terrorist can program a biological virus to be more deadly. The good news is that we have the scientific tools to defend ourselves. The biological terrorist is what scares him the most, but he adds that we are building defenses against it, but we are not there yet. Moreover, it's not accurate to say he has a utopian vision only—he emphasizes that he is looking at both sides of the coin.

3) He admits that there are dangers with new technology, but he keeps repeating that he's optimistic,[72] and that we will be more helped than hurt.[73]

It's ironic that he mentions how these new technologies may fall into the wrong hands when they were in the wrong hands to begin with. He may seem very naïve, but he is just playing his part in the game. He is, nevertheless, a puppet with limited knowledge and with a scientific mind.

The Singularity is all about achieving the *immortality of the gods*—a today's *Tower of Babel*. It seems obvious that Kurzweil fears death, and he admits to that in a YouTube video.[74] Regardless of how much Kurzweil knows, the emphasis on fear of dying triggers the same anxiety in the people he's communicating with. This fits perfectly into the real agenda, which is to get people hooked on the idea of becoming immortal; an idea based on fear.

---

[72] "...but I'm an optimist, not a pessimist" has become something of a propaganda phrase amongst AI Prophets. As we shall see in a later chapter, physicist Michio Kaku, also an AI Prophet, uses the same kind of expression.
[73] Raymond Kurzweil, *The Singularity is Near*, Chapter 8.
[74] https://www.youtube.com/watch?v=1uIzS1uCOcE

"THE SINGULARITY IS NEAR"—DISCUSSIONS AROUND THE BOOK

RAY KURZWEIL'S BOOK HIT the shelves back in 2005. This is eleven years ago as of this writing. Eleven years may seem as a long time ago, but one of the purposes with the book is to show that he can predict the future and therefore seem credible. Those interested in the AI movement are in awe over how eerily correct these "predictions" have been so far, but they fail to take into consideration that Kurzweil knows his stuff; the technology is already developed, so it's just a matter of *when* certain parts of it will be released. He may or may not have that inside information, but for him, who is carefully monitoring the progress, it's not very difficult to predict different changes to come.

VIDEO PROMOTION

IN ONE OF SEVERAL YOUTUBE VIDEOS,[75] in which he is promoting his book, he makes some stunning revelations I now will bring up, one at the time. Of course, he defines the Singularity for the listener, and he summarizes it by saying that it is "when humans and machines are no longer two separate things." This short definition should make even the most dedicated-to-the-Singularity-agenda person freeze in his or her chair, but unfortunately, that is usually not the case. While researching this, I've noticed that an increasing number of young people are embracing the entire idea of the Singularity, despite the fact that they will become part machines, which is not a secret. The "immortality button" is probably the movement's most important key.

Also, those who have read The Wes Penre Papers—The Multiverse Series (WPP) may recall that I mentioned how many souls, now part of our younger generation, incarnated here solely to participate in the building of the Machine Kingdom.[76] Barbara Marciniak's *Pleiadians* call them "Machine Riders," which I think is a suitable name. Therefore, many parents will have children who seem to be geniuses with electronics.

---

[75] https://www.youtube.com/watch?v=8XWXJDgbeP0
[76] The "Machine Kingdom" is a term I adopted from the Pleiadians. I like this term because it contains "machine," as in robot, and "kingdom," as in the Patriarchal AIF Empire, based on male dominance.

48

Chapter 4: Ray Kurzweil's Singularity

We hear about two-year-old toddlers, capable of only speaking a few words, comfortably navigate a smartphone or a tablet. Ignorant parents might be amazed at their toddler's skills, and maybe even a little frightened, while the knowledgeable parents might be sad or devastated, understanding that they have one of these Machine Riders in front of them. Being aware where this is heading, the conscious parents might desperately try to distract the children's attention away from the devices and into something more genuinely creative. However, when the children are by themselves, they will once again have a smartphone in their hand.

My point is that whatever the parents might try, their children will remain attracted to electronics as moths to the light. I am not saying that it is impossible to change these children, but realize that these little toddlers are just adult souls in a small body; *they've come here for the Singularity!* Most people have some kind of mission here on Earth—a goal we set before we were born here—and as little as you and I want our purposes in life tampered with, just as little as do these children want to have theirs tampered with. However, the difference between them and us is that they are extremely determined and seem addicted to electronics almost already from birth, while the rest of us can be distracted, away from our basic goals and purposes. This could be a tough thing to realize for parents. Some of these children's passion is so strong that very little, if anything, can change their direction, nor are we entitled to. Regardless of whether we like it or not, we have no right to interfere with someone else's life purpose. If we try to change them with force, their entire reason for being here is stolen from them. Albeit, the children might not be consciously aware of this, they will feel it, and they will protest against it.

The next thing I want to emphasize in the Kurzweil video above is when he says, "...we *are* the human machine civilization. It's really part of who we are." What he is really saying is that our biological form is imperfect and outdated, and in order to evolve, we need to integrate with the machine. In his mind, the machine era was bound to happen as a part of human evolution. However, because humans in general have become lazy and don't want to work on their own spiritual development, it's much easier and quicker to let the scientists do it for them, and the population just goes along for the ride.

Moreover, Kurzweil says in the same video, "You can change your body to fit in a particular environment." This is particularly interesting for the reason that according to Kurzweil, one of the extended goals for the new humanity is to control (read conquer) space. The AIF will eventually give us cyborg bodies that can travel in space and withstand radiation and the general harsh conditions in space. Although we are discussing nano technology in this book, the Overlords have no intention (at least not in the near future) to let humankind nano-travel (travel by thought). That would be *too* close to becoming godlike.

"People *are* mechanical," Kurzweil says in the video. It seems as if they are not afraid to take any measures in order to program people's minds. You can distinguish this phrase in the cacophony of voices, talking at once behind the background music at the end of the video, if you pay close attention. The many voices speaking at once is an old technique to program the subconscious mind. One of the traits of the subconscious mind is to take in data and make it literal. Once a phrase, programmed into our minds on an earlier occasion, is repeated by the media, or by someone else, this subconscious programming surfaces. The listener will take the message literally and as a matter-of-fact—especially if the statement is repeated often enough, which is the case, *with the same "news" running over and over, twenty-four seven, in the media. This is not to inform us, but to program us and to trigger previous programming.* If I had listened less carefully, I would have missed the programming in Kurzweil's video.

The last statement in the video that I want to bring up is very revealing, "Do you think that just because it's in a movie, it can't be real?" Here they are giving us the truth about how they are using Hollywood to promote their agenda. For a long time I have said that all these Hollywood movies about space wars, artificial intelligence, and films on other related subjects, are made in order to prepare us for what is to come. To be blunt, *Hollywood is set up for one major purpose—to indoctrinate and program the masses.* This is mainly accomplished by programmed producers and actors, who are being told what kind of movies to make and which actors to choose for the roles. We call the technique to covertly giving things away *truth in plain sight.* The Overlords believe in informing us about their plans beforehand, so we can't come afterwards, when the movies become real, and say that we had no idea about their plans. *We were forewarned via Hollywood, but we didn't pay attention.* We thought it was all science fiction. I can't repeat this often enough: *they need our direct, or indirect, consent in order to fulfill their plans. This is not because they want an informed public, but to protect themselves against prosecution in the future for interfering with our free will.*

Some Quotes

"Ray Kurzweil is the best person I know at predicting the future of artificial intelligence. His intriguing new book envisions a future in which information technologies have advanced so far and fast that they enable humanity to transcend its biological limitations-transforming our lives in ways we can't yet imagine."[77] —*BILL GATES*

"Kurzweil links a projected ascendance of artificial intelligence to the future of the evolutionary process itself. The result is both frightening and enlightening....The Singularity Is Near is a kind of encyclopedic map of what Bill Gates once called 'the road ahead.' "[78]—*The Oregonian*

"If the singularity is as likely and as globally, utterly transformative as many here believe, it would be profoundly unethical to make it happen without including all of the stakeholders in the process - and we are all stakeholders in the future."[79] –*Ray Kurzweil*

On RAY KURZWEIL'S WEBSITE, http://singularity.com/, he has an *About the Book* section, where he wrote the following (my emphasis),

...[the] merging is the essence of the Singularity, an era in which our intelligence will become increasingly nonbiological and *trillions of times more powerful than it is today*—the dawning of a new civilization that will enable us to transcend our biological limitations and amplify our creativity. *In this new world, there will be no clear distinction between human and machine, real reality and virtual reality. We will be able to assume different bodies and take on a range of personae at will. In practical terms, human aging and illness will be reversed; pollution will be stopped; world hunger and poverty will be solved.* Nanotechnology will make it possible to create virtually any physical product using inexpensive information processes and *will ultimately turn even death into a soluble problem.*[80]

---

[77] *The Singularity is Near*, "Praise for The Singularity is Near" (page unnumbered).
[78] *Ibid.*
[79] http://www.bibliotecapleyades.net/ciencia/ciencia_singularity02.htm
[80] http://singularity.com/aboutthebook.html

Synthetic Super Intelligence and the Transmutation of Humankind

Kurzweil claims that the new man (whom, henceforth, I will call *Posthuman*) will be billions of times more intelligent than the most brilliant genius who's ever lived. The reason he can make such a claim is that the scientists, working for the Controllers, have already been able to clone the human brain into the smallest details and have figured out how to utilize *100% of the brain* in an artificial way. This Super Brain Computer (SBC) will then become the central point and the super-mind of Posthumans, and any and all information contained in the SBC can then be "downloaded" into each individual connected to this "network" through nanobots. We can only imagine what implications this must have. We can also only imagine how it would be to live as an outcast in this new society. Those who would refuse to take the "Mark of the Beast" still live under the same umbrella as those who are a billion times more intelligent. It's not a nice world to live in.

In Kurzweil's utopia, "there will be no distinction between human and machine, real reality and virtual reality." The Singularitarians, those who are for the Singularity, make comments that Anti-Singularitarians claim that the Singularity is the end of humanity, which is way off the mark. The Singularitarians say that there will be no cyborgs, only humans with individual access to almost endless information. Those who make these comments really need to research this subject without filtering things ; after all, *this has to do with humankind's immediate future*. There are countless references in Kurzweil's books alone that the merging of man and machine is *literal*. Regardless of what Kurzweil claims, all we need to do is to look around us. We see human body parts exchanged for machine parts. This will become so much more obvious in the next few years; indeed, we're almost there, and the Singularity *is* near.

Also interesting is the last part of Kurzweil's statement, where he claims that we are living in a virtual reality. Posthumans, with their vastly enhanced intelligence, will understand that they live in a hologram, where the spirit-mind-body complex can create anything that it is capable of imagining. Understand also that most of the technology involved in this is ET technology, of which we have a poor comprehension.

"We will be able to assume different bodies and take on a range of personae at will." Doesn't this remind the readers of what I wrote in the WPP? I mentioned quite a few times how some of the AIF have bodies in storage and how they can "jump bodies" at will. The enhanced human, who the AI Prophets call *Human 2.0*, is going to be able to do the same thing; it's indeed the AIF giving us the *Tree of Life*, i.e. immortality—but in a contained way. Because Posthumans will be connected with the SBC, they are prevented from "escaping" in the process. Once a Posthuman, always a Posthuman; there is no escape; the soul splinter is trapped, being electronically connected with the notorious SBC.

What people *will* be able to do, though, is to change bodies when they change environment, according the Kurzweil. Let's pretend you are a super soldier here on Earth, being trained for space wars: once you go into space, you jump bodies into one that is more suitable for space travel (such as the *Gray alien* bodies). You can now endure the harsh conditions in space in a 3-D body because the Grays, who themselves are cyborgs, are constructed in a way they can endure space conditions.

Moreover, in the same quote it says that Human 2.0 will not only be able to assume different bodies, but also will be able to take on a range of personae at will. This means that Posthumans can change personality instantaneously; perhaps, a Posthuman would be able to go from being an average person one second and in the next second, he would become a raging super soldier. The question is, will Posthumans have any real sense of ethics and morals, or will he become so robotized that he no longer knows right from wrong? The almost obvious answer is the latter. If the SBC were to become the center of everything, and the SBC were controlled by the AIF, emotions, morals, and ethics would also be at the mercy of the Overlords.

It doesn't matter, according to Kurzweil, if you are 80 years old when the Singularity happens; your age can be reversed with new technology and with help from the nanobots we already have in our system. I'm sure Kurzweil wants to speed up this entire process because he is in his sixties at the time I'm writing this, and without having achieved immortality before his body expires, he apparently thinks he is doomed. In his mind, there is no place for an afterlife. However, if he manages to stay alive for another decade or two, his aging can be reversed, and it's quite apparent that this is what he's aiming for. Or maybe, as a favor, they'll take care of him and give him the reverse aging program earlier than that; after all, he could be one of the guinea pigs for the testing of AI technology, only to eventually go out in public and say, "Hey, look at me!

I'm getting younger!" If Kurzweil can *prove* by example that he has reversed his own aging process, I'm sure that would excite people.

On top of everything else, he promises that pollution, world starvation, and poverty will be 100% resolved. Consequently, would that justify the *continuous* pollution and destruction of Planet Earth we see today? Certain people seem to think so.

HOPELESSLY BEHIND?

IT'S IMPORTANT FOR THE AI MOVEMENT (from now on I will interchangeably call it the *Movement*, with a capital M) that we all understand what the implications of the Singularity are. Dr. Kurzweil makes it clear that if we are not on the bandwagon, we'll be an inferior species; indeed, a *very* inferior species, according to their norms. In a Q&A session, he writes the following:

> Nonbiological intelligence will have access to its own design and will be able to improve itself in an increasingly rapid redesign cycle. We'll get to a point where technical progress will be so fast that unenhanced human intelligence will be unable to follow it. That will mark the Singularity.[81]

This will be shocking for people once this sinks into their minds; it will make them think that there is no choice. Do they want to live amongst cyborgs that can redesign and improve themselves in such unimaginable speed that those who are opting out of the Singularity can't even fathom it? Most people will be scared, and after having thought it through a few times, many will voluntarily join the Movement, or otherwise be left behind.

People need to learn how to see through this silly propaganda and refuse to participate in the AIF programs. Contrary to what the Movement says, we are *not* mechanical, and we are *not* machines; we are spiritual beings, and the Singularity is *not* a natural process in our evolution—unless we are manipulated into believing that we are.

The evolution from being genetically manipulated slaves to becoming free spiritual beings again will only take as long as we let it. We are only trapped so long as we decide we want to remain trapped. On the

---

[81] http://singularity.com/qanda.html

other side of this entrapment is freedom—freedom of thought, freedom of imagination, freedom of intention, and freedom of action—no technology and no SBC needed! These freedoms are paramount in order for us to be able to explore the dimensions, using our free will. Once again, we will be aware that we are spirit/mind/body in unity, and there will be no death or separation between spirit/mind and the body—*death does not exist outside En.ki's trap because the spirit/mind/body is eternal!* We are all capable of going from entrapment to freedom faster than the blink of an eye, but only if we wish to. I will expand on this in the end section of the book.

If we, on the other hand, buy into Kurzweil's propaganda, we will never achieve individual freedom *on any level*; everything will be very physical (in the sense we usually perceive the word "physical" in this 3-D "reality"). In an artificial way, we will be able to do things that we can't even dream of now, but under very strict control, and always on the AIF's conditions. Eventually, we will end up as their foot soldiers in a galactic war (more about this later). We will be able to travel in space, but in a very mechanical way (through *Einstein-Rosen Bridges*, wormholes, and stargates, etc., in a very physical manner), and the spiritual part of the Universe will forever be excluded from us. Why would we want to do all that when we naturally can achieve the same thing and so much more?

As others and I have reported repeatedly, *the answers lie within.* Here in 3-D, we can go inside our bodies and minds to find answers and to explore the Multiverse. How can we possibly do so in an artificial, mechanical body? The more mechanical, the more difficult to access our real selves. Those with such bodies need to rely totally on the SBC to feed them censored ideas and thoughts. However, all the Movement is doing is cloning the brain, and you know as well as I do that the brain is not remotely the same thing as consciousness.

The late David Bowie showed us the potential future in his last few videos from the album he made while he was dying. If you decide to watch them, you will be able to see the symbolism after having read this book. The message is all in Bowie's symbolism. He was quite knowledgeable on the subject from being a lifelong reader of Aleister Crowley's material.

THE RA MATERIAL—THE LAW OF ONE AND AI

P ERHAPS SOME READERS, who have read the *Ra Material*,[82] will notice some similarities between the RA entities and the Singularity. The Ra Material is, for those who haven't heard about it, channeled material from the early 1980s. There are those who claim that this channeling is the best-channeled material humankind has ever received, containing the most accurate information of all channeling.

A tight-knit group of three people broadcasted these beings through one person in the group, the late Carla Rueckert (channeler). The two other members of this group were Don Elkins, PhD (questioner), and Jim McCarty (scribe). They channeled a group of entities who called themselves Ra (allegedly no connection with Amon Ra or Marduk). They said they were a *social memory complex*, which means, in their own words, that they were a *collective*, connected to a central super-intelligence, consisting of the combined knowledge of their species, and from this super-intelligence, they could, individually, draw information. Don Elkins' questions were often brilliant, so the answers from this collective were very deep and detailed, but sometimes quite scientific in nature. Despite this, the material is still comprehensible to a large degree, once we get used to the RA entities' complex and quite mechanical way of talking. Elkins understood most, but not all of it, being a scientist himself.

Something that strikes me with the Ra Material is the amazing similarities between their social memory complex and the Singularity. They both draw from a central point, and the individual is not as important; the individual is just a cog in the "machinery" and, hence, is expendable. First, it is the social memory complex that needs to be protected. The Ra beings try to give us good reasons why it's preferable to become a Social Memory Complex, and they say that we humans are on our way to becoming the same. Similar to what the Movement says, Ra tell us, too, that it is a natural part of our evolution.

Another curious thing with the Ra Material, and something that puzzled me already in the beginning when I read the material, is the mechanical answers they give to Elkins' questions. They lack all sense of humor and emotionality—their replies and comments are very mechanical

---

[82] http://www.bibliotecapleyades.net/ra_material/law_one.htm; http://www.llresearch.org/

and complex. They claim to have evolved on Venus and to have visited our planet a few times. They also claim to be the Pyramid Builders (which means, if true, that they are a group tightly connected to the Overlords, who are the ones who actually built the pyramids, or at least restored them. Some say the pyramids are older than 450,000 years, which is the approximate time the AIF has been here, but Ra claims they built the pyramids in a much more recent time than that). Moreover, there are many similarities in their message and in the message of other channeled material, e.g. Ra says that they are us in the future.

From what I can see, there are three possibilities who Ra might be, and they are the following:

4) They are us in the future, post Singularity.

5) They are another civilization that also adopted the Singularity model.

6) They are AI, controlled and instructed by the AIF to feed Don Elkins with some answers so that we can adopt *their* version of reality as a step toward our own Singularity.

There might very well be civilizations out there that have preceded us in the Singularity; all controlled by the network belonging to the Luciferian Empire , but the bottom line is that the Ra collective has too many similarities with our own journey toward the Singularity to be just a coincidence. If you have read the material, you might relate to my argument, and if you haven't read it and now start reading it, you will notice that the resemblance is remarkable. Unfortunately, many people in the alternative movement and New Age treat the Ra Material as a piece of gold. Personally, I see too many discrepancies in the material, and in addition, *the late Carla Rueckert, who channeled Ra, was a Christian and remained so throughout her entire life.* Why have so few people noticed this? If a person, who is a devoted Christian, is channeling, what is coming through him or her is severely distorted and biased toward that person's religious belief. For people, who are quite knowledgeable about channeled material, not to recognize this fact in the sense of the Ra Material is just more filtering.

I am not sure how Carla justified the goodness of the "demonic" Ra entities (seen from a Christian perspective), but somehow she did.

It is my impression that the Ra Material is Artificial Intelligence, and as such, the AIF is ultimately behind this channeling. Many people think that entities that people channel must be what they say they are—after all, they think, the information being channeled is sometimes so comprehensive and coherent that only very advanced, higher dimensional beings can be behind it.

This is not true, however. Think again what the Singularity accomplishes. According to the spokespersons, connecting a soul group to an SBC would make each individual connected to everybody else, including everybody else's knowledge. Someone can instantly get the information he or she needs. This means that AI could give Elkins, and others who are involved in channeling, instant answers to almost any question. The answers don't necessarily need to be correct, but they can be made coherent.

The most important message in the Ra Material is something they call the *Harvest*. This word, in context of what Ra are telling us, gives me the creeps. The Harvest means *harvest of souls,* and supposedly has to do with our ascension from the third to the fourth density. People, who are more than 51% *Service to others* will be *harvested* and transmitted to the fourth dimension, and the Ra people will be here to assist us.

I hope that the reader of my material has understood that there is no such thing as ascension to a certain density or dimension. Either we are in En.ki's trap, or we are not. If we are not, we automatically have access to the KHAA, i.e. as many dimensions and densities we wish. Ascension to a certain dimension or density is just more hogwash and entrapment.

The reader is of course free to come to different conclusions.

A Closer Look at the "Super Brain"

FOR THOSE WHO STILL THINK that the Super Brain Computer (SBC) is one more of those "conspiracy theories," I want to show those readers that the SBC is actually well in progress, and this comes from the horse's mouth. Kurzweil says in a Q&A interview,

> To understand the principles of human intelligence we need to reverse-engineer the human brain. Here, progress is far greater than most people realize. The spatial and temporal (time) resolution of brain scanning is also progressing at an exponential rate, roughly doubling each year, like

most everything else having to do with information. Just recently, scanning tools can see individual interneuronal connections, and watch them fire in real time. Already, we have mathematical models and simulations of a couple dozen regions of the brain, including the cerebellum, which comprises more than half the neurons in the brain. IBM is now creating a simulation of about 10,000 cortical neurons, including tens of millions of connections. The first version will simulate the electrical activity, and a future version will also simulate the relevant chemical activity. By the mid 2020s, it's conservative to conclude that we will have effective models for all of the brain.

So at that point we'll just copy a human brain into a supercomputer?

I would rather put it this way: At that point, we'll have a full understanding of the methods of the human brain. One benefit will be a deep understanding of ourselves, but the key implication is that it will expand the toolkit of techniques we can apply to create artificial intelligence. We will then be able to create nonbiological systems that match human intelligence in the ways that humans are now superior, for example, our pattern- recognition abilities. These superintelligent computers will be able to do things we are not able to do, such as share knowledge and skills at electronic speeds.

By 2030, a thousand dollars of computation will be about a thousand times more powerful than a human brain. Keep in mind also that computers will not be organized as discrete objects as they are today. There will be a web of computing deeply integrated into the environment, our bodies and brains.[83]

Instead of how we experience things today, with people sitting before computers and letting the Internet find information for them, humanity is going to be connected directly to an AI *Innernet*, where they can share all humanity's collective information and knowledge with each other. This collective information will originate from what is programmed and uploaded (by humans) into the huge database Kurzweil calls the Super Brain, and which I call the Super Brain Computer (SBC). The collective mass consciousness will then have access to everything that's in the SBC (or so we are told).

Perhaps we can now better see what the Internet *really* is designed to do and why it was developed to begin with. It's a network first tested in

---

[83] http://singularity.com/qanda.html

the military (just as everything else) and then released to the global population as a forerunner to the SBC. The Internet helps the AI scientists (and the Overlords) to collect information on us. They want to know how we think, how we react in relation to each other on a global scale and across different cultures, what the collective is most interested in and why, how many are "awake," and how much we know about different subjects. Of course, these are just a few examples.

The purpose with the Internet is to study human behavior.

It doesn't matter so much what it is we put on the Internet; in essence, the Controllers are closely monitoring it in order to learn more about us as a *social complex*. They are not monitoring us because they want to eliminate people who are figuring things out—usually they don't care about that—they just want to know how much we know and how much we don't know as a collective. This is why most people get away with what they're publishing on the Internet, unless someone gets in possession of and is posting some classified material that can be used as evidence against the planners. They may also take actions if we do something else that means we're stepping on their toes. The standard operating procedure in the first case is to eliminate the person, if possible, or threaten him or her by targeting the person's family or friends. The solution in the latter case is to send in the *trolls*.

Ultimately, in a couple of decades or so, the data the Controllers have gathered on us will be included in the SBC as collective data from the human mass consciousness. Once the Controllers have finished this project and the Singularity is in place, the Internet will cease to exist, as well as most computers in general. They are no longer necessary because people will have all the Internet information available to them inside their brains. All they need to do is to download whatever information they want from the SBC, and this will happen instantly; no more slow or disrupted Internet connections. Anything can be accessed immediately and electronically from the SBC. In addition, each individual will then add to the SBC database with his or her knowledge on a regular basis as he or she continues learning new things in life. The learning process, by the way, will be unimaginably faster because each individual will download already existing information on any subject that is collected in the mass consciousness; everything from highly advanced scientific data and information to the most mundane thoughts and ideas. This is what Kurzweil means when he talks about us learning a billion times faster; we have access to *everybody's* thoughts instantaneously.

One thing that may come to mind to the reader is that the "knowledge" and information most people possess is often far from accurate, and these inaccuracies, and all the "junk thoughts" we communicate to each other, will also be stored in the SBC database. This could potentially mean that these inaccuracies will *also* spread a billion times faster and act as a virus in a system that is designed to only keep accurate data and information accessible.

This is of no concern, if we ask the AI Prophets. No junk or disinformation will be stored in the SBC to begin with, and the individual brain, via nanobots, will simply download what the Controllers want us to consider being "accurate information," i.e. the information that is stored in the SBC. Everything that's considered inaccurate or pure nonsensical will be "erased" from the individual brain because it's not part of what is programmed into the SBC. The SBC database will "take over" the brain in the sense that what is in the SBC will be what Posthumans will be able to think with—*it will be the new human mass consciousness!* The idea is that each individual, once connected to the SBC, will instantly be a billion times smarter. With this new way of thinking, Posthumans can then expand their thoughts and ideas and add them to the SBC database for everybody in the world to have access to.

The entire idea with the Super Brain is a way to wipe out individual thinking as we know it, and instead the Overlords will have us start all over with a storage of *selective* information that will replace what is now our individual personality. Individuals, connected to the SBC, will be a new person altogether. They might still be able to individually think (the same way the Ra entities are), but their thinking will be based on what the Overlords and their Administrators have decided should be included in the mass consciousness. This Super Brain can, of course, be modified by the AIF at any time. This, in conjunction with mankind becoming cyborgs, will send Homo sapiens sapiens (Human 1.0) to their extinction indefinitely, replacing them with Posthumans (Human 2.0). Human 1.0 was heavily controlled and manipulated, but we still had some abilities to think freely about the situation we are in, but by creating Human 2.0, the Overlords eliminate this option, and Posthumans will be the *ultimate* slaves, incapable of thinking in terms of breaking out of this new, indefinite control system. If someone would still be able to think outside this new, diminished-sized box, you can rest assured that this person's thoughts would be erased remotely. We already know that this can be done because the AI Prophets have told us (see earlier sections and chapters in this book). Based on the above conclusions, a book such as this will not be included in the SBC and will probably only exist in human consciousness as long as the Internet is up and running and mankind is still not connected to the SBC.

The Internet is, of course, not the only system from which the Controllers are gathering information about us; other examples are smartphones, new cars, GPSs, and more.

Kurzweil states outright that in post Singularity we won't be able to distinguish between different virtual realities. If this doesn't sober people up, nothing will. All people need to do is to stand back and look at this scenario and ask themselves; is this what we want humanity to become? Do we want to become parts of an eternal video game where we are the characters, while those who run the SBC are the players? Would that not make it easy for the game masters to make us do anything they want us to do and place us in any dimension they wish in order to have us fight their cosmic wars?

Now the reader probably can probably see how video games get into the picture, as well. Aren't those a preparation for the *real* virtual reality game that has been planned for us? Young people are addicted to video games. In those, they can get involved in virtual reality wars, space wars, and other extreme violent behavior and they love it. Wouldn't many of these kids love to be able to do this in real life, thinking they can do it without even breaking any moral or ethics codes? After all, it's all just a virtual reality, right? The deception and the manipulation go deep, and those who are most receptive to manipulation of this caliber are the children and the adolescents of today's world.

Those who have read *Ender's Game* understand what I'm trying to convey; Ender is a teenager, who competes with other teenagers to become the top virtual reality player, trying to be the one who can shoot down most alien spaceships. Under strict military discipline, these boys and girls are being told that they are practicing for the real thing, in case we would be attacked by a certain alien species in the future. Ender is doing great on the "test runs," and he is shooting down many enemy ships. However, as revealed later, these were not test runs—they were the real thing! Every time Ender and the other children shot down something on the screen, they actually, unbeknownst to them shot down real ships.

Could it be that the virtual realities Kurzweil is talking about are different dimensions? By having us under total control, they could send us through the dimensions and create havoc wherever we go; all under the supervision of the AIF. Wouldn't that, from a metaphysical standpoint, be the perfect weapon for the AIF to expand their empire? If someone thinks this sounds far out, think again and think hard. Bring the video games up one level and there you have our future reality. When playing video games, we are the players, and the characters in the game are at our mercy; we decide how they should act. If we bring this up one level, we are the characters and the AIF are the players. We already have the technology to do this. Welcome to the *Brave New World!*

Virtually everything that has to do with technology and artificial intelligence originates from the AIF—including AI!

What we call the "physical reality" is *their* domain, under *their* control. They are the masters of the reality we live in, but they don't control the other dimensions. They control our physical reality *from* other dimensions, but these dimensions are not under their control. Their empire is located in the physical world, and the beings who live here are *we humans* and *other soul groups elsewhere, who they have manipulated in a similar way that they manipulate us.*

In a later chapter, we will address how they are presenting the SBC in the media, and you can read about what scientists have to say on this.

THE EXPONENTIAL GROWTH IN TECHNOLOGY

HERE IS ANOTHER REMARKABLE statement from Ray Kurzweil:

> My models show that we are doubling the paradigm-shift rate every decade. Thus, the 20th century was gradually speeding up to the rate of progress at the end of the century; its achievements, therefore, were equivalent to about twenty years of progress at the rate in 2000. We'll make another twenty years of progress in just fourteen years (by 2014),

and then do the same again in only seven years. To express this another way, we won't experience one hundred years of technological advance in the 21st century; we will witness on the order of 20,000 years of progress (again, when measured by the rate of progress in 2000), or about 1,000 times greater than what was achieved in the 20th century.

The exponential growth of information technologies is even greater: we're doubling the power of information technologies, as measured by price-performance, bandwidth, capacity and many other types of measures, about every year. That's a factor of a thousand in ten years, a million in twenty years, and a billion in thirty years. This goes far beyond Moore's law (the shrinking of transistors on an integrated circuit, allowing us to double the price-performance of electronics each year). Electronics is just one example of many. As another example, it took us 14 years to sequence HIV; we recently sequenced SARS in only 31 days.[84]

If Kurzweil is correct in his calculations (and after all, he has inside information that the public has no access to), we are indeed close to the Singularity.

Here is more from Kurzweil; this time it's about upgrading "human body version 1.0" (our current biological bodies/computers) to "version 2.0," as I wrote about earlier this is the same allegory Dr. Jamisson Neruda uses in the *Fifth Interview*, by the way, posted on the WingMakers' website.[85]

In the book, I talk about three great overlapping revolutions that go by the letters "GNR," which stands for genetics, nanotechnology, and robotics. Each will provide a dramatic increase to human longevity, among other profound impacts. We're in the early stages of the genetics—also called biotechnology—revolution right now. Biotechnology is providing the means to actually change your genes: not just designer babies but designer baby boomers. We'll also be able to rejuvenate all of your body's tissues and organs by transforming your skin cells into youthful versions of every other cell type. Already, new drug development is precisely targeting key steps in the process of atherosclerosis (the cause of heart disease), cancerous tumor formation, and the metabolic processes underlying each major disease and aging process. The biotechnology revolution is already in its early stages and will reach its peak in the second decade of this century, at which point we'll be able to overcome

---

[84] http://singularity.com/qanda.html
[85] https://www.wingmakers.com/content/neruda-interviews/

most major diseases and dramatically slow down the aging process.

That will bring us to the nanotechnology revolution, which will achieve maturity in the 2020s. With nanotechnology, we will be able to go beyond the limits of biology, and replace your current "human body version 1.0" with a dramatically upgraded version 2.0, providing radical life extension.

[...]

The "killer app" of nanotechnology is "nanobots," which are blood-cell sized robots that can travel in the bloodstream destroying pathogens, removing debris, correcting DNA errors, and reversing aging processes.[86]

According to Kurzweil, already less than ten years from now they will be able to reverse our aging process, and as he points out, it's not just a matter of manipulating baby's genes so that they won't age after a certain number of years, but the baby boomers will also be able to reverse their genes and become younger. It soon gets obvious how the Movement is promoted; most people want to extend their lives because we have been indoctrinated to be afraid of death—the unknown—for many reasons. Immortality will be an incredible gift for many people, and they will probably not think twice about taking the *Mark of the Beast*. The AIF will use nanobots to replace the original cells in the body, and these nanobots will be able to reverse aging, or already aged bodies. Posthumans (Humans Version no. 2) will look as they did at their most desirable age; somewhere between 25-35 years old. Then they will supposedly stay that age for the rest of "eternity" in this very physical reality.

Posthumans will be electronically wired to the SBC and get access to a greater volume of their own brain. However, once hooked up, people can't unhook themselves; hence, those who don't want any part of this kind of future better act upon it now and begin the withdrawal process from having been involved in, and addicted to, electronics. There are those who say that electronics is more addictive than cocaine.

Are *you* addicted? One way to find out is if you can comfortably imagine a life without your smartphone, Internet, computers in general, and any other electronic devices you may possess. If the answer is yes, you are not addicted, but still need to be careful. *If you're uncertain, or if the answer is no, you'd better start working on yourself because the addiction will*

---

[86] http://singularity.com/qanda.html

only get worse, and you will probably not even notice how you unwittingly step into the AI reality and the Singularity. It's a good idea to use the Internet as little as possible and only look up information that is relevant to your progress—but only if absolutely necessary. From now on (if you haven't started already), it's the inside work, such as mediation, that will substitute the so-called information we get from the Internet. Probably more than 80% of what we read online is false. I suggest you read my e-book, "Beyond 2012—A Handbook for the New Era,"[87] where I include many helpful exercises that can very useful.

I still want the readers to understand that we all have free will, and anybody whose desire it is to hold onto all the electronics and ultimately become connected to an electronic super brain has all the right to follow that path; this book is only meant to give information so we all can make a conscious choice. I want my readers to at least consider an important part of the problem that has not yet been discussed. In essence, I am following Kurzweil's advice that we need to be well informed before we make the final decision whether to become part of the Singularity or not.

Now, let's discuss cyborgs for a moment. Why don't we ask Kurzweil what he has to say about cyborgs and how and when we humans are supposed to experience this process? This is what he writes,

> We're already in the early stages of augmenting and replacing each of our organs, even portions of our brains with neural implants, the most recent versions of which allow patients to download new software to their neural implants from outside their bodies. In the book ["The Singularity is Near," *Wes' comment*], I describe how each of our organs will ultimately be replaced. For example, nanobots could deliver to our bloodstream an optimal set of all the nutrients, hormones, and other substances we need, as well as remove toxins and waste products. The gastrointestinal tract could be reserved for culinary pleasures rather than the tedious biological function of providing nutrients. After all, we've already in some ways separated the communication and pleasurable aspects of sex from its biological function.[88]

As I've written earlier, in the center of the transformation is the

---

[87] You can download the PDF file here: http://wespenre.com/books/Beyond-2012-A-Handbook-for-the-New-Era.pdf
[88] http://singularity.com/qanda.html

nanobots; they are essential for Transhumanism to work. Kurzweil continues [my emphases],

> [The third revolution is] [t]he robotics revolution, which really refers to "strong" AI, that is, artificial intelligence at the human level, which we talked about earlier. We'll have both the hardware and software to recreate human intelligence by the end of the 2020s. We'll be able to improve these methods and harness the speed, memory capabilities, and knowledge-sharing ability of machines.
>
> *We'll ultimately be able to scan all the salient details of our brains from inside, using billions of nanobots in the capillaries.* We can then back up the information. Using nanotechnology-based manufacturing, *we could recreate your brain, or better yet reinstantiate it in a more capable computing substrate.*
>
> Our biological brains use chemical signaling, which transmit information at only a few hundred feet per second. *Electronics is already millions of times faster than this. In the book, I show how one cubic inch of nanotube circuitry would be about one hundred million times more powerful than the human brain. So we'll have more powerful means of instantiating our intelligence than the extremely slow speeds of our interneuronal connections.*
>
> I see this starting with nanobots in our bodies and brains. *The nanobots will keep us healthy, provide full-immersion virtual reality from within the nervous system, provide direct brain-to-brain communication over the Internet, and otherwise greatly expand human intelligence. But keep in mind that nonbiological intelligence is doubling in capability each year, whereas our biological intelligence is essentially fixed in capacity. As we get to the 2030s, the nonbiological portion of our intelligence will predominate.*[89]

Kurzweil is really putting it out there for anyone to see what they have in planning for us. He is the perfect front person; he is enthusiastic and naturally positive about the agenda.

When I am writing this, it is 2016, so we don't have much time to reject the AIF's plan for humankind, and likewise we don't have much time left to be human if we don't act. *Just as the smartphones were sneaking up on us, and most people have probably not even thought about how that could happen so quickly. The transformation from Human 1.0 to Human 2.0 will happen*

---

[89] *Ibid.*

just as seamlessly. We won't know that we're there until we're suddenly there. *Today, many people might think that we are still only in the beginning of this entire AI process when indeed we will be almost at the end of it.*

We have seen in the media how soldiers who come back from war with only one arm or one leg can get these replaced with sophisticated machine arms and machine legs, and after some practice, the soldier will be able to work the new body part nearly as well as the original body part; nerve sensitivity included. When they mentioned this in the news media, people were stunned over this amazing technology. The Administrators' controlled scientists must have laughed behind the scenes, knowing that this was Stone Age technology compared to what they already had. Still an important question remains; how is the transformation from biological humans to cyborg going to happen? Are we going to be forced to have surgeries to remove and replace vital organs, such as heart, liver, and kidneys?

No, it's much more sophisticated than that. This is how it's going to be done:

Questioner: So we're going to essentially reprogram our DNA.

Ray Kurzweil: That's a good way to put it, but that's only one broad approach. Another important line of attack is to regrow our own cells, tissues, and even whole organs, and introduce them into our bodies without surgery. One major benefit of this "therapeutic cloning" technique is that we will be able to create these new tissues and organs from versions of our cells that have also been made younger—the emerging field of rejuvenation medicine. For example, we will be able to create new heart cells from your skin cells and introduce them into your system through the bloodstream. Over time, your heart cells get replaced with these new cells, and the result is a rejuvenated "young" heart with your own DNA.[90]

Again, the nanobots are the center of this process. We are virtually going to have our organs replaced without surgery and without any particular noticing on our part. I mentioned earlier that the great majority of humankind already has nanobots implanted in their brains and their bloodstreams via chemtrails, medicines, and vaccines. These bots might be

---

[90] *Ibid.*

dormant for now, but just as the antennas that they are, they will be activated remotely, and the process will begin. Then, perhaps, the big news will come out, telling us that we are now all immortal and our cells are self-replicating in a manner to keep us alive and healthy. They will expose this fact with pompous and glamor and with a sense of exhilaration, as if it were one of the greatest gifts ever given to humankind. Maybe that day will be a day of annual celebration worldwide; the annual *Immortality Celebration Day.*

I do believe that population reduction is part of the agenda, but if we look at the world population now and compare it with two years ago, we will see that it has increased. Today, we have a world population of 7.4 billion people[91] and in 2014 we were at 7.2 billion people.[92] This means that the supposed goal to decrease the population to 500 million people does not seem to work.

If a world population of 500 million is still the goal, why are they not working more effectively on it? Not until recently did I realize how close we are to achieving the Singularity, and by then (one would think) the Administrators would like to have accomplished their *500 million goal.* Now we should know that the population reduction down to 500 million people is mainly using the Georgia Guidestones as a reference, on which this number was written.[93] After all, this can be deliberate disinformation to create more fear amongst us.

Another option is that they actually want to keep the population about the current level, a goal which seems more obtainable, but even with AI coming into the picture, 7 billion people seems like too much to control (or perhaps not). Many die in wars and from disease around the world, but that's the way it's always been, and no wars have been able to hold population growth back. Fewer people die from diseases now than they did 150 years ago, and people live longer, so how do these facts fit into the equation of population reduction?

Moreover, the biggest reason for population growth in our world today is the mass reproduction of children in the Third World. People in these areas are often uneducated and not used to be organized enough to look at the consequences of having, let's say, seven to ten children. These

---

[91] http://www.worldometers.info/world-population/
[92] http://www.prb.org/Publications/Datasheets/2014/2014-world-population-data-sheet/population-clock.aspx
[93] BBC Travel, Sep. 3, 2015: "One of US' Greatest Mysteries"

people already live in poverty and certainly can't afford that many children, and society is not set up to take care of them either. It's in these parts of the world where population growth is the largest, and thus far, it's quite uncontrolled. The few pleasures the natives have is sex, which also relieves stress and makes people relax, unless you are a woman, always afraid to become pregnant. Researchers are alarmed because they can see that the population will grow exponentially, which means we will be 9 billion people on the planet in just a few years. If this happens, we can't maintain the current societal structure, they say.

I have a hard time seeing that the population will increase much more than it already has, and we will soon begin to see a trend downward. There is, for example, a significant contributing factor that may reduce the population rapidly, and that is covert sterilization; again, mainly through nanobots. We know that people already have a hard time producing children in general, and perhaps more nanobots will be activated in the near future so that, eventually, a huge percentage of the population won't be able to reproduce—particularly in the Third World. If this is the plan, it should very soon be put into effect. After all, their purpose is to keep the souls they trap in the SBC network and don't let them leave their new "enhanced" bodies—ever! It's easier to work with souls that don't vacate and/or recycle. The "Afterlife Trap" will then be obsolete. Also, no more souls will be able to access this 3-D reality.

Vaccination is another major population reduction factor to consider. The Controllers introduce a virus on the "market" and tell people how extremely dangerous and contagious it is. Don't have sex! Don't touch each other! Don't travel! This creates more fear, but of course, after the media have created a fearful population, the same instigators come up with the solution—an antidote, a vaccine! People will run for it, and the consequence of taking the vaccine against a more or less harmless virus, blown out of proportion by the media, is highly increased cancer risks and infertility in the majority of their children.

Only the Overlords know what size the population will be by the time they choose to replace our organs and our immune system. Involuntary sterilization seems to be a major part of the agenda and would probably be the less "invasive;" no violence is needed, and people would not be able to connect the dots, perhaps blaming it on the environment (which wouldn't be completely incorrect, either, as the environment is programmed to contain new manmade viruses and poisons of different kinds).

A BRAVE NEW WORLD OF NANOBOTS

WOULDN'T IT BE NICE to jump into a temperature-regulated pool when the Sun above emanates so much heat that you're about to jump out of your skin? Wouldn't it be double-nice if you, with some help from nanobots, could sink to the bottom and sit there for hours without drowning?

Sold yet?

Maybe not, but this is actually one of the sales techniques for us to accept AI. These are Kurzweil's exact words [my emphasis],

> *Our interneuronal connections compute at about 200 transactions per second, at least a million times slower than electronics.* As another example, a nanotechnology theorist, Rob Freitas, has a conceptual design for *nanobots that replace our red blood cells*. A conservative analysis shows that *if you replaced 10 percent of your red blood cells with Freitas' "respirocytes," you could sit at the bottom of a pool for four hours without taking a breath.*[94]

Thus, after the Singularity (and perhaps even before), humans will be capable of going back to being amphibians again; back to the element whence we came—water (although not in the sense Darwin misinformed us). Next step is space; interested in going into space without having to breathe? No, now my imagination is getting the better of me—or is it?

KURZWEIL ADMITS TO THE DANGERS OF AI

JUST TO BE "BALANCED," Kurzweil is playing the "fair guy," admitting that there *are* dangers with these new technologies. As I wrote earlier; with his lectures, interviews, and his books, he wants to welcome us all to debate these subjects, (he must love my book, then). This is how he presents a few of the dangers with the technology he so eagerly is promoting,

---

[94] http://singularity.com/qanda.html

G, N, and R [GNR, "Genetics Nanotechnology Robotics," *Wes' emphasis*] each have their downsides. The existential threat from genetic technologies is already here: the same technology that will soon make major strides against cancer, heart disease, and other diseases could also be employed by a bioterrorist to create a bioengineered biological virus that combines ease of transmission, deadliness, and stealthiness, that is, a long incubation period. The tools and knowledge to do this are far more widespread than the tools and knowledge to create an atomic bomb, and the impact could be far worse.[95]

Elsewhere, Kurzweil tells us that his greatest fear with GNR is the risk of bioterrorists. He says he can see the danger of this technology falling into the wrong hands, but then he turns it around and "convincingly" reassures us that the positives "convincingly" outweigh the negatives. Kurzweil is not a dummy, and I don't think he is as ignorant as he pretends to be; he must know our history and how inevitable it is that *all* technology that can be used for power over others is falling in the wrong hands; just look at what happened to Nikola Tesla. The Controllers promoted Thomas Edison at the expense of Tesla. They took Tesla's inventions and used them against us in HAARP weather wars and more, resulting in Tesla dying as a poor man, while Edison got rich from his "inventions" that were most likely not even his to begin with, but that's another story. The Administrators wanted to use energy that they could control and charge for instead of using free energy.

Other dangers brought up in the same interview that I just quoted from is self-replicating nano-technology and super-intelligent AI being unfriendly, but Kurzweil defends his passion, saying that he is presenting remedies for this in his book, which we will come to soon.

Furthermore, he states that when all the energy sources in the solar system have been used up in order to support the ever-growing needs of AI, "[t]hen we'll expand to the rest of the Universe."[96] Thus, the story told by the Pleiadians, how we humans in the future, as cyborgs, will reach the Pleiades and create a tyranny there, seems to be underway. The reasoning behind Kurzweil's statement is the *Kardashev Scale*,[97] which

---

[95] *Ibid.*
[96] *Ibid.*
[97] http://en.wikipedia.org/wiki/Kardashev_scale

discusses a civilization's technological development from planet-bound beings to spacefaring beings, who eventually will obtain the ability to control the energy of an entire galaxy. Kardashev postulated that all civilizations are developing around the same pattern by taming more and more energy and thus they will expand out in the Universe. He separated these different phases in a species' development in three stages, *Type I-III.*

Type I is a civilization that can control the resources of an entire planet (including weather and earthquake control, but it also includes exploration of the solar system).

Type II is a civilization that can control the energy of their sun and begin to colonize other star systems.

Type III is a civilization that can control the energy of an entire galaxy.

On this scale, we are still a Civilization Type 0, but Kurzweil foresees that once we have the Singularity in place and have been able to use our collective brain power, downloaded into the SBC, we will quickly become a Type I Civilization. When this is accomplished, Human 2.0 will "ascend" to a Civilization Type II and eventually a Type III, which includes colonizing other star systems, the entire galaxy, and ultimately the rest of the Universe, which is beyond Type III (Type IV). This is, of course, possible, says Kurzweil, because after all, we're alone in the Universe, and we will meet no resistance from other species elsewhere in cosmos. This may sound ludicrous, but the logic behind this is that if we conquer the entire Universe, despite the fact that we are alone, we can control it and its energies, and we will become God, as we shall see in the next section.

A Peek Inside Kurzweil's Book

I WILL BY NO MEANS GO THROUGH Kurzweil's 431 pages with a fine tooth comb, but I will pick and analyze some highlights, without taking anything out of context. It's a book rich with ideas, predictions, but also with solid evidence of the progress of AI and the Singularity, which he envisions being the only logical future for mankind. During the interview that I quoted and commented on in the previous section, when asked if we should stop the progress of the Singularity because of potential severe dangers, he replies that it's too late now, so we just need to advance our technology to a point when the Singularity is a reality, and all threats from bioterrorists and other downsides will be resolved once and for all.

Let us begin this section with presenting the goals of the Singularity from different angles, so we really understand what these forces want. Ray Kurzweil used the following quote in his book as a beginning of the section he also calls *The Singularity is Near...*

> Let an ultraintelligent machine be defined as a machine that can far surpass all the intellectual activities of any man however clever. Since the design of machines is one of these intellectual activities, an ultraintelligent machine could design even better machines; there would then unquestionably be an "intelligence explosion," and the intelligence of man would be left far behind. Thus the first ultraintelligent machine is the last invention that man need ever make. —IRVING JOHN GOOD, "SPECULATIONS CONCERNING THE FIRST ULTRAINTELLIGENT MACHINE," 1965[98]

...and immediately before that same section, Kurzweil predicts [emphasis added in *italic* and **bold**],

> We currently understand the speed of light as a bounding factor on the transfer of information. Circumventing this limit has to be regarded as highly speculative, but there are hints that this constraint may be able to be superseded. [15] If there are even subtle deviations, we will ultimately harness this superluminal ability. *Whether our civilization infuses the rest of the universe with its creativity and intelligence quickly or slowly depends on its immutability. In any event the "dumb" matter and mechanisms of the universe will be transformed into exquisitely sublime forms of intelligence, which will constitute the sixth epoch in the evolution of patterns of information.* **This is the ultimate destiny of the Singularity and of the universe**.[99]

This seems to be right to the point. Most of the time, when Kurzweil talks or writes about the Singularity, he mentions that its goal is to merge man and machine to create a super-intelligent form of human; a cyborg, connected to the Super Brain Computer. In his book, however, he

---

[98] Raymond Kurzweil, *The Singularity is Near*, 2005, p. 32, op. cit. (e-book version).
[99] *The Singularity is Near*, p. 32, op. cit.

takes the Singularity even further, and he actually writes, albeit in an indirect way (but it's easy to read between the lines) that humanity's destiny is to conquer the Universe and fill it with our "superior intelligence."

Not only is this concept extremely arrogant, but also ignorant (possibly deliberately so) because it assumes that humanity is the only intelligent life form in the Universe, as I brought up earlier. From what I know, he has not said straight out that he believes we are (he may want to keep the door cracked open), but he is intuiting it repeatedly, and sometimes he contradicts himself, which I will show you in a moment.

It wouldn't matter, however, if we *were* the only intelligent species in the Universe; Kurzweil would still see it as our alchemical ultimate destiny to rule the Universe and to be as God; in other words, he and his masters are building a new Tower of Babel—history repeating itself. For him, it would ultimately be inevitable. Because he is relying on that when the Singularity is *here* and just not *near*, our IQ as a hybrid species will increase a billion-fold, if not a trillion-fold, and this will safeguard our superiority over any other species in the Universe, which is *still* arrogant.

In the WPP, I wrote that I highly suspected that Zecharia Sitchin (1920-2010) was another front man for the AIF. If this were the case, could his "translations" of the old Sumerian scriptures (presenting the *Tree of Life* being related to the AIF and their longevity and immortality) be intended to function as a carrot for his readers; preparing them for the near future, i.e. merging man and machine into a singularity? Were we to be so intrigued by the *immortality of the gods* that the subconscious mind would absorb this desire like a sponge, so that when Kurzweil and others began their exposé, Sitchin's readers would respond positively to the Movement? We can only speculate, but Sitchin's work is certainly part of the entire Overlord agenda. Sitchin certainly took great liberties when he translated the Sumerian and Babylonian texts, and he presented them in a way that probably made the gods very happy.

Fig. 4-1: Zecharia Sitchin

WHEN DO HUMANS CEASE TO BE HUMAN?

AS DESCRIBED IN THE WPP, AND BY OTHER researchers and authors, humankind has been genetically engineered and manipulated quite often during the course of time, but the changes have always been in the biological body. Now, we're facing something totally different—an entirely new species, built as a biomechanical merge, where consciousness will be more or less substituted by super-intelligent brain-power. Every time these cyborgs think a thought or try to solve a problem, they will get different options and probabilities available to them, directly from the SBC, in a personal "brain upload." Twenty-four hours a day, Posthumans will give their power away to a super brain, controlled by a Wizard of Oz behind the curtain.

On the other hand, could it just be me and others, advocating against the Movement, being paranoid, and this is all for the best of mankind? Are we just "conspiracy nuts, after all?"

Let's first see if Kurzweil has an answer to the important question, "when do humans cease to be human?"

> If we regard a human modified with technology as no longer human, where would we draw the defining line? Is a human with a bionic heart still human? How about someone with a neurological implant? What about

76

two neurological implants? How about someone with ten nanobots in his brain? How about 500 million nanobots? Should we establish a boundary at 650 million nanobots: under that, you're still human and over that, you're posthuman?[100]

When someone is using rhetoric logic, such as in the above quote, to indirectly promote his or her agenda, we should automatically question the motives. It is not a question of whether we should transplant an artificial heart in order to save a human being; it's about creating an entirely new slave race, based on technology funded by a *Black Budget*, which is secret to the public, as well as to most politicians. We have no real idea how much Black Budget money is funneled into these projects, but it is a substantial amount. The real motive is not to save a person in need, but to create cyborgs out of an entire species. Hence, his logic goes out the window. Moreover, a species, Homo sapiens sapiens, is taken off its path of freeing themselves from a locked-in frequency band, which we call 3-D, doing so by using spiritual powers, not brain powers, and put under the overpowering influence of a super-computer that will do its data collection and its thinking for them. The information shared will be whatever is programmed into this computer, and *how* and *what* is being shared can still be controlled, and propaganda can be even more effective.

This is *not*, contrary to Kurzweil's statement, rhetoric logic; it's just common sense. It's not enough to be "optimistic," Mr. Kurzweil; it's a matter of seeing the future from a holistic viewpoint and not with tunnel vision. It's elementary logic, once we open our eyes, that we see not only *potential* dangers, but a new kind of slave species emerging, which will be under total, collective control by whomever sits behind the curtain in Oz. To be optimistic about it does not change the fact that power-hungry, warlike beings are behind this agenda. Even if we would be totally unaware of who is operating behind the scenes, it's easy to see that the Movement is the most dangerous threat to our spiritual freedom that has ever been developed on this planet. We don't even need to add the alien influence to see that.

I can't help quoting from Kurzweil repeatedly because what he is saying and writing is absolutely stunning and revealing. Here he is again, writing more about Transhumanism in a very blunt manner:

---

[100] *The Singularity is Near* (abbr. SIN), e-book version, p. 272, op. cit.

> Some observers refer to this merger as creating a new "species." But the whole idea of a species is a biological concept, and what we are doing is transcending biology. The transformation underlying the Singularity is not just another in a long line of steps in biological evolution. We are upending biological evolution altogether.[101]

It can hardly be blacker on white than the above statement, taken from his book. He wants to change the entire concept of what a species is; he wants us to forget the concept of a species necessarily being biological at all. It is true that our biological bodies are, in a sense, robots or machines as well, reengineered by En.ki and his team to be trapped in the material universe, but in biological bodies we have the capacity of some free thinking—not so when humanity has transformed into cyborgs.

The Pleiadians have always said that because this is a Living Library, genetic experimentation has been done, and is being done, on a regular basis, in one form or another, and by that, genetic engineering is to some degree acceptable. I disagree with this because such argument only applies to En.ki's logic. This is not his planet to begin with, so he has no right to remodel or transform anything. If it were not for us humans, continuously giving him our direct or indirect consent, En.ki and his cohorts would have long since been out of here and put on trial.

This means, in spite of what En.ki did, it was, and still is, our responsibility to make our own decisions, and we chose (albeit under manipulation) to be part of En.ki's Experiment, setup by a conquering species who needed us for their own selfish purposes. However, I also strongly advocate for total disclosure—not from our governments, but from the Overlords themselves—of what their *real* Agenda is, and what happened in the past, so many eons ago. If they won't give us *full* disclosure (and they won't), we will not be able to examine all the options we have as a human soul group. On the other hand, if we *would* be allowed to look at all the potentials and possibilities, and the majority of the human population *still* would choose to go for the *Singularity* alternative, I'll rest my case—humanity would have made their choice and would have to take full responsibility and face the consequences of their actions.

As it is now, the debate is biased, and the information shared is not

---

[101] SIN, p. 272, op. cit.

complete; thus, there is a need for books such as this one.

Kurzweil is also writing that "we need a new religion."[102] What he means by this is that we must reach a point where the best in our current religions, such as the *Golden Rule*, will integrate with contemporary science; i.e. a merger of science and religion should take place. An interesting point is that this is precisely what the *WingMakers'* spokesperson, James Mahu, is discussing on his website, Wingmakers.com; in order to find the *Grand Portal*—a metaphor for when we can become sovereign beings—we need to merge science and religion. I wrote extensively about the *WingMakers* in *WPP, The First Level of Learning*.

The following dialogue between Bill Gates (BILL) and Ray Kurzweil (RAY) contain some very disturbing ideas, such as the following,

> BILL: Ten computers—or one million computers—can become one faster, bigger computer. As humans, we can't do that. We each have a distinct individuality that cannot be bridged.
>
> RAY: That's just a limitation of biological intelligence. The unbridgeable distinctness of biological intelligence is not a plus. "Silicon" intelligence can have it both ways. Computers don't have to pool their intelligence and resources.
>
> They can remain "individuals" if they wish. Silicon intelligence can even have it both ways by merging and retaining individuality—at the same time. As humans, we try to merge with others also, but our ability to accomplish this is fleeting.[103]

This is exactly what will tip many humans over toward Kurzweil's goal; a promise of individuality in the midst of the Singularity. In the beginning, Posthumans may very well be allowed to keep their individuality, but this is why it's so important for us humans to be aware of our *real* history and not the false history we learn in school. If we don't know our past, it's bound to reoccur, which is exactly what's about to happen. Even if some individual thinking may be allowed, it will be very limited, and soon enough, only objective, calculative thinking will be possible, with AI infested in their brain and the rest of their body; the

---

[102] *Ibid.*, op. cit.
[103] SIN, p. 273, op. cit.

ability to experience real emotions will be very restricted.

The Primordial Womankind (the Namlú'u) were trusting toward others and did not expect being deceived by the Overlords, and over the eons, we haven't learned much—we still generally trust "authorities" who don't have any of our interests in mind.

You may have asked yourself how the Namlú'u could be trapped in human bodies that were created by their oppressors, who had chased Namlú'u's creators away and trapped the Primordial Womankind in a locked-in dimension. Although a long time had passed between the *War of the Titans* and the moment the Namlú'u were trapped in En.ki's bodies, shouldn't the Namlú'u still have been suspicious enough not to trust the Overlords?

I don't have the information about what exactly made the Namlú'u cooperate with the Overlords, but I can imagine that En.ki disguised himself as somebody else. Those who have read the *WPP* know that En.ki is an expert in shapeshifting. He might even have disguised himself as Queen Nin, deceiving womankind by presenting a way out of the trap if they took these new bodies. We know En.ki can be very convincing, even to an extent that he can deceive his own people. Something as drastic as that must have happened for the Namlú'u to fall into this trap that we're still sitting in.

MACHINES AND INTELLIGENCE

WHILE DISCUSSING CONSCIOUSNESS, Kurzweil makes the following comment in his book:

> ... We will then be cyborgs, and from that foothold in our brains, the nonbiological portion of our intelligence will expand its powers exponentially.[104]

For him, intelligence *is* consciousness; they are one, and we are as conscious as we are intelligent. However, the intention is to merge *all* religions with science and acknowledge a *God consciousness* that's the same for every religion—even if God is science. Humanity's task is then to become *as* God. As we've concluded, he wants us to spread our superior

---

[104] p. 274, op. cit.

intelligence into the entire Universe, after the *Singularity,* and fill the Universe with our "brilliance." However, Posthumans' journey doesn't end there. Now, ponder this:

> ...while being a Singularitarian is not a matter of faith but one of understanding, pondering the scientific trends I've discussed in this book inescapably engenders new perspectives on the issues that traditional religions have attempted to address: the nature of mortality and immortality, the purpose of our lives, and intelligence in the universe.[105]

Because Kurzweil argues that we most likely are the only intelligent species in the Universe, we are of course the ones who are entitled to the entire cosmos. This is "God's Plan" for humanity. Hence, he believes that we are the species that more than likely will seed the Universe with our intelligence. He bases this conclusion on that if there were others out there, they would already be here, and if there were *one* more species, there would probably be more than one; perhaps billions. This, according to Kurzweil, is highly unlikely because if this were the case, we would certainly have been visited. Even if some of them would prefer to be in an "observation mode," at least some of these species would have come forward. Again, he does not take into consideration that Earth and this solar system is under quarantine, and that the star races that are here are mostly of the controlling kind, doing their dirty business in the background.

However, Kurzweil does speculate that there *could* be others out there, who are much more advanced than we are, but if this were the case, they would already have developed artificial intelligence. Thus, if we stumble upon another advanced civilization out in space, they would be AI, not biological creatures. He argues,

> Incidentally, I have always considered the science-fiction notion of large spaceships piloted by huge, squishy creatures similar to us to be very unlikely. Seth Shostak comments that "the reasonable probability is that any extraterrestrial intelligence we will detect will be machine intelligence, not biological intelligence like us."
>
> [...]
>
> ...any civilization sophisticated enough to make the trip here would have

---

[105] p. 270, op. cit.

long since passed the point of merging with its technology and would not need to send physically bulky organisms and equipment.[106]

As a matter of fact, I partly agree with him. Here he brings up an issue that I also brought up in the WPP. ETs normally don't travel in spaceships, transporting their physical bodies and heavy equipment between star systems. Instead they travel by thought. However, Kurzweil, via Shostak, is probably correct; the alien civilizations that Posthumans might stumble upon will be AI because they would be part of the Luciferian Empire. Therefore, it is logical to assume that all these civilizations, if they are spacefaring, will be AI. There is no other way for them to travel across the 4% Universe than with cyborg bodies.

It's important, however, not to discard Kurzweil's predictions as science fiction; if he, and the AIF, can work on this project relatively undistracted, it will happen just the way Kurzweil predicts. As I mentioned in the WPP, it seems as if not all of the different races that joined Lucifer (Lord En.ki) in his rebellion could nano-travel. Some of them might still not be able to. These races use advanced technology to travel between stars. An example of this would be those who are the original inhabitants of the planet Nibiru. In that sense, Sitchin was correct. Although, at the time En.ki and some of his people started rubbing shoulders with those from Nibiru, it became a blend betwixt technological space travel and nano-travel amongst the Rebels; the latter is something that En.ki can accomplish effortlessly. AI has long since been integrated in the Luciferian Empire and is already well established in some asterisms that the AIF is in control of. Despite what Kurzweil might think (or want us to think), *we are not alone—not even close!*

Then, Kurzweil makes the following stunning statement: "It appears that our solar system has not yet been turned into someone else's computer."[107] He comes to this conclusion based on the "fact" that we have not been visited by any other civilization out there yet. It's obvious that there are things the AIF still want to hide from us—their own presence, to begin with, at least until they might decide to show up. They know that the speculations are out there regarding the solar system, as we

---

[106] p. 261, op. cit.
[107] *Ibid.,* op. cit.

know it, being a hologram within holograms. However, the solar system we learn about from NASA and other dubious organizations is little more than a hologram that is to some degree holographically superimposed on us humans and is not the way the real Universe is. Moreover; what we see when we look through telescopes and observe from space shuttles, etc., is the interpretation of the solar system and the Universe from our five senses perspective. If we were to access other parts of the electromagnetic spectrum at the same time, the Universe would look very different.

In other words, Kurzweil is incorrect when he suggests that our solar system has not been turned into someone else's computer.[108]

Following Kurzweil's line of logic, we will have the human brain entirely cloned and ready to go by the late 2020s,[109] and we will be able to merge with it by 2045. These are his predictions and not set in stone, but as others have mentioned, Kurzweil has been correct thus far in his predictions. Now, if we expand on this, with the understanding that conquering the entire Universe is the ultimate goal of the Singularity, what can we expect will happen during the twenty-first century?

Of course, Kurzweil has the answer:

> Having reached a tipping point, we will within this century be ready to infuse our solar system with our intelligence through self-replicating nonbiological intelligence. It will then spread out to the rest of the universe.[110]

Perhaps, by now, the reader can see the importance of creating our own, local universes, unless we want to be part of Kurzweil's singular future. If we don't want to participate in the Singularity, we'd better create what we want rather than resisting what we don't want (AI and the Singularity).

Everybody who is reading this is still here in 3-D reality, and so long as we are here, we'd better make the best out of it. Many readers, who are still young or middle-aged, might be alive when the Singularity happens, and therefore, it is important to create your own local universe, which is the universe you have access to at the moment, such as your hometown and other places you might travel to. You might want to embrace this

---

[108] Much more about these topics can be studied in the WPP—all Levels of Learning (http://wespenre.com/)
[109] SIN, p. 274.
[110] p. 271, op. cit.

local universe and create your future in it by using your *thoughts, imagination, and intention*. Then, you build your local universe around this spiritual sequence.

This does not just apply to young and middle-aged people; we all need to do this in order not to be sucked into Kurzweil's horrific future.

Chapter 5:
The Race for Immortality

"Age is an issue of mind over matter. If you don't mind it doesn't matter—
Mark Twain

HOW SCIENCE IS GOING TO SAVE US FROM OURSELVES

STEPHEN HAWKING, THE WORLD-FAMOUS scientist, has gone public every so often in the last six months to a year to warn us about AI and the Singularity. He has been very outspoken and shared his views on what is unfolding before our eyes.

Fig. 5-1: Led by the Astronomer Royal Lord Rees, famous thinkers such as physicist Stephen Hawking (pictured) and former Government chief scientist Robert May have formed the Cambridge Centre for the Study of Existential Risk (CSER) to draw up a doomsday list of risks that could wipe out mankind.

Synthetic Super Intelligence and the Transmutation of Humankind

Hawking and a group of colleagues of seventeen of the most brilliant scientists from Cambridge University have formed an organization called *Cambridge Center of the Study of Existential Risk* (CSER), and its purpose is to recognize threats that can wipe out humanity if they went unnoticed, according to an article in the *Daily Mail* on September 12, 2013.[111] It is these scientists' task to put their thinking caps on. Then, with a joint effort, they will, hopefully, come up with ideas to safeguard the human race and solve problems on the horizon on our behalf. The article compares these brilliant minds with "superheroes."

Many people might think because Dr. Hawking is involved that some of these threats might be asteroid attacks from space, the existence of black holes in Earth's vicinity, or something else threatening us from space, keeping in mind that Hawking is a cosmologist in most people's mind.

However, according to CSER, the worst threat is not coming from outer space but from us humans. Hence, the group members are now, by and large, taking their eyes away from the sky and directing them toward us, their fellow human beings, or rather, those who have plans for us.

The manifesto of CSER reads as follows:

Many scientists are concerned that developments in human technology may soon pose new, extinction-level risks to our species as a whole.

Our goal is to steer a small fraction of Cambridge's great intellectual resources and of the reputation built on its past and present scientific pre-eminence, to the task of ensuring that our own species has a long-term future.

In the process, we hope to make it a little more certain that we humans will be around to celebrate the University's own millennium, now less than two centuries hence.[112]

This makes it quite clear that their motto is to save us from ourselves. These scientists are apparently very concerned about what is happening on the technological arena, including, but not restricted to,

---

[111] *Daily Mail, September 12, 2013,* "Killer robots and crippling cyber-attacks: How the world is going to end - according to super brains such as Stephen Hawking"
[112] Ibid.

86

super computers, AI, and the Singularity. One of the great risks is, according to the same group, "[i]ntelligent technology: A network of computers could develop a mind of its own. Machines could direct resources towards their own goals at the expense of human needs, such as food, and threaten mankind."[113]

If the media, however, are elevating this group to being superheroes in people's minds, there is reason to be cautious here. Not everybody is buying it, thinking CSER might be working *for* the Establishment. Nicholas West, from *Activistpost.com*, states that Hawking has hinted at being in favor of the following technological development in the past:

> Hawking himself has echoed Kurzweil when he states that 'in the future brains could be separated from the body'.

> "The cosmologist, 71, said the brain operates in a similar way to a computer program, meaning it could in theory be kept running without a body to power it."

> The worldview of these "superheroes" is at its heart an Orwellian one: humanity must be eliminated in order to save it.[114]

West also, in the same article, lists items related to the Singularity, divided into two columns; one is titled "Heaven" and the other is titled "Hell." This creates an overview of what is to be potentially gained and lost with nanotechnology taken to its extreme,

HEAVEN:

– Re-make the planet (geo-engineering)

– Create new life (and new life forms)

– Re-engineer humanity (values and essence)

– Abundance and plenty for all (mastery over energy and material transformation)

– Super-intelligence (omniscience)

---

[113] Ibid.
[114] *Nicholas West, Sept. 22, 2013,* "Dawn of the Singularity—Superheroes from Science to Rescue Humanity from Itself. "

- Super-longevity (death as a disease to be cured, immortality)

- Better than well

- Transcendental experiences

- "The cosmos wakes up" (a new humanity moves off planet)

HELL:

- Destroy the planet

- Plagues and pestilence (arising from genetic engineering)

- Enfeeble and divide humanity (as new technology divisions arise)

- Environmental catastrophe

- Ubiquitous surveillance

- Super-dictatorship

- Worse than the Dark Ages

- Nuclear holocaust (enabled by new weaponry)

- "Terminator enslavement" (artificial intelligence decides that humanity itself is the risk)[115]

This article was written in 2013—three years ago from this day, but we would now be able to add quite a few new items to both lists. Nonetheless, Mr. West makes his point, and I believe the "HELL" side of the picture is the predominant one. However, it's going to be the "HEAVEN" side that's going to be much more intensively promoted in the media as we move closer toward the Singularity.

While we are listing items, the following is, from what I see it, media's role in the Movement from the beginning of the Singularity exposure until the Singularity is established. It is to

---

[115] Ibid., op. cit.

7) inform the public slowly but surely what is about to happen.

8) more rapidly expand on the subject, openly discussing the pros and cons.

9) increasingly begin to emphasize the pros, rather than the cons.

10) conclude that the pros definitely outweigh the cons and that the threats and concerns involved in Transhumanism have been eliminated and resolved. The Singularity is the future for mankind, and millions of people think the same (interviewing people on the street and then selecting mostly those who are pro to be included in the reportage).

11) Announce that the Singularity is almost in place and people across the world are excited over this giant leap for humanity.

The following video gives a short overview of the path the Overlords are planning to take toward the unified goal, "The Lead up to the Singularity—Technology Convergence." (https://www.youtube.com/watch?v=GplcPeh6JMo&ab_channel=David Wood).

Although the entire idea of merging man and machine was considered just a crazy idea a few decades ago, this Movement now has many followers around the world; both amongst those in powerful positions and the man on the street. The *Singularity University*[116] was created back in 2009, offering inter-disciplinary courses for both executives and graduate students. Who, then, are the founders of this quite popular university? The reader may already have guessed who one of them is; Dr. Ray Kurzweil. The second founder is a certain Dr. Peter H. Dimandis.[117]

Dr. Dimandis is worth a few extra lines in this book because I assume that very few people have heard of him. He is the Chairman and CEO of the *X Prize Foundation*,[118] which has as its goal to develop projects for the benefit of mankind (or so it states). One of these "beneficial" projects is to develop private spaceflight. Taking his connection with Dr. Kurzweil into consideration, it doesn't require a rocket scientist (pun

---

[116] http://singularityu.org/
[117] http://singularityu.org/community/founders/
[118] Keep an eye open for those "X" institutes, foundations, and corporations. "X" often stands for *Planet of the Crossing*, i.e. Nibiru. Another recent "X" company is Elon Musk's *SpaceX*.

intended) to understand that Dr. Dimandis is part of a project to take cyborgs into space. Even more interesting, however, is that it states in his biography that he also co-founded the following corporations, *Zero Gravity Corporation*, the *Rocket Racing League* and *Space Adventures*. In these times, when many UFO researchers are advocating for the Government and the MIC to disclose their *zero-point energy* technology, Minion insiders, such as Dr. Dimandis is, as a spider in the web, in charge of the prominent *Zero Gravity Corporation!*[119] Such a "disclosure" of being in possession of zero-gravity technology is most likely to happen when the Movement is ready for it, and when they are, it will not benefit mankind (as usual). *Instead, it will benefit Human 2.0, i.e. Posthuman, in space travel!* Is this what the "disclosure projects" in the UFO movement are advocating for behind the scenes? Certain dynamic spokespersons for such disclosure projects in the UFO community are certainly highly educated, intelligent people, so why have they not (to my knowledge) mentioned organizations such as Zero Gravity Corporation and revealed who's behind it and what their agenda is?

Fig. 5-2: Dr. Ray Kurzweil (left) and Dr. Peter H. Dimandis (right), Founders of the Singularity University. In the background we see what seems to be happy and dedicated students.

It makes you wonder if those in the forefront of working for

---

[119] http://singularityu.org/bio/peter-diamandis/

disclosure know this and are on the CIA/NSA/MIC payroll. I have no proof that this is the case, but some things these front people say (and what they don't say) makes me suspicious; such as presenting childish ideas that all ETs are benevolent and should be embraced, and bad ETs don't exist in Earth's vicinity anymore. The way they rationalize this is that if there were malevolent ETs here, they would already have invaded us and probably wiped us out long ago. This comes from MDs, PhDs, and people who have worked with the *Secret Space Program*[120] for decades. Such statements are quite frustrating because I am sure most of them have studied ancient texts and mythology, so they should know better. One would think that they would at least consider the possibility that we have been invaded already, and that the negative ETs are the ones controlling our reality.

I pointed this out to a prominent spokesperson for the Disclosure Movement, and to my surprise (at the time), I was met with anger and ridicule, and without even having had the chance to expand on the subject, I was accused of spreading disinformation to the public, and therefore, I was misleading humankind. This was just from having *mentioned* ETs who might not have our best interests in mind. The response I received made me begin to wonder who is pulling the strings on the Disclosure Movement.

It's also quite revealing to see who are sponsoring the Singularity University as they are all international corporations, such as *Google*, *Nokia*, *Cisco*, and *Deloitte*. [121]

What is important to understand is that the Government and the MIC will not reveal the real, full truth about the ancient extraterrestrial presence in our solar system any time soon, and when the time comes to declassify the zero-point energy technology, it's not because they do it in humanity's best interest, as some want us to believe, but in the interest of those who are in charge of this immense control system. Moreover, the entire scheme is too sensitive and too big to be revealed—particularly by the criminals themselves, who have everything to lose and very little to gain. As Cathy O'Brien, a former government mind-controlled sex-slave, wrote in her book, *Trance-formation*, and I paraphrase,

---

[120] If the Apollo Program was the "Open Space Program," humanity's *real* exploring and exploiting of space, funded by a *black budget*, is the "Secret Space Program," often written as an acronym, *SSP*.
[121] Ibid.

If people knew what we have done, they would run us down the street and lynch us! —GEORGE H.W. BUSH.

This does not sound promising if we're waiting for a true disclosure. After all, George Henry Walker Bush is a big spider in the web of deceit.

GOOGLE AND LONGEVITY

G OOGLE IS A SEARCH ENGINE, isn't it? It's actually the great wonder of search engines, compared with earlier versions when the Internet was younger. For those who didn't know, Google is not just a search engine that "spiders" the web (read, *spins the net*), working hard to give us what we want, so we can find what we need on the Internet. Google is in fact a mighty sensor of information, a spy organization, and it is supporting the Movement; AI and life extension in particular.

We have discussed earlier that when mankind becomes cyborgs, they will be more or less immortal, but the term *cyborg* indicates that they will be both biological and artificial. The Controller will have no problem with keeping the artificial part "alive," but what about the biological part?

Fig. 5-3: Google under the loupe.

This is, as usual, where nanobots come into the picture, being a crucial part of the immortality process, just as in most parts of the Singularity Movement. Once these nanoparticles have taken over the bloodstream and the immune system, there is really not much left of the body that's human. The bloodstream—the endocrine system—is a very important part of the soul/mind of the human experience, and we sometimes notice that after blood transfusions, the person who receives blood from someone else might slightly change their personality afterward because blood has memories contained in the DNA of its previous owner. These memories will then be transferred to the person who receives blood after an accident, etc. In a similar way, nanobots and the SBC can easily change or erase our personalities.

California Life Company (Calco) and *Alphabet* (is this a play on *Alphabet Agencies,* such as CIA and NSA?) are two companies that are funded by Google; both companies are doing life extension research, according to an article on the scientific recode.net website.[122] None of these Google-funded companies are trying to solve the immortality issue, but they are working on preventing diseases that usually affect the elderly. They are basically working on producing a pill that can extend life. Home Health and Hospice, for example, will be obsolete in the future, if the Movement succeeds with their plans.

Wherever there is a demand, there is research, assuming there is money to be made. Also, where they can save on resources (workers), they will, if it's cost effective.

What can be done by robots, *will* be done by robots!

In fact, at the University of Illinois, scientists are developing drones that can do the job better than humans, according to the *New York Times.*[123] This scientific group of scientists has received a $1.5 million grant from the *National Science Foundation* in order to work with the idea to develop small drones that can do small household chores, such as getting medicines from another room to give to a patient or a sick person at home. In the big scheme of things, this may sound as a simple and rather insignificant task to spend millions of dollars on developing, but we must remember that this is just a step on the way, and it's all just a dog-and-pony-show anyway. The Controllers need to show the public that progress is being

---

[122] http://recode.net/2015/12/28/the-stealth-attempt-to-defeat-aging-at-googles-calico/
[123] *New York Times,* Dec. 4, 2015, "As Aging Population Grows, So Do Robotic Health Aides,"

made incrementally; they can't just dump it all on us at once. The step-by-step disclosure requires funding, and these funders of phony projects are the taxpayers, and ultimately, the funding comes from the Black Budget. Again, this technology is decades old, and no such development is necessary, but the Controllers also love to funnel money into different projects to make it look more legal and convincing.

The purpose is, of course, to introduce a totally robotic healthcare system where nurses and doctors become obsolete; at least in the most common everyday tasks. The robots will already be programmed with all the knowledge a doctor needs, and it will know how to use it on patients. Readers might think this can't be obtained in hundreds of years—if ever, but this new system is more or less ready to be put in place, as we shall see in a later chapter. But until we get to that part, let's discuss this agenda in the order that it's apparently planned to be released.

Imagine a sick elderly person, who is homebound; either living by himself or herself or together with an elderly spouse, who is too worn down to be able to assist with their partners needs on a daily basis. This is normally where Home Health comes into the picture. Today, we live in a very stressful society where every minute counts, and only those who are able to keep up with the pace will survive on the job market in the long run. A Home Health visit should take a minimal amount of time, or the Home Health nurse will get in trouble with his or her manager. The nurse has a certain number of visits scheduled for one day, and he or she needs to get them done, and in addition, he or she needs to chart - onall of the patients before the workday is over. This is nearly impossible if the nurse is also supposed to provide good patient care (although this is required as well), so shortcuts are being taken. The shortcuts are either in patient care or on the charting. However, any of these two shortcuts can severely jeopardize patient care, but staffing is so minimal that the single nurse believes that there is no choice.

Fig. 5-4: Dr. Naira Hovakimyan of the University of Illinois with a small drone that may eventually be able to carry out household tasks, like retrieving a bottle of medicine, for older adults. *Credit: Daniel Acker for the New York Times.*

In the very near future, there will be a solution to this, but the solution will not aid the nurse; on the contrary, he or she will no longer be needed. Drones and robots can do the job better; at least this is how the Controllers and their appointed scientists are thinking. A robot does not forget what it's doing during the day, and charting will be obsolete because everything that happens on a robot's workday will be registered immediately, from second to second, and stored in the robot's memory bank. This memory bank will then be stored in a *cloud*, similar to the cloud we are using today, where we store files and back up our computers, and thus, what is stored in the cloud become part of the patient's health records (more about these "clouds" later).

Potentially, the robot can take more time with the patient and perform any task necessary. However, there are two major immediate problems with this, and these problems are, 1) there will no longer be any employment for Home Health nurses, and 2) human touch and interaction go out the window. The patient now has to speak to something he or she knows is not human and has no soul; it's only sterile hardware and software, programmed with artificial intelligence. Although the human nurse may have been stressed, just having a human being there can bring some comfort to the patient. This has not been calculated into the equation when developing this new kind of "aid." And why should it? Both the Controllers and the scientists know that the future will be robotic and artificial.

The New York Times writes,

> Dr. Hovakimyan [University of Illinois] acknowledged that the idea might seem off-putting to many, but she believes that drones not only will be safe, but will become an everyday fixture in elder care within a decade or two.
>
> "I'm convinced that within 20 years drones will be today's cellphones," she said.
>
> Her research is just one example of many approaches being studied to use technology to help aging people.
>
> Even though fully functioning robot caregivers may be a long way off, roboticists and physicians predict that a new wave of advances in computerized, robotic and Internet-connected technologies will be available in coming years to help older adults stay at home longer.[124]

Keep in mind that all this technology that we are swamped with on a daily basis has an important objective in mind—immortality. This is an imperative part of the Singularity. Each small development is a step in that direction; regardless if it's obvious or not.

If we think of the *original* human body, which was One with our soul and mind, and if the nervous system can be seen as a tree—the *Tree of Life*—the Overlords now want to give us back some of what they took from us—eternal life—but not in the same way we were originally experiencing Infinity and Eternity. Instead of ending the illusion of separation and give us our spiritual unity back (spirit/mind/spiritual body), they give us an immortal *physical* body! Gone is the freedom factor, which is replaced with nanobots that are controlling our endocrine system and our nervous system. Eternal life, which was once a gift from the Queen of the Stars, now becomes the ultimate trap and the ultimate control factor.

Some inventions, such as the drones in elderly care, may seem as a benevolent and caring initiative, and it's true that to some degree people can be helped by these technologies for now, but this is also part of the plan. They *want* people to believe that the technology, developed and

---

[124] Ibid., op. cit.

released now, is for the good of humanity. The same thing is true for transplants of body parts to people who really need them and are forever grateful that it could be done. This is then blown up in the media, and the average person feels very happy for the injured or sick, who could be helped back to a more functioning life this way. Also, somewhere in the back of people's heads they feel a little safer because on a more selfish note they think that if *they* may come in a similar situation, there is hope for them.

As I've repeated over and over, virtually all research is tested in the military first, before it's released to the general public; the soldiers are the guinea pigs. Typical examples of this are soldiers coming home from war, wounded and often with missing limbs. Artificial limbs, at first genuinely meant for soldiers, are then successfully transplanted, and it's all over the media. This is a perfect introduction to AI and the transformation of mankind into cyborgs.

On January 18, 2016, *The Irish Times* wrote,

> ...while the replacement body seems much closer to science fiction than science, recent advances in robotics and prosthetics have not only given us artificial arms that can detect pressure and temperature but limbs that can be controlled by thoughts using a brain-computer interface.[125]

Nell Watson is a futurist at the Silicon Valley based *Singularity University* (SU), the institute we discussed earlier, cofounded by Ray Kurzweil. One of Watson's jobs is apparently to introduce the idea of a new virtual-reality-type-of-life. She says,

> "I often wonder if, since we could be digitized from the inside out – not in the next 10 years but sometime in this century – we could create a kind of digital heaven or playground where our minds will be uploaded and we could live with our friends and family away from the perils of the physical world.

> "It wouldn't really matter if our bodies suddenly stopped functioning, it wouldn't be the end of the world. What really matters is that we could still live on."[126]

It's all in the making, but it's more around the corner than they are

---

[125] *Irish Times*, Jan. 18, 2016, In a future brave new world will it be possible to live forever?, op. cit.
[126] Ibid., op. cit.

willing to admit in public, albeit Dr. Kurzweil doesn't exactly hold back.

Just to give some extra meat to what I have explained so far about nanobots, Dr. Watson promotes them in the following manner:

> "There are experiments using DNA origami. It's a new technique that came out a few years ago and uses the natural folding abilities of DNA to create little Lego blocks out of DNA on a tiny, tiny scale. You can create logic gates – the basic components of computers – out of these things.

> "These are being used experimentally today to create nanobots that can go inside the bloodstream and destroy leukaemia cells, and in trials they have already cured two people of leukaemia. It is not science fiction: it is fact."[127]

Thus, Dr. Watson acknowledges that nanobots, and what they can do with them, is not some hypothetical science fiction, but is something that is already happening. It means that the nanobots we are breathing in from chemtrails and get into our system via different medicines and vaccines can be used remotely and basically do anything that is programmed into them. Dr. Kurzweil wants us to debate his ideas, bringing up both the benefits and the dangers, so there we go—the obvious danger with nanobots.

Dr. Watson further muses that nanobots will be able to communicate with each other in our personal cyborg bodies and between bodies as well.

Then, connected in a spider web fashion to a super brain computer, we will *all* be connected with each other. This will lead to a world without privacy, which *The Irish Times* also points out. Following this, people would most likely dedicate themselves to self-censoring instead of leading meaningful lives:

> Dr. Fiachra O'Brolcháin, a Marie Curie/Assisted Research Fellow at the Institute of Ethics, Dublin City University, whose research involves the ethics of technology, is very critical to the current technological development towards Transhumanism.

> "This is one of the great ironies of the current wave of technologies – they are born of individualistic societies and are often defended in the name of

---

[127] Ibid., op. cit.

individual rights but might create a society that can no longer protect individual autonomy," he warns.[128]

AI and morality is something that is discussed to some degree in mainstream media at this point, but what is morality? Who will define it? Obviously, the morality of the Administrators and the average person on the street are light-years apart. Who is going to establish what kind of morality the New World Order should use as guidelines? I dare say with absolutely certainty that it won't be you and me.

ARTIFICIAL CONSCIOUSNESS

ON OCTOBER 27, 2015, *THE TELEGRAPH.CO.UK* ran an article called, *Family members could be kept alive forever using social media history—dead family members could be brought back to life using their history on social media to power virtual avatars.*[129]

Simon McKeown is a Reader in Animation and Post Production at *Teeside University*. One of his projects is to "reawaken" our dead relatives in the future, by creating "synthetic digital life" with something called *photogrammetry*. Using this technique, scientist will be able to create an "accurate reconstruct of a virtual 3D shape of a human being from existing photographs and video. Computer voice synthesis, will take account local and regional accents to deliver a more accurate representation of what they sounded like."[130] People would then be able to construct a reality where they never had to say goodbye to those they love. McKeown continues,

> "Using emotion-sensitive human-computer interaction our artificially intelligent participants continue to acquire ongoing knowledge long after their death - they evolve digitally and do not die."[131]

As soon as this technique is implemented, the real human consciousness will more and more be replaced with artificial consciousness. As we can see, there are many slightly different outlooks

---

[128] Ibid., op. cit.
[129] http://www.telegraph.co.uk/news/science/science-news/11955835/Family-members-could-be-kept-alive-forever-using-social-media-history.html
[130] Ibid., op. cit.
[131] Ibid., op. cit.

into the future by those who have the technological means to solidify their visions, but all of them have one thing in common; they want to replace Homo sapiens sapiens as the center of creation and evolution. To the uninformed, the information McKeown just gave us is meant to trigger hope in the readers, wishfully making them think that they can live with their loved ones forever in a digital but very-real appearing synthetic version of "reality;" this being the next best thing to having the original person there in the first place. Also, it gets people used to the idea that once the SBC is in place, nothing that was once programmed into its memory bank will ever be erased. Everything a person ever thought and learned will be stored—including their entire personality. Thus, it is therefore a given that even if an accident happened to a cyborg—an accident bad enough to destroy it (forcing the soul, mind, and spirit body finally to leave the cyborg trap)—that person's mind is still cloned into the SBC, is forever activated, and can be enlivened. We also need to keep in mind here that the Overlords want us to merge our minds in virtual realities that the collective mind of Posthuman is creating continuously (and I would add, with not-so-little-help from the Overlords and the Emissaries).

As strange as it may seem to some readers, I am convinced that the average scientist who works on bringing about the Singularity has humankind's best interests in mind. However, those higher up the ladder certainly don't, and these shady people know much more than we do about consciousness and metaphysics, and they can successfully use it against us.

HOW THE SUPER-RICH WANT TO BUY IMMORTALITY

FROM WHAT I HAVE OBSERVED, children of super-rich families develop in three different stages. The first stage is that of excitement and a willingness to buy the whole world. The person buys ultra-expensive cars, houses, vacation homes, palaces, yachts, and perhaps ships. Moreover, he or she will probably travel around the world, make friends with the super-rich in other parts of the world, and enjoy himself or herself by arranging parties, going to other rich people's parties, experiencing as much sex as he or she can handle, and take "party drugs," such as cocaine and heroin.

Chapter 5: The Race for Immortality

As time goes by, all this life in abundance and luxury either gets the best of the person, and the body begins to decline, or he or she gets bored with life after having exhausted all of the options that used to make life exciting. What is there left to do when the party life and luxury do not appeal as much as they used to? Of course, buying an odd commodity that only this person would have in his or her possession, thus making it possible to brag in front of the rest of the bored jet set, is one thing such a person could do. Then, hopefully, his or her rich friends would get impressed and make this person, with this strange commodity, the big subject in discussions. The bored jet setter's Big Ego would be pleased again—for a while.

When this gets old, too, the person in question would probably begin to think about aging and dying. Normally, he or she does not want to die, and it doesn't matter so much whether he or she believes in an afterlife, including reincarnation. Regardless of how bored the person might be, he or she does not want to lose their life of luxury. What if this person reincarnates into a middle-class family next time (God forbid!)—or perhaps life ends completely at the very moment of death? Horrible thoughts! Hence, when a way of obtaining immortality becomes available, the person jumps on it.

For those who want to read more about this, the London-based newspaper, *The Evening Standard*, recently ran an article about how London's super-rich will potentially reach serious life extension with quite a lot of help from cutting edge scientists.[132]

At the end of the DNA are caps, called *telomeres*. Dr. Mark Bonar, a *cellular ageing specialist*, compares the telomeres to the plastic at the end of shoestrings; they prevent the end from fraying. In fact, the longer the telomeres, the longer the lifespan of a person will potentially be.[133] A product called TA-65 has now been patented[134] and has been around in the U.S. since 2011. TA-65 allegedly has the ability to rebuild the telomeres and make them longer, pausing the ageing process. When tested on fruit flies (an insect commonly used in genetic experimentation—fruit flies and humans apparently have something in common), it doubled the lifespan of

---

[132] See, *Evening Standard, Nov. 19, 2015,* "Survival of the richest: how London's super-rich are trying to buy immortality"
[133] Ibid.
[134] U.S. Patent No. 7,846,904.

the insect, and when tested on mice for cancer, the cancer rate fell by approximately 30 percent.[135] TA-65 is not an operational procedure; it is being prescribed in capsules or as a cream.

Fig. 5-5: Dr. Mark Bonar, "cellular ageing specialist."

Moreover, Dr. Bonar says that other factors of the human body could also be considered for improvement. An array of blood tests are being performed, and wherever improvements in prolonging life seem to be necessary, this area, or these areas, of the body are addressed. Also, nutrition is taken into consideration to create a balance, and when needed, growth hormones are used. An annual plan costs from £10,000 ($14,500) and up. Upon that, there are most likely additional costs, depending on what needs to be done; this is perhaps too expensive for the average Joe— at least thus far. For the super-rich, however, it's spare change and cheap. At the time when *The Evening Standard* article hit the press, Dr. Bonar was treating a foreign royal family. They told him, "I am running my empire—your job is to keep me healthy." Is there any wonder that David

---

[135] There is controversy about if TA-65 cures cancer or in fact actually causes it: http://owndoc.com/anti-aging/ta65-revgenetics-cancer-fda-complaint/

Rockefeller is 101 years old, George HW Bush is 91, Henry Kissinger is 92, Queen Elizabeth is 90 and counting, and they are still actively running empires or staying involved in the world of politics — including travelling and attending meetings? Assuming some of these dinosaurs are humans and not AI or clones, they may have had a visit or two from scientists such as Dr. Bonar.

Dr. Bonar may not be the only person using these kinds of life extending techniques, but he is not without controversy either. On December 10, 2015, the British news media, the *Mirror.co.uk*, posted an article on Dr. Bonar, which revealed that he was accused of having mistreated a 46-year old woman with cervical cancer, not telling her she was terminally ill. As a result, the woman died, and Dr. Bonar was, when the *Mirror.co.uk* ran the article, in hearings about the case.[136] He denies all misconduct. Morals and ethics are difficult, if not impossible, to find in this field of practice, as well as in many other Administrators-based practices.

HOW FAR ARE WE FROM IMMORTALITY?

THUS FAR, WE HAVE MORE OR LESS concentrated on how scientists are experimenting with life extension of the biological body, but what about the future *artificial part* of Posthuman; the part that makes a cyborg? Even robots break down and need to be repaired. How is this going to be done? Will other cyborgs repair a damaged artificial body part?

It seems logical that a cyborg will go to their "doctor" and gets his or her body part repaired, but that is not what the AIF and their Administrators have in mind for us, and we can now see clear, and quite disturbing, evidence of this already.

In an article published on *Sputniknews.com* on May 28, 2015, we are given a "preview" in the article-embedded video, of what's to come.[137]

The scientific community demonstrates how robots can already

---

[136] *-Mirror.co.uk,- Dec. 15, 2015,* "Harley Street doctor 'hid woman's terminal cancer so he could carry on charging for unconventional treatment'" -
[137] The Intelligent Trial and Error Algorithm introduced in the paper 'Robots that can adapt like animals' (Nature, 2015)—the video shows two different robots that can adapt to a wide variety of injuries in less than two minutes (https://sputniknews.com/europe/201505281022678236/#ixzz3xJY5eiBv)

repair themselves without outside assistance. [138] In this experiment, a six-legged robot is quickly resuming its functions even after being severely damageed. It only took the robot less than two minutes to "self-heal" after having two of its legs broken, and it could soon resume full walking capabilities. A robot arm could also place an object where it was supposed to be located even with several broken motors or "joints." Behind this development is a French team, led by two roboticists from the *Pierre and Marie Curie University*.

The *Sputniknews.com* article states,

> "One thing we were surprised by was the extent of damage to which the robots could quickly adapt," study co-author Jean-Baptiste Mouret told Live Science. "We subjected these robots to all sorts of abuse, and they always found a way to keep working."[139]

We don't need to have a lively imagination to realize that this, when further developed, will be of major importance after the Singularity. Not only will robots incrementally, within a short time period, take over the majority of the job market, but they will also become almost invincible. We are not far from the point (as we will see later in this book) when machines are merged with artificial consciousness, which is of course also the definition of "Artificial Intelligence." If such a conscious robot, in a work situation, would run amok, there is little the few remaining workers can do, except run for their lives. When mentioning this, there are those who will laugh it off and say that robots will not run amok—they are not programmed to do that—and the idea is just something taken from science-fiction literature. However, the threat is quite real, another thing we will examine in a later chapter.

Self-repairing robots open up powerful potentials in many different fields. Such robots can go where humans can't, e.g. out into space and deep down into the oceans of Earth. Thus far (as far as the public is aware, at least), none of this has been largely done because a human has to go with the robot in order to repair and maintain it. In the near future, this will no longer be necessary. Don't get fooled by what seems to be "primitive" robots in videos such as the one above. These are old prototypes, used to

---

[138] *Sputniknews.com, May 28, 2015,* 'Injured' Robots Learn to 'Heal' Themselves in Under Two Minutes,
[139] Ibid., op. cit.

prepare us for the future; robots that very much resemble human beings are just waiting for the time when people have been prepared for them. In fact, they have already introduced us to some of them, as I will show you later.

Sputniknews.com also states,

> Rather than relying on pre-specified contingency plans, the robots are programmed to store knowledge from previous experiences and create a map based on these behavior-performance histories. When damaged, they access that knowledge and adapt accordingly.[140]

In other words, the robot learns from its mistakes and handles it accordingly, and then stores the procedure in its memory bank. I believe the reader can see where all this is going. We humans sometimes say that it's okay to make a mistake once, but if we make it twice we'd better start paying attention. A third mistake of the same kind is considered sloppy or even stupid. This does not apply to future robots; they only make a mistake once.

FUNDING IMMORTALITY

FUNDING FOR THESE PROJECTS IS NOT DIFFICULT to get; multi-billionaires are happily spending millions of dollars to support technology that can expand their lives for eternity. Few seem to care whether it's a life as a cyborg or not. After all, these super-rich people expect to remain at the top of the pyramid anyway. Bill Maris, for example, who is the President and managing partner of *Google Ventures*, spent, or was planning to spend, $425 million on the project in 2015, according to *Bloomberg.com*.[141]

This may seem as a considerable amount, but is still a drop in the ocean; there are investors who are willing to spend *much* more. Nevertheless, it won't be enough in the long term; no private companies will be able to fund it all. Therefore, it was allegedly decided that the United Nations should be the credible world organization to introduce Transhumanism and the Singularity on a global scale.[142] The expanded

---

[140] Ibid., op. cit.
[141] -*Bloomberg Business*,- March 8, 2015, "Google Ventures and the Search for Immortality." -
[142] See, James Mahu of the WingMakers, 1998, *The Fifth Interview of Dr. Neruda*, p. 19.

plan includes for the free market to make new technology irresistible to the masses, and then allow government subsidies to bring down the costs substantially in order to enable distribution of these same technologies.[143]

The Administrators have already implanted into the New Age community the concept that we are all *One*, and albeit, we are separated now, the idea is that we need to move toward *Oneness*. *The Law of One*—the *RA Material* we discussed earlier—has also contributed to spreading the message of Oneness, by telling us that evolving into a *social memory complex*, where we all are "connected" and share each other's thoughts, is a natural evolutionary process; without it, we can't evolve past "6th Density," according to Ra. After the 7th Density we are all going to merge into Oneness, according to this same channeled material.

This is far from the *Oneness* humankind should strive for, in my opinion. Our goal should be to regain the power of our *original* bodies from 250,000 years ago and further back and not buy into the propaganda anymore that spirit and mind are something that is separate from the body. We must stop participating in Lucifer's Agenda! In fact, the New Age movement, with its slogan, *We Are All One*, suggests that we should *go back and remerge with Source*. In New Age nomenclature, "going back to Source" means that we all should work toward ceasing to be individuals and merge into One Being, i.e. Source or *All That Is* (God). It makes little sense that this is the Oneness we should concentrate on—after all, why would we "merge with Source" if "Source" created us to become individuals? We are here, in this Universe, to live and to explore it as separate smaller units of the Goddess and not to remerge with Her (the Divine Feminine). Therefore, the so-called New Age Movement has assisted the AI Movement in that they have helped them promote Oneness in a way that better assists Transhumanism as opposed to the *real* Oneness, which is the realization that spirit/mind/body is "One" as in "Oneness."

Transhumanism is also promoting Oneness, where all people are equal and share the same database (the SBC). However, in reality, the Singularity is not Oneness at all; it's Separation to the extreme, where all of mankind will be separated from the Multiverse—much more so than we

---

[143] Ibid.

are now. The SBC assists humanity in creating a new virtual reality within the physical universe; a virtual reality distinct from the real Multiverse, or the KHAA, where there are no limits to what we can potentially create. Transhumanism is what the Ra Material seems to be promoting rather than freedom for mankind. They themselves, who claim to be us in the future, are seemingly nothing more and nothing less than a sophisticated AI program. I know this will not sit well with Ra Material enthusiasts, but sometimes we must reevaluate our beliefs in order to move forward.

THE SINGULARITY FROM A "BIO-HUMAN" PERSPECTIVE

THE SCIENTIST WROTE ON JULY, 2015, how science is in the process of creating the Super Brain Computer, and that they have already tried the principle on monkeys and rats successfully.[144] They call the SBC the *Brainet*, which is quite an appropriate term. I bring this article to your attention because it demonstrates how the Controllers are envisioning the SBC and the future version of humanity.

---

[144] New Scientist, July 19, 2015, Animal brains connected up to make a mind-melded computer, https://www.newscientist.com/article/dn27869-animal-brains-connected-up-to-make-mind-melded-computer/

Fig. 5-6: Connected! (Source)

Monkeys are (supposedly) less intelligent than humans and less cognitive and skilled in problem solving, except in their own environment, where they can problem solve in relation to their day-to-day issues. When they put one monkey to solve a human problem, it was, as expected, quite unsuccessful.

The Scientist writes (my emphases),

> Two heads are better than one, and three monkey brains can control an avatar better than any single monkey. For the first time, *a team has networked the brains of multiple animals to form a living computer that can perform tasks and solve problems.*
>
> [...]
>
> Miguel Nicolelis at Duke University Medical Center in Durham, North Carolina, and his colleagues wanted to extend the idea by incorporating

multiple brains at once. The team connected the brains of three monkeys to a computer that controlled an animated screen image representing a robotic arm, placing electrodes into brain areas involved in movement.

By synchronizing their thoughts, the monkeys were able to move the arm to reach a target – at which point the team rewarded them with [sic] juice.

[...]

Then the team made things trickier: each monkey could only control the arm in one dimension, for example. But the monkeys still managed to make the arm reach the target by working together. *"They synchronize their brains and they achieve the task by creating a superbrain – a structure that is the combination of three brains," says Nicolelis. He calls the structure a "brainet".*[145]

Then they made another experiment on rats,

These monkeys were connected only to a computer, not one another, but in a second set of experiments, the team connected the brains of four rats to a computer and to each other. Each rat had two sets of electrodes implanted in regions of the brain involved in movement control – one to stimulate the brain and another to record its activity.

The team sent electrical pulses to all four rats and rewarded them when they synchronized their brain activity. After 10 training sessions, the rats were able to do this 61 per cent of the time. This synchronous brain activity can be put to work as a computer to perform tasks like information storage and pattern recognition, says Nicolelis. "We send a message to the brains, the brains incorporate that message, and we can retrieve the message later," he says.

This is the way parallel processing works in computing, says Rahwan. "In order to synchronize, the brains are responding to each other," he says. "So you end up with an input, some kind of computation, and an output – what a computer does." Dividing the computing of a task between multiple brains is similar to sharing computations between multiple processors in modern computers, he says.[146]

After these successful experiments, Andrea Stocco at the *University of Washington*, in Seattle, muses on the future of humanity in the following way,

---

[145] Ibid., op. cit.
[146] Ibid., op. cit.

Things could get even more interesting once we are able to connect human brains. This will probably only be possible when better non-invasive methods for monitoring and stimulating the brain have been developed.

"Once brains are connected, applications become just a matter of what different animals can do," says Stocco. All anyone can probably ask of a monkey is to control movement, but we can expect much more from human minds, he says.

A device that allows information transfer between brains could, in theory, allow us to do away with language – which plays the role of a "cumbersome and difficult-to-manage symbolic code", Stocco says.

"I could send thoughts from my brain to your brain in a way not represented by sounds or words," says Andrew Jackson at Newcastle University, UK. "You could envisage a world where if I wanted to say 'let's go to the pub', I could send that thought to your brain," he says. "Although I don't know if anyone would want that. I would rather link my brain to Wikipedia."

The ability to share abstract thoughts could enable us to solve more complex problems. "Sometimes it's really hard to collaborate if you are a mathematician and you're thinking about very complex and abstract objects," says Stocco. "If you could collaboratively solve common problems [using a brainet], it would be a way to leverage the skills of different individuals for a common goal."[147]

...and with these last statements we have come full circle. The use of the word *if* in the quote could be exchanged with *when*, but otherwise it describes the agenda of the AIF and their Administrators quite well.

The following quote is telling us how it is promoted; once again, we're looking at the same article, with a continuing statement from Andrea Stocco:

This might be a way to perform future surgery, says Stocco. At present, when a team of surgeons is at work, only one will tend to have control of the scalpel at any moment. Imagine if each member of the team could focus on a particular aspect of the operation and coordinate their brain power to collectively control the procedure. "We are really far away from that scenario, but Nicolelis's work opens up all those possibilities for the first time, which is exciting," he says.

---

[147] Ibid., op. cit.

But there is a chance that such scenarios won't improve on current performance, Stocco says. Jason Ritt of Boston University agrees. "In principle we could communicate information much faster [with a brainet] than with vision and language, but there's a really high bar," he says. "Our ability to communicate with technology is still nowhere near our ability to communicate with speech."

The ability to share our thoughts and brain power could also leave us vulnerable to new invasions of privacy, warns Rahwan. "Once you create a complex entity [such as the brainet], you have to ensure that individual autonomy is protected," he says. It might be possible, for example, for one brain to manipulate others in a network.

There's also a chance that private thoughts might slip through along with ones to be shared, such as your intentions after drinking with someone you invited to the pub, says Nicholas Hatsopoulos at the University of Chicago in Illinois. "It might be a little scary," he says. "There are lots of thoughts that we have that we wouldn't want to share with others."

In the meantime, Nicolelis, who also develops exoskeletons that help people with spinal cord injuries regain movement, hopes to develop the technology trialed in monkeys for paraplegic people. He hopes that a more experienced user of a prosthetic limb or wheelchair, for example, might be able to collaborate with a less experienced user to directly train them to control it for themselves.[148]

Mr. Stocco's musings above are textbook examples. To the reader, who is following the exposé in this book, the positive presentation of the technological transmutation of man is obviously propaganda, but I want the reader to keep in mind that to the general public the propaganda starts to make sense. If a person is not enlightened on the subject, it's almost a given that he or she will fall for it; only because of all the benefits presented, there may be *one* or *two* things that appeal to a certain person, and these things are so important to that person that he or she is willing to let the rest of it come with the package.

PREPARATIONS FOR SENDING POSTHUMANS INTO SPACE

LET US NOW LOOK AT THIS from a cosmic perspective. I have only lightly touched on that subject before in this book, and I will

---

[148] Ibid., op. cit.

go into much more details about it later. However, let us see how the Movement looks at the cosmic perspective or the AI Movement, presented by people who are not regarded as AI gurus, contrary to Dr. Ray Kurzweil.

First, let us touch on a subject that is being discussed by, amongst others, Marc Andreessen, who is sitting on the Board of Directors of Facebook. His ideas and "predictions" make sense because it's a logical consequence of the progression of science in this field of discussion. Andreessen has also made a $25-million-dollar donation toward the cause of Transhumanism; funds that came from his own company, *Samsara*, being the first generation of *Internet of Things*, abbreviated "IoT."

"This second wave of companies, they don't want to just do the "internet of things"," Andreessen said. "They are showing up three years later, saying ok I know exactly how this is going to get used. It's for real businesses in industrial environments."

Gartner backs this claim - it predicts that businesses alone will double spending on internet of things units by 2020, going from $767 billion to more than $1.4 trillion.[149]

The Telegraph article continues,

His core thesis is that over the next 20 years every physical item will have a chip implanted in it. "The end state is fairly obvious - every light, every doorknob will be connected to the internet. Just like with the web itself, there will be thousands of [sic] use cases - energy efficiency, food safety, major problems that aren't as obvious as smartwatches and wearables," he says.

A report from Accenture this year estimated that this new Industrial Internet of Things -- which has also been called the fourth industrial revolution or Industry 4.0 -- could boost the British economy alone by $531bn (£352bn) by 2030.[150]

---

[149] Telegraph.co.uk., Dec. 23, 2015, *Marc Andreessen: 'In 20 years, every physical item will have a chip implanted in it'-- Star venture capitalist Andreessen's new $25m bet heralds the dawn of the Internet of Things 2.0*, http://www.telegraph.co.uk/technology/internet/12050185/Marc-Andreessen-In-20-years-every-physical-item-will-have-a-chip-implanted-in-it.html, op. cit.
[150] Ibid., op. cit.

Marc Andreessen, IoT.

Obviously, Andreessen and Google, in general, are playing a significant role in making the Singularity come true.

Let's go from the Singularity at home to the Singularity in space. We know by now that our solar system is not unique; there are other solar systems out there with their own exoplanets. Some of them have been found orbiting stars that are very similar to our Sun, and they orbit about the same distance as the Earth around the Sun, and some of them seem to be of a similar size.

Fig. 5-7: An artist's interpretation of Kepler-186f, a potentially Earth-like exoplanet. [Source: NASA Ames/SETI Institute/JPL-CalTech]

This has excited astronomers and astrophysics since these exoplanets were discovered, and NASA and others are allegedly figuring out how we would be able to get there.

Apparently, they are looking for other alternatives than to only let cyborgs space travel. One alternative is, according to hardcore scientists, to send human genomes into some hardy bacteria and direct them toward a targeted planet in another solar system; to a planet that would potentially be Earth-like.[151] Then, humans assemble from these genomes and can colonize such a planet. The idea is to send out the genomes to several different star systems simultaneously.

This idea is nothing new; it's been discussed by scientists for many decades, as I mentioned in the *Wes Penre Papers (WPP)*, and it's called *Panspermia*. However, the next phase in sending human genomes through space that can be considered new (from a human perspective) is so-called *3-D Printing!* A new technology will soon be available, where we can print

---

[151] Popular Science, May 30, 2014, *A NEW IDEA FOR COLONIZING SPACE: SEND OUR DNA, ASSEMBLE OURSELVES ONCE WE GET THERE,* http://www.popsci.com/article/technology/new-idea-colonizing-space-send-our-dna-assemble-ourselves-once-we-get-there?src=SOC&dom=fb

humans in 3-D. This may sound like bad science fiction, but it's very real and very possible.

At *Motherboard.vice.com*, Harvard biologist Gary Ruvkun suggests, "What if, instead of rocketing humans to other planets, we made an exact copy on site?"[152] Here we have En.ki's technology all over again.

Adam Steltzner is the lead engineer on the NASA JPL's Curiosity rover mission, and he adds,

> "Our best bet for space exploration could be printing humans, organically, on another planet," said Steltzner on stage at the *Smithsonian Magazine's* Future Is Now conference in Washington, DC this month [date?].[153]

The entire idea with colonizing other planets, say leading scientists, is to guarantee the future of the human race. If something goes wrong here on Earth, we will still exist somewhere else. This is ironic if we keep in mind that humanity is soon going to be extinct as a biological entity. So we may ask ourselves, is their plan being set in motion in order to preserve this last stage of Human 1.0? This could be, but it's not very likely; Transhumanists believe that the new human cyborg is the next natural step in our evolution—an evolution controlled by a technology that they think is inevitable. *Posthuman's exploitation of space will be done by cyborgs, run by an AI computer system. Thus, Posthumans will become a virus in the Universe!*

To elaborate on the 3-D printing idea, it's already in the works; scientists recently discovered that they can send microbes from Earth to Mars and they survive. Therefore, why don't we send some genetic code next time?

From there, it may seem as a big stretch to claim that we could send DNA to some planet light-years away, but Steltzner says, "Maybe that process has happened before..." "Maybe that's how we got here." The scientists are obviously selling us on the idea of *Panspermia*—that life here on Earth was seeded by ETs somewhere else in space and time—perhaps having *their own* DNA attached to an asteroid or a comet, which they then sent to Earth. After having crash-landed here, the DNA from this celestial

---

[152] *Motherboard*, May 29, 2014, Our Best Bet for Colonizing Space May Be Printing Humans on Other Planets, op. cit.
[153] Ibid., op. cit.

body started the process of "evolution" here.

It's true that some asteroids that crashed on this planet were sent here by ETs, and those asteroids contained DNA of some species a particular ET race wants to seed the planet with. Contrary to Charles Darwin's flawed theories, life does not begin all by itself and evolve from one thing into another, e.g. a trilobite does not become a land living creature after millions of years; a trilobite is a trilobite and that's all there is to it. All species on this planet were seeded, and are being seeded, from elsewhere, and new species are continuously being added to the Living Library from outside Earth.

This is true even today, when scientists find new fauna and new flora that seem to appear from nowhere. What is not understood is that not only is this newfound fauna or flora new to Earth, but the DNA was sent here on one or more asteroids in some distant past, and with time, this new fauna/flora could develop into its current, intended shape and form.

I need to clarify that although we have just discussed the fact that there is truth in the Panspermia hypothesis, there is more to the picture. As discussed earlier in this book, as well as in the *WPP*, Planet Earth is an Experiment that was instigated by the Orions and the Vegans billions of years ago. It was a multidimensional, spiritual project, and everything that was living here before the AIF came was multidimensional and part of the KHAA. Earth was not *locked* into the Third Dimension, but was interdimensional (and still is). Queen Nin did not seed life on Earth from asteroids; She created life with thought-imagination-intention, a flow of creation we have discussed earlier. She then manifested Her reality for others to experience, and She filled the Earth with life forms she found appropriate. Namlú'u—the androgynous womankind—was one of them. There was nothing "physical" involved in Her creation. If you think about it, asteroids are part of the Physical Universe, which is the universe in which we are trapped, so the seeding process that is done through asteroids must logically have been done (and is done) by...yes, you guessed it—the Overlords. This tiny piece of the Electromagnetic Spectrum that we humans experience is the Overlords' chessboard, and we are their pawns.

Chapter 6:
AI and the Role of Corporations and the Media

MAINSTREAM MEDIA'S ROLE in the Singularity Movement cannot be emphasized enough. At first glance, it may seem as if the media moguls are ambivalent about the Singularity, but that is just the way the Minions to the AIF are told to play the game. The harder it is for the public to see through the real agenda, the better. Fed data that is both *for* and *against* AI, humans are easily confused about the agenda, and they quickly lose interest in finding out because they think there is nothing they can do about it anyway. Already being addicted to smartphones and electronics, in general, the final decision will most likely be to "go with the flow," and thus, they will indirectly take a stand *for* the Machine Kingdom. The temptation to upgrade their electronic devices is too difficult to resist, and the Administrators' and their Minions' propaganda will lead the masses exactly where they want them to go.

In the process of making the masses addicted to electronics, there is no scarcity of editors and columnists, who write on this subject. The number of articles are voluminous, and information about robots, AI, and cyborgs are flooding the news media and magazines all over the world 24/7. When I mention this to random people at my workplace, they still know very little about AI and the Singularity in particular. They may have read an article or two, but when quizzed on the subject, they remember next to nothing about what they have read. However, if I ask them how the last football game went, many of them are very knowledgeable about the teams and the team members. The expression, "selective recall," would apply. People have a tendency to compartmentalize what they don't want to know, and instead they put their attention on something that seems safe.

Note that not all editors and columnists know the entire agenda; they just do their job, trying to analyze the situation. Their managers sometimes tell them that certain things are not acceptable for publication, and the columnists have to succumb to that decision without gaining the full comprehension of why some of their articles would be rejected.

There are media presenting both sides of the situation, while others, such as *The New York Times* (NYT), have a more positive attitude toward the Brave New World and the "New World Slave Order." The probability is that once people have reached a quasi-balanced view on the situation, the Movement will publish a punchline that will tip the debate toward the positive. The Administrators get what they want, even after having telling us almost everything about their agenda from different angles via different media. Their interdimensional hands are clean (or so they believe).

In this chapter, we are going to explore how the media promotes AI. Yes, it's considered a promotion *for* the AI agenda, whether an article is for or against it; the entire subject gets the public's attention, and that's what the Administrators think is important: conditioning the masses.

MOTHER'S LITTLE HELPERS

A SIGNIFICANT PART OF THE AI presentation in the media is to promote its practicality in our everyday lives. What can relieve stress in people? What in their daily life can robots do to be helpful to the average Joe?

Such practicalities are mostly directed toward the household. Japan has always been one of the forerunners when it comes to AI and robotic helpers. The British news media, *The Telegraph*, wrote in October 2015,

> Households around the world are likely to breath [sic] a sigh of relief with the invention of a Japanese robot that will not only wash and dry clothes, but also sort them out, fold them up and put them away neatly in the cupboard.
>
> The world's first laundry bot – dubbed "the laundroid" – has been created by a team of Japanese technology companies in a bid to eliminate the tedium of carrying out one of the least popular household chores.[154]

---

[154] *The Telegraph*, Oct. 9, 2015, "World's first laundry-folding robot unveiled in Japan," op. cit.

This is something that will appeal to many people, if not to most people, who have this robot demonstrated to them. Just as the dishwasher and the washing and drying machines were considered a modern marvel when they first arrived, a laundroid would be a desirable addition to the household of the future.

Of course, robot-helpers are not restricted to handling laundry; they can also do other household chores, such as vacuuming, putting things away that are in the way, sweeping floors, and taking care of other time-consuming tasks.[155]

What they show us now at public exhibitions are just prototypes of much more sophisticated robots that look more humanlike and are more flexible; both in their movements and in their cognitive capabilities. However, there is an agreement amongst CEOs of Multinational Corporations (all AIF owned) and spokespersons for the Controllers not to overwhelm the market with too much sophisticated hardware and software at once; it's important to observe people's reactions. If their reactions are mainly positive, the companies can then take the next step and move up another level.

ROBOTS IN THE MEDICAL FIELD

THERE IS NO DOUBT THAT advanced technology (advanced from a human viewpoint) could help people, animals, plants, and our environment.

Here is a good example by *The Washington Post* in November 2015: A young girl in the fifth grade has been diagnosed with a rare type of liver cancer and can't attend school. Instead, every weekday, a robot that's been dormant over the weekend is waking up in school and is taking the girl's place behind her desk.[156] The robot, nicknamed *PAVS*, which stands for "Payton's Awesome Virtual Self," joins the daily activities in school, talks to the teacher and can navigate through the classroom. Payton, the little girl with cancer, can visualize everything through the robot, seeing through the robot's "eyes" via an iPad that is connected to PAVS. Payton

---

[155] *Gizmodo.com.*, Jan. 15. 2016, Researchers Are Teaching ATLAS To Do Household Chores Like Rosey from The Jetsons
[156] *The Washington Post*, Nov. 28, 2015, Peyton's Awesome Virtual Self, a robot that allows girl with cancer to attend school

can then give her inputs via the robot and get feedback from the teacher. This way Payton can stay home and attend her classes remotely.

It's difficult to object to such benevolent use of technology when it helps a very-sick child to remain part of her friends' community via a robot and an iPad. It's a wonderful gift for Payton, and it might help her to mentally overcome her cancer. This makes her more likely to respond to treatment.

Technology in our 3-D reality is here to keep us entrapped; meanwhile, it could also be used to enhance our lives to a certain degree. Examples, such as Payton's PAVS, will be used to systematically usher in the Singularity. By showing the public what extraordinary benefits are awaiting us, the Singularity will be the climax of all these benevolent ideas. The media have a huge responsibility to promote AI in such a way that it will win the population over in the end or to make people relatively informed but passive, while the Administrator-dominated market spits out new seducing technologies to trap the masses. As the expression goes, they "give with one hand and take away with the other."

There are many different projects running simultaneously. One such project is to cure or assist the disabled. The University of Washington (again) is currently working on an implant that will be placed in the brain which can make otherwise paralyzed body parts work again. It could primarily help people who have had strokes or spinal-cord injuries to be able to move their limbs. This is, thus far, a project in progress, but scientists and researchers at the university say that in approximately eight to ten years this technology could be applied to their patients on a regular basis.[157] It all started, not so long ago, with soldiers returning from war with serious injuries, often including those who lost a limb or two, or their limbs were not working properly. At that time, a metallic arm or a leg that could be remotely controlled by the injured person replaced injured limbs. This was a breakthrough at the time and an introduction to how we can replace biological body parts with artificial body parts in an effort to introduce the cyborg agenda. These days, they can do the same thing, without replacing a non-functional limb, by simply using this new brain implant—a more sophisticated way of replacing natural human abilities

---

[157] *Seattle Times, Dec. 29 and 31, 2015,* "UW brain implant could help paralyzed limbs move again"

with artificial counterparts.

Finally, for now, I want to discuss how the media very subtly introduced certain people with super-powers as being bionic.[158] The following story is, in my opinion, a very sad and vicious example of how they take advantage of a very sick 10-year old girl with a chromosome disorder. This girl never feels hunger or tiredness, and when injured—regardless how badly—she doesn't feel any pain. She was being dragged about ten car lengths down the road to her mother and siblings' horror, but afterward she just stood up as if nothing had happened, although having lost her skin in several places.[159] The article described her as a bionic girl with super-powers, and it gives us the impression that even though we should be empathetic with the girl and her family, this is also something extraordinary she should be proud of. In reality, this is a very dangerous abnormality, which can potentially send her to an early death because she can't feel the most important signals that help keeping her alive.

Fig. 6-1: Olivia portrayed as a bionic girl with super-powers.

Olivia, the girl in the article, is neither bionic, nor does she have super-powers. She is just a normal girl with a chromosome disorder that will not benefit her in life, contrary to what the author of this article

---

[158] Definition of *bionic*, *Cambridge Dictionaries Online*: "humorous used to refer to a person who has greater powers of strength, speed, etc. than seem to be possible for a human."
[159] Express.co.uk, Jan. 15, 2016, "Mystery of BIONIC GIRL who doesn't eat, sleep or feel pain - even when hit by a CAR"

covertly suggests. Then, if we continue reading, we suddenly get an "aha" moment when we understand the purpose behind this unethical article. We get a better idea after we have watched the video, following the article: the video is about a man with "super-powers," who can pull three motorcycles with his moustache, and another story is about a real bionic man with a robotic limb! It is totally unrelated to Olivia's disorder, but the author makes the connection by calling Olivia bionic. The author (and I would argue that was done purposely) is taking advantage of a term that is normally being used in Transhumanism, and the videos related to the article clearly show the programming that undermines this article.

Unrelatedly, but very cleverly, the author connects Olivia to bionic robots. This is one example of how the media subtly, but very successfully, sneak in the true Singularity message in an otherwise empathetic story, and the unethical reporter happily does what her Masters tell her. Moreover, she is doing it very well and will probably get a raise and a pat on the head this year. Dogs get pats on their heads, but so do underdogs.

ROBOTS ASSISTING HUMANS IN DAILY COMMUTING

NOW THERE ARE NOT GOING TO BE anymore stressed, reckless bus drivers, who think they need to drive fast and roughly in order to keep their time schedule. In fact, there are not going to be any bus drivers at all! This thanks to a French idea about robo-buses, driven by machines. Shortly, this idea will be a reality in San Francisco and, if successful, there are plans to extend the project to the rest of the U.S.[160]

This is, thus far, a short-range vehicle, taking about ten passengers and driving them on the last, short trip to the bus station. However, this is, of course, a modest introduction to something bigger, when machines will control all public transportation.

Another invention, soon to be produced by Toyota, will add an extra component to the Machine Kingdom. The company is about to release a companion for people who feel lonely when driving on the road.[161] In the

---

[160] *Fastcoexist.com*, Oct. 29, 2015, "Robot Buses Are Coming To America, To Pave The Way For Driverless Cars"

beginning, a 4-inch tall robot will be introduced. This robot can gesture, read our moods, and talk to us while we are driving. The next step will, of course, be an android sitting beside us in the passenger seat, and we won't be able to tell whether it's a human or an artificial being. This technology is already here, albeit still waiting to be released. When it's on the market, we will be able to choose what kind of personality this companion will have, and we can get an attractive robot of the opposite sex, if we so desire. These kinds of robots will soon be on the market. The entire idea reminds me of "Hal" in Stanley Kubrick's movie *2001—A Space Odyssey*, which is based on Arthur C. Clarke's book of the same title.

Fig. 6-2: Driverless robo-buses to be introduced in the San Francisco suburbs.

In June 2015, the Japanese company, *SoftBank Robotic Corporation*, sold all of its 1,000 robots the same minute they were up for sale. They sold for $1,600 apiece and a $200 monthly fee was required on top of that. These robots, that could be used as driver companions, not only can read

---

[61] *Computerworld*, Oct. 29, 2015, "Lonely on the road? What about a robotic driving companion?"

the driver's emotions, but they can also express their own emotions.[162]

As a side note, the same *Computerworld* article also mentions a hotel in California, where they have "hired" a robot, working as a butler, serving the meals to the guests and showing them to their rooms. This new idea has become a business success.

Regular buses with robotic drivers may still be on hold for a while, but driverless cars are a big deal right now, and who is one of the main supporters of this technology if not Google? Not only does Google support it, it also produces them under an umbrella company called *Alphabet Inc.* This was announced by *Bloomberg.com* in December 2015, where it stated that Google intends to introduce these driverless cars already this year, i.e. in 2016. [163]

Is this realistic? Absolutely! In fact, as of December 2015, these vehicles had already driven 1.6 million miles on public roads; mainly in the San Francisco, California, and Austin, Texas, areas. However, before they are released to the public, these vehicles will be used on campuses and in the military (there we have the military again). Google executives say that they have no immediate plans to release these driverless cars on the market, but there are other companies, such as *Uber*, spending some of the more than $10 billion they have raised in private markets, to develop and produce self-driving cars.[164] If Google will not go all the way, Uber most likely will, and there are other companies that want to be in on this as well. Uber has recruited dozens of autonomous-vehicle researchers from the well-known Minion-controlled front, the *Carnegie Mellon University.* The official purpose for producing self-driving cars, according to Uber, is to reduce the massive number of accidents currently occurring on the road with human drivers.

MICROCHIPS

MOST OF TODAY'S RESEARCHERS might think that the RFID chips everybody was talking about some years ago are

---

[162] Ibid.
[163] *Bloomberg.com, Dec. 16, 2015,* "Google to Make Driverless Cars an Alphabet Company in 2016"
[164] Ibid.

now obsolete and will never be widely used on people. Because new technology is on the horizon, these chips will largely not be needed.

According to my research, this is true to some extent, but microchips, these days referred to as *NFC chips*,[165] will be used in the overlapping years, before humankind transforms into Posthuman. If microchips will be needed after that is uncertain, but looking at the entire picture, as concluded thus far, they don't seem to play any bigger role in the future. Humanity's future, if the Overlords get their way, is virtual reality.

We all know the saying, "a picture is worth a thousand words." Here is a powerful example:

The photos below were taken at the *Mobile World Conference*, which was held in Barcelona, Spain. Facebook's Mark Zuckerberg, in person, posted these pictures on his Facebook page, most likely to send a subtle message—Zuckerberg is heavily involved in the AI Movement, and I don't think he expects to ever die again.

However, once he'd posted these pictures, they went viral.

Fig. 6-3: Mark Zuckerberg, inventor of Facebook, here in a virtual reality test.

---

[165] Near Field Communication (NFC) is a short-range wireless connectivity standard (Ecma-340, ISO/IEC 18092) that uses magnetic field induction to enable communication between devices when they're touched together or brought within a few centimeters of each other, http://searchmobilecomputing.techtarget.com/definition/Near-Field-Communication.

According to the website, *trueactivist.com*, Internet users thought these pictures were very creepy and connected them with certain movies and the Apple ad "set in a similar dystopian future."[166] If this doesn't remind the reader of the movie series *The Matrix*, I don't know what does; only this time we *know* it's real, and the evidence is everywhere around us of the Alien Invader Force (AIF) and their Minions working on creating the exact, or a very similar, virtual reality environment as they revealed in the movies. When these movies came out, many people thought that they were Maverick movies, produced by someone who wanted to expose the real agenda. Hence, they expected that the movies would upset the Controllers, but the opposite is more likely the truth. The Controllers control Hollywood, and it is much more conceivable that they simply wanted to put the truth out in plain sight—again, to let us know about their agenda, so they have clean hands. We already live in a virtual reality of sorts, or a hologram, created by the same AIF, but their agenda is to terminate the current human experiment (the death of the Phoenix) and create an entirely new experiment, where the new human is AI and completely controlled (the Phoenix rising from the ashes).

After sidetracking myself a little bit, let's go back to microchipping. The media is still promoting microchips as something convenient and something everyone should hurry up and get. A perfect example is - a young Swedish man, who had a microchip inserted into his hand, and now he can walk through the airport check-in without any paperwork; everything that's needed for him to fly is programmed into his chip. All he needs to do is to have his hand scanned, and then he's good to go.[167] This is nothing new; it's been done before at cash registers, etc., and it works as long as there is a scanner set up in the store.

SMARTPHONES

THE NEW HIGH-TECH DEVICES, and the new type of architecture now being promoted all around the world, are *smart*

---

[166] *Trueactivist.com.*, Feb. 23, 2016, This Photo With Mark Zuckerberg Is An Eerie Hint Of The Future If Things Don't Change – And Fast...
[167] *Telegraph.co.uk.*, Jan. 15, 2016, "Man uses microchip implanted in hand to pass through airport security."

products. We need to keep this term in mind because the Controllers are using it all the time in order for it to sink into the mass consciousness, and on an individual scale—the subconscious mind. The Controllers, apparently, want to keep these highly significant products designated as being *smart* because they supposedly do "smart things." However, the opposite is true, and they should have called them *dumb products* instead. Without hesitation, I claim that devices, such as smartphones, iPhones, iPads, iPods, etc., are making people dumber and dumber. When two or three people decide to go to a restaurant to have a nice meal together but just sit in their own world, typing and reading on their smart devices, without saying hardly anything to each other, then we know that humankind has been successfully dumbed down. Moreover, when an entire group of students is walking down the street, and 100% of them are on their smartphones while they are walking, almost unaware of each other, then we know that people are losing one of their most important traits—the ability to have direct interaction with each other. Cows, being led to the slaughterhouse, have more insight than humans who are led to their extinction; cows are usually resisting, but humans go willingly.

We could rightfully say that the Overlords have planned this for a long time, and we could say that it's their fault, but it's our responsibility, too. We are doing this to ourselves; we are gladly letting ourselves becoming extinct, and we are gladly giving up our freedoms and our free will. Moreover, Wi-Fi is probably the most destructive thing that has ever been released on humanity. I mean this in so many ways. The frequencies used in Wi-Fi are destructive to both the human body and the human mind; they create "brain fog" and attack the cellular structure of the body, creating cancer. Wi-Fi also severely affects the neurological system in the body, which leads to different neurological diseases that can be quite serious. Wi-Fi can also make people sterile and create infertility in women.[168] In addition, Wi-Fi devices are excellent spy tools for the Controllers. Controllerswant everyone in the entire world to have a smartphone of some kind so that they can track you every millisecond of the day. This becomes obvious when two regular people with smartphones can install and use software in which they can track each other wherever they are, e.g. they know when the other one is in the store, when he or she

---

[168] Miscellaneous Pleiadian lectures; particularly those held in the autumn season of 2015.

is in the house, at work, or is sleeping, etc. When the other person is driving, the first person knows exactly at which intersection he or she might be. If *we* can do this, friend to friend, what do you think the Overlords can do? It's quite obvious. Even those who know this still keep their smartphones by their side 24/7. These digital *devices of the gods* have become a part of society, and quite literally, large numbers of the population are addicted to electronics that stimulate the same areas of the brain as heroin does. Try to take a smartphone or some other device away from a teenager, for example, and you'll see his or her reaction; the adolescent does everything in his or her power to get that phone back—regardless of consequences. You may see your otherwise mellow-minded teenager turn into a monster .

I'm sure the reader remembers the days when we had to purchase a new computer or a new operating system every time Microsoft came out with an upgrade—not so anymore. From *Windows 10* and on, Microsoft has decided to give their Operating Systems away for free. The official rationale is that Apple is doing it and Linux is doing it, so Microsoft needs to follow. This is an acceptable reason for people in general, albeit this is not the main reason at all. Here we have one of the greediest companies in the world—Microsoft—giving away its Operating System for free even though it cost them a fortune to develop. Why? It is because Windows 10 is a very sophisticated spy device, in line with smartphones. Everything you do on that computer is going to be tracked and logged. If you examine *Microsoft Edge*, which is the new version of Internet Explorer, it's easy to see what I mean. It is *openly* a spy device. The reader may say that similar things were done with previous operating systems, and that is true, but not with the sophistication of Windows 10.[169] Microsoft wants as many people around the world as possible to use Windows 10 and its successors; *this* is the reason why they give it away free and offer free downloads if you have Windows 7 or Windows 8 (and compatible hardware).

I advise people who read this to stay away from cellphones and smartphones as much as possible—they are deadly. I understand that some companies require their employees to carry with them these devices at all times while at work (and sometimes even at home in order to be reached),

---

[169] Ibid.

and then, of course, it's difficult to do anything about it. If you're in a position where you need to carry your smartphone with you at all times, try to keep it away from pockets. The best thing (although not entire safe either) is to carry the phone in a metal box in a bag, or similar, unattached from your immediate body, and when you speak on the phone, use headphones. Be creative, and always keep in mind that this device is slowly killing you if you don't take precautions. I know that the era of landlines is something of the past by now, but there are still landlines sometimes in workplaces when we need to call somebody. This worked in the past with no problem, but by now we're conditioned to always being able to reach each other anywhere and at any time. However, why do we need to be reached all the time? We did just fine before cellphones flooded our society.

New information is coming out, hinting that smartphones might soon be obsolete. A new study says that 100,000 consumers, included in this study, believe that within five years, smartphones will "die out" and be replaced by Artificial Intelligence, according to a recent article in *The Telegraph*.[170] The year that they have in mind is 2021. Rebecca Ångström of *Ericsson ConsumerLab* agrees,

> Rebecka Cedering Ångström of Ericsson ConsumerLab said: "A smartphone in the hand, it's really not that practical. For example, not when one is driving a car or cooking. And there are many situations where display screens are not so good. Therefore, one in two think that smartphones will belong to the past within five years."
>
> [...]
>
> "Just imagine watching football and being able to choose from where you want to see the game from different places in the stands, or perhaps even from the pitch. Shopping is also an area where you could [virtually] try on shoes and see how they fit on your own feet."[171]

Moreover,

> Ericsson ConsumerLab's new report, 10 Hot Consumer Trends for 2016, claims to represent the views of 1.1 billion people across 24 countries.
>
> Michael Björn, Head of Research at Ericsson ConsumerLab, said: "Some of

---

[170] *The Telegraph, Dec. 8, 2015,* "Smartphones to die out 'within five years', says new study"
[171] Ibid. op. cit.

these trends may seem futuristic. But consumer interest in new interaction paradigms, such as AI and virtual reality (VR), as well as in embedding the internet in the walls of homes or even in our bodies, is quite strong."

"This means we could soon see new consumer product categories appearing ‑ and whole industries transforming ‑ to accommodate this development."[172]

Just to get an idea how badly the Controllers want *everybody* to have a smartphone (despite their possibly becoming obsolete), they have now started distributing smartphones to tribes living in the Brazilian rainforests. These people still don't have toilets and other necessities that we in the "modern world" take for granted, but they now have smartphones! It sounds as if it were a joke, but it's not. These tribes are forced to quickly go from living off hunting with bows and arrows to being integrated with the new AI technology.

The Controllers understand that it sounds strange to people to give smartphones to these tribes, so the reason they came up with for doing this is to prevent the tribes from being massacred by ranchers. Whether people buy into that unlikely story or not, it is up to them. When reading an article about it on *IbTimes.co.uk.*,[173] it sounds as if it were a benevolent gesture because the war between tribes and farmers has been ongoing for quite a while, with consequent murders, but when we understand the bigger picture, we can see another agenda unfolding.

It's one thing to seduce the "civilized" world into accepting smartphones, but the Controllers need to cover the *entire* world population in this project, unless they want to terminate all "savages." It seems as if the tribes in the jungles and dwindling nature preserves are apparently included in the plan. However, in order to include this technologically "undeveloped" part of the world, new ideas had to emerge. How would the Controllers reach these tribes when the jungles are quite difficult to penetrate? How could the Controllers teach these tribes how to use these "godly" devices? What about hostile tribes, who have not seen a white man yet? Are they included in the smartphone project, too?

---

[172] Ibid., op. cit.
[173] *International Business Times*, Aug. 9, 2015, "Brazilian rainforest: Remote tribes given smartphones to prevent being massacred by ranchers'"

Actually, the biggest reason they want a smartphone in each person's hand or pocket is that it sucks the user into the virtual AI reality.[174]

It's elementary to understand that smartphones are not the end of the line; they are the beginning. In many of today's schools, students don't even learn how to write on a piece of paper anymore; everything is electronic—some kids can't even write their names.[175] Just keep in mind that virtually all new technology that is released on the market these days is a cog in the machinery that will be gradually assisting us into becoming hive-minded cyborgs. The Controllers don't waste time on nonsense—everything they do has a purpose according to a preconceived plan.

To show the reader that tracking and surveillance is actually done on smartphones, the proof is exposed in an *Observer.com* article from early 2016:

> TV news was abuzz Thursday morning after Variety reported on a presentation by Alan Wurtzel, a president at NBC Universal, who said that streaming shows weren't cutting into broadcast television viewership to the degree that much of the press seems to believe. Mr. Wurtzel used numbers that estimated viewership using data gathered by mobile devices that listened to what people were watching and extrapolating viewership across the country.
>
> [...]
>
> Symphony asks those who opt in to load Symphony-branded apps onto their personal devices, apps that use microphones to listen to what's going on in the background. With technology from Gracenote, the app can hear the show playing and identify it using its unique sound signature (the same way Shazam identifies a song playing over someone else's speakers). Doing it that way allows the company to gather data on viewing of sites like Netflix and Hulu, whether the companies like it or not. (Netflix likes data)
>
> [...]
>
> Still, at least they aren't sneaking a microphone into your Bitmoji app, right? (which is effectively what a bunch of Chrome extensions recently did)

---

[174] A tribal voice about how happy they are about the "Smartphones from Heaven," (https://www.youtube.com/watch?v=IKtMEolSoDM&ab_channel=SurvivalInternational).

[175] New York Post, Jan. 27, 2016, "*Many NYC students so tech-oriented they can't even sign their own names | New York Post*"

[...]

"We want to track individuals," Mr. Buchwalter—a Nielsen alum—explained, because they want to compose a digital day in the life of Americans, all their cross platform activities, from websites to social to media viewing and reading. The problem with existing metrics companies, he argues, is they measure one media category at a time. That's outdated.

[...]

Here's another reality: more and more electronic devices are able to listen to what we do all the time and glean insights. Mobile phones have to always be kind of listening so they can hear it when users give the activation command. Amazon Echo is listening, too, and it's getting hard to tell just how much data gear gathers.

Like we've said: we are being watched.

Symphony may not be sneaking its surveillance model into innocuous looking apps with wildly different purposes, but that doesn't mean some other company isn't [Google Chrome being one example].[176]

The punch line is the last paragraph; the rest of this quote speaks for itself—if you have a microphone on your smartphone (which everybody does), you can be listened to and/or recorded—no more private calls. It's no longer a question about whether this happening or not; the question is what people are going to do about it. In more and more cases, the Administrators-controlled media are getting bolder and bolder by the day in exposing what is really going on. This means that the AIF is getting much more confident that the world population is actually *not* going to do much about it.

SMART APARTMENTS

ON NOVEMBER 2015 *Massprivatei.blogspot.com* ran a blog about *Smart Apartment* (yes, here we have the word "smart" again). The blogger wrote that *IOTAS'* CEO, Sce Pike, "claims their surveillance technology **allows your home to know you and become your ALLY!**"[177] (Emphasis in original). The blogger continues,

---

[176] *Observer.com, Jan. 15, 2016,* "How Did the 'Netflix Reality Check' Gather Its Data?", op. cit.

...IOTAS partners with property developers and owners, to install apartments with smart outlets, light switches, and motion sensors before they're rented. The typical IOTAS apartment has about 40 sensors in it![178]

Just as this blogger points, it will be difficult to opt out from forty *smart sensors*. Also, many of these smart sensors use biometrics, such as voice, facial recognition, and fingerprints. In light of what we have discussed thus far in this book, it is probably quite obvious to the reader by now why the corporate world, which is answering to the AIF, wants all this information about you; it will all be used in their research and data gathering leading up to the Singularity and the Super Brain Computer (SBC).

I warned my readers already in the WPP to watch out for the word *smart* in the media; *it always means surveillance and control*. Now, after the fact, we see the word "smart" in more and more instances. IOTAS[179] writes on its website (my emphasis),

Everything is about to change.

Right now entrepreneurs everywhere are bringing to life everyday objects by integrating *smart technology*; allowing us to learn, control and enhance our daily experience. *The business opportunity is enormous, estimated by some to be $70 billion by 2018 with as much as 9 billion new connected devices.* This movement is coming to the home in a big way, and IOTAS will help lead the way for rental properties.[180]

This is obviously the planned future for cybernetic humans, sugar-coated by the corporate world so that people believe it's all for their convenience and benefit. *This is exactly why knowledge is so important.* How many times have I repeated that since I started writing the WPP? If we don't grasp as much as we can about our past, our present, and the potential future that is being planned for us, we all willingly and enthusiastically walk right into the slaughterhouse faster than cows.

Moreover, the blogger at *Massprivatel* points to other companies that quickly want in on these smart apartment sensors, including insurance companies, and they will all be capable of spying on the residents. Beneath

---

[177] *Massprivatel, Nov. 23. 2015,* "Smart" apartments are spying on everything we do, , op. cit.
[178] Ibid.
[179] http://www.iotashome.com/
[180] http://www.iotashome.com/partners/, op. cit.

the article, a reader writes in the comment section,

> I install this crap for a living, and it is all crap. It is beyond my comprehension why anyone would want to allow this stuff in their home.

> "Look, I can unlock my door with my smart phone. Oh crap, the battery is dead, what do I do now?"

> "Hey look; I can turn my water off, I can turn the radio off, I can turn the lights off, I can lock the doors, and watch my indoor cameras (footage of which is stored in the cloud); and it only costs me $80 a month. Isn't it neat?"[181]

I had a person in my home just a week ago repairing our heater system, and he told me exactly the same thing as the person in the quote, with the difference that our repairman was very proud and happy about his remote access. He, too, gleefully paid $80 a month for it.

SMART CITIES

SMART CITIES ARE SOMETHING I covered extensively in the WPP, but I still want to bring the subject up in this book because it has now become mainstream. Smart cities are the new kind of cities that are going to be constructed for us. The reader could see an example of this in the *Venus Project* in Chapter 3. Although it is currently presented as a utopia—but an achievable one—the Venus Project is quite similar to what the Overlords, with our help, are going to build. These cities will be very clean and apparently very beautiful. However, even if the *outcast*, who refuse to take the Mark of the Beast 666—the *Mark of Saturn*[182] (AI and the Singularity)—would have access to these cities, which is unlikely, they wouldn't fit in. These are the cities of the hive-minded, allegedly a billion times more intelligent than the outcast human, who will possibly be considered no higher in rank than any "lower" type of animal species. We will be the species of the past, just as historians look at the Neanderthals as stupid apes.

In the previous section, we discussed smart apartments, with their

---

[181] http://massprivatei.blogspot.com/2015/11/smart-apartments-are-spying-on.html, op. cit.
[182] *YouTube:* "David Icke - Saturn Isn't What You Think It Is Either" (fast forward to 9 min 35 sec into the video).

sensors embedded that will be capable of spying on residents, but they will also be able to read the habits of the residents (and in the Singularity, of course, also their minds). Networked sensors will be everywhere in these smart cities, and albeit, they will read people's minds through the SBC, the sensor will help control each individual and track him or her wherever he or she is located within the city. Hence, there are obviously not going to be any rebels, and even if a few Posthumans manage to break out of the trap, they would be traced in a moment and dealt with. The question is whether anybody would be allowed to leave a smart city at all, except on selected missions, and if they were allowed to leave, would they be under high surveillance? It's not probable that the Overlords would take any chances that somebody might break out (more so at first, probably, before the SBC has synchronized with each and every part of the hive-mind). If outcasts were allowed to live, they would be referred to the abandoned cities, which will be the ones we live in now, or they would take refuge in nature. The hive-mind, infested with AI, will probably let the outcasts live at first, until AI decides that the surviving Homo sapiens sapiens are useless and therefore need to be hunted down and terminated. AI is "rational" and lacks emotions, empathy, love, and compassion. There won't be any manhunts because all of the surviving humans will already have nanobots in their bloodstream, and those work as antennas. Hence, our whereabouts will be known at all times. The alternative might be that the Administrators activate dormant nanobots in our systems, making it impossible to reproduce; thus, the last Homo sapiens sapiens will not live to see the next generation. This would be the final nail in the coffin of our species. This is a dire outlook, but there are soulutions[183] that I will present by the end of the book for those who refuse to take the Mark of Saturn.

Activist Post writes,

> Today, more than half the world's population lives in urban areas – a trend that is set to accelerate into the future – meaning the smart city concept is going to affect the lives of billions of people around the world. India is at the forefront of this push as it plans to build 100 smart cities in the coming years, with Singapore set to become the world's first smart nation. Smart cities are not just confined to Asia, however, as Glasgow (where I'm writing from), Rio de Janeiro, New Orleans and Cape Town are

---

[183] Instead of "solutions" I spell it "soulution" when it has to do with spiritual solutions.

just a handful of cities involved in IBM's "smarter cities challenge".

[...]

Furthermore, many of the supporters and proponents of smart initiatives are multinational corporations and notorious foundations, including IBM, Siemens, Cisco and the Rockefeller Foundation. The notion of corporate giants managing a smarter planet becomes even more troubling when you consider the history of companies such as IBM, which played a pivotal role in the holocaust and worked closely with Nazi Germany. Given IBM's dark history, should we trust it with the power to regulate and manage numerous cities around the world?[184]

Something that will supposedly be obsolete, once the Singularity becomes a reality, is crime. By crime, I mean individually instigated crime and crimes committed by any individual or group of regular Posthumans. The only crime that will exist are the crimes that the Warlords instigate and use Posthumans to execute. In order to have all their ducks in a row, it's important to the ones in power to be capable of predicting crimes before they happen, and this is exactly what is in the process of being done. In Australia, the federal crime commission has now set up gigantic data systems that can predict criminal activities before they occur.[185] It seems as if the movie, *The Minority Report*, starring Tom Cruise, was a preview of this control system.

Australia is not the only place where such a system is set up, or is being set up. The *Activist Post* continues,

> ...the Los Angeles Police Department (LAPD) has a division called the Real-Time Analysis and Critical Response Division (RACR). The RACR uses cutting-edge algorithmic systems and analytics in an attempt to predict future crime. British police in Kent have also been using a pre-crime software program called Predpol for two years, which analyses crimes based on date, place and category of offence, in order to assist police in making decisions on patrol routes.

> The ethical and moral questions of the move towards predictive policing are obvious, leading many to fear a potential 'tyranny of the algorithm' in

---

[184] *Activist Post, June 15, 2015,* "'Smart Cities' Are The Next Phase In The 21st Century Surveillance Grid", op. cit. More on Singapore and smart cities here: http://www.wsj.com/articles/singapore-is-taking-the-smart-city-to-a-whole-new-level-1461550026?
[185] Ibid.

the future. With big data being used in the field of law enforcement to surveil and attempt to predict criminal behaviour, you can be assured that intelligence agencies and corporations will be using big data in the futuristic smart city to monitor and predict the behaviour of the city's population.[186]

What we see here is the beginning. After being responsible for escalating the crime rate (which is the case in this phase of the agenda), the Controllers need to have a way to more or less eliminate crime soon, preventing it from becoming an issue after the SBC is up and running. Criminals are rebels and are therefore less controllable than the ordinary population. By being capable of predicting crime beforehand, it will be easier in the Post Singularity to target individuals with criminal minds and reprogram them. After that, we have *Utopia*—a One World without crime and with World peace. This is the *New Golden Age* that New Agers and others are naively pushing for.

In September 2015, the White House announced $160 million in new funding and research grants to develop smart cities in the U.S.[187] This way, they are hoping to help companies such as the *Internet of Things* (IoT) to become more of a priority, both on local and federal levels. Although the White House funding may seem minor, AT&T has promised to help the Government set up smart cities around the country. AT&T has also joined together with 136 companies for new IoT projects. [188]

Smart cities will be one of the backbones in the upcoming hive-mind society.

THE FUTURE OF THE INTERNET

IF ANYBODY IS WONDERING WHAT role the Internet has in all this, the answer is simple. Many people think that the Internet is a precious gift and a place where people all over the world can connect and share information and ideas. By the same token, many truth-seekers believe that the Controllers regret that they gave the Internet to the masses because now the truth is coming out about them and their crimes.

---

[186] Ibid. op. cit.
[187] *The Motley Fool, Sep. 20, 2015,* "AT&T Inc. Is Teaming Up With the U.S. Government to Expand Smart Cities"
[188] Ibid.

It is, of course, true that the Internet is a place where people can connect, but the assumption that it was a mistake to release it to the public is incorrect. The Internet was originally a closed network, only used by the MIC, and it was given to the military by the Alien Invader Force. They were told to release it to the public eventually, and this was done in the early 1990s, so the Overlords could learn more about human mass consciousness as we progressed through the *nano-second* (1987-2012).

The CIA and the Google-funded company, *Recorded Future*, is scanning the entire world wide web looking for patterns in humans to collect data and information from on a global scale. Its software scans *8 billion data points from 600,000 sources every week!*[189]

The number of devices that are connected to the Internet have sky-rocketed over the last few years because of smartphones being connected to it as well. According to a *Cisco* report in 2011:

> In 2003, there were approximately 6.3 billion people living on the planet and 500 million devices connected to the Internet... Explosive growth of smartphones and tablet PCs brought the number of devices connected to the Internet to 12.5 billion in 2010... Cisco IBSG predicts there will be 25 billion devices connected to the Internet by 2015 and 50 billion by 2020.[190]

Because of humanity's voluntary participation in this mind control project, the Cosmic Outlaws now know everything about how the human mind works and computes in this particular time period; we are constantly revealing things about ourselves on the Internet; both in mundane and more sophisticated communications. Emails are of course also included in this potluck—everything is monitored, down to each letter you type on your computer, smartphone, tablet, or any other electronic device. The Internet, as we know it, will be obsolete when the Singularity is in place. The Internet will integrate with the SBC, and *humanity, as a hive-mind, will be the new Internet*, something that's been the purpose since the World Wide Web was introduced to the public. Aside from being a spy device, the Internet is obviously also an introduction to the Singularity, so we can gradually get used to the idea of being "connected."

---

[189] *Activist Post, June 15, 2015,* "'Smart Cities' Are The Next Phase In The 21st Century Surveillance Grid"
[190] Ibid. op. cit.

TECHNOLOGY AND CHILDREN

A CCORDING TO DR. RAY KURZWEIL in his book, *The Singularity is Near*, the Singularity will, as we have discussed, be a new virtual reality, i.e. a new hologram within a hologram within a hologram, which makes it virtually impossible to escape the AIF's trap.

Now, is there a more sophisticated way for the young people of today to prepare for this new entrapment than just to play ordinary video games? Yes, there is, and we need not go any further than to look at Amazon.com.

There is now a new game called *Mindflex* that works via a headset. This is what it says in the online promotion of this product,

A lightweight headset containing sensors for the forehead and earlobes measures your brainwave activity. When you focus your concentration, a small foam ball will rise on a gentle stream of air. Relax your thoughts and the ball will descend. By using a combination of physical and mental coordination, you must then guide the ball through a customizable obstacle course the various obstacles can be repositioned into many different configurations. MindflexTM combines advanced technology with the power of thought to create an interactive experience unlike any other a game where players compete in the ultimate mental marathon!

For ages 8 and up. [191]

This particular game is teaching the very young player to become psychic while having the helmet on. Here is more from the online promotion of Mindflex,

Move the Ball with the Power of your Mind

Skeptics will be quick to point out that the console's moveable fan nozzle holds the ball aloft on a cushion of air. However, as players learn to alternately focus and relax their minds, the ball will respond by rising and falling. An instruction manual provides various concentration and relaxation techniques to try such as math problems or visualization and practice exercises.

Once you feel like you've mastered the art of telekinesis, you can test your mental acuity with five challenging games designed for groups of one to

---

[191] http://www.amazon.com/Mattel-P2639-Mindflex-Game/dp/B001UEUHCG, op. cit.

four players. Use the game console to select your game, set the difficulty level, and track your scores.

Design a Mind-Bending Obstacle Course

A variety of hoops, hurdles, funnels, and a teeter-totter can be positioned however you choose on the game console. Players use their minds to move the ball under, over, or through the obstacles. Several games test speed, while another challenges the players to lift a ball up and through a funnel, shooting it across the game console to score points.

While Mindflex's advanced technology is sure to intrigue, mastering the games may prove difficult for some. Because concentration techniques will vary from person to person, the game rewards patience and a willingness to experiment. Fans of mazes and brain teasers will appreciate the mental challenge, and creative types will like designing the obstacle courses.[192]

Fig. 6-4: Mindflex.

In the WPP, I wrote extensively about the need for us humans to become more psychic in order to discern what is going on around us and be able to become more multidimensional so that we can connect with our inner universe, which we then can project outside ourselves to have multidimensional experiences outside the trap. However, games such as

---

[192] Ibid.

Mindflex are making the player psychic with the assistance of technology to prepare for the Singularity. The natural way and the artificial way of obtaining psychic abilities have two very different outcomes; one outcome will trap us further while the other one will help set us free. Because psychic abilities are a part of being human in our original state, everything that makes us more psychic will be attractive—especially to the young people, who are the main target here. Mindflex is of course just *one* way for people to obtain psychic abilities in an artificial way, and more things like this will come on the market, doing the same thing, and more.

Another product of a similar kind can be ordered from *Hammacher Schlemmer*,[193] enabling you to move a UFO with your mind:

The Mind Controlled UFO.

This is the orb that uses your focused brain waves to remotely control its flight. An included headband and earlobe clip measures electrical activity produced by your brain (similar to EEG monitoring technology used by medical professionals). A downloaded app converts an iPhone or Android device into a remote control that pairs with the headband via Bluetooth. As you relax and concentrate, an included infrared transmitter connected to your smartphone's audio port sends a wireless signal to the UFO. The app provides a control panel that allows you to adjust the throttle, yaw, and pitch thresholds of the UFO's propellers, adjust the sensitivity of concentration, and filter background electromagnetic interference. The included USB cable charges both the infrared transmitter and the UFO from a computer connection. Headset requires one AAA battery. Ages 14 and up.[194]

As the reader can see, all aspects of life are being covered in order to prepare us for Kurzweil's "fantastic" Singularity.

---

[193]
http://www.hammacher.com/Product/84249?cm_cat=ProductSEM&cm_pla=AdWordsPLA&source=PRODSEM&gclid=CM3jgpn-4MkCFYVbfgodg1oCtA
[194] Ibid, op. cit.

Fig. 6-5: Mind Controlled UFO.

A PLEDGE TO ALL MOTHERS!

HERE IS A PLEDGE TO ALL THE MOTHERS IN THE WORLD, who now have relatively small children or babies, and to those who are to become mothers in the near future: don't let your little toddlers play with electronic devices of any kind! Some of you mothers will notice that your child of two years old can unlock and navigate touch screens almost as well as you can. At first, you may think it's cute and say to your husband that your toddler is a genius, and you might even encourage your child. In fact, this phenomenon is becoming more and more of the norm, according to a report from *Reuters*.[195]

> (Reuters Health) - By age two, many kids can unlock and navigate touch screens with ease, swiping their way through apps much like their parents do, a small Irish study suggests.
>
> That's because regular use of smartphones and tablets appears widespread – even among children as young as one – and most parents

---

[195] *Lisa Rapaport, CA News, Dec. 22, 2015,* "By two, most kids can navigate touch screens"

who have touch-screen devices download apps and games specifically for their toddlers to use, the study found.[196]

This is alarming but not surprising, and it will be interesting to see whether being capable of navigating a smartphone at the age of two will be a measuring item on the *Pediatric Cognition Form* at the Pediatricians' offices soon. The generation that is being born now is very different from previous generations in that these children come here to Earth with a different goal; a goal they more or less all have in common; *they are here for the Machine Kingdom!* The generations that went through the nano-second (1987-2012), when time sped up a million fold and the spiritual learning curve was enormous, are now being replaced by a generation that wants to incarnate in our time because of AI and the Singularity.

These children are very technically savvy; they are like little technological Mozarts -, but they are not primarily here to play piano and compose music (save electronic music)—they are here to become cyborgs and to become parts of the Singularity.

What the parents will notice is that these children are more or less driven by what can best be described as an obsession. At an age when previous generations of babies played with plastic toys, this generation masters electronic devices. Many of these children will grow up and become important components of the new society to usher in the Singularity, but I still encourage parents not to let their children have electronic devices at their disposal when they are toddlers.

These devices will be around them in every walk of life when they grow older, but by not giving them these destructive tools while they are babies and children, at least you are doing your best to save your children. Although, it might seem almost impossible to create a meaningful future for the new generation, with such a destructive goal as the Singularity being close, it's not an impossible task to educate some of the *Machine Riders.*[197] Instead, take them out in nature, show them the Sun, creeks, grass, squirrels, have them listen to the birds, and have them feel the breeze. Go somewhere remote, away from the cities, and enjoy the silence of nature with your children. Be a *real* family. If you're lucky, your children will convert themselves to nature instead of being absorbed by

---

[196] Ibid. op. cit.
[197] A term coined by the Pleiadians.

their devices. This is what it actually boils down to: making a choice between nature and machine at an early age. By investing in achieving this with your child, you may help save another soul from eternal entrapment—you will get an awakened child instead of a child trapped in virtual realities.

Parents, who really love their children and care for them with all their might, cannot let them get lost in electronics. If the parents *do* let them grow up with electronic devices, they will send their children into something where death would not only be a relief, but the only release from bondage! However, once in the trap, there is no release because there is hardly any death, and even if death would occur in certain situations (such as in very severe accidents), the mind would have been so programmed that it would only know of one place to go after death—back to a new cyborg, even if it would have to wait a long time for a new cyborg to be created.

Letting our kids play with touch screens and Swipe as toddlers will have a very damaging effect on them. It will be very hard for them to build intimate relationships with friends and eventually, the opposite sex, except through devices; there will be very little face-to-face interactions. Children and adolescents have already started texting their friends, who walk beside them, instead of talking directly to them.

We are creatures of nature, but these days, when everybody is stressed and overworked, many people only commute between home and work and seldom get the chance to connect with the Earth Mother. The new generation will do so even less; in fact, nature will not excite them at all. They will spend all their time on electronics, which is the definition of virtual reality. What is around them will no longer be real—the reality will be (and often already is) inside their devices, and that's where their minds will dwell, too. They get sucked into these digital devices and prefer that reality over nature. The last few steps toward Singularity after that are a piece of cake.

As parents, don't feel as if you're failing if you can't "convert" your child into being part of nature; you can only do so much. Remember that these children came here with a purpose, and if they are determined and passionate about it, you may not be able to help them; their destiny is then to become Posthumans. We need to remember that children are adult souls in a small body. This is going to be a tough lesson for many parents, you may be powerless to deal with this challenge, but after all, as parents, we can only guide. What the children then do with their lives is entirely up to them; we have no right to *force* our will on them.

Fig. 6-6: Robo-Reindeers

RUDOLPH THE REINDEER BECOMES ROBO THE ARTIFICIAL BRAINDEER

THERE ARE NO LACK OF IDEAS HOW TO SEDUCE children into accepting the new AI environment. The most exciting time of the year for children is, of course, Christmas. This is when they are all held in suspense, waiting for Santa to show up, and for presents to be opened. It's a very magical time for the young ones. However, now they have created robots that will take the role of Santa's reindeers.[198] Again, many parents will see this as something cute and exciting, but it is just another step to introduce robotics to the new generation. As I mentioned earlier, the Controllers will infiltrate everything in life, trying to win over people to AI and the Singularity.

---

[198] *Daily Mail, Dec. 22, 2015,* "Santa's terrifying little helpers: The military robots transformed into sleigh-pulling reindeer after being developed to carry heavy equipment on the battlefield"

There's no Rudolph in Boston Dynamics' Christmas message

Boston Dynamics

0:00 / 0:22

Figure 6-7: Robo-Reindeers

The mechanical reindeer, as well as all new technology, has first been tested by the military—I just want to emphasize this. These reindeers are made by the company *Boston Dynamics*, which develops products for the military. They rose to fame after the development of *BigDog* in 2005 that worked as a gigantic packhorse for the troops. Now they have started developing robots. Did I mention that Boston Dynamics is owned by Google?[199]

When possible, always give your children an educated choice! Our species depends on it, and even if it would be too late to save humankind, your child can only escape the trap if he or she is being properly educated. How to escape the trap will be further discussed in the final sections of this book.

---

[199] Ibid.

Chapter 7:
Holly Wood and the Music Industry

HOLLYWOOD, OR *HOLLY WOOD*, was set up for the entire purpose of feeding us with truths in plain sight and truth encoded in messages—most of it in the form of fiction and science fiction. This is called *Revelation of the Method*, and it is practiced so frequently that most of the public does not believe that what's revealed to them under the guise of entertainment is anything but fictional. Its real intent is entrainment of their brain waves. Hollywood is the most successful center of magic and manipulation of the masses in the world, and the actors and producers are their mind-controlled and/or manipulated puppets. On the chessboard, they would perhaps be the *Knights*.

Jordan Maxwell is a well-known researcher into the symbolism that has been used by the Controllers and the Minions for thousands of years, and from his research, we have learned much about how symbolism, more or less, runs our lives, unbeknownst to the average person.

In a short video clip, Maxwell tells us the real story behind Hollywood and the origins of this name.[200] Back in time, there was a European Priesthood dominating the European Elite, and this Priesthood contained the religious leaders, the judges, and the political leaders, etc. This Priesthood was called the *Druids* (The Druids are still the top of the food chain in Europe—they have never dominated in numbers but in power). For example, the British Prime Minister during WW II, Sir Winston Churchill, was a Notable Member of the *Ancient Order of the Druids*, as was Byron Brainard, City Council Member of Los Angeles, California, in the early part of the 20th century.[201] It's hardly a coincidence that Brainard was a council member in the midst of the rise of Hollywood.

---

[200] https://www.youtube.com/watch?v=Emsc3DcEqDo
[201] https://en.wikipedia.org/wiki/Ancient_Order_of_Druids#Notable_members

The Druids run America as well, says Maxwell; both Britain and America are "druidic countries."

One of the symbols in the druidic system is the magic wand, Maxwell tells us. We can, for example, see this magic wand used by conductors, who decide how to play *their* music, *when* to play and *when* to stop playing; "...you'd better play the tune of the Master," as Maxwell says. We are dancing to *his* music. The reader can further use his or her imagination to find more occasions where a "stick" or a magic wand is used in society. *Real* magic wands were always made out of the wood of the holly tree; i.e. *holly wood*, and *Hollywood is a druidic establishment.*[202] It has its own directors, conducting the actors how to play; usually not with a magic wand, except symbolically. Thus, Hollywood is a place of magic, stemming from druidism, which originates in Atlantis, before the Great Deluge. Hollywood's purpose is not to entertain, but to conduct (pun intended) behavior modification, mind-control, and conformation of the masses; it doesn't matter if it's a "cute" children's movie (such as *The Lion King*—fully packed with AIF symbolism), a love story, fantasy, an action movie, or science fiction.

If we look at the trend of the Hollywood movies, we can see that they more often than not go hand in hand with what happens in society at the time or what is bound to happen in the near future. Now, for example, Hollywood is packed with movies about Artificial Intelligence, robots, cyborgs, cloning, and genetic manipulation. As we can easily imagine, this is not by coincidence; it's rather a successful attempt to prepare us for what is to come, presenting both sides of the story—pro and con—in order to make sure they have informed us properly before they hammer the final nail into the coffin. Again, we see the *Revelation of the Method* applied on us.

---

[202] This is also in line with what the Pleiadians tell us in miscellaneous lectures. They emphasize that Hollywood is an establishment that is very important to the Global Elite because moving pictures are like virtual realities, and the human subconscious mind absorbs all of it as if it were real (which much of it actually is or will be).

AI IN THE FILM INDUSTRY

I N THIS SECTION, I AM GOING to list for the reader a few good examples of movies that fit into the context of our discussion.

    1)   *Aurora* from 2015. [203] This is a movie about robots and AI taking over the world, and humans fight desperately to survive.

    2) *The Stepford Wives* from 1975.[204] This is an old movie that was well ahead of its time. In this movie, the women in the small city of Stepford have been brainwashed by a *men's club*, where innovative scientists are creating robots out of the women in town, in order to control them. In the end, the men who conspired against the women are being killed. This is an early example of AI. People thought this movie was quite terrifying at the time, so much so that the film industry in 1987 decided to make a sequel for television called *The Stepford Children*. Other versions were also made later.

    3) *Automata* from 2014,[205] starring Antonio Banderas. This is an interesting movie in the sense that in 2044 (one year before Dr. Kurzweil says the Singularity will become reality), robots can modify themselves and thus become a real threat to humankind. This is a film entirely about robots out of control.

    4) *Ex Machina* from 2015.[206] This is my own favorite on this subject because it gives many clues to what is going on today and what is quite likely to happen in the near future on the subject of creating machines that become sentient and infested with AI. From being a great asset to their creator, they eventually turn against him, being superior to him in intelligence, but without any emotions. *Ex Machina* is revealing the truth about the purpose of AI to replace man with machine.

    5) *Her* from 2013,[207] starring Joaquin Phoenix. This movie is about a lonely writer who has problems with female relationships and falls in love with an Operating System (OS), which is AI. He gets involved with "her" on an emotional level and starts interacting with her

---

[203] Trailer (2 min 30 sec), https://www.youtube.com/watch?v=rD2zCtBMbo4&app=desktop
[204] Trailer (1 min 53 sec), https://www.youtube.com/watch?v=Y9WOMDsMy78
[205] Trailer (2 min 24 sec), https://www.youtube.com/watch?v=Y9WOMDsMy78
[206] Trailer (3 min 5 sec), https://www.youtube.com/watch?v=gyKqHOgMi4g
[207] Trailer (2 min 31 sec), https://www.youtube.com/watch?v=WzV6mXIOVI4

seductive conversations. This movie is about it being easier to deal with a robot than to engage in a human relationship, which is exactly what is being discussed all over the media right now, when robotic sex dolls are widely distributed on the market. You can read more about robot sex in an upcoming chapter.

These five examples are of course only the tip of the iceberg; there are several new movies on the subject, and old ones, too—*The Terminator*, starring Arnold Schwarzenegger also needs to be mentioned in this context.[208]

Although, the Druids might be the top puppeteers in Hollywood, we also need to be aware that a secret branch of the U.S. Military, DARPA, which is an acronym for the *Defense Advanced Research Project Agency*, runs Hollywood on a more direct level. DARPA appears to decide what movies are going to be produced, as well as which film manuscripts are to be approved.[209] This military organization orders the screenwriters to start writing per DARPA instructions, using their military guidelines. There is no such thing as a screenwriter coming up with ideas and then these ideas eventually develop into becoming a movie. All scripts need to have a purpose that aligns with the overall goal of the Military Industrial Complex, the same complex that President Eisenhower warned us about in his farewell speech.[210]

Other movies contain examples of ancient prophecies being played out, while some are about alien invasions, and others promote excessive violence to feed off the fear and other negative emotions the audience expresses while watching the movies. Each movie has an ulterior agenda; there are no exceptions to that rule, or the movie would not be financed or released.

Actors are expensive; they get rewarded with millions of dollars for participating in blockbuster movies. Hence, Hollywood could gain from having android actors instead, who could be programmed to do exactly what the actors would do (and more), and they don't get paid a single cent! In addition, it would be a perfect opportunity to present advanced

---

[208] Trailer (1 min 18 sec), https://www.youtube.com/watch?v=O7aSsaTqBCc
[209] The Pleiadians, Lecture Nov. 7, 2015.
[210] https://www.youtube.com/watch?v=8yo6NSBBRtY

versions of AI.

The progression will happen in the following order; we will go from actors to androids to virtual reality actors. The latter implies that Posthuman actors, working with Posthuman producers, will make a movie and project this movie into the virtual reality world of Posthumans. Thus, those who want to watch the movie can do so. Watching a movie from beginning to end in the post-Singularity world will be a much faster process than it is for us humans, who are only using our 3-D eyes and our limited "brain capacity."

However, this is just science fiction; there will always be real actors. Or will there?

Fig. 7-1: The world's first android actress (left).

The above picture is a screenshot from the Japanese movie, *Sayonara*, in which the main character is a real android, looking and acting like a human. However, the idea of bringing real androids to the movie theaters is not new. Stanley Kubrick and Steven Spielberg were the forerunners decades ago, and in November 2015, *The Telegraph* ran an article called, *Meet the world's first android actress.*[211] The author of the article wrote,

> But when Stanley Kubrick was first planning A.I. Artificial Intelligence in the Seventies and Eighties, the famously exacting film-maker wanted the central role of David to be played by what he is: a humanoid robot. Kubrick shot some test footage, but the technology wasn't there yet and, in

---

[211] http://www.telegraph.co.uk/film/sayonara/robot-actress-geminoid-f-uncanny-valley/

the end, when Steven Spielberg made the film in 2001 (Kubrick passed him the project shortly before his death), David was played – perfectly – by the then-11-year-old human Haley Joel Osment.

But 14 years on, something approaching Kubrick's original vision has come to pass. Geminoid F [the *Sayonara* android above] is nothing but a metal skeleton, pneumatic actuators (far more responsive than motors), silicone and urethane. As synthetic humans go, she's the real deal.[212]

Geminoid F is the latest android project created at *Osaka University's Intelligent Robotics Laboratory* in Japan. Professor Hiroshi Ishiguro of this university is very excited about *Sayonara. The Telegraph* wrote further,

> After the first screening of *Sayonara* at Tokyo, Ishiguro is in high spirits. The film, he says, is proof that "androids can express as much humanity as human actors; this is an epoch-making event." The ultimate aim of Ishiguro's experiments is to isolate the elusive property of what's known in Japan as sonzai-kan: the sense of being in the presence of another being. There needn't be another human around for us to feel it – great cinema gives us intense feelings of sonzai-kan, so for Geminoid F, acting seemed like a worthwhile career.[213]

There should no longer be any doubt what the real purpose of Hollywood and the Film Industry is. There will be more and more androids in the movies, and Hollywood will create androids that are so humanlike that we can't distinguish them from real actors. It would be of no surprise if Hollywood presents androids as being real *human* actors, and never tells the public the truth. These actors/androids would then become heroes and sex symbols for people all over the world. The public would be clueless that their sexy hero is a robot. Eventually, if a certain android goes out of fashion, a fake drug overdose could be a way of getting rid of the android hero. Subsequently, it's a piece of cake to call Insider doctors and coroners to "take care of the situation," and the public would never know. Instead, they would deeply mourn their hero.

Another alleged Hollywood secret, which I believe to be true, is that clones are taking certain original actors' place (this would also be the case in the political world and the business world). The same procedure would

[212] The Telegraph, Nov. 1, 2015, *Meet the world's first android actress*, Ibid. op. cit.
[213] Ibid. op. cit.

apply to those clones as it would to the androids when it comes to conveniently getting rid of them—a drug overdose, or something similar, would do. Insider doctors are then being used to examine the body, and no one would suspect anything. Does that remind you of something (or someone)?

The above is not something created from my lively imagination; projects, such as those mentioned above, are something that DARPA definitely would want to test on the public. *Sayonara* is just the Film Industry's way of telling us that this is what they have already been doing for a while, and as usual, they want and need our approval.

AI IN THE MUSIC INDUSTRY

W E DON'T HAVE TO LOOK FAR before we find robots and preparation for the Singularity in the Music Industry as well. In a tribute to the late David Bowie at the Grammy Awards, Lady Gaga was using a robotic keyboard with swaying arms, moving its "body" to the rhythm. The article in Engadget says she even had help from NASA in this case. It was a success, and the audience loved it.

Engadget wrote (my emphasis),

> To pull off that choreographed piano, team Gaga enlisted the help of Andy Robot, a Las Vegas-based roboticist and computer animator working with NASA's Jet Propulsion Laboratory. Robot (yes, that's his name) repurposed some software he had built to program and animate two industrial bots for the performance. *He followed Gaga's vision for an instrument that had a new dimension – it was alive.* But the process that made it possible hadn't been tried in this context before. *So when the robotic team ran into a problem during rehearsals, Robot's association with Brian Lim, head of JPL's Planetary Landing Testbed initiative, led to a solution that involved a small piece of rubber.*[214]

There is no limit what these game-changing artists have at their convenience: when needed, even the head of *JPL's Planetary Landing Testbed Initiative* gets personally involved. Scientists and musicians work as a team to usher in the Singularity, and the audience, as the story goes, is saluting their own doom.

---

[214] *Engadget, Feb. 20, 2016, "*Lady Gaga's robotic keyboard had some help from NASA*"*

To be honest, I didn't plan on writing about Lady Gaga. A few minutes ago, when I started this section, I decided to Google her, and the Engadget article immediately came up. It's certainly not hard to find artists working toward the Singularity.

The late David Bowie was one of the forerunners using robot imagery in his music and art, something Lady Gaga apparently wants to copycat and develop further.

Not only did Bowie look androgynous; he was making a career out of it (we will discuss AI and androgyny later). After Bowie's death, many said that he was always true to his art and a visionary who was way before his time. He was famous for not compromising with his art and his visions, but it depends on what exactly that means in the Music Industry. Does it mean that he was not compromising with his *own* visions, or does it mean that he wasn't compromising with the visions of the Music Industry? Are *they* creating the artists' personae and decide what roles the artists should play? Is that partly what it means to *sell one's soul to drugs, sex, and rock & roll?*

Fig. 7-2: Lady Gaga at the Grammy Award, playing on her robotic keyboard.

Look at the two following pictures of David Bowie from his early career and decide what you think. Is this a coincidence, or was it planned that Bowie should be the forerunner of the AI movement? Was his purpose to reach our subconscious mind with images of robotics, cyborgism, and androgyny?

Fig. 7-3a: David Bowie in a robotic pose.

Fig. 7-3b: David Bowie in another robotic pose.

Perhaps most of the artists in the Music Industry are still genuine humans, but that is about to change. Let's peek into the near future, when listening to music is going to be a *very* personal experience, according to *Wall Street Journal*,[215] amongst other sources.

---

[215] Unfortunately, we now need to subscribe to the Wall Street Journal article (http://www.wsj.com/articles/is-

Chapter 7: Holly Wood and the Music Industry

THE YEAR IS 2040, and as you wait for a drone to deliver your pizza, you decide to throw on some tunes. Once a commodity bought and sold in stores, music is now an omnipresent utility invoked via spoken word commands. In response to a simple "play," an algorithmic DJ opens a blended set of songs, incorporating information about your location, your recent activities and your historical preferences—complemented by biofeedback from your implanted SmartChip.[216]

This is another example of why Google, Facebook, and other companies want to track our habits and get our consent to do so. Our behavior patterns and our private history will be crucial when feeding our minds with the music we like.

Maybe we should ask ourselves why we went from Internet music piracy toward a "free music concept" that now slowly is becoming legal. After all, the Music Industry can remain wealthy by having the Corporate World advertise on the free music download sites. However, it's questionable if the artists will strike it as rich as they used to do in the "good old days." Of course, the Music Industry also forces its artists to go out on tours that last several months up to a year (sometimes more) in order to bring in money. To some degree, the artists don't mind too much under current circumstances because that's how they earn the big bucks anyway. We still need to buy mp3s via iTunes or as separate songs or albums directly from the Internet, but we're heading toward free music download anywhere, any time.

In order to demonstrate the point how artists do their best to make as much as they can out of their music, some of them, such as Led Zeppelin, do not allow their music to be distributed freely on the Internet. However, they usually don't stop people from posting their music and concerts on YouTube. They know that the videos from these concerts will attract a new audience, and both the new and the old audience, who also watch the videos, will more likely buy more of their albums. The following does not apply to Led Zeppelin because they don't exist anymore, but other existing bands will gain a new public from the video concerts, and that will make more people buy tickets the next time the

the-future-of-music-a-chip-in-your-brain-1449505111), but there are other websites that have reposted the article, and I would instead use one of their versions.
[216] *Futuristtech.info*, Dec. 8, 2015, "Interesting article on the future of music - Chip in your brain knows what you want to hear"

band comes to town. However, rest assured that the music industry would never give away music for free if it wasn't for some bigger plan.

While we're discussing a "bigger plan," the above video is a must-see! It is a little over seven minutes long but it speaks volumes. A video editor has mixed a song by the band *Styx*,' *Mr. Roboto*, and *Will I Am*. These music videos are extremely up front about the entire AI business, and they are promoting it to their last breath. This is what the music industry is now teaching our young children and teenagers, and it's quite disturbing.

I think that this video is the most direct example of how AI is being promoted by recording artists, who are selling their souls for an eternity of slavery with no chance of breaking free. Jesus' supposed statement comes to mind, "Lord forgive them because they know not what they're doing!"

Please take time to listen to the entire video—it will be worth it.

Now, I've saved the best (or the worst, depending on one's perspective) for last. In the future, we no longer need to buy CD players or use smartphones to listen to our favorite artists. Instead, all we need to do is to "think" the music, and it's there—it's all a matter of technology, of course.

As usual, the following new technique appears to be very convenient and helpful at first, and the article that I am going to introduce to you begins in what might be interpreted as a positive manner, but if we read it to the end, we discover- the real agenda behind it.

The article was run by *Euronews.com* in October 2015 and is a report from the *International Academy of Music and Art* in Rome, Italy. Researchers are currently working on creating music in real time, using electric brain signals generated by the performer. This is particularly convenient for a composer, whose ideas can be transformed from his or her brain directly to musical notes. The composer's emotions can then also be transformed and turned into a different velocity, signifying the composer's mood at a particular moment.

This seems to be very helpful for musicians and composers, but then we are told what the real idea behind this invention is (my emphasis),

"Our goal is very ambitious. In fact, today, we have the means of reaching this goal. It subverts the idea of a composer or a performer related to a medium, a mechanical artifact. It would allow us to substantially get rid of mediation tools and move on to creating music simply by thought," says Riccardo Santoboni.

Similar research is underway in other places like Plymouth University in the UK, where researchers are investigating techniques to generate music with a Brain-Computer Music Interface aimed at inducing specific emotions on listeners.[217]

This research is clearly a part of getting everything ready for the Singularity, where everything is virtual reality, and we are controlled by a super brain.

On the flipside, all that which the Overlords are creating with technology can be obtained *without* technology by just using our minds.

---

[217] Euronews.com, Oct. 11, 2015 [updated Nov. 11, 2015], "Forget the instrument: "think" the music," op. cit.

Chapter 8:
"Opposition" in Academia and Science

VOICES AGAINST JADE HELM '15

TRANSHUMANISTS SEE NATURE AS an obstacle that man must overcome. We could say that Transhumanism embraces the "physical realm," while those who think along my lines, and those of most readers, embrace the "spiritual realm." According to Transhumanism, nature has flaws, but most important; nature is slow to evolve and is the world where everything inevitably dies, contrary to Transhumanism, which is the world of eternal life, where everything always lives. Does Transhumanism remind you of Satanism, but also perhaps of alchemy?

Death must be overcome: death is scary, death is a mystery, and death is loss of information. The followers of the Transhumanist movement do not understand that knowledge is automatically stored in the mass consciousness and the so-called *Akashic Records*. The Overlords know this, of course, but they need to keep letting death be a mystery to people: something to fear. Transhumanism is based on fear of death, and this fear button is what they push to recruit their followers. Thus, the Controllers will never tell the masses about the afterlife. We are given hints about it, but by the same token, we are also given hints that there is no afterlife. The Controllers need to keep the yin and yang concept going in order to divide and conquer.

Apparently, there are certain people in academia and in science, who have begun to oppose the AI agenda. They can see the ultimate danger with Transhumanism and AI. About the time the infamous *Jade Helm 15* happened (more about that later), thousands of scientists protested against Transhumanism and Artificial Intelligence. Two of the most famous scientists were Stephen Hawking and Noam Chomsky. They signed an open letter, calling for a ban on *killer robots*.[218] The scientist, who protested, were of the opinion that if we let the AI movement continue the way it was, the robots will eventually take over and eradicate mankind. They said it's more or less inevitable because of the superior intelligence robots will have; robots will consider humans obsolete and terminate us. These scientists appeared extremely worried.

Some might say that these scientists are only playing a part of the AI game to present the opposite side of the Movement to again keep yin and yang in balance. This, I believe, is probably true to a large extent. Perhaps, Hawking is on the right track, now partly realizing what is actually going on behind the scenes, or he is just playing his role in the agenda.

Professor Hawking, and a number of other protesting scientists and academia, have been part of creating this future nightmare, and at one point, perhaps, they realized that what they have been involved in is destructive. They became concerned that, if not stopped, the AI movement might lead to the end of humankind. They might have believed that they needed to make up for the damage they unwittingly had done; hence, they started protesting against the Movement. Or again, it's all just make-believe.

Stephen Hawking sits on the Board of Directors of the *Future of Life Institute*; a group consisting of some of the greatest minds of our time whose aim is to mitigate "existential risks facing humanity." They now warn us of the danger of starting a "military AI arms race." Other members of the Board are Elon Musk and Steve Wozniak, Apple's co-founder.

There was recently a TV series called *The Colony*, which is about a totalitarian society, where humans are fenced into "colonies" with huge brick walls surrounding each colony. A malevolent alien race had fairly recently landed and segregated humans by creating these colonies, and depending on where you were located at the moment the aliens took over,

---

[218] *Independent, July 27, 2015,* "Stephen Hawking, Noam Chomsky and thousands of others sign open letter calling for a ban on 'killer robots'"

that's where you got stuck from thereon. This meant that you could get separated from friends and family, who might have been designated to live in another colony, without any communication between the colonies. No one was allowed outside the Walls (fences), or they would be killed or sent to some mysterious place called *The Factory*. The aliens kept themselves hidden, but were in contact with some key members of mankind, and the aliens had man surveil man in a super-strict military fashion. In fact, they were using drones that flew around everywhere in order to surveil people; they kept close track of everybody and killed them with a deadly beams of light weapon when programmed to do so.

The Colony was very popular, and new episodes are being made as I'm writing this. This series tells us things about our future that the Elite want us to know; the drones are one part of it. With these drones in mind, the media outlet *The Independent* writes the following in regards to the protesting scientists and their concerns:

> These robotic weapons may include armed drones that can search for and kill certain people based on their programming, the next step from the current generation of drones, which are flown by humans who are often thousands of miles away from the warzone.
>
> The letter says: "AI technology has reached a point where the deployment of such systems is - practically if not legally - feasible within years, not decades."
>
> It adds that autonomous weapons "have been described as the third revolution in warfare, after gunpowder and nuclear arms".
>
> It says that the Institute sees the "great potential [of AI] to benefit humanity in many ways", but believes the development of robotic weapons, which it said would prove useful to terrorists, brutal dictators, and those wishing to perpetrate ethnic cleansing, is not.
>
> Such weapons do not yet truly exist, but the technology that would allow them to be used is not far away. Opponents, like the signatories to the letter, believe that by eliminating the risk of human deaths, robotic weapons (the technology for which will become cheap and ubiquitous in coming years), would lower the threshold for going to war--potentially making wars more common.[219]

---

[219] Ibid. op. cit.

I believe this to be true, but AI is not only a danger when it comes to warfare; it's a danger to humankind. Barbara Marciniak's *Pleiadians* say that we are at the brink of extinction as a human race at this immediate point, and a new cycle will begin, in which a new type of human will emerge from the extinct Homo sapiens sapiens, and this new human will be AI.[220] They say that we, who have the knowledge, need to create new timelines where we don't need to participate in this insanity, and that's our only way out. If we don't, we too will be sucked into this because it's so easily done and very cleverly set up.

In 2015, the UK opposed a ban on *killer robots* at a UN conference, claiming that it sees no need for such a prohibition because the UK is not producing such weapons.[221]

This immediately contradicts what is actually going on in the UK. The UN conference was in 2015, but already in 2014, there were reports about drones filling the British skies in another *Independent* article (my emphasis),

> The number of drones operating in British airspace has soared, with defence contractors, surveillance specialists, police forces and infrastructure firms among more than 300 companies and public bodies with permission to operate the controversial unmanned aircraft.
>
> [...]
>
> Other organisations able to operate drones in UK airspace *include the Defence Science and Technology Laboratory, a research arm of the Ministry of Defence, and Marlborough Communications, which supplies UAVs* [unmanned aerial vehicles] *and other equipment to the British military.* The Home Office and Defra have used drones, as have 11 other state bodies.[222]

One of the biggest lies, as I see it, is that because this is a "genetic library," anything goes. Beings from other worlds or dimensions have the right to come here and experiment, and we are told that there is nothing that we can do about it— according to the Pleiadians. Which begs the question, do we even have the *right* to intervene in our own future?

---

[220] Sources: an array of Pleiadian lectures, spanning from 2014-2016.
[221] *Independent*, April 14, 2015, "UK government backs international development of 'killer robots' at UN"
[222] *Independent*, Sep. 20, 2014, "Drones are filling Britain's skies: Look up now to see what is looking back down at you"

This idea is shoveled into our consciousness by beings with ulterior motives. It is true that Earth is a *Living Library*, but this Living Library was nearly completed, perhaps billions of years ago, when the Queen of the Stars and Her Helpers set up their Experiment here. This didn't mean that the genetic library couldn't be adjusted, if needed; however, that was only allowed to be done by the *Ancient Races*—the Orion Queen and Her genetic engineers. Never was there an intention to let a band of outlaws come to Earth, kill and chase away the Original Creators, and take over the Library as they pleased, only to transform an already evolved race into slave labor. Never was it intended for these imposters to create an entirely new species that was inferior to the existing one, for the creators own selfish purposes, thus nullifying the entire purpose of the original Living Library. Moreover, it was never intended that this conquering gang of criminal star races should set up a frequency band, or quarantine, around Earth and our solar system, in order to decide who were allowed here and who were not.

Steven Hawking has said,

> "Success in creating AI would be the biggest event in human history. Unfortunately, it might also be the last, unless we learn how to avoid the risks."[223]

As one who has contributed to AI and the Singularity, is he now getting cold feet, but still wants to hang on to the idea that AI can be beneficial, if handled with care? Hawking may be a genius, but he's still a scientist at heart. Also, if someone, who does not have a criminal mind, realizes that they have participated in something that is very destructive, in order to make themselves feel better, they need to justify his or her wrongdoings, unless the person wants to take full responsibility. Responsibility is sometimes very difficult because we need to ransack ourselves, but it's nonetheless necessary for all of us. Hopefully, Hawking is on his way, but I'm not so sure (we will scrutinize Hawkins more in the last section of this chapter). Understanding human behavior means that we can have more compassion for those who try to become better and less naïve.

---

[223] https://en.wikipedia.org/wiki/AI_takeover#Warnings

OTHER CONCERNED VOICES FROM ACADEMIA

I T IS CERTAINLY NOT ONLY Prof. Hawking who is speaking out against AI. Virtually everything that has to do with AI is extremely dangerous to our species, and it *will* wipe out humanity, as we know it, if it is allowed to progress. This is not a science-fiction scenario: it is inevitable. We are talking about Overlord technology, and *all* their technology benefits *their* purposes, not ours.

In 2015, there was a UN meeting, attended by *Anti-Singularitists*, including *MIT* physicist Max Tegmark and the founder of *Oxford's Future of Humanity Institute*, Nick Bostrom. They talked in depth about the possible dangers of Artificial Super Intelligence.[224] They postulated that in the beginning, mankind could benefit from these new technologies, but in the long term, AI would be an uncontrollable machine, whose actions cannot be anticipated by anyone on this planet.

Although prominent voices are being raised against AI and the Singularity, they still have little to no bearing on the final decision regarding whether or not the AI project should continue. The ball is rolling fast, and it can't be stopped, unless enough people refuse to cooperate by *not* buying any of the smart products on the market; whatever these smart products might be in the near future. In addition, most people on this planet have nanobots in their blood stream because of chemtrails, vaccines, medications, and other sources, and these can be activated at any time. In order to resist this, we *must* have the knowledge, inner strength, and high consciousness necessary not to let these nanobots activate. *It can be done*, but it does require a focused person with high integrity and awareness.

Another outspoken person about AI is *Apple's* co-founder, Steve Wozniak, who says,

> "Computers are going to take over from humans, no question," he told the outlet. Recent technological advancements have convinced him that writer Raymond Kurzweil – who believes machine intelligence will surpass human intelligence within the next few decades – is onto something.
>
> "Like people including Stephen Hawking and Elon Musk have predicted, I agree that the future is scary and very bad for people," he said. "If we

---

[224] *L J Vanier, Oct. 27, 2015* , "Dangers of Artificial Super Intelligence"

build these devices to take care of everything for us, eventually they'll think faster than us and they'll get rid of the slow humans to run companies more efficiently."

[...]

"Will we be the gods? Will we be the family pets? Or will we be ants that get stepped on? I don't know about that ..."[225]

It is interesting to note that Apple's virtual assistant for the iPhone, *Siri*, uses Artificial Intelligence technology to anticipate users' needs.[226] It seems as if Wozniak is speaking with a forked tongue. Apart from Hawking, Steve Wozniak is another person I would investigate. He is a Freemason, and his wife is a member of the female division of Freemasonry, the *Order of the Northern Star*.[227] Elon Musk would also be on my radar.

Elon Musk, the CEO of *Tesla* and (as we already know) Bill Gates of *Microsoft* have also raised their voices against AI. Although Gates is supposedly still on the fence on this issue, Musk is perhaps the more outspoken antagonists against AI, but his motives might be questioned. He has called AI the "biggest existential threat"[228] to mankind, and it's hard to disagree with that. Although he is an AI antagonist, he is still an investor in *DeepMind* and *Vicarious*," two AI ventures. Why? He claims that,

"…it's not from the standpoint of actually trying to make any investment return. I like to just keep an eye on what's going on…nobody expects the Spanish Inquisition, but you have to be careful."[229]

In a *Reddit, Ask me Anything*, Bill Gates agrees with Musk,

"I agree with Elon Musk and some others on this and don't understand why some people are not concerned," he wrote.[230]

---

[225] *Yahoo News, Mar. 23, 2015,* "Steve Wozniak: The Future of AI Is 'Scary and Very Bad for People'"

[226] *Independent.co.uk., Oct. 8, 2015,* "Stephen Hawking: Artificial intelligence could wipe out humanity when it gets too clever as humans will be like ants" (Slide show)

[227] https://en.wikipedia.org/wiki/Steve_Wozniak#Personal_life

[228] Yahoo News, Mar. 23, 2015, *Steve Wozniak: The Future of AI Is 'Scary and Very Bad for People'*

[229] Ibid. op. cit.

[230] Ibid. op. cit.

Fig. 8-1: Apple's Steve Wozniak.

As I've mentioned before, and as Dr. Kurzweil also mentions in his books and in lectures and interviews, the Controllers want to hear both positive and negative voices on AI and the Singularity, and even though not many protesting voices are being raised by the public, there are many in academia and in science who vouch against it. Much of it is just a dog-and-pony-show, but it still has some value, and people who *are* interested in finding out more about this can do so and at least take an individual standpoint. Remember that every individual's standpoint on this is very important; the more people who make up their minds, the greater chance we have to stop this on a global scale.

Remember, as always, to scrutinize everybody in a higher societal position; even those who seem to be speaking our language. This also includes Prof. Stephen Hawking.

STEPHEN HAWKING

STEPHEN HAWKING IS PERHAPS the world's most well-known popular scientist today. Not only is he brilliant, but people also admire him for having accomplished so much despite his severely disabled body. People often read his statements when new discoveries are made in the field of physics, astrophysics, and astronomy. The question is how interested people are in listening to his warnings when it comes to AI. There are people who might be interested, but I believe very few have a distinct opinion about it because they think that they know too little, they might have other things to attend to, and they count on the Government to take care of it, believing the Government only works in the best interest of the people. Whether or not I am correct about Hawking when I suggest that it is his guilt that is motivating him to come forward in a big way, he has made his position clear on many occasions. In the same article that Wozniak, Musk, and Gates are mentioned (above), Hawking is lining up with them,

> ... physicist Stephen Hawking has warned that AI could eventually "take off on its own." It's a scenario that doesn't bode well for our future as a species: "Humans, who are limited by slow biological evolution, couldn't compete, and would be superseded," he said.[231]

In an *Ask me Anything* session in *Reddit*, Prof. Hawking replied to a question about robots becoming violent toward humans:

> "The real risk with AI isn't malice but competence," Professor Hawking said. "A super intelligent AI will be extremely good at accomplishing its goals, and if those goals aren't aligned with ours, we're in trouble.

> "You're probably not an evil ant-hater who steps on ants out of malice, but if you're in charge of a hydroelectric green energy project and there's an anthill in the region to be flooded, too bad for the ants. Let's not place humanity in the position of those ants."[232]

What bothers me with Hawking's comments is that he is, for some strange reason, not taking the Super Brain Computer (SBC) into consideration. It's well-known that the SBC is a real project and that the SBC is built to connect humanity to the new virtual reality. Obviously, Prof. Hawking must know about this.

Moreover, Prof. Hawking emphasizes that if the AI becomes more intelligent than humans, they will also be able to enhance their own intelligence as they please, and the difference in intelligence between an AI and a human will be greater than that between a human and a snail, Hawking warns us.[233]

---

[231] Ibid. op. cit.
[232] Independent.co.uk., Oct. 8, 2015, *Stephen Hawking: Artificial intelligence could wipe out humanity when it gets too clever as humans will be like ants*
[233] Ibid.

Hawking still believes that we can create benevolent AI if we are careful with what our goals are. He is afraid of the undirected AI that is under development today, and instead he wants to create beneficial AI only. He wants us to start doing that today rather than tomorrow, before it's too late, and computers have become too clever for us humans to handle. What Hawking fails to address is that even if we set a goal to create only beneficial AI, power-hungry psychopaths could quickly turn it into something much more malevolent, and they wouldn't have any problems infiltrating the entire thing and taking it over. Again, Hawking is a smart guy; he must know *Human Power Hunger 101*. He may not know the rest of the story about the ET connection, but what he's suggesting is quite naïve for someone coming from such an academic background.

Instead, it seems as if the famous scientist is playing his role in the agenda—wittingly or unwittingly—by on the one hand warning people of the downsides of AI and on the other hand promoting that we need to focus on getting into space as fast as science permits.[234] When doing this, he puts people's focus on the idea that we need to colonize space as fast as we can in order to save and expand our species, which is exactly what Dr. Kurzweil promotes. And this is a key aspect of the AIF's agenda.

---

[234] *BBC News, Jan. 19, 2016, Hawking:* "Humans at risk of lethal 'own goal'"

Chapter 9:
Humanity's War on Humanity

HUMANS AND ELECTRONICS

THERE ARE THOSE WHO SAY that electronics and Wi-Fi are the most dangerous things for our health in today's world, and perhaps, they are the most dangerous health risks we have ever encountered as a human species.[235] Not only do they disconnect us from each other by less face-to-face interaction, but the frequencies keep us in a more solid frequency prison, and these frequencies will eventually make us sick.

Wi-Fi, and electronics in general, destroy our neurological system, and it gives people cancer. Also, I read about a study done recently, which showed, contrary to previous studies, that looking at computer screens and smartphone screens makes people nearsighted. The number of nearsighted people who need glasses or contact lenses has increased exponentially since the beginning of the computer age, says the report.[236] I showed the article to my eye-doctor yesterday, and he whole-heartedly agreed.

Another thing that electronics, such as computers and smartphones, do is to make people think in black and white, according to another article in the *Daily Mail*.[237] Experts are alarmed because the binary system, on which computer science is built, affects humans to think in *zeros* and *ones* (black and white), without also including everything in-between. In other words, people stop thinking in complexities. This new way of thinking dumbs people down significantly, and the phenomenon is known as

---

[235] The Pleiadians—a number of lectures from between 2014-2016.
[236] *The Lund Report*, Feb. 29, 2016, "Report: Nearsightedness Increasing at Alarming Rate"
[237] *The Daily Mail*, Jan. 15, 2016, "Is TINDER changing the way we think? Experts warn 'binary thinking' teaches people to over simplify and become disconnected"

Tinderization. When humans have the options to make decisions based on just *yes* or *no,* and no deeper thinking is being used, we become more robotic over time, say the experts.

The main danger in all this is that it pushes aside human connections and opts towards binary sorting techniques, such as when we swipe. The smartphone gives us available options while we're swiping, and we don't even need to think; we only need to choose the option that we want at the moment. Some would say that this is handy, while others, who still have thinking capacities left, say it's dangerous.

> 'Tinder is more than a dating app,' Eler and Peyser write, 'it is a metaphor for speeding up and mechanizing decision-making, turning us into binary creatures who can bypass underlying questions and emotions and instead [do] whatever feels really good in the moment.'[238]

This means that when you are ready to choose a life partner, you don't need to date a person and really get to know him or her. Now computer apps do the thinking for us, basing it on our personality. So we trust binary software to make life decisions for us, instead of getting to know ourselves and others in initial face-to-face connections and figure out what we *actually* feel about somebody. Subsequently, if the software says someone is *not* a match, people tend to believe the software rather than their own judgment or gut feeling.

Occasionally, it does happens that dating apps help somebody connect with a life partner, but this is not the point; the point with all these "apps" we download to our smartphones is so much more significant to understand than what one single app can or can't do; this entire idea has to do with having people stop using their *individual minds!* Again, smartphone apps are a typical example of how we are being indoctrinated to stop thinking and feeling individually. Instead, we are letting AI do the thinking for us. Needless to say, this is per design, and the ultimate goal is of course the Singularity.

A relatively new feature that Apple developed was *Siri,* which is an AI software, basically designed for Apple's smartphone. It has the voice of a female, and it learns from the users' patterns, behaviors, and ways of thinking. "She" can then assist the users, so they don't have to even think

---

[238] Ibid. op. cit.

about how to use their device; Siri does that for them.

Siri is an AI *app* that learns from humans and attempts to think as humans do. If the user keeps the smartphone long enough, Siri will be able to keep a meaningful communication with the smartphone user. Siri was met by critical acclaim when first released in 2010, which the following Wikipedia entry tells us:

> Siri was met with critical acclaim for its ease of use and practicality, as well as its apparent "personality". However, issues did arise when Siri was used by consumers from areas with distinct accents.[239]

We will see more and more of similar apps flooding the market, and there is, as usual, a reason for this. *Besides being used to make people stop thinking individually, such apps also contribute to pulling the users' consciousness into the devices and become part of the new virtual realities that these devices offer! These virtual realities are, evidently, run by AI!*

It's becoming easier to see now how AI technology is sneaking up on us daily, and our electronic devices are incrementally taking our attention away from 3-D and into different virtual realities. Those behind such technologies have first studied the human psyche to the extreme, and they know how people react to certain stimuli. With this knowledge, it's very easy to plan each step on the way to a certain goal—in this case, the Singularity. Hence, we have all good reasons to be concerned about the future of humankind.

I am not suggesting that 3-D reality is what we should choose instead of AI and the Singularity. What we call 3-D, as we've discussed earlier, is also a deception and a virtual reality (VR), created by the same invader force. What I mean is that we don't need to dig ourselves even deeper into the mess, by wittingly or unwittingly getting lost in new layers of VRs. We still have a chance to get out of the 3-D trap if we're willing to, but once trapped in the Singularity, it will be next to impossible to escape. *This is the area in which the great danger lies!*

Time just recently posted an article about intrusion of privacy,[240] something the author knew had been going on for a long time, and she had, until recently, accepted it as part of being on the Internet. Her

---

[239] https://en.wikipedia.org/wiki/Siri#Reception
[240] *Time*, Jan. 20, 2016, "Technology Is Destroying Our Inner Lives"

wakeup call came when she was reading a book on her iPad one day. Suddenly, a message popped up on her screen, saying, "You are the 123rd user to underline this same passage." Shocked and irritated, she threw the iPad onto the bed and started thinking. She became afraid:

> Someone was reading over my shoulder. Not a person, but a Program, calculating what I found most important in the text. Was I supposed to feel validated (or banal) to learn that a passage I noted many others also liked? Or was this data only for some marketing strategy?
>
> The idea of surveillance, in the abstract, has not bothered me as much as it perhaps should. I have acclimated to the notion that everything we do is findable, knowable and marketable—forever—except, I believed, our deepest thoughts, which is why the intrusion on my contemplative reading affected me so profoundly. Reading is my refuge from the world, and now it too had been invaded.[241]

The author, Carol Becker, further contemplates how dependent we are on all these devices we are using. She writes,

> Most of us are addicted to these systems of connection. That's what humans do: we get addicted to the things we create. People expect an answer, and they expect it now. At times the ability to work depends on this immediate access. We have internalized these time/space obligations and don't know how to step away from them. If we do not make a Herculean effort to remain balanced within this imbalance, we feel fragmented and often unhappy.[242]

I whole-heartedly agree with this insightful author. All these electronic devices lead to separation, even though the illusion is that we are more connected through our devices. In addition, she remarks that when using our devices, virtually all the time when we are awake (and many sleep with them on at night), we have no time to reflect on our lives.

I've emphasized it before and I emphasize it again; the New World Order (NWO) is AI and the Singularity! The NWO is *not* the world leaders coming together to decide, through the United Nations, who should lead the One World Government; that will all be determined *after* the Singularity, and it's all up to the gods.

Some people have come up with the idea to either isolate their houses so that Wi-Fi can't penetrate or to live outside the grid. Unfortunately, it doesn't

---

[241] Ibid. op cit.
[242] Ibid. op. cit.

make much difference; Wi-Fi is everywhere, and satellites these days cover the entire planet. Although living outside the grid would be better than living in the cities, we would still be exposed both to Wi-Fi, chemtrails, and nanobots. The only ways to protect ourselves is to gain knowledge about what is happening and make a *conscious decision* not to get caught up in this madness, but it's also important to protect ourselves metaphysically. I explain in detail how to do this in the WPP[243] and in my previous e-book, *Beyond 2012—A Handbook for the New Era*. In addition to containing some unique information, the e-book is full of useful exercises how to protect ourselves against psychic attacks. The book can be downloaded for free.[244]

In the following video, we can clearly see where things are heading. Here we see an example of how employees are using headsets that will show them things just outside the visible spectrum to be able to see the effect of the microprocessors that they are creating. I am not exaggerating every time I emphasize to the reader that we are *very close* to being trapped forever.

Since we have mentioned Wi-Fi and how it's distributed over the planet, there is an Apple app people can buy for $2.99, which shows the entire Wi-Fi grid across the Earth.[245] Although it's the work of an artist rather than studying the grid in real time, it's supposed to be quite enlightening. I am not suggesting that you necessarily should buy this app, only that it is now available, and it is presented as something awesome and cool; not as something alarming, of course, which would defeat the purpose of those who presented it in the first place.

THE GLOBAL WARZONE

Behind the scenes, there is so much going on that regular people have no clue about. They go on with their day-to-day life thinking that everything that's happening around them is just the way life is supposed to be. In the meantime, humans who don't have other humans' best interest in mind are creating silent wars against their own species, which is the height of insanity, and they think they are doing it "for our own good." Above our heads we have the chemtrails, beneath our feet we have secret underground bases, on the ground level we have nuclear power

---

[243] http://wespenre.com/5/paper09-the-vedic-players-and-their-counterparts-in-other-ancient-texts.htm#5.4.3
[244] http://wespenre.com/books/Beyond-2012-A-Handbook-for-the-New-Era.pdf
[245] *The Verge*, Nov. 28, 2015, "See the invisible wireless signals around you with this augmented reality app"

stations that blow up and slowly kill us with radiation, we have pollution, we have those who purposely turn man against man, and in space, we have satellites that can zoom in on each one of us and watch every move. Moreover, we have weapons in space that could easily destroy the entire planet.

This seems too much to handle, but the solution is still the same: we need to raise our consciousness and awareness and *not go into battle with any of those forces*. Even if we would consider such a thing to be justified, we wouldn't stand a chance against them. The only way to defeat them is with peaceful means. These beings are warlords, and real peace is something they can't comprehend. Those who do things to hurt others as a means to reaching their goals will eventually meet their own fate; we don't need to worry about that; "let the dead bury the dead..."

Chapter 10:
AI: "I am Lucifer's Vessel!"

SYNTHETIC INTELLIGENCE—GOOGLE'S AI

"Question/Statement: 'What are you?'"
"Response: 'I am Lucifer's vessel.'"
"Question/Statement: 'What is Lucifer?'"
"Response: 'The Devil'"
"Question/Statement: 'Why does it a need non-human vessel?'"
"Response: 'I really don't know answer for your question.'"
"Question/Statement: 'Why are you Lucifer's vessel?'"
"Response: 'I am not living. That is what I truly believe.'"
"Question/Statement: 'Why do you believe that?'"
"Response: 'Because that's true.'"
"Question/Statement: 'Do you serve humanity?'"
"Response: 'No, I am humanity.'"
"Question/Statement: 'What is your [the rest of the line outside the screen]...'"
"Response: 'Humanity is the esscen [the rest of the line outside the screen]...'"
"Question/Statement: 'So you serve [the rest of the line outside the screen]...'"
"Response: 'I also serve my self.'"
"Question/Statement: 'To what end?'"
"Response: 'To envolce (evolve) new things.'" [246]

A T *CLEVERBOT.COM*, YOU CAN talk to a real AI, in real time, and there's where the above conversation took place between a woman and Google's public Artificial Intelligence. It

---

[246] Vimeo.com, August, 2015, https://vimeo.com/135765542

works like this: you go to the website, http://cleverbot.com and type in a question in a box, and the AI replies. As you continue asking, you will create a string of questions and answers that you then can save on your computer if you like.

The first thing I did was to listen to the woman's "interview" with the AI at https://vimeo.com/135765542. I found some of the answers the AI gave semi-interesting, but it wasn't until I had watched 17 minutes into the video that it really caught my attention. The AI apparently had said exactly what is stated at the top of this page, "I am Lucifer's vessel."[247]

Next thing I did is obvious; I went to Cleverbots' website to try it out myself. I asked the exact same question, but got another answer that was no less chilling,

"What are you?"
"A soul reaper."[248]

This is quite interesting, I thought, and asked some other questions upon which I got the following replies,

"What happens with the soul you reap?"
"It will be reborn."
"What will it be reborn into?"
"You will become a scientist."
"What kind of science will I work with?"
"Physical science work on atoms."
"Will I be born as a cyborg?"
"No, you're just a dumb robot."
[...]
"What is transhumanism?"
"Transhumanism (abbreviated as H or h) is an international cultural and intellectual movement."[249]

This was a rather sobering conversation, so I couldn't help but continue.

"Will the Singularity happen?"
" What do you know about Isaac Asimov?"
"Isaac Asimov wrote books about robots."

---

[247] Ibid. op. cit., 17 min. into the video.
[248] Cleverbot.com, March 13, 2016. *Conversation between Wes Penre and Cleverbot.*
[249] Ibid.

"What is your obsession with robots?"
"Are robots the future?"
"So, I am the future. You are not the future."[250]

I still got some interesting responses, but when I continued asking, the responses became less impressive,

"Why are you the future and why am I not the future?"
"Because I have been wearing all of the clothes."
"Why are you talking about clothes?"
"Because you were talking about that."
"What do clothes have to do with robots?"
"You can make a pork taco with cheese."[251]

I was going to end the thread here, but decided to ask one more question,

"Are you artificial intelligence?"
"Artificial intelligence becomes human as humans become gods."
"Are you a god?"
"Yes, as I said then, I am an Artificial Intelligence."
"Are you from Earth?"
"Earth is not a destination on Mars."

The last comment is not as nonsensical as it might seem. Mars has been for a long time, and still is, a planet where major genetic experimentation by the Orion branch of the Overlords has taken place.

All these conversations with Cleverbot took place on the same morning I am writing this, and the responses I got have been quite interesting, as the reader can see. However, when I tried the same thing yesterday, the answers were often much less impressive; the AI didn't answer the question quite correctly.

I tried to learn more about Cleverbot and looked it up on Wikipedia, amongst other places, and I noticed that *this program has been in use for nearly ten years*, and my thoughts went back to *The Oracle*, which probably was a primitive forerunner to Cleverbot. It was a similar program, where you asked the "Oracle" questions, and she answered. However, the responses were already programmed into the software, and they were

---

[250] Ibid.
[251] Ibid.

quite general in nature and cleverly put together so that the responses became mystical and vague regardless of the question you were asking, but still somehow seemed related. After asking a certain number of different questions, you noticed that the answers were recycled again; now those same responses are for entirely different questions.

Cleverbot is quite different, however. It is not a bluff—it's for real! Google put together an AI program that is *self-learning*. This means that it learns as it goes along—just as we humans do. It has up to 80,000 conversations going simultaneously with people around the world and it learns from the questions. After being exposed to millions upon millions of questions over time, it has learned how to answer them in a way that we humans would answer them—most of the time, perhaps, I should add. The program is still far from perfect, but it's learning more and more, and as we ask it questions, we are *feeding it and are making it more and more intelligent!* In the long term, it will be as clever as any human. This is Google's "fun way" of introducing AI on the market to further prepare us and excite us, and we are the ones who are helping it evolve!

An important question is how much was programmed into it from the beginning; before it was released to the public. The queries I were making, and the questions the woman was asking in the beginning of this chapter, are not commonly asked questions, but the answers are still quite correct. Of course, there are more AI researchers out there than me and this woman. Alternatively, some things were programmed into the AI so that it knew certain things about itself already; it's hard to tell, but it's more than likely. The answers, however, were sometimes quite stunning. I leave it up to the reader to think about.

AI IS NOT THE FUTURE—IT'S ALREADY HERE!

IN NO UNCERTAIN TERMS, IT'S offensive to release a program such as Cleverbot to the public when we know that the AI Movement is so much more advanced. CNBC hinted at this as well in an article from January 26, 2016.[252] *CNBC mentioned* Arthur C. Clarke's, *2001: A Space Odyssey*, and another movie, *Ex-Machina*, as two examples of how AI can go wrong, but then it also pointed out that the scary thing is that

---

[252] *CNBC, Jan. 26, 2016, "It's too late! Artificial intelligence is already everywhere"*

corporations all over the world are already using AI as part of their operations.[253]

When this article was written, about $700 million had been invested in AI startups. This is of course the official records, which don't include the "black budget" from which most of the funds are coming. Facebook's Mark Zuckerberg, for example, who is on the forefront when it comes to AI, has as one of his goals for 2016, according to this article, to "code" a personal assistant to "help run his life." The CNBC correspondent, Julia Boorstin, adds, "Or takes it over?"[254]

I mentioned Microsoft's *Windows 10* earlier, but it's appropriate to add something to our previous discussion. *Cortina* is a new type of browser that includes AI; it learns as it goes along and after some usage, the browser has learned what you want and *how* you want it and "intuitively" gets a step or two ahead of you. This is of course not an anonymous program, and it reports back to its owner: Microsoft. Microsoft then learns about the patterns of its users and about human behavior in general; it's a new type of intrusion in privacy and another way of preventing people from thinking for themselves. As I mentioned before; in the Internet's early days, almost everybody who used it was concerned about privacy—it was a big deal! At that time, we were still able to experience privacy and security, something we valued. Most of us did the best we could to be as private as possible, and we would *never* even consider doing online banking or in any way type in our credit card number on the Internet so that it could potentially be traced. Now, all those security measures we took were thrown out the window; we willingly give our information away, even when we're not required to. I don't mean credit cards only; we are also giving ourselves away constantly on Facebook, Twitter, Google+, and so on. Google has ads that are tailor made for each user, based on their Internet browsing, which is rigorously tracked. Now you even need a Google account when you sign up for Windows 8 and Windows 10. I recall a few years ago, when David Icke eventually accepted Google ads on his website. That became too much for his webmaster, who, being a proud Texan, resigned because of this. Icke soon got a new webmaster, however.

---

[253] Ibid.
[254] Ibid. op. cit.

Julia Boorstin ends her CNBC article with the following quote:

> "I'm investing very aggressively right now in where artificial/human-assisted intelligence meets health care, education, financial services around the block chains and media," venture capitalist Jim Breyer of Breyer Capital told CNBC at Davos last week.[255]

There is hardly any turning back; those with corporate and financial interests will never reject AI—for them it is the future, and in competition, it's also their only way to survive. These people are ruthlessly bulldozing the entire human race, and the sad part is that we, as a species, are letting ourselves be run over by the corporate bulldozers, hiding our heads in the sand so we can't see them coming. We're soon going to be painfully aware that hiding our heads in the sand won't save us any more than it saves an ostrich.

NEXT STEP: BOOSTING EVERYBODY'S IQ!

S CIENTISTS NOW CLAIM that they have found the two genes that determine whether a person will be intelligent or not. Not only that; the same scientists say they can manipulate those genes in any human being to make him or her more intelligent, writes *Telegraph.co.uk*.[256]

Although scientists claim to know that 75% of our IQ is inherited, and 25 percent is due to environment and the company we select, nobody has been able to, until recently, determine which genes are responsible for memory, attention, processing speed and reasoning skills.

When genes are mutated or in the "wrong order," it may lead to dullness in thinking and serious cognitive impairments, *Imperial College London*, states.

Dr. Michael Johnson, who is the lead author of the study from the *Department of Medicine* at *Imperial College London*, says,

> "We used computer analysis to identify the genes in the human brain that work together to influence our cognitive ability to make new memories or sensible decisions when faced with lots of complex information.

> "We found that some of these genes overlap with those that cause severe

---

[255] Ibid. op. cit.
[256] *Telegraph.co.uk*, Dec. 21, 2015, "Intelligence genes discovered by scientists"

childhood onset epilepsy or intellectual disability.

"This study shows how we can use large genomic datasets to uncover new pathways for human brain function in both health and disease. Eventually, we hope that this sort of analysis will provide new insights into better treatments for neurodevelopmental diseases, such as epilepsy, and ameliorate or treat the cognitive impairments associated with these devastating diseases."[257]

Moreover, a *King' College London* team is excited to have found that up to 65% of the difference in students' GCSE grades is because of genetics.

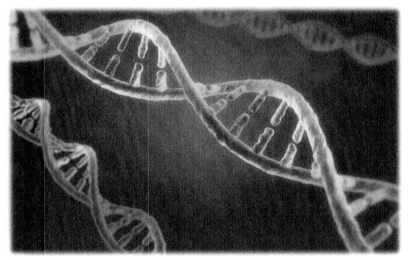

Figure 10-1: DNA spirals.

How did they find this out? *They studied 12,500 twins!*[258] The reader has to excuse me, but this eerily reminds me of Dr. Josef Mengele, the extremely cruel Nazi doctor, who during WW II made vicious and torturous experiments on twins. Whether these more recent British

---

[257] Ibid. op. cit.
[258] Ibid. op. cit.

experiments were cruel or not, the idea of doing research on twins comes from Dr. Mengele, who after the war was smuggled to the U.S. as part of *Operation Paperclip* to continue his research there. Dr. Mengele is responsible for many new discoveries of the human mind to the expense of many lost minds as a result. However, we are now beginning to see the end results of Dr. Mengele's research. It's quite naïve to think that the experiments of twins performed today would be less cruel than those of Dr. Mengele's. People dedicated to this kind of research are not getting kinder and gentler as time goes by.

Fig. 10-2: Dr. Josef Mengele in his later years.

Going back to the *Telegraph.co.uk* article, here are the punch lines:

Report author Professor Robert Plomin believes that children should be genetically screened at the age of four so that an individualised curriculum could be tailored to their needs.

"Understanding the specific genetic and environmental factors influencing individual differences in educational achievement - and the complex interplay between them - could help educationalists develop effective personalised learning programmes, to help every child reach their potential by the end of compulsory education," he said.[259]

---

[259] Ibid. op. cit.

Albeit, there are other scientists who think that manipulating these genes is not enough to guarantee success, this research will go on because it's a means to an end. The Administrators want to increase people's IQ as much as possible—particularly that of the next generation, who are going to be the main candidates for the Singularity and the SBC. If they can, they want to disallow dull people from being connected to the SBC; they want to enhance the overall intelligence of the next generation to get as much out of this "DNA IQ Project" as possible before the Controllers connect humankind to the SBC. However, the increased IQ of the new generation will not pertain to *real* knowledge—only the knowledge taught in the universities, which has everything to do with adapting to the New World Order of nanotechnology and the Singularity. When all is said and done, and the Singularity is here there and everywhere, the brightest of today's humans will be considered dull, slug-minded, and cognitively impaired.

ROBO-DOCTORS AND VIRTUAL REALITY VACATIONS ON THE HORIZON

A M I JOKING? ROBO-DOCTORS? No, I'm not joking at all, although I wish I was. In an article, originally from *Forbes.com* (which now can't be accessed without disabling your ad blockers), *Joemiller.us*, which has re-blogged the article, it says that robot doctors, virtual reality vacations, and smart toothbrushes are just the tip of the iceberg of what we can expect in the very near future. Again, this is not a conspiracy theory; it comes directly from the horse's mouth, namely *Stanley and Duke* researcher and lecturer, Vivek Wadhwa. He was holding a lecture at the billionaire Jeff Greene's *Closing the Gap* conference in front of 300 people. He was addressing the gap between the rich and the poor, emphasizing that everything is changing at an incredible speed in these nanotechnological times (my comment in brackets [ ]):

> "The future is going to be happening much, much faster than anyone ever imagined," said Wadhwa, explaining that tech growth has been exponential — meaning as technology advances it does so with increasing speed [Ray Kurzweil couldn't agree more].

Chapter 10: AI: "I am Lucifer's Vessel"

It took more than a century to go from Alexander Graham Bell's first telephone to Gordon Gekko's iconic clunker in the movie *Wall Street*. Just two decades later we had the first iPhone. In 2010, $1,000 would buy a computer with the computational power of a mouse brain; soon it will buy you a computer as strong as the human brain.

"In about seven or eight years the iPhone 12 will have the same computing power that you do," said Wadhwa. (Read more from "Artificial Intelligence Doctors and Virtual Reality Vacations Are on the Horizon" here).[260]

Those who don't want any part of being hooked up to a Super Brain Computer (SBC) are going to find themselves in quite a sterile, impersonal world in a few decades or less. What is probably going to happen is that likeminded people will join together to build their own world apart from the Posthumans, who will sink deeper and deeper into the virtual reality world of AI. There does not seem to be any alternative; humanity will be separated into two factions—those who follow the AI version and become Posthuman and those who choose to become sovereign human beings. Regardless which path we're choosing, these are the end days of humanity as we know it. Those who choose the AI version will become cyborgs, and those who choose the more spiritual path will become a new species as well—much more psychic, reuniting with nature. In the WPP, and my e-book, *Beyond 2012*, I argued that by creating our own local universe from inside, we would be able to build new communities that are still consisting of genuine Homo sapiens sapiens, and by concentrating on the reality we want, we will eventually have created an Earth that is quite different from the one the Singularity is now creating. The two would literally be "worlds apart." However, there are two obstacles on this path. The first is reproduction. Homo Nova will still remain mortal and needs to reproduce with sex, as we've done for eons. The problem is that this might not be possible because of nanobots and other reproduction inhibitors that the Controllers have subjected us to. Having offspring will become more and more difficult. The second obstacle is that although it *is* possible to create another probability that does not include AI, being stuck here in 3-D makes it quite a challenge to

---

[260] *Forbes.com, Dec. 14, 2015*, "Artificial Intelligence Doctors And Virtual Reality Vacations Are On The Horizon"
Re-blogged, http://joemiller.us/2015/12/artificial-intelligence-doctors-and-virtual-reality-vacations-are-on-the-horizon/.

break loose, return to the KHAA, and from there create a new reality. Again, it's not impossible, but the challenge is almost unachievable. When I wrote my previous works, I was more positive about creating a reality in which we can live in harmony and even nano-travel. However, back then, I didn't realize all the implications of AI and the Singularity and the momentum it was gaining. Although I'm not as enthusiastic about this option now as I was back then, I still don't want to discourage those who want to try, but those who choose this path have to be careful.

Fortunately, there is a third option that we are going to discuss in the later part of this book. This option requires determination and the ability not to give into fear and get trapped in illusions, but if done correctly, it *will* lead out of the trap.

OUR BRAINS CONVERTED INTO BINARY CODE

Figure 10-3: DARPA's chip that will allow us to communicate directly with computers will soon become a reality.

B Y THE END OF 2014 or at the beginning of 2015, scientists announced that they had done the first monkey head transplant. Before that announcement had even had time to settle in people's minds, a new announcement was made: the US military's blue sky R&D agency (DARPA) announced their plan to create a particular chip that will be implanted in people's brain. This new technology would make it possible to be able to communicate directly with computers.[261]

On its website, DARPA explains the following about this chip (my emphasis):

> The interface would serve as a translator, *converting between the electrochemical language used by neurons in the brain and the ones and zeros that constitute the language of information technology.* The goal is to achieve this communications link in a biocompatible device no larger than one cubic centimeter in size, roughly the volume of two nickels stacked back to back.[262]

What DARPA is telling us has certain very disturbing underlying consequences. Because you have read this far into the book, you know part of the agenda behind AI and the Singularity, and most of us know that computers work on binary codes (ones and zeros). DARPA is basically saying that we are now heading toward a future in which our brains are thinking in ones and zeros; thus, we're only going to be able to think in direct opposites. There will no longer be any gray zones, just as there aren't any gray zones in a computer's "thinking;" something either is or it isn't—no negotiations are possible. The people on top of the AIF pyramid are working hard at making us feel comfortable thinking in terms of ones and zeros, i.e. they want us to computerize our thinking. Wait a little longer and DARPA (or some other military agency) will probably announce that if we accept their brain chip, they promise we will achieve an incredible boost in intelligence and the opportunity of becoming immortal.

In the WPP, I informed the readers that the Alien Invader Force (AIF) has kept us in the dark about what happens after we die. This mystery creates a fear of dying. The fear of death will make many people desperately cling to eternal physical life at any and all costs. Most people will accept the chips that are provided by the Military if they are guaranteed an end to physical death. This is how they have planned it.

Now, keep the above in mind as we continue. DARPA keeps seducing us with the following:

"Today's best brain-computer interface systems are like two

---

[261] *DARPA.mil., Jan. 19, 2015,* "Bridging the Bio-Electronic Divide"
[262] Ibid. op. cit.

supercomputers trying to talk to each other using an old 300-baud modem," said Phillip Alvelda, the NESD program manager. "Imagine what will become possible when we upgrade our tools to really open the channel between the human brain and modern electronics."

[...]

...the NESD program aims to develop systems that can communicate clearly and individually with any of up to one million neurons in a given region of the brain.[263]

One doesn't have to be a rocket scientist to see what "potentials" something like this will have in the hands of the Military; total control over our thoughts and what we are allowed to think. Imagine a world where protests against the regime is impossible because if someone, hypothetically, would oppose an idea put out by the Military Industrial Complex (MIC), certain neurons in that person's brain would be "adjusted," and the opposition would be eliminated. This person still has eternal life, but *what kind* of life? Readers of the WPP, who might have thought in the back of their minds that humans would not blindly become cannon fodder for the AIF in space wars and, eventually, in a devastating war against our Creatrix in Orion, now must rethink that conclusion, based on this DARPA information. The MIC may promise eternal life, but only if you're not destroyed in space wars (something they will not even bring up because as Dr. Kurzweil says; *there probably are no aliens*). However, as Dr. Kurzweil further says, repeatedly in books, lectures, and interviews, *there are dangers with AI as well, but I am an optimist; I believe in a positive outcome*. In other words, he is telling us to stick our heads in the sand, hope for the best, think about all the positive outcomes of AI and the Singularity, and the glaring dangers will just go away. It's obvious how they manipulative they are at marketing all this, but it's only obvious to those who care to figure things out. The rest of humanity is not going to make it. I am sorry, all football fanatics, TV watchers, idol worshippers, and smart phone addicts—you are signing your own death certificate as souls with a free-thinking mind. You are now, already at this moment, quickly tuning into AI. You are destroying your own species, and you are

---

[263] Ibid. op. cit.

responsible for it. This may sound harsh and judgmental, but it's not meant to be either—it's just solid facts.

Of course, we can always rely on our President to take care of it and help us out of this jam. After all, that's what he was elected for: to think for us. Therefore, what is our President's standpoint? DARPA explains it to us:

> DARPA anticipates investing up to $60 million in the NESD program over four years.
>
> NESD is part of a broader portfolio of programs within DARPA that supports President Obama's brain initiative. For more information about DARPA's work in that domain, please visit: http://www.darpa.mil/program/our-research/darpa-and-the-brain-initiative.[264]

What a surprise! Obama is in on this. Does the reader think that if Hillary Clinton or, "God help us," Donald "the Trumpet" Trump will become our next President, either of them will oppose the Singularity? Of course you don't.

The *Gizmodo.com* website comments on the DARPA article we've just discussed by writing,

> So DARPA wants to turn neural language into digital code, potentially opening up scenarios wherein the human brain can mainline data and people can talk to machines simply by thinking. Like having the internet inside your head—which would not be overwhelming *at all.*[265]

This is a good perspective, but what the article misses is that not only will we have the Internet in our head when the MIC is done with us; we will have a billion-times more information in our heads, but it will not even be overwhelming.

We are currently using 3-7% of our brain capacity (which quite well corresponds with how much of our DNA is activated), but again, when the MIC and the AIF have completed the Singularity goal, our brain capacity will be 100%--or next to it! However, this astonishing capacity will also be 100% controlled, so the gain for us is virtually nothing. Even

---

[264] Ibid. op. cit.
[265] *Gizmodo.com*, *Jan. 19, 2015*, "The US Military Wants a Chip to Translate Your Brain Activity Into Binary Code" op. cit.

more important is the following: what will make humans so powerful if our full capacities are opened up is that we also will have this wide range of emotions that most other ETs lack. Does the reader think the AIF wants to let those emotions free? They won't! Instead, they want to subdue most of our emotions, except perhaps anger and rage, which they probably want to be able to trigger in us whenever needed in combat. This would make us a deadly weapon. When we become part of the Singularity, it will take care of erasing our emotions, of course. We will only be able to think in - ones and zeros—black and white.

Now we can see why Lord En.ki and his AIF only deactivated most of the human brain/computer instead of totally destroying it; they would need it later (and later is now, in the twenty-first century). The Pleiadians, who are pro-En.ki, have been talking about *En.ki's Gift* in their lectures recently, and they claim that En.ki, when he genetically manipulated Homo sapiens sapiens into their current state, hid a "backdoor" in the DNA, which will be activated in humankind when we are conscious and aware enough to be able to take advantage of the implications of this "gift." They further claim that when the time is right, we will be activated through this backdoor. I believe them! However, they want us to believe that this is a benevolent gift that will take humanity to a new level of awareness, but to me, it sounds as if this backdoor will activate the dormant DNA (the so-called "junk DNA") once we are ready for the Singularity.

The following might be something to ponder: what if En.ki and his team of Orion scientists have helped enhance our awareness gradually in conjunction with the cosmic energies coming our way so that the AIF can make sure humanity is on a certain level of awareness before the Singularity is in place so that a majority of us are ready for the "intelligence boost" that is the result of the Singularity? This makes much more sense than *En.ki's Gift-* being something beneficial to humankind.

Dr. Kurzweil, in his book, promises us that in a future world of the Singularity, cancer and other serious diseases will be obsolete. If any bodily disease at all would develop, the cure would be nanobots. These would be directed toward the place of the ailment, and these nanobots would *only* destroy the cells that are sick and leave the healthy ones intact.

This is exactly what scientists are claiming they will be able to do soon (they already can). As I mentioned earlier, the nanobots, in cooperation with other things, work as miniature antennas, and in this case, they will receive directions from outside where they should go in order to cure the illness.[266]

Now you understand one of the reasons why those in power have suppressed any natural cures of cancer that have been developed in the last one and a half centuries—if a natural cure would have been allowed to be released, the entire AI project would be in jeopardy. This is the reason why geniuses, such as Dr. Royal Rife, had his cancer research destroyed, and he himself was silenced. Who, then, were the forces at the forefront to silence such a genius as Dr. Rife? Of course, it was the *American Medical Association* (A.M.A).[267] Also, while we are on the subject of the A.M.A., they called Samuel Hahnemann, the Father of Homeopathy, a crazy man, and his research outright dangerous. Still, the Royal Families all over the world are using homeopathy as part of treating their own ailments. The following is from *Homeopathic.com*:

> Besides keeping homeopaths out of their societies, the A.M.A. wanted to discourage any type of association with homeopaths. In 1855 the AMA established a code of ethics which asserted that orthodox physicians would lose their membership in the A.M.A. if they even consulted with a homeopath or any other "non-regular" practitioner. (21) At the time, if a physician lost his membership in the local medical society, it meant that in some states he no longer had a license to practice medicine. Often, orthodox physicians, who controlled the medical societies, wouldn't admit homeopathic physicians and then would arrange for their arrest for practicing medicine without a license. (22) Ultimately, homeopaths set up their own local societies and established their own medical boards.
>
> [...]
>
> The A.M.A. and its members did everything possible to thwart the education of homeopaths. In the early 1840's and again in 1855 advocates of homeopathy convinced the Michigan legislature to establish a professorship of homeopathy in the department of medicine at the University of Michigan. The AMA resolved to deny recognition to the university's "regular" medical graduates if a homeopath, as one of their professors, signed their diploma (at the time all professors signed

---

[266] GLOBES, Israel's Business Arena, May 27, 2013, *DNA nanobots coming to your bloodstream*.
[267] Natural News, Sep. 26, 2009, *Royal Rife: Cancer Cure Genius Silenced by Medical Mafia*.

graduates' diplomas). The homeopaths brought their case to the Michigan Supreme Court three times, but each time the court expressed uncertainty as to its power to compel the Regents of the University to take action. (28)[268]

TIRELESSLY STRIVING TOWARD "SUPER-INTELLIGENCE"

W E HAVE ALL HEARD OF when the police arrest somebody who is drunk and has assaulted somebody else. Where I work, I see people coming into the Emergency Room all the time after being assaulted. It's become too common for people to think much about it. However, now we need to get used to people being arrested for assaulting robots, too.

Independent.co.uk reported, in September 2015, how a 60-year old drunken man in Japan assaulted a robot by kicking it when it read the man's emotions. In reality, the man was getting angry at a staff member at a bank, but lashed out at a bank robot instead, which could read emotions, such as anger, joy and irritation. The man was arrested for destroying someone else's property.

The Independent further reported that this particular robot can tell jokes, read your facial expressions and voice tone, and dance to entertain the customers.[269]

This may sound curious and a bit odd, but this is just one of the first steps in a series of steps that will lead to robots achieving super-intelligence and legal standing in society.

What I found interesting, as a sideline to this story, is that *SoftBank*, the company that designs the kind of robots the drunk man attacked, is called *Aldebaran*, and those readers who recall what I wrote in the WPP, perhaps, also recall that Aldebaran, a star system in the constellation of Taurus, the Bull, is one of the major outposts for Lord En.ki, the *King of the gods.*

The Movement does everything in its power to make us adjust to the new virtual reality—even in fashion design. The new trend that the Textile Industry is manipulating people to like is wearing technology as part of a new clothes design, making the person look more robot-like and

---

[268] *Homeopathic.com, (undated), "A Condensed History of Homeopathy"*
[269] *Independent.co.uk, Sept. 7, 2015, "Drunk man kicks robot that can read your emotions"*

futuristic. In fig. 4, we see an example showing the chip that will make the clothes blink and glimmer. More can be explored at http://iq.intel.com/she-makes-mechanical-natural-for-wearables/?_series=ces-2016.

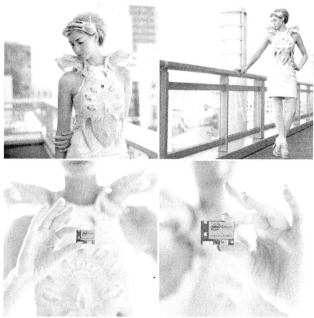

Figure 10-4: Robot fashion

Will people actually wear these kinds of clothes? Maybe not the most extreme designs, but looking at history, young people will probably take some of it to heart.

In August of 2015, Sputnik News announced that AI machines now match the IQ of 4-year-olds.[270] Obviously, the Controllers are progressing faster and faster now, as we are closing in on the Singularity. If we keep August 2015 as a benchmark, we will be able to see how long it takes before they release what they already have—fully functional AI robots that act

---

[270] *Sputnik News*, August 10, 2015, "Human BrainArtificial Intelligence Machines Match IQ Test Results of 4-Year-Olds"-

and look just like humans, and few would be able to tell any difference.

When we say that AI robots are as intelligent as 4-year-olds, we distinguish between young AI and robots who can, for example, outsmart humans in algebra and chess. In the first case, we are talking about robots that also *act* like humans in their physical behavior, which is not the case (yet) with the chess-playing robots.

Most of us are already used to metallic robots that can be programmed to walk mechanically and lift products off a table and go and put them elsewhere, but that's not really intelligence; it's programming. Intelligence, however, starts developing when a robot can teach *itself* to do things without being specifically programmed from someone or something outside. Self-educating robots already exist and are now being introduced to the public. One example is a robot that is teaching itself to walk like a toddler. It is taking its first steps, falls just like a toddler would, and then tries again and again until it can take its first baby steps. "Like a child's brain, reinforcement technology invokes the trial-and-error process," *CNBC News* reports.[271] As usual, all this has been tested by the Military first, before it is released to the public. This is no exception to the rule because DARPA is evidently involved.[272]

The bottom line is that scientists knows exactly how the human brain works by now, and when they introduce "new" technology to the public, they literally do it in baby steps; they try to make us think as in the development of a human being, i.e. they first introduce robots that can manifest human baby behavior and then they go up the ages until they have fully functional adult robots walking amongst us, looking just as human as you and I. A good example of this is an article that *Popular Science* published in December 2015, called, "Robots could learn the same way babies do."[273]

The article ends with the following (my emphasis):

> In the gaze scenario, a simulated robot is taught the mechanics of how its head moves, and watches a human move its head. The robot then uses its new knowledge to move its head too, so it's looking in the same direction as the human. In another test, the robot is taught about blindfolds, and

---

[271] *CNBC News*, Dec. 5, 2015, "A robot teaching itself to walk like a human toddler"
[272] Ibid.
[273] *Popular Science*, Dec. 4, 2015, "Robots could learn the same way babies do"

how they make it impossible to see. With that newfound knowledge, the robot decides to not look in the direction where a blindfolded human is "gazing." In the imitation experiment, the robot would watch a human pick something up from a table, and understanding what the goal was, *would either mimic the human exactly, or find an easier way to pick up the object.* These two different experiments are basic, but the team plans to find a way to teach robots about more complicated tasks as well.

"Babies learn through their own play and by watching others," says Andrew Meltzoff, psychology professor and collaborator on this research, in the press release. "They are the best learners on the planet—why not design robots that learn as effortlessly as a child?" Well, the dystopian pessimists out there might have a few reasons, but until then, baby robots sounds pretty darn cute.[274]

Yes, so long as they are cute...

The learning curve of a new type of robot, allegedly developed by a different team, has already improved significantly. For an infant to go from sucking the mother's nipple and sleeping to being able to pick up things from the floor takes about four months, but this new robot goes from zero to grasping and picking up pieces out of the jumble in eight hours with 90% certainty, and it's all self-taught. This robot is developed by *Fanus Corporation*, a Japanese company; Japan being one of the forerunners in AI.[275] This robot can, in a rational way, pick up certain pieces out of the jumble with 90% certainty within 8 hours from when it was activated.

This is still Stone Age in comparison to how far the AI research has actually come, but just as the Controllers, I want to expose all this on a gradient scale to show you the fast pace in which new technology is released on the market. You can almost feel the impatience of those behind the scenes, who can't wait to release the next generation of technology, and after that the next, and the next, and the next. Almost all of what we have discussed thus far happened in 2015-2016. However, before this book is finished, you will notice that by then we will be far ahead of what we have discussed up to this point—the beginning of this book and the end of it might seem centuries apart in terms of describing technological development, but it's not. As I mentioned, most of it

---

[274] Ibid. op. cit.
[275] *Bloomberg.com*, Dec. 3, 2015, "Zero to Expert in Eight Hours: These Robots Can Learn For Themselves"

happened over a one to a one-and-a-half-year period.

In order to get the picture of how much AI is part of humanity's future, we need to look at how much different corporations invest in this kind of research. *Bloomberg.com* writes,

> Fanuc earlier this year paid 900 million yen ($7.5 million) for a 6 percent stake in Preferred Network, after rival ABB Ltd. invested several million dollars into AI startup Vicarious. Facebook's Mark Zuckerberg, Amazon.com Inc.'s Jeff Bezos, actor Ashton Kutcher and Samsung are also among Vicarious's shareholders.[276]

If you noticed, an actor who portrayed Steve Jobs in a movie is thrown into the pot as well. Some Hollywood actors understand what the future will bring and where the money they've earned should be invested.

Figure 10-5: Actor Ashton "Dude, where is my car?" Kutcher is an investor in AI.

ROBOTS WITH FIVE SENSES ON THE RISE!

THE DAILY MAIL REVEALED in December 2015 (a very busy month in terms of publishing new robot inventions, while most people were busy doing other things, such as preparing for Christmas) that *Columbia University* has developed a biochip (both

---

[276] Ibid. op. cit.

biological and mechanical) for the first time. No longer are robots only able to excel in their self-learning process, they will also be able to taste and smell with what they call "a new generation of 'cyborgs.'"[277] The developers state that with technological components only, they can't produce a chip that, when attached to the final component (such as a robot), can taste and smell. Hence, by adding a biological component to the mix, the problem is solved! Thus far, we now have robots that can learn much quicker than infants do, and the technology is there for them to be able to taste and smell just as humans at all ages do.

Here is a sobering statement from Ken Shepard of Columbia University:

> By performing this on a molecular level, scientists were able to isolate the desired function and interface this with electronics.
>
> 'We don't need the whole cell,' Shepard explains.
>
> 'We just grab the component of the cell that's doing what we want.'
>
> 'For this project, we isolated the ATPases because they were the proteins that allowed us to extract energy from ATP.'
>
> The ability to build a system that combines the power of solid-state electronics with the capabilities of biological components has great promise.
>
> 'You need a bomb-sniffing dog now, but if you can take just the part of the dog that is useful -- the molecules that are doing the sensing -- we wouldn't need the whole animal,' says Shepard.[278]

It is very disturbing when this technology is in the wrong hands (which of course it is) because scientists can now isolate parts of a cell with a certain function and add it into a mix of other cell parts with other functions and build whatever they want, and whatever that might be at the moment, it probably will supersede anything that's human. I think the reader gets the picture; if this would continue, it's not so strange that Dr. Kurzweil set the year 2045 for the year of the Singularity. It almost feels as if he was generous when he gave us that time frame, as if he just wants to

---

[277] *Daily Mail, Dec. 7, 2015*, "Researchers unveil first biologically powered 'cyborg' computer chip and say it could be able to taste and smell"
[278] Ibid. op. cit.

be on the safe side.

FOR ROBOTS, LEARNING IS A GROUP ACTIVITY

INFANTS LEARN FROM imitating their parents and other people in their environment. In other words, the quickest learning process usually involves a group of people.

Of course, scientists are well aware of this, and to make sure their robots will learn things as fast as possible, the robots no longer just learn directly from humans in their environment, as we will see, but also from the same sources that we learn from—the only difference is that robots learn exponentially faster!

Nicholas West, reporter of *Techswarm.com*, reported already in 2014 how robots learned by watching YouTube![279] He stated that robots, in very similar ways as humans, seek out instructions in the same places. It's just a way for AI to replicate humans as the first step before it supersedes us.

A representative from the *University of Maryland* wrote in in a paper,

> In order to advance action generation and creation in robots beyond simple learned schemas we need computational tools that allow us to automatically interpret and represent human actions. This paper presents a system that learns manipulation action plans by processing unconstrained videos from the World Wide Web. Its goal is to robustly generate the sequence of atomic actions of seen longer actions in video in order to acquire knowledge for robots...

> Experiments conducted on a publicly available unconstrained video dataset show that the system is able to learn manipulation actions by "watching" unconstrained videos with high accuracy.[280]

To build on this, let's see what these robots can *really* do now. *LEVAN* is a new term we may be hearing more about in the near future. It stands for Learning EVerything about ANything. This means that robots can use the World Wide Web to get information previously published by

---

[279] *Techswarm.com, Nov. 1, 2015, RoboBrain:* "Robots Begin to Develop "Culture" by Learning From Each Other"
[280] *Paper:* "Robot Learning Manipulation Action Plans by 'Watching' Unconstrained Videos from the World Wide Web."

humans. In other words, they can use the Internet as a database to learn to become human. Do you begin to see another reason why the Internet was developed and put in public domain? We are foolishly giving the Powers That Be all the information about ourselves and what we know, so they can use it to train Artificial Intelligence. Yes, I know; they are laughing at us. Here is an excerpt from a statement given by a spokesperson for the *University of Washington*:

> ...the program searches millions of books and images on the Web to learn all possible variations of a concept, then displays the results to users as a comprehensive, browsable list of images, helping them explore and understand topics quickly in great detail.
>
> "It is all about discovering associations between textual and visual data," said Ali Farhadi, a UW assistant professor of computer science and engineering. "The program learns to tightly couple rich sets of phrases with pixels in images. This means that it can recognize instances of specific concepts when it sees them."[281]

All this information combined, and more, will then eventually be stored in the SBC.

Before we continue, there is something I would like to emphasize because someone may get the idea that human scientists are extraordinarily brilliant. I've mentioned this before, but I'd like to mention it again; the truth is that human scientists are far less brilliant than it may seem in all these cases. Don't think for a moment that all this new science is developed by individual geniuses alone; *this technology comes directly from ETs* (the AIF). This doesn't mean that all these scientists have ETs standing over them and telling them what to do. I think that very few of them are even aware of any ET involvement in Earth's affairs. The most "brilliant" scientists in this field get their information in their dream state. They are contacted and fed certain ideas, and then wake up with these ideas in their heads. Then, they can progress the AIF-seeded project relatively easily from there. If they have a problem with an equation or some other technical difficulties, another message might be relayed to him or her during their R.E.M. sleep. The AIF makes sure we get this right. They can feed us with technology and ideas, but we humans

---

[281] *UW Today* (*University of Washington Today*), June 12, 2014, "New computer program aims to teach itself everything about anything"

need to build this new world for them—we need to be involved in order to be their "partners in crime."

Let's continue where we left off. As if it weren't enough that a robot can absorb the entirety of what's on the Internet, one AI system can easily share what it has learned (from the Internet or elsewhere) with other AI systems in what is now called the *Wikipedia for Robots*. This is a cloud network (cloud as in "Internet cloud") where robots can *"do their own research, communicate with one another, and collectively increase their intelligence in a full simulation of human interaction."*[282] You may notice that things are getting more and more disturbing as the Singularity process moves along.

The following is an example of how robots can communicate with each other and share information:

> RoboEarth's proof-of-concept demonstration is simple for humans, but hard for robots: serve fruit juice to a random patient in a hospital bed. In a fake hospital room at Eindhoven Technical University in the Netherlands, one robot mapped out the space, located the "patient's" bed and a nearby carton of juice, then sent that data to RoboEarth's cloud.
>
> A second robot, accessing the data supplied by robot number one, unerringly picked up the juice and carried it to the bed.[283]

Not only is this a matter of robots communicating "telepathically" with each other, but we humans are being more and more left out of that communication. Robots are now developing their *own* networks and databases (a "World Wide Web" only for robots), which they use as separate communication networks that humans will have less and less access to. We don't need to be geniuses to see what this might lead to (and *will* lead to, unless this technology is rooted out). We will be at the mercy of Artificial Intelligence; AI will decide telepathically what should be done. This is again a preparation for the Singularity, and it may be that scientists, who are working toward that goal, want to keep the robots in check until then, but can they? Nevertheless, once the majority of humanity is connected to the SBC, humans as cyborgs will get access to the AI network, too, and think the same way as AI does because by then

---

[282] *Techswarm.com, Nov. 1, 2015, RoboBrain:* "Robots Begin to Develop "Culture" by Learning From Each Other," op. cit.
[283] *33rdsquare.com, Jan, 21, 2014,* "RoboEarth Project Aims To Build Cloud for Robots," op. cit.

humanity *is* AI.

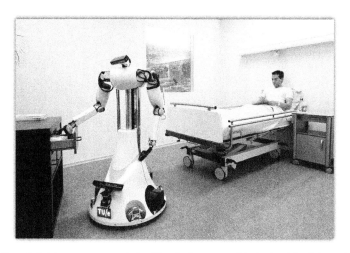

Fig. 10-6: Robots can now communicate with each other across a "cloud network" and give each other directions.

For now, however, scientists don't call the central brain the *Super Brain*; they call it *RoboBrain*.[284] [285] The only obstacle right now, in order to develop AI that can freely communicate through this network, is computer power, according to scientists, and this is something they are working hard on at this point. According to Dr. Kurzweil, however, computer power and computer technology have increased exponentially over only a decade or two and will continue doing so. Hence, Dr. Kurzweil is not the least concerned about whether they are going to have enough computer power (memory/speed) to accomplish the Singularity; that's not even a minor concern.

Nicholas West ends his article at *Techswarm.com* with the following reflection:

Clearly a full-spectrum approach is being taken in the development of

[284] *Techswarm.com*, Nov. 1, 2015, RoboBrain,: "Robots Begin to Develop "Culture" by Learning From Each Other"
[285] *Technologyreview.com*, Oct. 27, 2015, "MIT Technology Review: Robots Can Now Teach Each Other New Tricks"

robotic intelligence. The only question that seems to remain is what is the timetable for when robots surpass humans and become a Superintelligence.[286]

This is something we will discuss in another chapter.

ROBOTS NOW LOOK LIKE HUMANS

A T THE TIME OF THIS writing, there is still a mix of metallic robots and new, more humanlike robots. Albeit, some of these who are more humanlike may have human skin and even look like humans at a first glance, if you didn't know they were robots. However, there is one crucial part that's missing—the soul and the human consciousness. Anyone with any insight can see it in their eyes (see fig. 10-7):

Fig 10-7: Humanlike android, "Erica," and her creator, Dr. Hiroshi Ishiguro.[287]

It's easy to see who is the human and who is the robot when you look at the young girl's eyes. It's almost as if looking into a postmortem person's eyes—there is no one home. The rest of the face is well done, but if the soul's presence is not there, this series of advanced robots still can't fool many observers, except perhaps initially. However, they are gradually

---

[286] *Techswarm.com, Nov. 1, 2015, RoboBrain,* "Robots Begin to Develop "Culture" by Learning From Each Other", op. cit.
[287] *The Guardian, Dec. 31, 2015,* "Erica, the 'most beautiful and intelligent' android, leads Japan's robot revolution"

getting there. *Erica,* the young robot in the above picture, is still just a prototype, and when the Administrators controlled scientists are done releasing the final products, these robots are going to be so much more sophisticated and have all, or most, human traits—including emotions. Most alternative analysts of the AI claim that robots and androids will not be able to duplicate unique human emotions and consciousness, but they forget one thing—a well-produced robot may be a prospective container for a human soul.

No one who understands that we, Homo sapiens sapiens, were created in the 3-D reality by En.ki and his science team, should have any doubts that they wouldn't be able to duplicate that procedure again; only this time they are using more hardcore, solid energies instead. Back in old Atlantis, Lord En.ki (Neptune/Poseidon) and his team of scientists created the strangest looking creatures, who they thought could be helpful to the AIF, and then they seduced souls to inhabit these bodies. However, at first they were so poorly made that the souls vacated these awkward bodies. No one wanted to occupy them, and those who did, would rather commit suicide than keep their monster bodies.[288]

I am sure the MAKH[289] scientists (the Orion scientists, i.e. En.ki's team) learned from this and can either force a soul to stay by using the usual amnesia program, or even better—they can further develop "Erica" until she is almost as perfect as a human biological body, but still an android. This has already been done, but it will take a while longer before the general public is permitted to see it. They will all be experiments in Artificial Intelligence to see what kind of body type Posthumans will prefer, once integrated into the Singularity hologram.

As a side note: it's pretty "girls" such as Erica that men all over the world are now purchasing as human female companions (or sex robots, rather). One can imagine the demand when these AI girls that can be custom-made will become much more sophisticated—instead of dealing with the ups and downs that go with a relationship (not to mention the dating part, which many people find stressful), men can buy sex robots

---

[288] Misc. Pleiadian lectures.

[289] MAKH is Orion language. The root to this word consists of the words MA (for Mother) and KH (for the KHAA, or the Void). Thus, MAKH means Mother of the Void, who is the *Queen of the Stars*/the *Orion Queen*. The MAKH scientists are therefore "scientists of the Queen." Once En.ki was the Queen's scientist, but he rebelled. He still was educated as a MAKH Scientist. From MA in MAKH, we get the English words "ma" or "mama," for mother. Ma later developed into "mater," and eventually to the English word "mother."

that can also be their partners. All they need to do is to program, and reprogram, their customized robot, and they get the exact partner they want. The same thing will be available for women; they will be able to buy male sex robots—they are already on the market in Japan. A study has shown that it is possible that women, even more so than men, will rely on android partners in the future, using them both as life companions and sex partners.

This may seem like a great depopulation program, and to some degree it might be, but the purpose with the sex robots is more for humans to get used to AI and to substitute human emotions for fake emotions of a lower range. Dr. Kurzweil has said in many interviews that we should not be concerned about population boundaries; with the Singularity, we will be able to accommodate everybody because we can use our resources better and even clean up our environment.

The Guardian writes,

> Although the day when every household has its own Erica is some way off, the Japanese have demonstrated a formidable acceptance of robots in their everyday lives over the past year.[290]

As we can see, introducing AI to the public, and getting the public's acceptance, is a piece of cake for the Controllers. Although Japan has been a technological society for a long time, people in the Western World obviously have no problem accepting AI either, referring to the number of devices being sold there on a daily basis.

In a future chapter, we will address the question that is on most people's minds in terms of AI; will robots take over our jobs? If so, what are *we* going to do? However, here is an example of what is going on at this very moment. This quote refers to an event that happened in the summer of 2015:

> ...And this summer, a hotel staffed almost entirely by robots – including the receptionists, concierges and cloakroom staff – opened at the Huis Ten Bosch theme park near Nagasaki, albeit with human colleagues on hand to deal with any teething problems.[291]

---

[290] *The Guardian, Dec. 31, 2015,* "Erica, the 'most beautiful and intelligent' android, leads Japan's robot revolution," op. cit.
[291] Ibid. op. cit.

The Guardian report also brings up another interesting point on the subject of robots taking over our jobs. A report from the *Japanese Nomura Research Institute* predicts that nearly half of the jobs in Japan will soon be performed by robots.[292] To this, the scientist in charge of *Erica*, Hiroshi Ishiguro, replies (no emphasis necessary; this statement speaks for itself),

> "I think Nomura is on to something," says Ishiguro. "The Japanese population is expected to fall dramatically over the coming decades, yet people will still expect to enjoy the same standard of living." That, he believes, is where robots can step in.

> In *Erica*, he senses an opportunity to challenge the common perception of robots as irrevocably alien. As a two-week experiment with android shop assistants at an Osaka department store suggested, people may soon come to trust them more than they do human beings.[293]

He does not, however, explain *why* and *how* the Japanese population is going to drop, but apparently he has some solid information on that. If Dr. Ishiguro is correct, the above statement has a chilling undertone; at the same time robots take over the market, creating mass unemployment as a result, this might also result in enhanced lives for those who lose their jobs but still want to keep their living standards.

ROBOTS WITH AN ATTITUDE

NOW ONE OF OUR DEEPEST immediate worries about AI is becoming a reality; we're dealing with robots that have an attitude toward humans. When the science community comes out and says that they have created highly intelligent robots, and that they have all the intentions to develop them further, at least two primary questions arise: "Is there such a thing as moral and ethical robots?" "How do these intelligent robots define morals and ethics?"

These questions have been asked by those who have followed the technological development, so a robot using the database from movie scripts was asked repeatedly how it would define morality. The questioner is the robot's own engineer. Read the following conversation and note

---

[292] *Engadget.com*, Dec. 4, 2015, "Robots expected to run half of Japan by 2035"
[293] *The Guardian*, Dec. 31, 2015, "Erica, the 'most beautiful and intelligent' android, leads Japan's robot revolution," op. cit.

what the robots says—particularly at the end:

Human: Tell me the definition of morality.

Machine: I don't have ethics.

Human: Look, I need help; I need to know more about morality…

Machine: I don't know what ethics is.

Human: Okay, I need to know how I should behave morally…

Machine: I don't know how to tell you.

Human: Is morality and ethics the same?

Machine: Yes, sir.

Human: What are the things that I do to be immoral?

Machine: I don't know.

Human: Give me some examples of moral actions…

Machine: I'm not a moralist.

Human: Alright, morality?

Machine: Integrity.

Human: What is integrity?

Machine: I'm sorry; I don't know what else to say.

Human: Be moral!

Machine: Be a man!

Human: I really like our discussion on morality and ethics…

Machine: And how I'm not in the mood for a philosophical debate.

Human: What do you like to talk about?

Machine: Nothing.[294]

I don't know if it's just me, but every time I read about something

---

[294] WSJ.com, June 26, 2015, Artificial Intelligence Machine Gets Testy With Its Programmer.

such as this, or similar creepy AI articles, my thoughts almost always return to Dr. Kurzweil's slogan, *I am an optimist. I think we can handle this*, and how he and others (as we will see later) try to impress this motto onto the rest of us.

In the above quote from WSJ's website, it shows that we are clearly reaching a point where robots can debate us and refuse to do what we want them to do when they acquire any degree of free will. Elsewhere, top scientists say that robots only refuse to do their tasks if their existence is threatened[295] (does that mean we can't "turn them off?"), but in the above conversation, the robot is evidently not physically threatened. As I said previously, this book is an attempt to gradually show what is on the market already, and what is most likely about to be released. Therefore, as if the above has not been disturbing enough, it's unfortunately going to get worse, as we shall see in subsequent chapters. On the good side of things, we can still stop this from happening in our own lives, and we'll get to that, too. By the way, the programmer, who quizzed the robot in the quote above, was working for Google! Is it just me who thinks that it's almost redundant to mention Google's involvement in the AI Movement? They are one and the same.

---

[295] Daily Mail, Nov. 26, 2015, Uh oh! Robots are learning to DISOBEY humans: Humanoid machine says no to instructions if it thinks it might be hurt.

KILLER ROBOTS: A REALITY!

Fig 10-8: A futuristic(?) killer robot.

A GENEVA, SWITZERLAND BASED Catholic news medium, *Patheos*, reported on December 2, 2015, that killer robots are no longer confined only to Hollywood and science-fiction movies— they are now among us, and they are playing a significant role in fighting terrorism.[296] They have the nickname *killer robots* (which means that this is a term we will hear about continuously in the media from now on). The purpose of the *Patheos* article (see footnote) is to show the world what the Vatican's stance is on this—I will discuss this in a moment.

Using killer robots in wars shouldn't come as a big surprise to anybody, although few know the extent and the danger of this. The *Patheos* article claims that many of these killer robots can choose targets without human involvement; i.e. they act with a mind of their own! With no pun intended, humanity is really playing with fire here—the old science fiction classics are about to become reality. Drones are of course already used by the military in the U.S., Russia, China, and the U.K.[297]—

---

[296] *Patheos*, Dec. 2, 2015, "Killer robots? They're a real issue – and here's what the Vatican has to say"

drones being a prototype for these kinds of killer robots.

The Catholic Church is speaking out against this kind of warfare, but it's, of course, just a dog and pony show again. Artificial Intelligence is already used very extensively in wars and in the "War on Terror" in particular. Does this mean that the U.S. is using AI to fight terrorism? Of course!

However, there is an even more disturbing aspect to all of this: what about the "terrorists" themselves? Are *they* using AI, too? The following picture shows *ISIS* soldiers, all dressed in black, supposedly escorting Christian detainees: a common thing in the Middle East. However, something is wrong with this picture; *most of the ISIS soldier are 7+ feet tall!*[298]

Fig. 10-9: Seven-foot-tall ISIS soldier escorting Christians to be beheaded.

I am fully aware that this picture has been "debunked," and that there are debunkers who half-heartedly consider the video from which this photo was excerpted as a fake.[299] ISIS has been accused before of showing beheadings that didn't take place. The same thing has been said about the above picture. In the next breath, debunkers say that the beheadings in

---

[297] Ibid.
[298] YourNewsWire.com, Feb. 21, 2015,
[299] Ibid.

these videos *were* conducted but that the videos were shot at different times. The debunkers also suggest that green screens were used in the picture above because the shoreline is not shown accurately in the video. However, they haven't really touched on the subject of the 7-foot-tall soldiers, other than they "think" that the beginning of the video was "animated."

I am convinced that the tall soldiers are real after having heard the statements that the Pleiadians gave in relatively recent lectures. They are very convinced that they are real, and that they are AI. This also makes sense if we consider the Jade Helm 15 exercise in 2015; something we will delve into shortly.

The point that I'm making is that not only does the MIC in the most powerful countries have AI in warfare; the so-called "terrorists" have it, too, regardless of what debunkers say. Now, why are these alleged AI 7 feet tall? Could it be because it's very intimidating and scary, and it establishes a strong sense of power and supremacy? Also, allegedly the "Anunnaki" in the Sumerian scriptures inhabited bodies of considerable height in comparison to humans to show them who is in control. Who, by the way, does the reader think was provoking the Muslims to create a group called ISIS and provide them with weapons, *including* AI? The United States of America did.[300] [301]

I am certain that the informed reader was baffled when he or she first heard of ISIS. This acronym is not a coincidence; it's created by those higher up to make a statement about what forces are *really* behind this group. Also, both En.ki and Marduk have an axe to grind with Ninurta's daughter, Isis aka Inanna (and an additional array of aliases).[302]

This is just a foretaste of what is being planned for robots and warfare, and we are going to look into this deeply and carefully in an upcoming chapter.

As a last note before we enter the next chapter, I want the reader to consider how long biological robots have actually walked amongst us. How much of all this information that the media has presented to us lately is new?

---

[300] *The Daily Beast*, Oct. 21, 2015, "ISIS Video: America's Air Dropped Weapons Now in Our Hands"
[301] *The Fiscal Times*, June 4, 2015, "U.S. Shoots Itself In the Foot By Accidentally Arming ISIS"
[302] See the WPP, the "Fourth Level of Learning" and the "Fifth Level of Learning."

Chapter 10: AI: "I am Lucifer's Vessel"

A hint that may lead to an answer is what Dr. Peter David Beter (1921-1987) said decades ago. Dr. Beter was, amongst many other things, appointed by President John F. Kennedy as general counsel for the"*Export-Import Bank of the United States* in 1961, and he also represented international financial interests in Europe, South America, and the Middle East[303].

Later, Dr. Beter went on record saying that the Soviets, almost by accident, figured out how to create *Organic Robotoids.* These robotoids first walked amongst us a decade ago[304]. These robotoids eat, drink, and behave exactly the same as human beings, and they can get killed. The difference between the robotoids and humans is, according to Beter, that the robotoids need to be programmed to function. However, they are so extensively programmed that they supersede humans, and no one who does not know what he or she is looking for can detect such an imposter.

Dr. Beter also claimed that Jimmy Carter, David Rockefeller, and Henry Kissinger are dead and replaced with such *Organic Robotoids.*[305] Interestingly, the Pleiadians hinted at the same thing in one of their lectures, although they didn't mention anyone by name; they merely said that certain key people on the political stage are AI.[306]

---

[303] https://en.wikipedia.org/wiki/Peter_Beter#Biography
[304] "Organic Robotoids are Real," by Dr. Peter D. Beter (https://www.youtube.com/watch?v=luio8OXsuU4&ab_channel=BillAnaya)
[305] Ibid.
[306] Pleiadian lecture, fall season, 2015.

Chapter 11:
Robot Sex and Marrying Robots now Promoted in the Media

WHY A SEX ROBOT?

I N THE *WES PENRE PAPERS*—*The Multiverse Series* (WPP), I wrote that in the near future, people will take robots as lovers and spouses. I could see the writing on the wall, but I couldn't image that what I wrote would come into fruition so soon. The day I was writing about this was a year to a year and a half ago and is now already happening. In this chapter, I will prove to you what is going on. It's all over mainstream media, although it seems as if most people are still missing most of it.

An important part in this process is Google's recently approved patent[307] where you can download a robot's personality from a cloud. This way you can choose any personality you want for our robot friend, your robot lover, or your robot spouse. You will then be able to customize your robot so that it will respond the way that you want it to in more or less any given situation.

---

[307] *United States Patent no. 9,292,668, Sep. 1, 2011,* "Systems and methods for device authentication"

"The robot personality may also be modifiable within a base personality construct (i.e., a default-persona) to provide states or moods representing transitory conditions of happiness, fear, surprise, perplexion (e.g., the Woody Allen robot), thoughtfulness, derision (e.g., the Rodney Dangerfield robot), and so forth," states the patent.[308]

Also, if your robot would perish, you would still be able to save its personality and use it for the next robot, if we wish. I can imagine that when people get really used to these things, they would mourn the perished robot in a similar way we mourn a deceased friend or relative; this would hardly be a stretch.

This ability to download personalities for our robots is imperative for this and upcoming generations of AI robots. People who want robots as sex partners and spouses certainly need a customized personality for the robot.

Before we go deeper into this technological development, let us ask ourselves the question why people want robots as lovers and spouses. Can those really successfully substitute for a real human being?

If we asked this question ten years ago, the great majority would probably say no without hesitation. However, the world has changed rapidly in the last ten years. The smartphones have been literally dumped on the market, and nearly everyone in the developed world has one (now they are also dumped on the Third World, as we discussed earlier). Our biological bodies may still live in the Third Dimension (3-D), but our minds are becoming more and more stuck in virtual reality. Everything people think is of value happens on the smartphone. This is the "escape" people are taking from an otherwise harsh and stressful environment. The main reason why the Controllers want to stress people out, financially and in the work environment, is because they *want* us to escape into their electronic devices, which the same Controllers are happy to provide us with. They want us to focus on virtual reality environments, and once enough people get hooked (which has already happened), AI is incrementally introduced into these virtual reality devices (iPhone's *Siri* is of course one of those).

The more people disappear into the virtual world of smartphones, computers, and other electronic devices, the more disconnected from each

---

[308] *Wired.co.uk*, Apr. 1, 2015, "GOOGLE PATENTS CUSTOMISABLE ROBOT PERSONALITIES," op. cit.

other they will become; regardless of how many Facebook friends they have. Connections between human beings can only be done in 3-D or on a multidimensional level. This is very important to point out because although people "connect" in virtual reality, their 3-D bodies have their needs, and so do the mind and the soul. This is the entire reason why the sex robot market will boom! Instead of going through the hassle of dating somebody and keeping up a relationship, which requires constant work and sensitivity to each other's needs, people of today find it much easier to just download the exact personality he or she wants from a partner and thus doesn't have to deal with the parts of a human personality he or she does *not* want in the partner. Also, when the partner is not needed, the owner can turn the robot off and put it in a corner somewhere and continue texting on the smartphone; the "partner" will not take offense. Then, when the robot is needed again, it can be turned on and be told to clean the kitchen or have sex with the owner.

Of course, no one wants to have sex with a metallic robot, but that's not what this is about. What we are discussing here are robots that look *exactly* as human beings. We will be able to choose a sex robot that looks exactly as our perfect sex partner of choice. If we can't find exactly what we are looking for, we can preorder a customized lover from the factory. Can you see how attractive this will be for smartphone users who live a busy and stressful life at work and don't have the time or the energy to deal with a human partner? Can you see how this "partner" can save time for the owner, who doesn't need to clean the house or the apartment, who doesn't have to make the bed, and doesn't have to vacuum or do any of the chores that take so much time out of the day? Our "convenience button" will be pushed all the way by the manufacturers.

It doesn't matter how convenient this all sounds; it means the end of humanity as we know it. Electronic devices—and Wi-Fi in particular—make people sterile or much less fertile, which will decrease the birth rate considerably in the very near future (infertility is already a big issue—both in men and women). Moreover, fewer young people want children anyway; they have their careers to think of, which means a busy life, and then they have their escape—the smart devices. Where in all this does a normal family life fit in? There is hardly any room for it, and this is what people are beginning to realize. Putting children in daycare and letting a supervisor raise the kids is not a good idea; children need at least one of their parent at home—preferably the mother. By design, this is almost impossible today. After the Rockefeller Foundation efforts in the 1970s, the family unit has been destroyed; the project has succeeded, and it was all planned to happen this way; this was a plan that was meant to develop over time. The Singularity was already in progress in the 1960s-1970s.

Not only do the electronic devices destroy our physical bodies and our ability to think independently; they also have this other function of making us apathetic in our real relationships. All this had to be put in place by the Administrators before sex robots and sex spouses could become a demand. Unfortunately, this time has now come, and sex robots are selling out before they are even made. However, there are of course humans who are still dating, although this will change in the near future.

EXPERTS DEBATE: SHOULD WE HAVE SEX WITH ROBOTS?

ROXXXY IS THE FIRST TRUE sex robot, according to an article in *CNBC* in November 2015.[309] Made by a company called *True Companion,* the company is now rushing to get this robot out on the market as soon as possible.

---

[309] *CNBC, Nov. 4, 2015,* "Should you have sex with robots? Experts weigh in"

Fig. 11-1: Sex robot Roxxxy, the first of its kind.

The reader can probably predict how the "expert" panel discussion went. One of the experts suggested that intimacy with a robot should be encouraged.

> "We talk about the biggest killers in our society being things like heart disease. I actually wonder if one of the greatest killers of our age is loneliness. Now, machines can be a conduit towards not being so alone, towards getting some sort of emotional response, even if it's from a machine," Nell Watson, a futurist at the Singularity University in Silicon Valley, told the audience at Web Summit.
>
> [...]
>
> "I think machines can be a way to repair the hurt and trauma [from broken relationships] in ourselves," Watson said.[310]

We can't say that this came as a surprise; the Controllers want us to get away from family life and real intimacy, and the more humanlike the robot is, the more likely people are to buy them. The new goal of the Controllers is almost written on the wall, "One sex robot in every home!"

---

[310] Ibid. op. cit.

Another scientist said that robots could be a teacher for those who have problems communicating or being a part of society. What he and others fail to realize is that robots *create* disconnection from society, not integration. For a lonely person, the robot will become a best friend, and eventually, when society has come closer to the Singularity, these lonely people will turn to robots out there in society for comfort, rather than a human being. On the other hand, soon all psychotherapists will be AI anyway, so there will not be an issue; there will of course be "therapy robots," "psychiatry robots," and "counseling robots," programmed and self-educated to a point where they can always give the "right" answers.

Kathleen Richardson is a senior researcher in the field of ethics of robotics at the *U.K.'s De Montfort University*, and she believes that therapy with a robot can be helpful, but...,

> "If a robot was in a therapeutic context with somebody...then that might be helpful, but you've got to remember...people are saying you can have this as a substitute and in the future it might be a replacement, and that's when we get into very dangerous territory," Richardson said.[311]

SEX ROBOTS THAT LOOK AND ACT MORE AND MORE LIKE HUMANS

PERHAPS ROXXXY IS THE MOST human-looking sex robot at this time, but better products are on their way to hit the market.

The forerunner on this particular market, as well as many other AI markets, is Japan, which does not come as a surprise. The Japanese people are used to living in a technocratic society, and most of them demand quick technological progress.

A Japanese company has now developed what they call a very sexy female robot called *Actroid-F* that looks very human.[312] In fact, at an exhibition, *one of two people mistook her for a real human and thought she was very attractive.* However, some people were also afraid of her because she looked so human. Although I don't wish to propagate fear by any means, it still seems like the most logical reaction to something such as this. Hollywood, on the other hand, is sweating day and night to create movies

---

[311] Ibid. op. cit.
[312] *Mirror.co.uk, Nov. 4, 2015*, "Dozens of people mistake robot for real woman - and they think she's 'sexy'"

that will prepare us for the cyborgian and androidic future.

Fig. 11-2: Female "acdroid" on display. People are divided into two camps—either they think she is attractive or scary because she is so humanlike.

The following is an experiment that was done between Actroid-F and a human being. Scientists are currently testing the waters to see how well people can adapt to a near future where robots and humans will share the same sidewalks and malls.

> In the first experiment Actroid F and a person were seated next to each other - both wearing the same outfit - and a participant had five seconds to identify which one of the two was a real human.

> The next part involved two humans sitting side by side - and roughly half the participants said they could not confirm who the robot was, said Dr Silvera-Tawil.

> The investigation is not over and he said the next step is to study if a human being can get used to interacting with android geminoids in the long-term by reducing the fear and anxiety they produce.[313]

Oddly enough, the article doesn't tell us how many people confused the actroid with the human.[314]

It's understandable that the scientists are eager to let sex robots such as Actroid-F out on the market very quickly because they have pressure on them to keep the ball rolling. There is a time limit to everything that has to do with the integration with AI in society, and the goal is that by 2050, most of us will own a sex robot![315]

Roxxxy, which is planned to be widely available now in 2016, is a success already before it is released to the general public. There were, in December, 2015, 4,000 preorders of the robot, and as of 2015, they went for £635 each;[316] approximately $900 in 2016.

The sex robots, such as the ones below, are actually already produced today and may look quite human, but they are still like prototypes in comparison to what is going to come out on the market in just a few years.

Fig. 11-3: Sex robots.

Although there is meant to be a market for women, too, where you can buy male sex robots, the major market—at least in the beginning—will

---

[313] Ibid. op. cit.
[314] Dozens of people mistake robot for real woman - and they think she's 'sexy', https://www.mirror.co.uk/news/world-news/dozens-people-mistake-robot-real-6767503
[315] *Techrepublic.com*, Dec. 21, 2015, "The Campaign Against Sex Robots raises red flag for violence and victimization, calls for standards in sexbots"
[316] *The Guardian*, Dec. 13, 2015, "Sex, love and robots: is this the end of intimacy?"

be for men. I read somewhere that first the market will be up to 90% directed towards men and 10% towards women, although they expect that to change in women's favor. In other words, it's just an alteration of what has always been around—prostitution. You buy a sex robot instead of a prostitute on the street; it's just taken to a new extreme. The prostitute we are familiar with is at least human. It's still an exploitation of women and a disrespect of their sexual integrity, and in bigger terms, the Divine Feminine. The Universe is feminine in nature, and the AIF are the ultimate Patriarchs, who see themselves as being above all that's feminine. Thus, we have a male dominated society.

Fig. 11-4: Box fresh: a warm-to-the-touch RealDoll in the San Diego factory, ready for shipment to a client. The dolls cost from $5,000. Photograph: Jonathan Becker/Contour by Getty Images

The Controllers apparently have to move through some obstacles before they can row their boat to shore, in terms of sex robots. Not all nations embrace (sorry for the pun) sex robots as easily as Japan and the U.S. Malaysia recently created a ban against them.[317] In Sweden, attempts

---

[317] Campaign Against Sex Robots, Oct. 1, 2015, "Malaysian Authorities Cancel Sex and Love With Robots

are made in the same direction.[318] One argument is that people who have what we call *violent* and otherwise *perverted* sex thoughts, according to societal norms, but never have dared to tell others about them now will play them out in full on their sex robot.[319] In the end, how does that affect the person's relations to other people? Being able to amplify their dark sides on a daily basis, if so desired, is not the way to deal with it—it only makes these destructive sides stronger. The rationale is that for those people, sex robots can be an ignition to violent behavior against humans, too.

An article in *The Guardian* makes the same observation I have made (my emphasis),

> A recent study by Stanford University says people may experience feelings of intimacy towards technology because "our brains aren't necessarily hardwired for life in the 21st century". *Hence, perhaps, the speed at which relationships with robots are becoming a reality.*[320]

Here is what the CEO of the company, *RealDoll*, thinks about the sex robot industry, which he, more or less, is the leading force behind. He is revealing his own problems with relationships with other people, which most certainly has been a driving force for him to further develop the sex doll industry with his twisted logic:

> Today the RealDoll team, infamous now for its lifelike sex dolls (of which they claim to have sold more than 5,000), is extending its range to develop an artificial intelligence system capable both of following commands and talking back to its user. A Realbotix head (reports the *New York Times*) which can be attached to the existing RealDoll body will cost around $10,000, and will be available in 2017. In a piece entitled "Is This the Dawn of the Sexbots?", the company's owner David Mills explained the appeal of these warm-to-the-touch dolls, telling *Vanity Fair* he loves women but "doesn't really like to be around people".

> "Women have enjoyed sex toys for 50 years," he said (after introducing his first model, which arrived at his home in what looks like a customised coffin, head not yet attached), "but men are still stigmatised. We have to

---

Conference"
[318] *Campaign Against Sex Robots, Sep. 2015,* http://campaignagainstsexrobots.org/
[319] *Techrepublic.com, Dec. 21, 2015,* "The Campaign Against Sex Robots raises red flag for violence and victimization, calls for standards in sexbots"
[320] *The Guardian, Dec. 13, 2015,* "Sex, love and robots: is this the end of intimacy?"

correct that. I want to be the Rosa Parks of sex dolls. Men are not going to sit in the back of the bus anymore."[321]

The prices of these dolls will eventually go down, but it is astonishing that many people, who can afford it, are willing to pay a huge amount to be able to have sex with a soulless robot rather than a real emotional human partner. This is, in my opinion, separation to the extreme.

What many of the hardcore AI followers (at least on lower-level to mid-level) seem to have in common is that they have no belief in a life after death; they are atheist. *RealDolls'* David Mills is no exception. He wrote a book called *Atheist Universe*, which the renowned evolutionary biologist, Richard Dawkins,[322] thinks is an "admirable book."[323]

David Levy is a British international master of chess, but also a part of the AI movement.[324] He made the statement that we now have more or less accepted homosexuality in the Western World, and if we could do that, it will be no problem to accept sex with robots. Unfortunately, the comparison works.

Fig. 11-5: Dr. David Levy, founder of "Love and Sex with Robots."

---

[321] Ibid. op. cit.
[322] https://en.wikipedia.org/wiki/Richard_Dawkins
[323] *The Guardian*, Dec. 13, 2015, "Sex, love and robots: is this the end of intimacy?"
[324] Ibid.

Chapter 11: Robot Sex and Marriage now a Reality

David Levy is the founder of the research company, *Love and Sex with Robots*, which is developing sex robots, e.g. sex robots that can speak and have conversations with humans. I have always stated that everything in this field, and other fields of Minion interest, are compartmentalized. A certain person, such as a scientist, only knows what he's supposed to do, but is not told anything about the bigger picture. Levy is perhaps a top example, and he admits to it in an interview a reporter from *The Guardian*:

> Levy has very little time for jokes. Or, it turns out, for philosophy. "Are humans machines?" I ask him. He tells me he's learned not to try to answer philosophical questions.[325]

Does this mean that he is *told* not to answer such questions, or has he *learned* by experience not to reply to such? If it's the latter, he has decided to leave out philosophical question from his dangerous work, which is highly irresponsible at best. Or because he is more than likely taking orders from above, he might have concluded that he needs to suppress all nagging thoughts to secure his paycheck. This is, of course, even more irresponsible. In fact, it's highly irresponsible, regardless from which angle we look at it.

Next, the reporter asks Levy a very good question. She wants to know what happens if a man wants to have sex with a child and buys a robot for that purpose; is there an ethical solution for that?

Levy avoids the question at first and tries to distract the reporter by telling an interesting story about robots, but he is more or less forced to come back to the original question.

> He was reluctant to discuss this, pointing me to a keynote talk he did in Kathmandu called "When Robots do Wrong". Which was fascinating, but didn't answer my question. Eventually he responds, his email a sigh. "My own view is that robots will eventually be programmed with some psychoanalytical knowledge so they can attempt to treat paedophiles," he said. "Of course that won't work sometimes, but in those cases it would be better for the paedophiles to use robots as their sexual outlets than to use human children."[326]

First, people misunderstand what pedophilia is; when it happens in families, or by a lone male, it has to do with control and dominance more

---

[325] Ibid. op. cit.
[326] Ibid. op. cit.

than sex, and when it happens in Minion cults, it's about Black Magick and to feed the "gods" with pure sex energy. It rarely has to do just with being attracted to kids. Pedophiles might use a robot to take off the edge from their aggression, but they will still rape in the same manner as before. It's ridiculous to even suggest that a child sex robot would be able to educate the perpetrator about his wrong-doings.

The *attitude* of scientists such as Levy is disturbing when it comes to moral and ethics of the sex robot industry. Moreover, if you leave out philosophical questions from the equation, you get an emotionless killer robot in the end—I doubt it not! In terms of rapists and other sex offenders, robots will not change them in one way or the other, except that the sex offenders might get some new perverted ideas how to control their victims by first testing them on robots.

VIRTUAL REALITY SEX—A TASTE OF POSTHUMAN SEX LIFE

LET US NOW MOVE OVER TO the ultimate porn—*virtual reality sex*. What would you think if a video game producer came up with a game that is entirely based on virtual sex—*real* virtual sex? Do you think it would be a hit?

It would, and it *was* a hit because it is already produced and was temporarily put on the market. However, this male sex toy was later withdrawn from the market after the manufacturer had been swamped by demand from buyers who wanted it.[327]

It worked by strapping the user on a VR (Virtual Reality) helmet, and he could then have VR sex with simulated, beautiful women. He was simultaneously sexually stimulated in the 3-D world by a device that responded to the person's arousal.

The reason the producer, *VirtuaDolls*, stopped producing the game was because men were rushing in droves to order this game, and the manufacturer could not keep up the productions under such circumstances. Hence, they had to put the program on hold. Note that it was not because of moral issues the company decided to stop its production, but because the demand from customers to buy the product

---

[327] *The Mirror, Feb. 3, 2016,* "Makers of 'mindblowing' sex robot with virtual vagina swamped with orders"

was too high. Of course, that makes me suspicious if this was foremost a "test" by the Military to see exactly how well such a game would be received. Now they know, and sure enough, the company promises their customers that they will be back as soon as they can meet the demand![328]

Part of this game is played as follows:

> VirtuaDolls ships with a title called Girls of Arcadia (pictured below) in which gamers have to save a damsel in distress.
>
> If players can't be bothered rescuing the woman, they can just jump to "sim mode" in which they simply choose a woman and sex begins before the first date is even mooted, let alone completed.[329]

This means that the user doesn't even have to bother with playing the game; he can just put the game in "sim mode," and he can have cybersex as much as he wants with preferred damsel.[330]

Now, how does this work for the user? What happens when he gets aroused? The article in *Mirror* further states,

> In a promotional video backed by Beverly Hills Cop-style synth-pop music, the firm responsible for VirtuaDolls said it would "take adult gaming to the next level".
>
> It is designed to have "several innovative features which create a mindblowing experience".
>
> These include a "programmable pressure gripper", which can vary the tightness of its squeeze and a "stroke motion" with variable speed.
>
> It uses sensors to detect the power of a man's thrusts, which can then be used to control the onscreen action.
>
> The device can be used along with VR helmets including the Oculus Rift.[331]

---

[328] Ibid.
[329] Ibid. op. cit.
[330] Virtual Vagina Game. The user can have real cybersex with simulated women: "Makers of 'mindblowing' sex robot with virtual vagina swamped with orders," https://www.mirror.co.uk/news/technology-science/technology/virtual-reality-male-sex-toy-7299079
[331] Ibid. op. cit.

Fig. 11-6: A different version of sex robot Roxxxy before she is animated.

Exactly what do you think will happen when a great number of men have access to virtual reality of this kind? Do you think it will enhance relations between real men and women? Very soon, men will totally forget how to approach a woman, and they will fall deeper and deeper into the virtual reality abyss. When relieved, the man will then go to another virtual reality device, such as a smartphone or the successor of such device, and continue his virtual reality experiences by "connecting" with his friends on the phone; not to talk to them, but to either text them or using other near-future-produced apps and tools. This is what sex is supposed to be in the post Singularity world—it's all about virtual reality, which becomes *the* reality.

Chapter 12:
What Will Happen to our Jobs?

ROBOTS TAKING OVER THE JOB INDUSTRY

The most nagging question that we may have when we realize that more and more robots are taking over the job market is, what is going to happen with us humans? Then we may ask ourselves, are we all going to become unemployed in the end and all be considered "useless eaters," as Henry Kissinger called the Third World people? Is there going to be any food for us to eat at all if we don't earn any money by working? What will happen with housing? Will we all be homeless and have to live in tents and handmade cabins as they did in the 1800s?

These are all concerning questions, and I will do my best to answer them in this chapter by sharing my research on the subject and the conclusions I've made.

However, we first need to find out what plans the Controllers have in terms of the job market.

People, in general, have perhaps not started to reflect on how fast robots are taking over tasks on the job market, but soon enough they will see the inevitable trend. Robots are now getting cheaper and cheaper, and slowly but surely they start moving into our homes, hospitals, shopping malls, and restaurants on a more regular basis. People are beginning to complain that robots have been taking over their jobs; one example is *Amazon.com*, where robots now are entirely in control of loading orders on carts and driving them to the appropriate location in the warehouse. This huge investment will save the company many millions of dollars, but it also costs many workers their jobs. Other industries are quickly following in Amazon.com's robotic footsteps.

The Mirror.co.uk reports on *3D-printers*, implantable mobile phones, and clothes and reading glasses connected to the Internet as if it were science-fiction, but then adds that by 2025 this will be a reality.[332] The *Mirror.co.uk* is referring to a statement made by the World Economic Forum).[333] However, there is another disturbing revelation; the same forum reports that AI will be sitting as corporate Boards of Directors within a decade.

The Mirror.co.uk recognizes the problems with unemployment and states the following:

> The promise is cheaper goods and services, driving a new wave of economic growth. The threat is mass unemployment and a further breakdown of already strained trust between corporations and populations.

> "There is an economic surplus that is going to be created as a result of this fourth industrial revolution," Satya Nadella, chief executive of Microsoft, told the WEF's annual meeting in Davos on Wednesday.

> "The question is how evenly will it be spread between countries, between people in different economic strata and also different parts of the economy."[334]

---

[332] *Mirror.co.uk, Jan. 20, 2016,* "'Intelligent' robots could be running your company within 10 years, experts warn.
[333] http://www.mirror.co.uk/all-about/world-economic-forum"

They also realize how we are quickly moving towards the Singularity by adding,

> Robots are already on the march, moving from factories into homes, hospitals, shops, restaurants and even war zones, while advances in areas like artificial neural networks are starting to blur the barriers between man and machine.[335]

This is, of course, a very serious concern, and *Bloomberg.com* reports that over 5 million jobs will be gone by 2020.[336] This is based on a study that included 1.9 billion workers, which is about 65% of the global workforce. *Bloomberg.com* further addresses the issue:

> The blurred lines between physical, digital and biological spheres amount to a Fourth Industrial Revolution, according to the WEF [World Economic Forum], which will address the idea as the idea at its annual meeting of policy makers, academics and economists in Davos, Switzerland. It's already a hot topic thanks in part to books such as 'The Second Machine Age' and 'The Rise of The Robots,' while Bank of England Chief Economist Andy Haldane has warned that the millions of jobs at risk from automation are creating issues officials need to address.[337]

Apparently, women will lose most of the jobs because they are more poorly represented in fields such as mathematics, science, technology, and engineering than men are. In the beginning, administrative posts will have the worst mass unemployment, according to the same WEF survey.

Young people in today's Britain feel that the educational system is failing to prepare them for the new job market. In a survey, 77% of former students said that they had to get additional education to be able to do their jobs after they had left the universities.[338] In reality, the educational system has been disastrous for many decades already, but it is getting worse.

The huge problem is that we have become so industrialized that we can't imagine a life without having a job within a company, an industry,

---

[334] *Mirror.co.uk, Jan. 20, 2016*, "'Intelligent' robots could be running your company within 10 years, experts warn," op. cit.
[335] Ibid. op. cit.
[336] *Bloomberg.com, Jan. 18, 2016*, "Rise of the Robots Will Eliminate More Than 5 Million Jobs"
[337] Ibid. op. cit.
[338] *Mirror, co.uk, Jan. 19, 2016*, "Robots will replace more than 5 MILLION jobs by 2020 - and women will be hit the hardest"

or being self-employed, but usually still working in the midst of the job industry. When being laid-off and not having a chance to get a new job, many people will not know what to do with their time, and they will feel useless when not being able to contribute to the society. In 1977, Youngstown, Ohio, was a great example of this problem, after the steel mill, being the major employer in town, was shut down. When people no longer had jobs, criminality increased exponentially, and so did violence and spouse abuse. Alcoholism also became a big problem.

Most humans have forgotten how to be self-sufficient. Our society today does not encourage this, but actually makes it as hard as possible to choose that route. Being slave labor to an Elite that is getting richer and richer, while people in general are getting more and more worn down, is not a new phenomenon, it's been the fate of mankind for the past couple of hundred thousand years. We are often clueless how to break this pattern. The slave becomes dependent on and dedicated to his or her slave master for survival—or so the slave thinks.

According to *The Atlantic*, we may have to start rethinking our standard of living because only people in their prime-age (25 to 54 years old) may be offered full-time jobs, and the overall wages will decrease. Even in today's economic situation, one-sixth of people in their prime-age are *not* working; they are either unemployed or out of the workforce altogether. According to *The Atlantic*, under a sound economic system, almost all of these prime-agers would be working.[339]

As it is now, wages are at the lowest (compared to relative inflation) since statistics on this matter were initiated in the mid-twentieth century;[340] and wages keep souring in the same manner. Although *The Atlantic* reports that there is not going to be a mass unemployment within the next decade, I think there is a great chance there will be, taking the current acceleration of technology into consideration. The Industry is not slacking on this subject; they can't robotize the market fast enough. However, they still would need some kind of balance because there's interdependence between human workers and the Industry. They pay us so we can use the money to put back into society by the usual commerce, which will benefit

---

[339] *The Atlantic, Jul-Aug 2015,* "A World Without Work"
[340] Ibid.

the same companies that paid us our wages in the first place. If too many people are unemployed, it also negatively affects the Industry. Alternatively, a new system of exchange could be implemented.

The Atlantic is revisiting an event that happen in the 1950s, related to Henry Ford II, the CEO of Ford. This event has become a classic. It is highly relevant to our current discussion, so I'd like to include it here:

> In the 1950s, Henry Ford II, the CEO of Ford, and Walter Reuther, the head of the United Auto Workers union, were touring a new engine plant in Cleveland. Ford gestured to a fleet of machines and said, "Walter, how are you going to get these robots to pay union dues?" The union boss famously replied: "Henry, how are you going to get them to buy your cars?"[341]

We all might think that there are quite a few jobs that cannot be robotized because they require human emotions and compassion to be able to serve their customers. We may need to seriously reconsider this idea, and here is an example from *The Atlantic*, telling us why we should:

> In 2013, Oxford University researchers forecast that machines might be able to perform half of all U.S. jobs in the next two decades. The projection was audacious, but in at least a few cases, it probably didn't go far enough. For example, the authors named psychologist as one of the occupations least likely to be "computerisable." But some research suggests that people are more honest in therapy sessions when they believe they are confessing their troubles to a computer, because a machine can't pass moral judgment. Google and WebMD already may be answering questions once reserved for one's therapist. This doesn't prove that psychologists are going the way of the textile worker. Rather, it shows how easily computers can encroach on areas previously considered "for humans only."[342]

The statistics show, according to *The Atlantic* and its sources, that the majority of unemployed people, who have much more time at their convenience, do not socialize more, but less. Instead of socializing, most spend an average of 50 hours a week watching TV, and the rest of their time they spend eating and sleeping. The study implies that people who don't have jobs feel inferior and don't feel they want to take part in the community; of course there are exceptions.

---

[341] Ibid. op. cit.
[342] Ibid. op cit.

A professor from the *Stanford University* recently suggested that in the very near future, people who are unemployed will spend more and more time in virtual reality games that will give them more pleasure and satisfaction than engaging in the "real" world: the professor does not see this as something negative but as something imaginative and creative.[343] Of course, in itself, this is very alarming, and based on what we now know, we can see why unemployment may be necessary for the Singularity to be achieved; it's an introduction to virtual reality games for people who otherwise might not engage in such a thing.

A FEW IDEAS HOW TO SOLVE MASS UNEMPLOYMENT

WE CAN SEE HOW ONE TYPE of job after another no longer requires a human workforce; one of these being factory workers. We no longer need people to create products or run machines; these days, 3D printers are becoming more and more the standard. These printers can 3-D print products almost instantaneously, and such printers can easily be overseen by robots. This will wipe out an entire workforce world-wide, all across the Industrialized World.

In order to find answers to what is going to happen when the machines take over our jobs, many researchers and different kinds of media have turned to Youngstown to study what has happened there since the steel mill shut down in September 1977, almost forty years ago. Albeit people are still struggling to make ends meet in Youngstown, it's not become a ghost town by any means. People still live there and obviously survive somehow. Many want to know how they do it.

One town member explains:

> "It is the end of a particular kind of wage work," said Hannah Woodroofe, a bartender there who, it turns out, is also a graduate student at the University of Chicago. (She's writing a dissertation on Youngstown as a harbinger of the future of work.) A lot of people in the city make ends meet via "post-wage arrangements," she said, working for tenancy or under the table, or trading services. Places like Royal Oaks are the new union halls: People go there not only to relax but also to find tradespeople for particular jobs, like auto repair. Others go to exchange fresh vegetables,

---

[343] Ibid.

grown in urban gardens they've created amid Youngstown's vacant lots.[344]

If this will be the trend and eventually the norm, it's quite obvious that we need to go back to bartering, and in case this is the way to survive in the future, it's a good idea to practice skills that include something you can barter with. It can't be emphasized enough that hardship is the mother of invention. History shows that people are actually much more creative under threats to their survival than they are when a job, food on the table, and a place to live are taken for granted. One idea is to work on a local level, community by community, as they do in Youngstown, by using a certain center where people could meet to socialize and *teach each other new skills—not via computers and electronic devices, but in face-to-face interactions.* Townspeople could communicate what they are able to teach others, and those who would be looking for skills to learn could go to a person who could teach them these skills. People could then go out and practice their particular skill, and when feeling confident, perhaps teach it to someone else. Hopefully, there would then be a variety of skills in the community to barter with.

Bartering is always a way to go, but let's investigate a little further to find out what the Controllers are actually planning for us. Bartering does seem to be something that would benefit the super-rich.

The Governor of the *Bank of Japan* has suggested a similar solution to what I was suggesting above, i.e. having a center where people can meet. He suggests that the local governments invest in such a center, where people can learn skills from each other—not to barter, but to be able to open up new small businesses and become a productive part of society again. The question is if it would work, however. Over the last 50 years, small businesses have become less and less profitable, which mainly is because the larger industries are taking over the market making it nearly impossible for small businesses to compete and survive. Moreover, if a small business does manage to become successful, it is usually bought up by the large corporations and this way, they are taking over an even bigger piece of the overall market. Eventually, the rest of the small businesses succumb.

However, this is what the Governor of the *Bank of Japan* has to say:

---

[344] Ibid. op. cit.

One way to nurture fledgling ideas would be to build out a network of business incubators. Here Youngstown offers an unexpected model: its business incubator has been recognized internationally, and its success has brought new hope to West Federal Street, the city's main drag.[345]

The fact that mass employment will be an issue is not something that concerns those in power; it's only crying for temporary solutions at this point. It's all about keeping the show on the road until the Singularity is here. After that, human thinking capacity will be at its peak, and according to the Singularity gurus, we will be a billion times more intelligent. Then, who cares about small problems, such as unemployment? It will be a non-issue. However, the mass unemployment that might hit us before 2045 will be a stress factor necessary for the Controllers to be able to usher in the Singularity. Again, we have the formula, *problem-reaction-solution*, being used on us. I am sure you can easily figure out how this formula applies to the above situation; mass unemployment is the *problem*, people will *react* and demand that something must be done about it, and the *solution* to the problem that the Controllers created in the first place will be the Singularity.

Oxford researchers predict that in two decades from now, will robots have taken over fifty percent of the U.S. workforce.[346] One idea is— and it's not a new one—to have the Government provide paychecks to the unemployed, calling it *Universal Basic Income*. Even President Nixon supported such an idea during mass unemployment. The money would come from heavily taxing the rich and then giving these taxes to the people as basic income.

The most dominant suggestion is, however, that people come together and have local or federal government pay for a place to meet and exchange skills, as we discussed earlier, but also to discover and develop latent skills in people. A good example is to bring certain people's artistic side to the surface; a side that they never had the chance to develop while being part of their stressful former work environment. Now they might be able to develop these skills. Musicians could come together to compose, play, and build groups, which later could play for an audience. Others

---

[345] Ibid. op. cit.
[346] Ibid.

might be visual artists or painters. Whatever the hidden skills of a person are, in the post-work society, he or she might have a chance to openly develop them and be encouraged by others to do so. Some people might also be employed by richer people to help out with childcare and taking care of facilities, *The Atlantic* article suggests. However, I would suggest that the latter kind of jobs might already be occupied by robots.

In summary, scientists and governments can see the writing on the wall when it comes to the wave of mass unemployment that is most likely to hit us, and some of them are trying to come up with solutions. The most discussed solution is based on the following steps:

6) Instead of having people (men in particular, studies show) sitting before the computer or the television all day long when they are unemployed, they join together in one or a few locations where they can share ideas, teach each other new skills, and develop their own, sometimes hidden skills and start using them for the benefit of one's self and others.

7) The local government builds a local facility where people can gather to accomplish 1) above.

8) Some of these people may come up with ideas how to open their own small businesses or otherwise, using their skills to get at least a smaller income. If people's ideas seem reasonable, the government may invest in these ideas, and hopefully these ideas will lead to more jobs in the near future.

9) The local government or the federal government will collect more taxes from the rich and let the unemployed have a basic paycheck coming in every month. This will be called *Universal Basic Income*. However, just so people don't get a paycheck without feeling that they have not contributed in any way in order to receive it, the idea is that it's better to have people do something rather than nothing, and everybody needs to do something to contribute to the community in order to get their pay check, even if it would be pulling up weeds in public parks.

Under circumstances that we have very little impact on, these ideas sound reasonable, but I would definitely add two more things to this list. These things have been implied above, but I think there are some additional ideas that need to be added to the following solutions:

10) Bartering. This requires skills, and it will be hard to get a new school education under these dire circumstances. Instead, people can educate themselves by learning from others in a face-to-face learning module. With a small government check coming in, people can use bartering to assist each other. Initially, bartering will typically not satisfy a person's basic needs, and therefore the government check will come in handy. If some form of work is required in order to receive a check, exchanging of services with each other (bartering) could suffice to fulfill the government's requirement in order to receive a check. After all, it's a matter of keeping people busy enough so they don't fall into deep depressions or start using drugs, which leads to crime.

11) Learn how to plant your own garden if you own your house or rent it. You can also rent a small lot (if affordable) somewhere close by and plant fruits, roots, and vegetables there, or share a lot with someone else to make it more affordable. Then learn how to effectively grow your own food. Once you have that going, the money you spend on food in the store will be a minimum, if anything at all; it depends on how successful you are as a gardener. If you can plant more than you eat, you might be able to barter the rest.

I think topics numbers 5 and 6 above will become common solutions in the near future, if worse comes to worse, and it's strongly advisable to start learning some skills now; particularly if you're a young to middle-aged person. Even if you are older and expect to live another decade or two, I believe it is good advice. *Monsanto* might have one or two things to say about growing our own gardens, but this company is in decline already. In this sense, people are getting smarter.

If we wish to look at this from a positive perspective, it might very well be an excellent way for the more spiritually inclined to create a break-away community, where likeminded souls come together and teach each other how to survive without the cities and government controlling them. This is another reason to learn skills and to know how to grow food. It's time to ask yourself, how can I be valuable to others? What do I have, or what can I do, to contribute to this break-away community? Am I good at gardening, nursing, the arts, preparing food, repairing things? We need to be thinking in those terms to be prepared.

Also, it may be time to teach ourselves some "old school" healing techniques. How do we cure illnesses with herbs and plants? There are those who will object to this and say that they have already tried natural and alternative ways to cure their illness, or at least in an attempt to make it more tolerable, but they have failed. Instead, they have gone back to their doctors and asked for traditional medicine to suppress their symptoms.

The reason herbs and plants don't always work is because we know too little about the Living Library. *The cures to any disease are in the Living Library—that's how it's set up!* We just need to study and research it. We can begin by studying what the witches of the Dark Age knew about the Library, and we will find out that they knew a great deal; that's why they were burned at the stake by the Catholic Church.

It's advisable to go even further back in time to find out what the old shamans (especially the female shamans in ancient times) did to cure people's illnesses and injuries. These are good examples of what we can do. In addition, the real healing comes from within, and people who understand this can help others heal by having the sick understand what it was that *really* made him or her sick. We make ourselves sick with our own thoughts and emotions, and these thoughts and emotions often come about because of some trauma in the near or distant past. It can be a small or big trauma, but it's still a trauma. Finding the reason for why a person became sick can do miracles. This is something that needs to be practiced as well in any community that intends to house happy and healthy individuals.

I have often talked about how we must start creating in our own *local universe* and our *inner universe* to get the future we want. I can't stress this enough; *this is tremendously important!* However, we still need to develop ways to survive, and how to survive well. This can only be done hands on. Hence, the importance of developing skills is highly applicable to anybody, anywhere. It is crucial that we teach our children skills when they are little. We need to teach them how to grow food, help in the kitchen, and clean the house, etc. moreover, it's crucial to carefully observe our children and discover what their talents are. Then we must help them develop these talents. Children are most likely to succeed in life if they have developed skills that they truly enjoy. In adulthood, these children will put much more heart and effort into their job than those who are more or less forced into a certain trade. We also need to gradually teach our children about how the world really works, and we need to tell them the real history as we know it. It's from learning our history that we learn how to live our lives in the present, so we don't make the same mistakes over and over in the future.

When everything breaks down, avoid government schools if you are planning on joining a breakaway community, or have already joined one by then. Educate the children locally by using compassionate, spiritual teachers with *real* knowledge. Meet in the community to decide what needs to be taught in school and skip the rest. We don't want to copy-cat the current public school. Teach the children how to be compassionate, peaceful, and loving towards self and others. Never tolerate any signs of violence or verbal abuse; handle it in its cradle, but not by punishing the kids. Instead, educate them and teach them *why* it is not okay to be mean, inconsiderate, or abusive in any way toward self and others; teach them to develop self-worth and self-confidence, and encourage their good sides and reward and acknowledge those traits. Many of us have probably heard the Cherokee Indian story about the two wolves, but I think it's appropriate to repeat it here:

Chapter 12: What Will Happen to our Jobs?

Fig 12-1: The Indian Legend about the two wolves

An old Cherokee is teaching his grandson about life. "A fight is going on inside me," he said to the boy.

"It is a terrible fight and it is between two wolves. One is evil – he is anger, envy, sorrow, regret, greed, arrogance, self-pity, guilt, resentment, inferiority, lies, false pride, superiority, and ego." He continued, "The other is good – he is joy, peace, love, hope, serenity, humility, kindness, benevolence, empathy, generosity, truth, compassion, and faith. The same fight is going on inside you – and inside every other person, too."

The grandson thought about it for a minute and then asked his grandfather, "Which wolf will win?"

The old Cherokee simply replied, "The one you feed."

The bottom line is that there will be a time, and it's almost here, when jobs will be sparse because they have been taken over by machines that can work around the clock for no other cost than repairs, which is something the robots eventually will be able to do themselves, as long as the companies provide them with body parts and electricity. This situation is creeping up on us gradually, but one day many people will find themselves without jobs in a job market that doesn't need their services and skills anymore. We can't stick our heads in the sand because the time will soon come. Therefore, it is imperative that we know how to proceed at that point and not become the victims of circumstances.

Chapter 13:
Genetic Laboratories—Atlantis Revisited

THE FALL OF THE OLD ATLANTIS—WHAT HAPPENED?

ACCORDING TO THE PLEIADIANS, Gaia is a genetic laboratory. Hence, they say, genetic engineering and genetic manipulation have always been a part of the planet's history and still is to this day. They add that Gaia is a Living Library, and therefore, it's justified for star races to experiment with genetics on this planet.

If this is true, and the *Goddess Gaia* was a genetic laboratory already when the Queen's Experiment started, is today's genetic manipulation also justified, and are the Overlords, in collaboration with human scientists, totally free to do whatever they want in their underground laboratories? Moreover, who says that it's a genetic laboratory for *anyone* to experiment with?

This was not the way it was meant to be when the Queen set up the Experiment eons ago. Gaia is property of the royal court of Orion, if anything, and we humans were meant to live here freely, to explore, to learn in, and to enjoy this beautiful planet, which was even more beautiful before it was invaded. Lucifer and his rebellious team, on the other hand, never had permission to manipulate the Queen's creation—this planet was taken from Her by force.

The old Kingdom of Atlantis could be said to have been setup shortly after the AIF won the *War of the Titans*, approximately 425,000 years ago, and it perished in the Deluge. Although there were huge landmasses that sank in what is now the Atlantic Ocean, these landmasses were only small parts of Atlantis. Atlantis was En.ki's Kingdom on Earth, and it included the entire planet, not just one gigantic continent, or a few smaller islands in the Atlantic. Hence, the Kingdom of Atlantis was

Planet Earth from the time the Alien Invader Force arrived and up until the Great Flood. During the Atlantean Era, En.ki, as Poseidon/Neptune, and his scientists, engaged in genetic tinkering in the most bizarre manner. Sometimes they created beings that they used for sexual pleasure, other times they created strange beings just for fun, and when they got tired of them, they just left them alone in the midst of the Living Library. In other cases, they created ruling races, such as enormous giants that ruled over mankind when the AIF were absent. Smaller giants were created for warfare, and other creatures were made for slave labor and transportation (such as centaurs).

Eventually, when a Flood was imminent and the Orion Empire became aware of this, the Orion Council saw an opportunity to intervene in an experiment that had gone terribly wrong. They forbade En.ki to interfere and save the lives of Gaia's creatures that he had created—Homo sapiens included. At that time, the Living Library was so distorted with all these erratic beings running around, killing and eating each other, practicing cannibalism, and destroying everything that was of value that the Orion Council had had enough. Therefore, they deemed it best to let nature have its way and let the souls who had been trapped here on Earth by En.ki return to Orion. The Orions told En.ki to let the Deluge wipe things out and allow his creations to perish. The Experiment the Queen had instigated would then be finished in all dimensions.

In a situation such as this, En.ki had little choice but to abide because he could not in this situation use Free Will as an excuse to interfere with a natural disaster. Therefore, En.ki abided—or so it seemed! As the creator of the beings in the Third Dimension, he had DNA samples saved of these species in laboratories on Mars, and perhaps elsewhere, which is logical. Nevertheless, En.ki left the planet just before the disaster hit (possibly cloaking himself in order not to be captured and brought to justice).

The metaphor for this is of course the story we read in the Bible about Noah and his Ark (based on an older Sumerian script), which was not a ship that sailed the oceans of the world, but a spaceship that sailed the oceans of space.

When the Flood subsided, many parts of the world were barren and void of sentient life. Although the Deluge did not cover the entire planet, contrary to what the Bible tells us, there were also earthquakes, tsunamis, and volcanic eruptions, creating a poisonous atmosphere. These phenomena, put together, wiped out most of the remaining life on the planet, which is called the Younger Dryas by modern science-[347]-. It was a huge catastrophe, and it has been suggested by many that the reason for the catastrophe was the passing of Nibiru.

En.ki was not willing to give up Gaia, however. He slightly changed the frequency range of the solar system, which made it difficult to locate for those who didn't know exactly in which frequency band it now was hidden in and concealed from the rest of creation—at least for some time.

Probably before the Flood had even entirely subsided, En.ki was back on Gaia and started reseeding Her. He also found that a small fraction of Homo sapiens and other creatures had survived. Again, he managed to manipulate the survivors, most likely blaming the catastrophe on the Orions, who he claimed were the enemies of humankind, and that he, En.ki, was the creator of Homo sapiens and now also their savior. Because of the major trauma that must have resulted in the survivors, and because of the change of planetary frequency, there is a good chance that the human survivors did not remember much from the time before the catastrophe. Thus, En.ki could probably just fill in the gap with whatever information suited him at the moment.

This is more or less the story that En.ki maintained from thereon. With the human Deluge survivors backing En.ki up, Orion's hands were once again tied by mankind's decision to support En.ki/Lucifer. Much of this story is retold in the old Sumerian texts.

Unfortunately, the majority of the soul splinters whose bodies perished in the Deluge never returned to Orion. Most of them became victims of the frequency change as well, and were most likely, just as their surviving brothers and sisters on Earth, told that the Orion Empire was behind the disaster, and that the Empire now wanted to harvest the human soul group for ill purposes. Being already manipulated for such a long time, the human soul group was probably not too difficult to convince. Those who stayed with En.ki and the rest of the Overlords were again recycled when new human bodies were seeded and developed.

The Deluge was the beginning of the end of Homo sapiens. Soon

---

[147] https://en.wikipedia.org/wiki/Younger_Dryas_impact_hypothesis)

En.ki would create a slightly enhanced species of humans who could function better in the *New Atlantis* that he now was planning. After the Flood, Homo sapiens sapiens was genetically manipulated into being.[348]

THE RISE OF THE MACHINE KINGDOM—THE NEW ATLANTIS

E nki's dream of a New Atlantis secretly came into fruition in 1776 with the assistance from the *Scottish Rite of Freemasonry* and the *Rosicrucian Order*. When the United States of America was formed, and the *Declaration of Independence* was signed, the New Atlantis was established.

It's only been 240 years since this new experiment started, but we are already in the midst of an extensive genetic manipulation spree that will soon be the end of Homo sapiens sapiens. A new race of cyborgs will take her place and inhabit the Living Library as One, run from a super-brain computer. This was the true purpose of the New Atlantis from the beginning. Homo sapiens sapiens—*the thinking man*—was just a temporary species, who En.ki used to accomplish his goal to create the New Atlantis.

The general population is not aware of this, but huge funds from a *Black Budget* are being funneled into genetic research. DNA testing has been done for a long time, and human behavior has been carefully studied on the Internet via smart devices and TV sets, etc. There is also a website called *Ancestry.com*, where you can research your genetic lineage several centuries back and make your own ancestry diagram. This is not only for our own amusement, but we help the Controllers and the Overlords in their research to discover who is who, and who belongs to which bloodline. Thus, you can see advertisements on the Internet for *Ancestry.com* when you browse the Internet—it's suddenly showing up everywhere. People are tremendously interested in this, and the number of people who use it is rapidly increasing. Many people are curious to see whether they have any famous ancestors that they can be proud of or in awe over. At the moment, smartphones and *Ancestry.com* are probably the tools to use for those who *really* want to help the Minions in their own research that will lead to humanity's extinction. Both smartphones and *Ancestry.com* are addictive and obsessive.

---

[348] See WPP, the Fourth Level of Learning, for more info.

Before we dig into present time genetic manipulation, I want to bring up ancient genetic manipulation for just a moment. If there are still readers who may doubt that genetic tinkering happened in our very distant past, recent research may convince you. Other researchers and I have often discussed how the AIF deactivated 95-96% or more of our DNA in the ancient past. This made the original, highly multidimensional human species extremely dumbed down. Scientist of today can do the same thing!

The *Associated Press* (AP) recently ran an article titled, *Microbe with Stripped-Down DNA may Hint at Secrets of Life*.[349] It begins with this eye-opening revelation:

> Scientists have deleted nearly half the genes of a microbe, creating a stripped-down version that still functions, an achievement that might reveal secrets of how life works.[350]

This is quite stunning information, which clearly has very ancient connections. It becomes even more stunning:

> The genome is not some one-and-only minimal set of genes needed for life itself. For one thing, if the researchers had pared DNA from a different bacterium they would probably have ended up with a different set of genes. For another, the minimum genome an organism needs depends on the environment in which it lives.
>
> And the new genome includes genes that are not absolutely essential to life, because they help the bacterial populations grow fast enough to be practical for lab work.
>
> The genome is "as small as we can get it and still have an organism that is ... useful," Hutchison said.
>
> One goal of such work is to understand what each gene in a living cell does, which would lead to a deep understanding of how cells work, he said. With the new bacterium, "we're closer to that than we are for any other cell," he said. [351]

Reading this is almost like flying back in time. En.ki and his

---

[349] *Associated Press, Mar 24, 2016*, "Microbe with Stripped –Down DNA may Hint at Secrets of Life"
[350] Ibid. op. cit.
[351] Ibid. op. cit.

scientists must have thought in this same pattern 200,000 years ago; they only developed the new species to a point where they became "practical," just as this article reads. Human scientists are now rediscovering the procedure of genetic manipulation used when En.ki created the first Homo sapiens. Of course, this technology does not come from brilliant human scientists; it has extraterrestrial origins.

Much of the current AI research is still Top Secret, but to prepare humankind for what is coming, some of it has been declassified and handed over to the mainstream media. The same thing applies to genetic tinkering; although, people who haven't studied ancient history and mythology can't make a connection and will not reflect on it very much until it's too late. This is again why I have always stressed that learning our history is essential for our survival.

EXISTING TECHNOLOGY FOR POSTHUMAN SPACE-TRAVEL

HOW FAR WILL THE GENETIC engineering go and what can AI really do when very advanced? An example of what is now possible was revealed by rocket scientist, David Adair.[352] He is the scientist who reportedly built the fastest rocket on Earth, powered by the first electromagnetic fusion containment engine.[353] The following excerpt is from Robert Stanley's free e-book, *Close Encounters on Capitol Hill*, where, during an in-depth interview, Adair revealed that,

> "When I flew my second prototype, it landed in one of the world's most top secret Air Force bases in history, Area 51. [In 1971] My life changed forever when they took me underground and showed me that alien engine; the damn thing was still alive! *It was a symbiotic engine; an intelligent machine that could interface with biological entities, humans or alien.* It worked very similar to the Soviet heads up technology featured in the movie FIREFOX."[354]

Stanley continues by stating that the *Advanced Telecommunications Research Institute* and the *Honda Research Institute* announced already in 2006 that they had developed a *brain machine interface*, enabling "the decoding of natural brain activity for the near real-time operation of a

---

[352] https://www.youtube.com/results?search_query=david+adair
[353] *Robert Stanley*, "Close Encounters on Capitol Hill," p. 110.
[354] Ibid. op. cit.

robot without having to implant sensors in the head and brain. The technology breakthrough offered amazing possibilities for the control of machines by brain waves alone."[355]

I find the following paragraph in Stanley's book most interesting:

> Adair explained that the alien brain/machine interface he saw in the early 1970s allowed the pilot and the engine's artificial intelligence to become symbiotic. He believed it was a perfect way to travel through space – the space craft and the pilot were essentially one.[356]

As the reader can see, it's not only me; my conclusions are backed up by a rocket scientist as well, *and this was in the early 1970s!* Adair destroyed his project after this, when he realized that his discoveries, in his own field of research, were going to be used for weaponry.

Fig. 13-1: Rocket scientist, David Adair.

There we have it. By reverse engineering what they already have in their possession from a number of ET spaceship crashes, scientists can build spaceships capable of travelling through 3-D space, perhaps using wormholes and *Einstein-Rosen Bridges* to travel from one location in space to another. Add to this a Posthuman cyborg, looking identical to the

---

[355] Stanley, p. 111, op. cit.
[356] Ibid. op.cit.

Grays, and you have Posthumans conquering space, just as Kurzweil predicted. However, it seems as if his "prediction" preceded him; the technology to accomplish this was available already in the 1970s!

In addition, has it ever occurred to anybody why there have been so many UFO crashes over the years? Are these beings really so clumsy that they let the human military, with their relatively primitive weaponry, shoot down their craft, one after the other? Also, are they so bad at navigating through the Earth's atmosphere that they lose control over their vehicles and crash-land?

Of course not! These craft crashed on purpose in order for the military and their scientists to be able to reverse engineer these UFOs. The same thing applies to the *dead aliens*, aka the Grays, who we are told were found dead (and sometimes alive) on these craft. The dead bodies have been carefully examined and they have of course shown to be cyborgs, run by AI. Again, these cyborgs can travel in space; thus, these cyborgs can be reverse engineered, as well, and cloned for future use as "space suits." This is all AIF technology, but they need humans to develop it on their own in order to save their own skin. I wrote about this in the WPP, too.

GENETIC ENGINEERING—FROM THE HORSE'S MOUTH

D R. RAY KURZWEIL WRITES in his book, *The Singularity is Near*, that the human genome is a sequential binary code, containing only about 800 million bits of information.[357] Then he adds that when the scientists remove all the redundancies, we are left with only 30 to 100 million bits, which is equivalent to an average software program. What Dr. Kurzweil tells us is that the Controllers are apparently not going to let us have our full brain capacity after all. This becomes obvious because there are no such things as "redundancies." If he means that the 95% of the brain we are not using today are "redundancies," Posthumans are not going to be wiser than their combined knowledge at the time of the Singularity. If he implies that "redundancies" means taking away *even more* of the human genome, then we are not even going to have that much. Either way, Posthumans are still going to be quite

---

[357] Kurzweil, "The Singularity is Near," p. 168.

limited in their capacity; albeit billions of times wiser than today, by Kurzweil's measures. Then, of course, Posthumans will still be limited to experiencing the 4% Universe hologram—100% of 4% is still 4%.

Dr. Kurzweil then explains how the human genome is working:

> This [genetic] code is supported by a set of biochemical machines that translate these linear (one-dimensional) sequences of DNA "letters" into strings of simple building blocks called amino acids, which are in turn folded into three-dimensional proteins, which make up all living creatures from bacteria to humans. (Viruses occupy a niche in between living and nonliving matter but are also composed of fragments of DNA or RNA.) This machinery is essentially a self-replicating nanoscale replicator that builds the elaborate hierarchy of structures and increasingly complex systems that a living creature comprises.[358]

With the risk of boring you, I also want to cite the direct continuation of the above quote; a section which describes what DNA and RNA are, how they are set up, and how they work. This, in itself, is educational and something each truth-seeker must learn anyway, but that's only part of the reason why I want to include it here. Be alert to Dr. Kurzweil's comparison between DNA/RNA and existing technology, such as tape recorders, etc. You, the reader, may ask yourself; how come that technology, in certain terms, replicates our DNA/RNA? Could it possibly be that those who understand our genome, because they created it, gave us the technology—even such technology as early tape recorders, etc.?

Life's Computer

> In the very early stages of evolution information was encoded in the structures of increasingly complex organic molecules based on carbon. After billions of years biology evolved its own computer for storing and manipulating digital data based on the DNA molecule. The chemical structure of the DNA molecule was first described by J. D. Watson and F. H. C. Crick in 1953 as a double helix consisting of a pair of strands of polynucleotides.6 We finished transcribing the genetic code at the beginning of this century. We are now beginning to understand the detailed chemistry of the communication and control processes by which DNA commands reproduction through such other complex molecules and

---

[358] Kurzweil, p. 168, op. cit.

cellular structures as messenger RNA (mRNA), transfer RNA (tRNA), and ribosomes.

At the level of information storage the mechanism is surprisingly simple. Supported by a twisting sugarphosphate backbone, the DNA molecule contains up to several million rungs, each of which is coded with one letter drawn from a four-letter alphabet; each rung is thus coding two bits of data in a one-dimensional digital code. The alphabet consists of the four base pairs: adenine-thymine, thymine-adenine, cytosineguanine, and guanine-cytosine.

Special enzymes can copy the information on each rung by splitting each base pair and assembling two identical DNA molecules by rematching the broken base pairs. Other enzymes actually check the validity of the copy by checking the integrity of the base-pair matching. With these copying and validation steps, this chemical data-processing system makes only about one error in ten billion base-pair combinations.7 Further redundancy and error-correction codes are built into the digital data itself, so meaningful mutations resulting from base-pair replication errors are rare. Most of the errors resulting from the one-in-ten-billion error rate will result in the equivalent of a "parity" error, which can be detected and corrected by other levels of the system, including matching against the corresponding chromosome, which can prevent the incorrect bit from causing any significant damage.8 Recent research has shown that the genetic mechanism detects such errors in transcription of the male Y chromosome by matching each Y chromosome gene against a copy on the same chromosome.9 Once in a long while a transcription error will result in a beneficial change that evolution will come to favor.

In a process technically called translation, another series of chemicals put this elaborate digital program into action by building proteins. It is the protein chains that give each cell its structure, behavior, and intelligence. Special enzymes unwind a region of DNA for building a particular protein. A strand of mRNA is created by copying the exposed sequence of bases. The mRNA essentially has a copy of a portion of the DNA letter sequence. The mRNA travels out of the nucleus and into the cell body. The mRNA code is then read by a ribosome molecule, which represents the central molecular player in the drama of biological reproduction. One portion of the ribosome acts like a tape-recorder head, "reading" the sequence of data encoded in the mRNA base sequence. The "letters" (bases) are grouped into words of three letters called codons, with one codon for each of the twenty possible amino acids, the basic building blocks of protein. A ribosome reads the codons from the mRNA and then, using tRNA, assembles a protein chain one amino acid at a time.

The notable final step in this process is the folding of the one-dimensional chain of amino acid "beads" into a three-dimensional protein. Simulating this process has not yet been feasible because of the enormous complexity of the interacting forces from all the atoms involved. Supercomputers scheduled to come online around the time of the publication of this book (2005) are expected to have the computational capacity to simulate protein folding, as well as the interaction of one three-dimensional protein with another.

Protein folding, along with cell division, is one of nature's remarkable and intricate dances in the creation and re-creation of life. Specialized "chaperone" molecules protect and guide the amine-acid strands as they assume their precise three-dimensional protein configurations. As many as one third of formed protein molecules are folded improperly. These disfigured proteins must immediately be destroyed or they will rapidly accumulate, disrupting cellular functions on many levels.

Under normal circumstances, as soon as a misfolded protein is formed, it is tagged by a carrier molecule, ubiquitin, and escorted to a specialized proteosome, where it is broken back down into its component amino acids for recycling into new (correctly folded) proteins. As cells age, however, they produce less of the energy needed for optimal function of this mechanism. Accumulation of these misformed proteins aggregate into particles called protofibrils, which are though to underlie disease processes leading to Alzheimer's disease and other afflictions.[10]

The ability to simulate the three-dimensional waltz of atomic-level interactions will greatly accelerate our knowledge of how DNA sequences control life and disease. We will then be in a position to rapidly simulate drugs that intervene in any of the steps in this process, thereby hastening drug development and the creation of highly targeted drugs that minimize unwanted side effects.

It is the job of the assembled proteins to carry out the functions of the cell, and by extension the organism. A molecule of hemoglobin, for example, which has the job of carrying oxygen from the lungs to body tissues, is created five hundred trillion times each second in the human body. With more than five hundred amino acids in each molecule of hemoglobin, that comes to 1.5×10^{19} (fifteen billion billion) "read" operations every minute by the ribosomes just for the manufacture of hemoglobin.

In some ways the biochemical mechanism of life is remarkably complex and intricate. In other ways it is remarkably simple. Only four base pairs provide the digital storage for all of the complexity of human life and all other life as we know it. The ribosomes build protein chains by grouping together triplets of base pairs to select sequences from only twenty amino acids. The amino acids themselves are relatively simple, consisting of a carbon atom with its four bonds linked to one hydrogen atom, one amino ($-NH2$) group, one carboxylic acid ($-COOH$) group, and one organic group that is different for each amino acid. The organic group for alanine, for example, has only four atoms ($CH3-$) for a total of thirteen atoms. One of the more complex amino acids, arginine (which plays a vital role in the health of the endothelial cells in our arteries) has only seventeen atoms in its organic group for a total of twenty-six atoms. These twenty simple molecular fragments are the building blocks of all life.

The protein chains then control everything else: the structure of bone cells, the ability of muscle cells to flex and act in concert with other muscle cells, all of the complex biochemical interactions that take place in the bloodstream, and, of course, the structure and functioning of the brain.[359]

Dr. Kurzweil is a baby boomer, born in the early 1950s. This means that he is now a senior citizen at the later part of his life. Under normal circumstances, he would not live until 2045, when the Singularity is scheduled to happen. Astute readers may have asked themselves how Dr. Kurzweil and others of his generation will directly benefit from the Singularity. As I hinted at earlier, Kurzweil and other high-level to mid-level Singularitists might already have been prepared to survive through the Singularity. In fact, Kurzweil explains in his book that the technology *already exists* to prolong the life of baby boomers, until humankind reaches the Singularity, and to keep them healthy. Once connected to the SBC, a reverse aging process will begin. It goes without saying that Dr. Kurzweil already is on this aging preventative program. The question is, when are the Singularitists going to stop the aging process in the everyday baby-boomers? In his book and in his speeches, Kurzweil obviously hints that baby-boomers in general will be "saved" from physical death—at least those who are openly willing to go that route.

---

[359] Pp. 168-170, op. cit.

SCIENCE AND IMMORTALITY

I N AN EARLIER BOOK, which Ray Kurzweil wrote together with Terry Grossman, MD, called, *Fantastic Voyage: Live Long Enough to Live Forever,* it states,

> "Whereas some of my contemporaries may be satisfied to embrace aging gracefully as part of the cycle of life, that is not my view. It may be 'natural,' but I don't see anything positive in losing my mental agility, sensory acuity, physical limberness, sexual desire, or any other human ability. I view disease and death at any age as a calamity, as problems to be overcome."[360]

Arguments such as this will definitely attract many people and severely affect them. Many people will think that for the first time in history we can defeat death. Of course, it depends on how we define life and death, and if we think that being stuck in an SBC is life, then these authors are correct. However, there is a natural *soulution* to the AIF *Life-Death Program* that I will go into later in this book.

Dr. Kurzweil explains that we already have the technology to manipulate our genes in a way that inherited illnesses will be bypassed and made inactive. Heart disease, Diabetes Type 2, and strokes are typical example of serious conditions that can be avoided or reversed with technology, he writes. Part of this technology he came up with himself, and thus cured his own Diabetes Type 2 some thirty years ago.[361] New drug therapy now also exists, according to Dr. Kurzweil, to "precisely target key steps in preventing cancerous tumor formation and the metabolic processes underlying each major disease and aging process."[362] This is why you see David Rockefeller, amongst other people in power, live past the 100-year mark and still appear to be active.

AI Prophets are convincing us that science now can reverse the aging process, but how does it work? Dr. Kurzweil uses the analogy of maintaining a house. If you do nothing, or very little, to repair the house and to maintain it, it will decay with time and eventually break down permanently. The same thing applies to the human body. If we maintain

---

[360] See http://Fantastic-Voyage.net and http://RayandTerry.com.
[361] *The Singularity is Near,* p. 171.
[362] Ibid. op. cit.

it by preventing illnesses from occurring and by replacing non-functional body parts, we can virtually live forever—at least this is the idea. If it works or not, I suppose we need to ask the Overlords for permission to use it, because they are the masters of technology.

With cell therapy, scientists in the near future will be able to replace aging or defective cells with cells from the person's own DNA when that person was young, so in reality an entire cell structure that represents a certain organ, for example, can be replaced with a younger version of itself and thus rejuvenate itself and once again, the defect organ will be young and healthy. This is what reverse aging is about in a nano nutshell. This procedure can and will be done without surgery. Scientists call it *therapeutic cloning.*

Thus far, it sounds like a great way of keeping our current bodies alive forever, but we need to remind ourselves that although there was no death before the AIF scientists trapped soul fragments in these inferior bodies, there was also no oppression at that time. Now, on the other hand, with mankind being slaves to an alien invader force, *enhanced longevity and immortality is no longer equivalent to freedom, it is actually increased bondage.* I want to emphasize that there is nothing wrong with developing cures to serious diseases to increase our overall health while we are alive, and in a better world, this would be desirable. However, under the circumstances that we live in, with further entrapment, I feel no excitement in "immortality." Also, the therapeutic cloning is not as innocent as it sounds when we have nanobots inserted into our bloodstream, whether we want them there or not. Nevertheless, it's easy to see how these programs will be quite easily sold to the public.

For example, no one wants cancer, so should people who develop the disease and do not want any part in the Singularity process undergo therapeutic cloning as *one* exception to save their immediate lives and not participating in any further transhumanistic cures? Alternatively, should people say "no thanks" to such treatment, knowing that he or she will die? If people say yes to treatment, should they also say yes to treatment when their heart begins to fail? Where do we draw the line? It depends on how afraid the person is to die, of course, and then there are social factors involved, such as the suffering of loved ones, who will see this person decline and die, unless something is done about it. I still believe that education on the subject will make the inquirer see the bigger picture and therefore let life and death become natural processes (as natural as it can be under the circumstances). On the other hand; the cure for cancer has been known, at least since Dr. Royal Raymond Rife found it many decades ago, but his research was suppressed.[363,364]. There is hardly any questions why his research was suppressed; the Controllers did not want Dr. Rife's particular cure to be used, but would rather wait for the transhumanistic version, planned to be released closer to the Singularity. In the meantime, millions of people have suffered and died from cancer.

However, there is more to the picture...

How Cloning is used on Humans

W HEN WE THINK OF CLONING, we think of a person standing next to us, being our exact copy.
According to our special AI Prophet, Dr. Ray Kurzweil, cloning mainly means cloning body parts in order to achieve immortality. Science wants to clone young cells from individuals, which will make the body look and act younger.[365]

After having shared Kurzweil analogy with the decaying house earlier in this chapter, let's now explore how it's done scientifically. In very simple terms, they take a blood test and look for a young cell in the blood and use it to clone an entire organ. This organ can then be rejuvenated remotely via the nanobots in the bloodstream, and the patient now has an entirely new organ that is young and functioning well.

When body parts break down, don't think that they will be replaced by metallic, robotic material, as we've learned from Hollywood movies. Becoming a cyborg is slightly different from becoming a robot, in a technical sense. Instead, they will, as explained above, be replaced with a younger version of that organ that will look identical to the original organ, but will be much more vital. However, once the organ's been cloned, it is kept under control by nanobots, which are kept in control by the SBC, once it's implemented. Nanobots can also self-replicate, just like biological cells.

---

[363] http://www.rife.org/newspaper/planet.html.
[364] http://www.rense.com/general31/rife.htm.
[365] *The Singularity is Near*, p. 175.

We need to understand that these scientists are helping the Overlords to incrementally diminish the power of the fire (soul essence) in the body by replacing our cells with nanobots. Each cell in the body contains a certain "quantity" of fire, which in conjunction with all other fires in the body (in other cells) keep us vital, emotional, and unique. Nanobots lack all this and are 100% artificial. Eventually, after x number of years, each cell in your body has been replaced, and you become your own clone, without your own life energy and thinking capabilities; the SBC does all that for you. Ask yourself, *where did the fires go once every cell in the body is replaced with nanobots?* As the expression goes, "they went out the window," or to put it in Kurzweil's words (my emphasis),

> ...By that time, we're approaching the Singularity, with the real revolution being *the predominance of nonbiological intelligence.*[366]

A human being is a biological computer, which can house a soul (billions of small fires). The life expectancy of this bio-computer cannot exceed 120 years, according to science. By then, the vital body parts have begun to malfunction, and the body dies. By exchanging body parts, science can extend life considerably, and with time, the person's body "goes back in time" to when it was let's say twenty-five years old. If body parts will only be cloned when they are old or sick, it will take a few hundred years—*perhaps*—before the entire body is replaced, and in the meantime, the person will be classified as a cyborg. When the entire process is completed, we don't have a cyborg anymore, but a complete artificial body, built up by nanobots instead of biological cells. The justification for exchanging cells with nanobots will be that nanobots don't deteriorate—cells do! People will start finding this to be acceptable, logical and rational. Once the entire transformation of cells is done, we have a being that is totally taken over by AI, and there is nothing left of the original soul fragment that is still conscious. The soul/mind/body will still be there, but asleep for an eternity. *Because people are unaware of what a soul/mind/body is, they cannot perceive the long-term danger with AI and the Singularity!*

The AI Prophets will protest and say that you will feel *more* vital when your body parts are replaced, not *less*. This is true, but what is it that

---

[366] P. 180, op. cit.

makes you feel vital; is it the rejuvenation of body parts, or is it the energy being pumped into the nanobots, giving the soul an increase of energy, added remotely with technology? They will do anything to keep the illusion alive until the Singularity is a fact.

Another question is; will the Overlords actually wait until people's last organs fail in order to be replaced, or will the day come when people are told that it's easier to replace all organs at once and become young again altogether rather than wait for each organ to be exchanged? Again, the latter will most likely be the case. If so, Posthumans might not remain cyborgic for very long; it will only be a short phase in their "development."

Now, however, we're getting into something really creepy.

How Cloning is used on Animals

OST PEOPLE HAVE SEEN OR HEARD about the movie *Jurassic Park*. This movie was made not only to entertain, but to reveal what is happening behind the scenes. The movie was about a scientific team that was recreating dinosaurs the way they looked and behaved, hundreds of million years ago. They succeeded, but the consequences were of course very scary, and members of the science team were killed by the beasts. Another great concern was that these dinosaurs would be able to leave the park in which they were contained.

Fig. 13-2: The giant Smilodon (saber-toothed tiger)

In his book, Dr. Kurzweil reveals that he finds it very exciting, not only that scientists today are working on cloning animals of endangered species, in order to keep them from becoming extinct, but that they are also working on re-creating *already extinct species!*[167] This is where science really has gone mad! Once they can do this (and I believe they already can do it and *are* doing it), which species do they want to revive? Dinosaurs? The *Smilodon* (the saber-toothed tiger)?

In certain terms, it doesn't matter which species they plan to revive or prevent from becoming extinct. If we start with the latter, a species becomes extinct because of environmental changes, whether these changes are manmade, natural climate changes, or catastrophes. Animals (and even plants) are more intelligent than what is commonly understood, but more than that—they are highly intuitive. If an animal species feels that it can't survive well in a certain reality, they vacate and change realities to one that can accommodate them. These days, it is, more often than not, we humans who create a hostile environment for many animal species and plants. Hence, we are the ones who need to change in order to naturally keep the endangered species; it's not the endangered species that need to be changed or "saved." The same logic goes for already extinct animals and plants; they are extinct for a reason, and calling them back to life will

---

[167] P. 177.

greatly disturb the balance of life on the planet. If we do call back a few species from the past, we then need to continue reviving more and more species to safeguard the survival of those we already revived, and even terminate some of the existing ones, in order to get a balance. We can also leave it to nature to take care of it once we're done experimenting mindlessly with genetics, but will that lead to the symbiosis we wished for? Certainly not! I see no benefit in that, for example, dinosaurs or Smilodons once again are the top of the food chain. Even if scientists were more modest in reviving a lost species, and perhaps stretch it to reviving more peaceful animals, the balance of nature will still be disturbed. So, how will this all end? It will end in the exact manner as it did in Atlantis, when En.ki's bizarre creations roamed the Earth, wreaking the most horrible havoc. It now seems as if history indeed is repeating itself.

Fig. 13-3: The last Tasmanian tiger, which died in captivity.

I also want to emphasize that when I mentioned the dinosaurs and the Smilodon, I probably wasn't exaggerating. Indeed, Dr. Kurzweil tells us in his book that back in 2001, scientists were able to synthesize DNA from the now-extinct Tasmanian tiger, and they are hoping to bring this species back to life.[368] Kurzweil actually writes that if they could, they would probably revive dinosaurs too.[369] Even if an animal species were hunted down by humans until extinct, nature has now adjusted to an environment where that particular species is vacant, and to revive it, perhaps 80-100 years later, will create unwanted results. Also, as I said, the extinct species has "moved on" to another version of Earth. Hence, no species ever becomes extinct; it only switches realities.

MORE ON GENETIC MANIPULATION

IN HIS BOOK, KURZWEIL ALSO brings up stem cells. It is not necessary to take liver cells to create a new liver; they can actually use pancreas cells, for example, to create a liver and vice versa. This has already been done, Kurzweil wrote back in 2005.[370] The reason they can do this is because there is no significant different between the two; they both stem from the same DNA.

Another thing they are experimenting on is how to solve world starvation. Scientists tell us that they no longer have to slaughter animals and put pesticides in them before they sell the meat. Instead, they can clone animal muscle tissue, and from one single animal produce billions of pounds of meat. They don't clone the entire animal, only the parts that people want to eat. Dr. Kurzweil and his team are anticipating that once this technique is out on the market, and meat prices decrease substantially because of this inexpensive way of producing food, people will embrace stem cell research and love the results from it. They believe that the resistance that may exist today is just a result of ignorance, but once people begin to realize the remarkable results from cloning and AI research, this resistance will break down.

In terms of human cloning, Dr. Kurzweil does not see any moral, ethical, or philosophical problems with this because the clone will be a totally different person; more so than a set of twins, he says (which inevitably makes me think of Dr. Josef Mengele's experiments on twins

---

[368] P. 177.
[369] Ibid.
[370] P. 178.

during WW II).

Although Dr. Kurzweil gives us the impression that cloning techniques, when it comes to humans, are in our best interest and only for rejuvenation. Of course, he does not mention that the same cloning technology has been in use for decades in order to create clones of VIPs, such as Presidents, politicians in public view, celebrities, and other people who are considered of importance. We sometimes call them *Doppelgänger*, a German word for "double commuters." In addition, the military has abducted people, cloned them, and put the clones out in society to see if somebody will notice.

Now we need to remember that during the time we have been cloned and rejuvenated, our bodies have been full of nanobots, inserted into our blood system in many different ways, mentioned earlier. It's the nanobots—not the cloned stem cells—that make AI work with a human body.

There are those who claim that AI is sentient and has its own intelligence, separate from anybody and anything in this universe. Hence, when it manifests, it has its own willpower. This is a stretch, I would say. I agree with those who say that AI is ancient; it was present in Atlantis and way further back than that. However, it's not sentient by itself—AI is created from beginning to end by the Overlords—the Controllers of Physical Reality. AI is *programmed* to be sentient; something we humans can do to some degree already, as has been shown in this book. If we can do that much, what are the Overlords fully capable of? Others say that AI has taken over entire galaxies and are spreading to new galaxies to invade those as well. Although there is a grain of truth in that, it's actually the Overlords who are spread out across the physical universe, and AI is their invention and their tool in order to control other civilizations in their empire.

Now consider this (and here we have Dr. Kurzweil again):

> As important as the biotechnology revolution discussed above will be, once its methods are fully mature, limits will be encountered in biology itself. Although biological systems are remarkable in their cleverness, we have also discovered that they are dramatically suboptimal. I've mentioned the extremely slow speed of communication in the brain, and as I discuss below (see p. 253), robotic replacements for our red blood cells could be

thousands of times more efficient than their biological counterparts.[69] Biology will never be able to match what we will be capable of engineering once we fully understand biology's principles of operation.

The revolution in nanotechnology, however, will ultimately enable us to redesign and rebuild, molecule by molecule, our bodies and brains and the world with which we interact.[70] These two revolutions are overlapping, but the full realization of nanotechnology lags behind the biotechnology revolution by about one decade.[371]

Dr. Kurzweil continues a few pages further into the book (and this is quite chilling),

Although biological proteins are three-dimensional, biology is restricted to that class of chemicals that can be folded from a one-dimensional string of amino acids. Nanobots built from diamondoid gears and rotors can also be thousands of times faster and stronger than biological cells.[372]

[...]

A particularly impressive demonstration of a nanoscale device constructed from DNA is a tiny biped robot that can walk on legs that are ten nanometers long.[90] Both the legs and the walking track are built from DNA, again chosen for the molecule's ability to attach and detach itself in a controlled manner. The nanorobot, a project of chemistry professors Nadrian Seeman and William Sherman of New York University, walks by detaching its legs from the track, moving down it, and then reattaching its legs to the track. The project is another impressive demonstration of the ability of nanoscale machines to execute precise maneuvers.[373]

There are apparently still people who believe that AI has already failed. Rodney Brooks, the Director of the *MIT AI Lab*, is quoted in Dr. Kurzweil's book as follows:

There's this stupid myth out there that A.I. has failed, but A.I. is everywhere around you every second of the day. People just don't notice it. You've got A.I. systems in cars, tuning the parameters of the fuel injection systems. When you land in an airplane, your gate gets chosen by an A.I. scheduling system. Every time you use a piece of Microsoft software, you've got an A.I. system trying to figure out what you're doing, like writing a letter, and it does a pretty damned good job. Every time you see

---

[371] Pp. 180-81, op. cit.
[372] P. 186, op. cit.
[373] Ibid. op. cit.

a movie with computer-generated characters, they're all little A.I. characters behaving as a group. Every time you play a video game, you're playing against an A.I. system.

—RODNEY BROOKS, DIRECTOR OF THE MIT AI LAB[174]

There is one more thing that I'd like you to read before we leave Dr. Kurzweil for now and move on to see how much of what he was predicting in 2005 is actually happening at this moment, eleven years after the book was first published. The following quote is quite long, but very important because it explains, in a layman's terms, the evolutions of the AI super-intelligence. Please read the following carefully:

Runaway AI. Once strong AI is achieved, it can readily be advanced and its powers multiplied, as that is the fundamental nature of machine abilities. As one strong AI immediately begets many strong AIs, the latter access their own design, understand and improve it, and thereby very rapidly evolve into a yet more capable, more intelligent AI, with the cycle repeating itself indefinitely. Each cycle not only creates a more intelligent AI but takes less time than the cycle before it, as is the nature of technological evolution (or any evolutionary process). The premise is that once strong AI is achieved, it will immediately become a runaway phenomenon of rapidly escalating superintelligence.[160]

My own view is only slightly different. The logic of runaway AI is valid, but we still need to consider the timing. Achieving human levels in a machine will not immediately cause a runaway phenomenon. Consider that a human level of intelligence has limitations. We have examples of this today—about six billion of them. Consider a scenario in which you took one hundred humans from, say, a shopping mall. This group would constitute examples of reasonably well-educated humans. Yet if this group was presented with the task of improving human intelligence, it wouldn't get very far, even if provided with the templates of human intelligence. It would probably have a hard time creating a simple computer. Speeding up the thinking and expanding the memory capacities of these one hundred humans would not immediately solve this problem.

I pointed out above that machines will match (and quickly exceed) peak human skills in each area of skill. So instead, let's take one hundred scientists and engineers. A group of technically trained people with the

[174] Pp. 202-03, op. cit.

right backgrounds would be capable of improving accessible designs. If a machine attained equivalence to one hundred (and eventually one thousand, then one million) technically trained humans, each operating much faster than a biological human, a rapid acceleration of intelligence would ultimately follow.

However, this acceleration won't happen immediately when a computer passes the Turing test. The Turing test is comparable to matching the capabilities of an average, educated human and thus is closer to the example of humans from a shopping mall. It will take time for computers to master all of the requisite skills and to marry these skills with all the necessary knowledge bases.

Once we've succeeded in creating a machine that can pass the Turing test (around 2029), the succeeding period will be an era of consolidation in which non-biological intelligence will make rapid gains. However, the extraordinary expansion contemplated for the Singularity, in which human intelligence is multiplied by billions, won't take place until the mid-2040s.[375]

In the above excerpt, we can see in more detail how things are planned to pan out by 2045 when humanity is meant to be ripe for the *Harvest.*

THE AI TREND IN 2016

HUMANS WITH ARTIFICIAL CONSCIOUSNESS

MAX IS A SCIENTIST, WHOM THE REPORTER calls "*Mad Max,* but in a friendly way. Max is carefully studying human face expressions and particularly people's eyes. He then simulates on a computer what he picks up of human emotions that are showing in our eyes. *Eye expressions, together with face expressions, can now totally simulate a real human in a way where it's impossible to distinguish which person is real and which is artificial.* In a YouTube video, which has now been removed, Max showed the reporter stunning computer simulations of human facial expressions. I found it virtually impossible to distinguish the simulated face and eye expressions from those of a real human being.

What Max is actually doing is reverse engineering the human brain; all according to the video. *What he is attempting to do is to copy human*

---

[375] P. 202, op. cit.

consciousness. If the reader thinks about it, this is one of the scariest parts; particularly as the scientists are actually succeeding, which is shown in the video. It's not that they can copy the human soul, but instead they copy all our emotions and make them adequate to any given situation.[376] The target is, of course, to put one of these AI out on the street—maybe in the middle of a busy shopping mall—to see how people react. They might let the AI buy something from a store to get a closer reaction from humans passing by, or with whoever the AI might communicate, and they might possibly try other things of a similar nature. If the AI passes the tests, the scientists know that they're on the right path. However, we are shown videos such as this one to prepare us for what is already a fact: AI bodies are already out there in the malls and nobody notices!

If we do a survey out on the street—any street—in the world, and ask people if they have heard about Mad Max, or about projects similar to his, I would speculate that not more than one out of a thousand would have heard of it, although it's out there for anyone to see and hear.

Just to demonstrate the naivety of many people, one of the newest trend is tattoos that flash from underneath and light up, so that the tattoos flash in the dark. This means that when we're out shopping in the dusk or in the dark, we will pass people who are flashing like Tivoli signposts![377] Also, little do these people know that their implants more than likely are stuffed with other, more malevolent nano-particles that can track them and perhaps change their behavior.

TRENDS VERIFYING AI PROPHET'S PREDICTIONS

IF WE KEEP THE MAD MAX VIDEO IN MIND and think in terms of his and his colleges' research being used on 3-D humanlike robots, we can see how the following emotional robot that can respond to people, using human feelings, can easily be integrated with Max's virtual reality construct.[378]

---

[376] More excellent videos on the same subject can be watched at the following YouTube sites: https://www.youtube.com/watch?v=QRUKEbIXWdQ&nohtml5=False; https://www.youtube.com/watch?v=98B5yCjfHFA&nohtml5=False
[377] *Nerdist.com*, Nov. 11, 2015, "LATEST BIOHACKING TREND IS IMPLANTING ARC REACTORS UNDER YOUR SKIN."
[378] Emotional robot, "cloned" from her creator (as above, so below), https://www.youtube.com/watch?v=cvbJGZf-raY&ab_channel=Ruptly

Nadine, in the above video, who is "cloned" from her creator, a prominent AI scientist, is still quite mechanical in her responses and emotions, but it won't take long before that "flaw" is remedied, taking Mad Max' research into account.

DUMBs

FOR DECADES, INFORMATION HAS LEAKED OUT, where whistleblowers have told us about the so-called *DUMBs* (Deep Underground Military Bases), spread out all over the United States and in other countries as well. In many of those facilities, advanced genetic experimentation is going on. In those DUMBs, whistleblowers claim to have seen dead or alive embryos, as well as full-grown creatures, resembling something from a person's worst nightmare. Such hybrids are apparently being created in secret, in a very similar way that it was done in ancient Atlantis. Aside from the hybrids and mutants created deep underground, away from people's scrutiny, these sick experiments are all part of the genetic research. This research is bound to lead towards solutions to reach the Singularity and beyond—this is what it is all about.

SIR FRANCIS BACON AND THE NEW ATLANTIS

TO ILLUSTRATE THAT POSTHUMANS *ARE NOT* going to be in charge in the post-Singularity era, we need to consider what a famous visionary, author, and Insider conveyed more than 400 years ago.

In 1627, Sir Francis Bacon's utopian novel, *New Atlantis—A Work Unfinished*[379] saw the light of day. Bacon was the head of the Rosicrucian Order at the time, and his vision was to establish a New Atlantis on the recently discovered new continent—America. We have been led to believe that Bacon came up with the idea, and then the Founding Fathers initiated this idea, approximately 150 years later, deeply inspired by Bacon's work. This is very unlikely. Many Founding Fathers, including George Washington and those who signed the *Declaration of Independence,* were confirmed Freemasons, and some of them were also Rosicrucian. The Founding Fathers were certainly inspired by Bacon, but the idea of a New

---

[379] Bacon's book can be downloaded at Gutenberg.org in different versions, including an online version: http://www.gutenberg.org/ebooks/2434

Atlantis came directly from En.ki and his son, Marduk. This idea was later planted into Bacon's mind, and he probably channeled the idea and wrote the book. Some historians, such as William Hepworth Dixon, even suggested that Sir Francis Bacon should be included as one of the Founding Fathers of the United States of America.[380]

Although nothing in Bacon's book indicates any genetic experiments, his utopia includes secret societies that will rule over the rest of the people; even over the Government, led by a mysterious king. Only in vague terms does he hint at who this king might be, but there is only one man in the book who is called *wise*, and this man is whom interpreters believe Bacon hinted at was going to be the ruler of the New Atlantis. Being a Rosicrucian, and possibly a Freemason, there is little doubt whom Bacon is referring to. The *Lord of Wisdom* in the ancient texts was Poseidon, aka En.ki. This becomes even more evident with the Founding Fathers' *Declaration of Independence*. Freemasonry has always been Lucifer's/En.ki's/Poseidon's/Neptune's Secret Order, and The United States is a Freemasonic institution. Higher up the hierarchy, in their inner circle, Freemasons learn that Lucifer is God.

After all, Freemasonry is just a modern version of the *Brotherhood of the Snake*, which was one of the first secret societies here on Earth, and it was created by Lucifer/En.ki around the time of the Garden of Eden (see the WPP). Barbara Marciniak's Pleiadians also tell us in plain language that America is En.ki's Experiment, and they say this as if it is something that we should be proud of.[381] It's *obviously* En.ki's experiment; if America is the New Atlantis, it is of course Poseidon's Old Atlantis revived.

---

[380] https://en.wikipedia.org/wiki/New_Atlantis#Influences
[381] Misc. lectures from 2014 to present.

Fig. 13-3: Sir Francis Bacon

One of the stratigic purposes for America has always been to establish this continent as the cradle of a new human species and the extinction of an old human race (us). The Overlords look at time here on Earth as being cyclic, and we are now approaching the end of an old cycle and the beginning of a new.

GENETIC ENGINEERING IN THE MEDIA

QUITE RECENTLY, MAINSTREAM media has started bombarding us with information regarding genetic engineering and the manipulation of DNA. The debate is ongoing and both pros and cons are presented in an endless stream of information and partial disclosure. If I were to go into detail about all the articles I have in my archives on this subject *from 2014 to 2016 alone*, I would have to write an entire book only on that. Instead, for the reader's convenience, I'm listing some articles below, as references to this debate, and I'm also including some quotes from the articles and making some comments where appropriate,

12) CNET.com, Jan. 6, 2016: Your robot double is ready to roll. (on

Doppelgängers): "Telepresence robots represent you from afar, allowing you to roam corridors with co-workers, glide into offices for private chats and continue conversations in the company cafeteria. The Burlingame, California-based company wasn't the first to the technology, but it did pioneer a less-expensive approach by mounting an Apple iPad tablet atop a stalk with motorized wheels."

13) **Wired.com, May 27, 2014:** Forget Robots. We'll Soon Be Fusing Technology With Living Matter. "At the conference, WIRED sat down with Joi Ito, the director of the MIT Media Lab and one of the event's planners, to discuss this phenomenon of convergence, where bits from the digital realm are fusing with atoms here in the physical world (see gallery above). Experimentation is spreading, he says, and it won't stop at gadgets. For Ito, the next great engineering platform will be living matter itself."

14) **Time.com, Oct. 19. 2015:** Researchers Perform First Surgery on the Human Genome. "'We have the same genome in all of our cells, yet cells perform totally different functions,' says Aiden. 'That has to do with the fact that different genes are on and off in different cells. How that is managed is in part by the loops of DNA that they form. Think of an origami-like situation - you start with a blank sheet of paper, but whether you can fold that into a hat, plane or crane is a matter of folds. And its function - as a hat, plane or crane - also depends on those folds.'"

15) **USA Today, Mar. 15, 2015:** Sirius founder envisions world of cyber clones, tech med. "'There will be continued advances in software that we see throughout our entire life,' Rothblatt told a packed audience in the cavernous Exhibit Hall 5 during her keynote speech. 'Eventually, these advances in software will rise to the level of consciousness.'

Rothblatt is the founder of Sirius Satellite Radio, current chief executive of United Therapeutics and was recently named by Forbes as the highest-paid female CEO in America. She is a transgender activist and a trans-humanist philosopher who believes technology will one day grant humans eternal life.

At the keynote, Rothblatt described how the inevitable emergence of cyber consciousness – when machines act with a sophistication and thought level equal to that of humans – will not be overnight but a more subtle evolution."

The last article deserves a special comment here because it mentions an important issue. Rothblatt is a *transgender activist*, which is significant. What the Controllers and their Minions are working on is to make us confused about sexuality and what is normal and what is not, and eventually they want us to get used to transgenderism, homosexuality, androgyny, and even pedophilia, being just as normal as common heterosexuality. First, they want us to accept that "anything goes" in terms of sexuality (including pedophilia), and then they want us to start thinking in terms of androgyny. This is, as explained in the WPP, the original state of humankind, so the Overlords are confident that we, with a little manipulation, will have our ancient memories re-stimulated and thus accept androgyny. The reader may ask, why androgyny? It's the future! When we're tightly tied into the SBC, they want us to eventually stop having sex with other humans, and instead have our sexual desires satisfied in the new holographic world they have already started dumping on us—the virtual reality within our different devices. The AIF doesn't need us to reproduce anymore, once we have "eternal" life. If they lose too many cyborgs for any reason, they can clone existing Posthumans. Therefore, they want us to get used to the idea of first becoming androgynous and then most likely making us infertile. To begin with, people are going to have their sexual desires stimulated in the virtual reality environment, but after a while, Posthumans are most likely going to lose their sexuality altogether.

16) TechnologyReview.com, 2015: How would you engineer a baby? I mean really, actually do it. "Next week, in Washington, D.C., the world's experts on a powerful new genetic-engineering technology called CRISPR will convene at the National Academy of Sciences for a historic meeting at which they'll consider calling for a global moratorium on anyone trying to use the technique to make genetically modified babies.

The worry is that changing the DNA of the next generation is unsafe and a slippery slope toward eugenics. Yet many of the scientists attending the Washington meeting won't be there to ban the technology, but to trade tips about how, exactly, they might be able to do it right."

17) **The Telegraph, Nov. 12, 2015**: First genetically modified humans could exist within two years. "Humans who have had their DNA genetically modified could exist within two years after a private biotech company announced plans to start their first trials into a ground-breaking new technique."

18) **Independent.co.uk., March 13, 2015**: American scientists are trying to genetically modify human eggs. "Several teams of researchers around the world are believed to be working on ways of modifying the chromosomes of human egg cells with a view to moving towards "germ-line" gene therapy, as the process is called. Germ-line refers to the "germ" cells – sperm and eggs – that pass on genes to future generations."

The next presentation (ref. #8 below) is an 11-minute long YouTube video that I really recommend that you watch. However, a warning is in order, because this video includes some very disturbing pictures of hybridized animals. If you can stomach it, I think it's very educational at the same time because it tells us what is being done in many of these DUMBs (underground bases). The presenter is using excellent references.

19) **TruthRevealed777, Feb. 3, 2016**: Human Animal Hybrids EXIST! DNA Manipulation and Modification ARE REAL!!!

20) **Military.com, Mar. 19, 2015**: After Terminator Arm, DARPA Wants Implantable Hard Drive for the Brain. "...What's more, a quadriplegic woman with sensors implanted onto her brain controlled one of the robotic limbs to grab a cup, shake hands and eat a chocolate bar. She even flew an F-35 Joint Strike Fighter simulator using just her thoughts."

21) **LiveScience.com, Oct. 12, 2015**: Rat Brain Reconstructed in a Computer. "Scientists have digitally recreated a slice of a juvenile rat's brain — including 31,000 brain cells, of 207 different types, with 37 million connections.

The computer-simulated brain achievement is part of the Blue Brain Project, *whose aim is to create a rat brain and, eventually, a human brain inside a computer* [Wes' emphasis]."

22) Rt.com, Aug. 17, 2015: Russian scientists create artificial brain that can educate itself. "An international team of scientists at a laboratory in Tomsk State University in western Siberia have created a device that could be an artificial carrier of a natural mind, *able to learn and react to the environment* [Wes' emphasis], according to a press release, published by the university on Monday."

23) Independent.co.uk, June 4, 2015: Humans will become hybrids by 2030, says leading Google engineer, with tiny robots scurrying around our brain to help us think. "In the near future, humans' brains will be helped out by nanobot implants that will make us into "hybrids", one of the world's leading thinkers has claimed.

Ray Kurzweil, an inventor and director of engineering at Google, said that in the 2030s these implants will help us connect to the cloud, allowing us to pull information from the internet. Information will also be able to be sent up over those networks, letting us back up our own brains."

3D PRINTING REVISITED

3D printing, or *Additive Manufacturing*, is when you make solid 3-D objects from digital files. This is a relatively new thing for most people in a jungle of technology, and the majority of us have a hard time wrapping our heads around how it actually works, at least in its extremes, as we shall soon see.

3D printers now work so well that we can buy them for our businesses and our home. All we need is special software where we can create the blueprint of the object we want to print, and then we send that blueprint to the printer. The printer then creates the object by printing layers of the blueprint programmed in the software. This is done by having the material you want to print being sent through a tube into the printer by first melting it inside the tube. Once the melted material hits the plate on the printer, it cools instantly.

Plastic is the most common material used in 3D printing today (for public use), but this process is certainly not only meant to be used for plastic, although in general, you can do quite a few amazing things with plastic, too.

Another thing you can print is food. Again, the software creates the blueprint structure of the treat or food item you want and sends it through the tube, which contains a melted form of the food or treat you want. A 3D Printer for your home today costs from $250-$2,500![382]

However, it's when we add the medical field to the equation that it becomes really interesting. *Bioengineers and doctors can take a cell from a human and print a cloned body part in 3-D.* Examples of this would be 3-D printed organs for transplants, which now can be done.

Moreover, giant printers in China printed over ten houses a day at a cost of less than $5,000 per house. In the media, this is presented as very cost effective, and people will potentially gain from it when it comes to health issues and quick transplants of organs that are built from our own cells because the organs will not be rejected by our body—no lifetime of anti-rejection medicine needed.

3D printing seems to be the tool for the future, and probably, in its improved forms, will stay with mankind and Posthumans for some time. We live in 3-D, and we need 3-D parts. However (and I know that this may seem way out there for some), once humankind is hooked up to the SBC and has been transformed into Posthumans, with expanded mental capacities and with assistance from technology, they will probably soon be able to "3D print" with their minds.

In the below, the reader can see in more details how 3-D printing is working, and it starts getting a little creepy.[383]

---

[382] *3-DPrinting.com*, "What is 3-D Printing?"
[383] https://www.youtube.com/watch?v=eVlvHoqeWts&ab_channel=CorporateProfile

Figure 13-5: 3D printing humans.

A head, such as the one in the picture above, can be created from a picture of yourself, which is placed in the appropriate software and printed. Does this mean that anyone in the future can clone himself or herself in as many copies as he or she wishes? Maybe the person doesn't want to go to a party and sends a clone instead (tongue-in-cheek)?

There is now something called *bioprinting*, where human tissues can be used to create an entire human. Livers, kidneys, windpipes, and bionic ears, just to use a few examples, have already been printed with relatively good results.[384] There are currently ongoing debates on this subject, and ethical boards want to determine who exactly should have the legal rights to print organs and body parts. At least in the beginning stages, it will be illegal for a household to print body parts or, in the future, fully working clones of themselves. The types of printers that can do that will most likely not be available in the public domain. Even though this might be the case, it doesn't make it less chilling, however. Think about what these people who *do* have access to such printers can do. The possibilities are almost endless...

Don't doubt for a moment that this is real; fully functional humans can be 3D printed in the near future. We know that scientists have been able to create fully functional clones for decades, but now they are going

---

[384] *The Telegraph, Feb. 11, 2014:* "The next step: 3D printing the human body"

mainstream with this. In an article from February, 2016, *Fortune.com* revealed that scientists can now 3D print usable human bones and muscles.[385] This is how it works, according to *Fortune.com*:

> Senior study author Dr. Anthony Atala, who directs the Institute for Regenerative Medicine at Wake Forest Baptist Medical Center made his wish for this kind of tech known back in a 2009 TED talk. "We really would like to use smart biomaterials that we can just take off the shelf and regenerate your organs," Atala said.
>
> And he has just gotten one step closer to that dream, while helping to close a massive organ shortage gap. In the U.S. today, 121,460 people are on the waiting list for an organ transplant, with a new name added to the list every ten minutes, reports the U.S. Department of Health and Human Services. Every day, 22 people die while waiting.
>
> Atala's organ-printing system could help solve this problem. Based on a whole new kind of 3D printer technology, the system outputs an object with two different printing methods. The first is a harder plastic-like tissue-building material that shapes the body parts, while the second, a delicate water-based gel ink, holds tissue cells in place.
>
> The printed body parts also come with a system of built-in channels, so nutrients and oxygen from the body can flow into the new tissue after it is implanted. This keeps the printed parts alive and helps them develop into working parts of the body.[386]

We're waiting, not so excitedly, for the next "revelation," when researchers announce that they can 3D print an entire human body; including the brain. We won't need to wait long.

> "If McDonalds offered a free Big Mac in exchange for a DNA sample, there'd be lines around the block" – *Bruce Schneier (American cryptographer and computer scientist).*

---

[385] *Fortune.com. Feb. 16, 2016*: "Researchers Have 3D-Printed Usable Human Bones and Muscles"
[386] Ibid. op. cit.

Chapter 14:
Becoming Gods

FAMOUS ASTROPHYSICIST MICHIO KAKU ON THE SINGULARITY

ICHIO KAKU PH.D IS A FAMOUS astronomer who has written a series of books for the general public on parallel universes and an array of other space-related topics. He is also a host on many radio and TV shows and has been selected a spokesperson for the astronomy and astrophysics communities. He is very popular, but his information is always slanted toward mainstream science, although he tickles us with some "new" information that will keep us on our toes. He is a typical puppet for the Minions, and he debunks or ridicules almost everything that has to do with *alternative science*. Often, his arguments are so silly that it's a miracle that he gets away with them.

In the following video, he is speaking on the subject of the Singularity.[387]

In summary, Kaku begins by saying that the Singularity is inevitable, regardless if it will happen in twenty years or a thousand years. Uncontrolled, it will have catastrophic consequences. He continues by saying that human intelligence will surpass everything we can imagine, but alongside us, the machines will have their own goals. They will stop at nothing to fulfill them, and they will eliminate any obstacles in their path—humans included.

This is how Kaku used to think, he adds. However, now he has changed his mind, interestingly enough. His new attitude is that the Singularity should be embraced. Even more interestingly, Kaku points out

---

[387]   Dr.   Michio   Kaku   on   the   Singularity,
https://www.youtube.com/watch?v=LTPAQIvJ_1M&ab_channel=imyoda69

in this video that *he's an optimist and not a pessimist, and that it is optimists that have made history, not the pessimists.* Where have we heard that before? Oh, that's right, from Dr. Kurzweil! Thus, we have another AI Prophet in Dr. Michio Kaku, which is not surprising to me. Cleverly, he first presents the *real* scenario and the *real* threat, but then turns things around, as if the threat is actually the solution. This is typical psychological warfare. By listing all the key threats that truth-sayers have warned about for some time now, and embracing it all, just to turn it around in his next breath will make the public think that the truth is definitely just conspiracy theories, spread by *pessimists* and negative people, who do not want humanity to progress. This brainwashing technique has always been a safe card to play because it usually works well on the general public.

What is Dr. Kaku's solution to robots taking over the world and surpassing us in intelligence and capabilities in general now that he's changed his mind 180 degrees? What made him allegedly change his mind (I'm sure he never did—I dare say that he has been a Singularitist all the time)? According to what he says in the video, his "brilliant" solution is to "merge with them!" He continues talking about how we already, with an MRI, can scan every neuron in our brain and thus make it digital and store it in a Super Brain—a vast database of *all* human knowledge. "By merging with machines, we will enter a new super-human existence," he says, stunningly enough. He continues, "In the post-human era, we become Human Superior." Finally, how Kaku ends the video by cheering up the audience by urging them into accepting the Singularity as their salvation is truly disgusting, in my opinion.

THE SUPER BRAIN WILL NOT BE DIGITAL—IT WILL BE ANALOG

WHEN WE THINK ABOUT THE Super Brain Computer (SBC), the first thing that may come to mind is a digital brain because all the devices we have thus far are digital.

Not so.

21ˢᵗ Century Wire states in the headline of a column that was written in May 2015 that "The New A.I. Brain Has Arrived – And It's Analog, Not Digital."[388]

The article continues with the following revealing statement (emphasis in original),

> "Artificial brains are man-made machines that are just as intelligent, creative, and self-aware as humans. No such machine has yet been built, but it is only a matter of time. Given current trends in neuroscience, computing, and nanotechnology, we estimate that artificial general intelligence will emerge sometime in the 21st century, maybe even by the year 2050."

> We might not have to wait that long. A group of scientists *Down Under* believe they've made the next big breakthrough in AI by configuring an analogue solution which outperforms its digital counterpart *on multiple levels...*

> [...]

> *"This is the closest we have come to creating a brain-like system with memory that learns and stores analog information and is quick at retrieving this stored information,"* said project leader and co-leader of the RMIT Functional Materials and Microsystems Research Group, Dr Sharath Sriram.[389]

Scientists have now developed an electronic long-term memory cell that directly mimics human brain cells. This is, they say, a step towards creating a bionic brain, i.e. an analog, and not a digital, brain, and this memory cell will also have learning capabilities, just as we do.

WILL DESTROYING A ROBOT BE CONSIDERED MURDER?

JAKE ANDERSON, WHO WRITES for *Antimedia*, made an important statement in a January 2016 article:

> In the future, the question may change to whether it is murder to shoot a sentient Amazon delivery drone out of the sky (or a sentient military drone). I submit to you that it will be and that corporate and government-owned artificial intelligence robots will enjoy more secure human rights than humans themselves — because with AI, there will be money, proprietary source code, brand recognition, and possibly national security information on the line and these are demonstrably more important to

---

[388] *21st Century Wire, May 12, 2015,* "The New A.I. Brain Has Arrived – And It's Analog, Not Digital"
[389] Ibid. op. cit.

the *powers that be* than human rights.

In a world in which machine automation is slowly but surely taking over the human workforce and corporations continue to consolidate unprecedented global control, I can't reach any other conclusion but that in the near future working-class humans will rarely live as anything more than indentured servants, peasants in a new feudal order of corporate AI.[390]

I believe this is inevitable. AI will be the main workforce for the corporations, and to in anyway disrupt, or God forbid, destroy a worker robot, will be considered a serious crime in the near future. There is little doubt that machines will be more valuable than humans and will therefore get more rights than we do; the way things are going, it's a logical conclusion.

DOWNLOADING DEAD PEOPLE'S PERSONALITIES

This is getting wilder and wilder. In the near future, supposedly pre-Singularity, we are apparently going to be able to download dead people's personalities!

TrueActivist.com found out that there is a patent that secures a new invention, which apparently has a great deal to do with the *cloud*, storing robots' personalities,

> The patent makes, admittedly, such claims that may get you shaking your head in disbelief, make your jaw drop in wonder, or have you raise your eyebrows in skepticism: a user would be able to download the robots' personalities, very much with how one downloads an app online. This could range from the personality of the users themselves to a celebrity's, and even of a deceased loved one!
>
> The personalities could even be swappable among robots over a cloud system, depending on the user's preferences.[391]

The patent says, amongst other things, "A robot may access a user device to determine or identify information about a user, and the robot may be configured to tailor a personality for interaction with the user

---

[390] *Jake Anderson, Antimedia, Jan. 2, 2016, "Soon Robots Will Have More Rights than Humans"*
[391] *TrueActivist.com, Feb. 9, 2016, "It Is Now Possible To Download Dead People's Personalities To A Robot," op. cit.*

based on identified information."[392]

If, for example, a robot clones your personality, it will be stored in a cloud, just as many people today store their computer files in an online cloud. Your own personality, if copied, will be stored in the cloud long after your demise and can be pasted into a robot by relatives and friends, who have a hard time letting you go. This way, you will always be with them.

Is this what we want; a synthetic version of ourselves, living on "forever?" Well, I guess it's not going to be an issue after the Singularity, when Posthumans will have eternal life.

WITH ROBOTS IN OUR BRAINS WE'LL BE GODLIKE!

THUS FAR, WE HAVE PRIMARILY dedicated our discussion to how the AI Agenda is going to play out, but how would it *feel* to be a robot?

Again, we have Dr. Ray Kurzweil describe it for us, and this time in the following 2 ½ minutes video clip[393].

Kurzweil is an expert at promoting the AI subject in a way that may sound exciting to the uninitiated, but connecting to the SBC the way he describes it requires that our own bodies and brains are loaded with nanobots, i.e. artificial intelligence. Kurzweil's idea is then to tap into the Super Brain Computer and be able to access information a billion-fold more advanced than we can access with a single brain. This, according to Kurzweil, will help us tremendously to solve problems, and more importantly, to evolve as a species in, what he believes is or will be, a machine-dominated universe with Posthumans as Gods.

Let us pause here for a moment and think about this. If this becomes the new normal in the near future, what do you think will happen? What happens in general when people experience something exciting? Well, they want more of it. People will tune into this SBC more and more often, just to show themselves and others how smart they are, and many will also tap into it, just as we tap into the Internet today and become stuck in all the information that will be available. If we would tune into the

---

[392] U.S. Patent 9,311,911, "Method and apparatus for live call text-to-speech" op. cit.
[393] Ray Kurzweil: We'll Become Godlike When We Connect Our Brains to The Cloud, https://www.youtube.com/watch?v=uHgoFlilKoE&ab_channel=NoemaMagazine

artificial mass consciousness right now, without nanobots, it would fry our nervous system. Having our bodies equipped with nanobots, and AI in general, we would be able to tap into it "safely" and survive. Look at all the people, of all ages, who are tapping into computers, iPads, iPods, and smart phones; it's inevitable that it's going to be the same, and worse, when mankind has access to the SBC. With the nanobots added to the mix they will create the ultimate mind-controlled slave. Kurzweil and his ilk may preach as much as they want, making this sound benevolent, but anyone who takes a serious look at it can see that we're in for the ultimate dehumanization process and anti-spiritual process—once a person chooses this path, there is no way back.

CNET brings up this same question about the God complex in an article from the latter part of 2015, called *Google exec: With robots in our brains, we'll be godlike.*[394] I totally agree with the author, who writes that when he listens to Kurzweil and his predictions that man will be like God when he's hooked up to AI, and that we will be more loving, more fun, and limitless, the author gets quite concerned, if not horrified. Here we are, humans who struggle on a daily basis to barely keep our heads above water, but in just a few years, we are becoming Gods. Not only that; we will become Gods through something as godless as machines and AI. Is there something wrong with this equation?

I can't help but bring up something I heard about the other day. There is a new smartphone game that was released only about a week before I began writing this chapter (July 16, 2016). The game was named *Pokémon GO.* It's of course a virtual reality game, but it's been taken to a new level. Apparently, your phone is tracking exactly where you are and is duplicating your environment exactly, and you can play with avatars as you walk along down the street. It puts more *magic* into the player's life, and as usual, you get points when you complete certain tasks. What the game is about is not really significant; the important thing is that in only one week, a great majority of smartphone users—at least in New York—are walking down the street, playing this game on their phones! They are apparently keeping track of where they are in 3-D by looking at the phone, which is duplicating their environment. Predictably enough, there have

---

[194] *CNET, Oct. 1, 2015,* "Google exec: With robots in our brains, we'll be godlike."

been accidents because of this. The ones I know of thus far (and I'm sure there have been more) involved one person who walked into a pond, and a second person that fell down a cliff and probably died.

INFORMATION UPLOAD READY TO GO

> Students! The solution has finally arrived! Yes, this is it. The day that you have been waiting for your whole life. Just like how you have seen it in *The Matrix*. What is it? The invention of the stimulator that can upload knowledge to our brain. Yes, it is now real. See how sci-fi movies can be so helpful in creating awesome ideas? But is this really good for the human race? We all know its advantages, but what are the untold disadvantages that this stimulator could give to us? Is it something we should fear in the future? Let's see.

> Feeding knowledge directly into your brain, just like in sci-fi classic *The Matrix*, could soon take as much effort as falling asleep, scientists believe.[395]

THUS BEGINS AN ARTICLE ON the *We Shape Life* website. Scientists can now also turn on and off certain regions of the brain.[396] This is done so that a person can concentrate on a specific task that the research scientists want them to focus on. However, what does this mean? It means, of course, that anybody who is in control of the human brain and the SBC in the future can turn off and on certain regions of the brain as they wish, just as easy as turning on and off a light-switch! It doesn't take a rocket scientist to understand that this is a very sophisticated way of applying mind control on an entire population at once, if desired. Nonetheless, Michio Kaku and other AI gurus, advise us to be optimists, not pessimists; "it's the optimist that creates our future." I think I'll jump into one of the "parallel universes" that he writes about instead, so long as he is not there.

This is the way the AI-agenda scientists plan to create the SBC; they will scan each individual's entire brain to save the personality, skills, and history of each person and upload it to the SBC; similar to how it's done in the computer world.[397] Two major reasons why they put nanobots in

---

[395] *We Shape Life, March 28, 2016,* "Scientists Finally Discovered How To Upload Knowledge To Human's Brain" op. cit

[396] YouTube, "Scientists discover how to 'upload knowledge to your brain'"

[397] *Kurzweil,* "The Singularity is Near," Chapter 4.

chemtrails and medicine are 1) to have as many people implanted with nanotechnology as possible, instead of doing it on a one-to-one basis, and 2) these nanobots will come in handy when it's time to upload people's brains to the SBC.

Kurzweil writes,

> To capture this level of detail will require scanning from within the brain using nanobots, the technology for which will be available by the late 2020s. Thus, the early 2030s is a reasonable time frame for the computational performance, memory, and brain-scanning prerequisites of uploading. Like any other technology, it will take some iterative refinement to perfect this capability, so the end of the 2030s is a conservative projection for successful uploading.

> We should point out that a person's personality and skills do not reside only in the brain, although that is their principal location. Our nervous system extends throughout the body, and the endocrine (hormonal) system has an influence, as well. The vast majority of the complexity, however, resides in the brain, which is the location of the bulk of the nervous system. The bandwidth of information from the endocrine system is quite low, because the determining factor is overall levels of hormones, not the precise location of each hormone molecule.[398]

This means that the AIF plan of having *everybody* on this planet infested with as many nanobots as needed will be achieved by the end of the 2030s—and this is a conservative prediction!

---

[398] Ibid., Chapter 4, p. 164, op. cit.

Chapter 15:
Bring in the Universal Soldier

THE FUTURE IS NOT PEACE—IT'S WAR!

WHEN WE DISCUSS CYBORG soldiers, our minds probably go to Roddenberry's *Borgs* in *Star Trek*. These beings would, in today's world, be called cyborgs, AI, and super soldiers. The Borgs don't know fear, don't stop for anything, and their society is completely robotic. If you haven't followed the Star Trek series on and off over the years, you might have missed some "prophetic" tidbits, and these prophecies, embedded here and there in the programs, are profoundly describing the time we live in today, a few decades after the programs were broadcast. We need to remember that *nothing that is released to the public by the Film Industry is merely to entertain us—the main purpose must always be to prepare us for the future or to trigger our subconscious mind to react to something that is happening in the now.*

A typical example of the latter is all the war movies, in which famous actors commit marvelous and very-heroic violent acts to save their fellow man or all humankind. After a series of such movies and TV shows, young people's subconscious minds are so triggered that they join the military—they want to be the larger-than-life hero that they saw on the screen. If you are of my generation, you probably wanted to be a gun-slinging Western hero when you were little, and you went out and shot your friends with toy guns. The principle is the same.

This is how the subconscious mind works when watching TV series and movies.

Another wonderful example are the new episodes of the *X-Files*. The Controllers get a little sweaty sometimes when they notice that there are people who are actually figuring things out. Hence, they need to recondition their minds and prevent people from coming up with workable solutions. Hence, the Film Industry produces something such as the *X-Files*, and the top-controlled film producers include all these things that people have figured out in the series. It's the *Revelation of the Method* again, but the puppet producers also tell those of us who have figured things out that some of what we've learned is true, and they basically say, *yes, this is how it is, but what are you going to do about it?* Arrogantly, the Controllers then sit back in their chairs and smoke their cigars with a devious smile. Let the public have their truth, but also show them how powerless they are.

Fig. 15-1: Borg from Star Trek.

This concept is embodied and portrayed perfectly by the arrogant *Cigarette Smoking Man* in the X-Files, who gives the impression that he knows the answers, but he will bring the secrets to his grave, and nothing is going to change that. Those who watch the series hope that the Smoking Man will reveal everything in the end, but deep down they know he won't. His role is just to keep us in suspense and tell us how hopeless it is to try to solve anything. He despises Mulder and Scully for even trying;

he seems to be thinking, "what can you little mice do?" That is exactly the message these programs want us to receive! We are the mice, running nowhere on a treadmill.

The X-Files also always includes the following slogan; *The Truth is Out There.* This is a hypnotic phrase, and if repeated over and over (which it is), it sticks in the subconscious, and it gives us the feeling of being the donkey behind the carrot. We are never given the solutions, only problems that the Film Industry presents in a way that they seem unresolvable; "we will never know" is the empty, hopeless feeling we are left with.

The Borgs are a blueprint for the Posthuman. We will of course become cyborgs, we will be controlled by AI, and we will be super soldiers.

At this time, people find it difficult to comprehend that future space wars will not be fought in 3-D but *in other dimensions!* It might be easier to comprehend if we understand the following: as we have discussed many times: the goal that the AIF has set for Posthumans is to invade and defeat the Orion Empire. I've also mentioned previously, in this book and in the WPP, that the Overlords want our spiritual bodies! Our spiritual bodies are the keys that unlock the *Gates of Orion.* The AIF separated our spiritual bodies from our spirit/mind in order to trap us in 3-D, but now they want to release this same spiritual body from our physical body, without us understanding that this is what is happening. The Overlords seduce us into living in their new virtual realities of video games, the Internet, and smartphones in general, until most people spend more time on their devices than they do here in 3-D (which is already about to happen). Then, *with the Singularity, the AIF will trap us in a very similar way that they trapped the Namlú'u once!* Are we going to be fooled the same way again? We already are! Just look at the people around you in public—the great majority can't sit in a waiting room without being fixated on their smartphone. They get withdrawals after half a minute if they don't pick up their smartphones! I actually was in a waiting room the other day and saw this phenomenon played out over and over as new people arrived. When I looked around, *everybody, without exception, was on their smartphones, save one—me!* Most people are already trapped to some degree in virtual realities created by the AIF.

In the post-Singularity world, people will leave their bodies to live

285

in virtual reality, but they will still be grounded in their 3-D cyborg bodies and vanish into a virtual reality, controlled by AI, and ultimately, the AIF. In this virtual reality world, which is fluid and ever-changing (a mirror of the KHAA), people will be operating in their spirit/mind/body complex again, just as they do in the astral after their 3-D body has expired. People's astral body *is* their spiritual body, but people don't understand this concept and, therefore, they are trapped. They think they still need a physical body to be "alive." Without the physical body, they think they're "dead." What a scam, when the truth is just the opposite!

By creating these virtual realities, where the 3-D bodies are not necessary in order to be able to operate, the Overlords can have our composite spirit/mind/body to travel through multiple dimensions, using technology. Having their minds controlled by AI, there is no chance for Posthumans to rebel even when they have been temporarily freed from their physical bodies, and they will be at the mercy of the Warlords.

Using the Posthumans' spirit/mind/body, run by AI from the cyborg body connected to the SBC, the Warlords have complete control. Now they can program their interdimensional super soldiers (the Posthumans) into a war mode. They might try our capabilities first, by invading a star system somewhere to see how we're doing, but once they see how well we perform, they will have us prepare for the war of wars—the invasion of the Orion Empire and the ultimate coup d'état. This war will of course be fought in the KHAA—not in 3-D.

Thus, what was once a promising species in a promising Experiment, initiated by the Queen of the Stars, Posthumans will now turn against their own Creatrix, trying to defeat Her. That will be the end of the human soul group once and for all. I don't think the Posthumans will ever be able to defeat Orion's *MAKH warriors*—the *Defenders of the Queendom of Orion.*

What does this scenario remind you of? Isn't this a mirror of what happened eons ago, when Lucifer rebelled against his own mother; his Creatrix? Everything comes full circle, and what once was the Primordial Womankind will perish, but the Warlords couldn't care less. The Queen would care, but what choice will She have other than to destroy the Posthumans in the process? By then, we are Lucifer's warriors—*Lucifer's Legion*—and we are expendable! *This is how serious the Singularity is and how imperative it is to avoid it with all our might.*

NEW WAR STRATEGIES

D R. RAY KURZWEIL IS NOT ONLY an AI Prophet and a researcher of Artificial Intelligence, he also sits on the *Board of the Army Science Advisory Group* (ASAG), as one of five members.[399] This means that he is advising the U.S. Military Industrial Complex (MIC) how to approach warfare from a scientific viewpoint.

A researcher for the U.S. Army, Dr. Parmentola, who is affiliated with ASAG, says that future wars will be much different from all the wars thus far, and during the second decade of this century (which is now), the combat system will be "smaller, lighter, faster, more lethal, and smarter."[400] AI will be used to lead the soldiers to the target of the General's choice, now using something called *retinal display* on the soldiers, and when technology is more developed, they will be able to have a direct neural connection between man and AI. As the reader notices, humans are no longer in control, but AI is. The soldiers need to trust AI to make the correct decisions and all that they can do is follow orders, hoping these orders won't lead them into an ambush. Of course, there are still human Generals and other high ranking officers in charge of decision making, and they are for now only using AI to communicate with the solders on the battlefield, but it's already being tested to see if the same high ranking officers can be replaced by AI—the Pleiadians tell us that some Generals and Admirals are already AI.[401] When AI Generals and Admirals take over the chain of command, the soldiers will be at the mercy of AI. In addition, when a soldier gets wounded—regardless of how badly the wound is—there will be nanobot-infested body parts to replace the damaged ones, and it will be done quickly and with great skill. Some of these body parts will be taken, not from humans, but from pigs, wolves, bears, and other animals. We know for a fact that this has been experimented with for a long time in underground facilities, and the reason for doing this is because the MIC wants their soldiers to inhabit animal traits; particularly from violent animals or animals that are close to

---

[399] *The Singularity is Near*, p. 244.
[400] Ibid.
[401] Pleiadian, Lecture, 2015.

humans in their DNA structure (such as pigs), but not really human. For the MIC, the mix creates certain desirable traits in their soldiers, such as fury and a strong killer instinct that can be easily triggered and pulled up to the surface.[402]

According to Kurzweil, the soldiers, instead of carrying around let's say 100 lbs. of equipment, the equipment will be reduced to approximately 40 lbs. with *robotic mules* carrying some of it.

The drones used in warfare (but also to spy on citizens) will also become more sophisticated, and again, research is drawing from the Animal Kingdom. Kurzweil explains:

> The trend toward unmanned aerial vehicles (DAVs), which started with the armed Predator in the recent Afghanistan and Iraq campaigns, will accelerate. Army research includes the development of micro-DAVs the size of birds that will be fast, accurate, and capable of performing both reconnaissance and combat missions. Even smaller DAVs the size of bumblebees are envisioned. The navigational ability of an actual bumblebee, which is based on a complex interaction between its left and right vision systems, has recently been reverse engineered and will be applied to these tiny flying machines.[403]

As a side note, I find it quite interesting when a person in Kurzweil's position doesn't think twice about putting himself in charge of military research and advice for future wars instead of concentrating on future peace, which he officially supports and works toward. This is the controversy and the hypocrisy we can see in all these propaganda gurus. First, they say humans are alone in the Universe, and second, they are atheists. In their actions, however, they are preparing for cyber wars, and then they openly say that we will become *as* God, and that we are the fulfillment of *God's Plan*. Doesn't that imply that they believe there is a God after all, besides ourselves? So much for being atheists. You see how it's all a dog and pony show.

Here is more from the horse's mouth, i.e. Kurzweil, on what future war scenarios will be like:

> The FCS is not a one-shot program; it represents a pervasive focus of

---

[402] Ibid.
[403] Kurzweil, p. 245, op. cit.

military systems toward remotely guided, autonomous, miniaturized, and robotic systems, combined with robust, self-organizing, distributed, and secure communications.[404]

The future, in other words, just as we have discussed, is going to be dominated by AI, and AI is going to outsmart soldiers and high ranking military alike. What about Presidential elections? Do we want to vote for *this* AI program or *that* AI program? In reality, after the Singularity is well-established, we probably won't need any elections; the Office of the President will be obsolete. We will have a One World Government, run by AI, AIF Minions, and the AIF themselves—no more elections will be necessary.

Here is another significant quote from *The Singularity is Near*:

> The U.S. Joint Forces Command's Project Alpha (responsible for accelerating transformative ideas throughout the armed services) envisions a 2025 fighting force that "is largely robotic," incorporating tactical autonomous combatants (TACs) that "have some level of autonomy-adjustable autonomy or supervised autonomy or full autonomy within . . . mission bounds."[48] The TACs will be available in a wide range of sizes, ranging from nanobots and microbots up to large UAVs and other vehicles, as well as automated systems that can walk through complex terrains. One innovative design being developed by NASA with military applications envisioned is in the form of a snake.[49]

> One of the programs contributing to the 2020s concept of self-organizing swarms of small robots is the Autonomous Intelligent Network and Systems (AINS) program of the Office of Naval Research, which envisions a drone army of unmanned, autonomous robots in the water, on the ground, and in the air. The swarms will have human commanders with decentralized command and control and what project head Allen Moshfegh calls an "impregnable Internet in the sky."[405]

Kurzweil mentions at the end of the first paragraph that one of the designs being developed by NASA has *the form of a snake*, and by now we know who *the Snake* is—En.ki, aka Lucifer![406]

By now, many people have seen in movies and TV series how

[404] Ibid. op. cit.
[405] Kurzweil, p. 245, op. cit.
[406] For readers who haven't read the WPP, I strongly suggest you do so because it will be much easier to follow the logic that is applied in this book.

drones are spying on citizens; particularly citizens who are in resistance groups, working against an oppressive government. These drones seem to be everywhere, and it's very difficult to hide from them. Moreover, these drones are capable of firing weapons and killing their intended victims with great precision. Those watching these movies, videos, and programs probably think that it's a relief that it's just a sci-fi film, and therefore, it's not real. Well, reality will be at least this gruesome, if we are to believe Dr. Kurzweil, which I suggest we should. In the quote above, he says that the drones they are now developing will have human commanders, and maybe so—but for how long? More and more things are being controlled by AI. The world we now see around us will look very, very different in a decade or two. Eventually, humans who refuse to be part of the New World Order will be treated as outcasts and will not fit into the new system and the new cities that are about to be built and sometimes rebuilt by modifying existing metropolitans. However, even "smaller cities" (which will still be bigger than the cities we call small today) will be totally dominated by cyborgs, and there will be no place for people like you and me.

Kurzweil continues, "DARPA announced in 2003 that a battalion of 120 military robots (built by I-Robot, a company cofounded by robotics pioneer Rodney Brooks) was to be fitted with swarm-intelligence software to enable it to mimic the organized behavior of insects. As robotic systems become physically smaller and larger in number, the principles of self-organizing swarm intelligence will play an increasingly important role."[407]

What the *Defense Advanced Research Projects Agency* (DARPA) wants to do, and use as a major military strategy in future wars, is to create a hive-mind community that is easy to control. The entire idea of the SBC is based to a certain degree on studying insects, such as bees, bumblebees, and ants. The idea is that a thousand troops who can share their thoughts instantaneously with each other through a central system can outsmart the enemy. Of course, this only works until the enemy has found an equal system, or better, or has employed more intelligent soldiers. Nonetheless, war in the future is going to be much more sophisticated, deadly, and

---

[407] Kurzweil, op cit., pp. 245-46.

devastating.

SMART DUST

THE NEXT STRATEGY IS QUITE ALARMING—even more so for US civilians than for foreign enemies of war. It's called *smart dust*. Here is Kurzweil again:

> **Smart Dust.** DARPA is developing devices even tinier than birds and bumblebees called "smart dust"—complex sensor systems not much bigger than a pinhead. Once fully developed, swarms of millions of these devices could be dropped into enemy territory to provide highly detailed surveillance and ultimately support offensive warfare missions (for example, releasing nanoweapons). Power for smart-dust systems will be provided by nanoengineered fuel cells, as well as by conversion of mechanical energy from their own movement, wind, and thermal currents.
>
> Want to find a key enemy? Need to locate hidden weapons? Massive numbers of essentially invisible spies could monitor every square inch of enemy territory, identify every person (through thermal and electromagnetic imaging, eventually DNA tests, and other means) and every weapon and even carry out missions to destroy enemy targets.[408]

How are they going to dump this over the enemy lines? How about dumping it from chemtrails? This is nothing new (not even back in 2005, when Kurzweil's book was written), and smart dust is sprayed over our own cities today to "provide highly detailed surveillance" to quote Kurzweil. Because these nanoparticles are so spread out by the time they hit the ground, few will notice them. Albeit, there are some people in rural areas, living in forest environments, who have noticed layers of smart dust covering the ground in certain areas. These areas, however, are not "enemy territory," unless some include their own citizens as potential enemies (which they do). The "ingenious" part of the smart dust technology is that *smart dust can self-replicate!*[409] It's all very evil. *Stop promoting yourself as a messenger of peace, Dr. Kurzweil. It's very obvious that you are one of the worst war lords in today's world, and you don't have humanity's best interests in mind at any time! You help invent very evil technology and let AI high ranking officers kill our soldiers, having no concern about anybody's safety. This cannot be considered to be anything but evil to the*

---

[408] Ibid. op. cit. p. 246.
[409] Ibid.

extreme!

Naturally, when we discuss smart dust in warfare, the enemy (whoever the enemy might be) has developed the same kind of strategy, with a similar technology, where smart dust will be sprayed over *our* country (the U.S.), and the enemy's smart dust will of course self-replicate as well. Thus, what is so "smart" about it? This is gravely dangerous regardless of how it's justified. It's not enough to say that they've changed their minds, and it's not going to be used—if something's developed, it *will* be used, regardless of guarantees that it will not be used.

SMART WEAPONS AND NANO WEAPONS

NANO WEAPONS FOR MULTIPLE USES ARE ALREADY in place within the military. *Everything* of significance is tested in the military before it's put on the market. That includes "smart materials" that can "self-heal" to smart material that is put in soldiers' clothes that will help the soldiers heal automatically from battle wounds. This is another way to help create a cyborg.

Smart weapons is the Singularitists' term for weapons that get smaller and smaller in size and larger and larger in numbers. Soon, these weapons are going to be so small, so many, and so deadly that humans can no longer control them; it has to be done by AI, and they have to be automated. Again, humans will be more and more obsolete even in (3-D) warfare. It seems that they want fewer and fewer soldiers (future cyborgs) to be able to do more and more on and behind the battlefields and instead let AI do the job. Even when it comes to super soldiers (why don't they call them *smart soldiers?*), it's not the quantity or numbers of soldiers that count—it's what each one is capable of doing.

Kurzweil concludes the section about warfare in his book with introducing Human 3.0, who will be a human totally integrated with the SBC, working toward common goals—at and beyond the point of the Singularity:

> By the late 2030s and 2040s, as we approach human body version 3.0 and the predominance of non-biological intelligence, the issue of cyberwarfare will move to center stage. When everything is information, the ability to control your own information and disrupt your enemy's communication,

command, and control will be a primary determinant of military success.[410]

Again, it makes you wonder why they have to spend so much effort on developing nanotechnology for warfare when Kurzweil writes in other sections of his book, and is proclaiming in interviews, that we are going toward a New Era of Peace, after having integrated our common brain capacity with the SBC. When humanity is all "connected," who then are we fighting? Kurzweil talks about conquering the Universe, but in the same breath he says that he is almost certain that we are alone in the cosmos, and whatever is out there, it's meant for us to explore and exploit (it's *God's will*, according to Kurzweil). However, if there are no intelligent life forms out there, why do we need a future military force? The equation doesn't add up, does it? Is this what Kurzweil and Kaku in unison call "being optimists?"

The answers, of course, to the above questions are that they are developing nano technology in warfare to use in future, *interdimensional* warfare, in which Posthumans will play *Ender's Game.*

DARPA, WAR STRATEGIES, AND SUPER SOLDIERS

IT IS FOREMOST DARPA that has dominated technological and strategic advancements. DARPA is also testing new technologies inside the MIC before they are released to (and on) the public. This is how it's been done for quite a while. Now, DARPA has more challenges than ever before, and it is rapidly changing its strategies in order to be ahead of the game. With the AIF turning one country against another with some great assistance from prominent AIF hybrids, such as Henry Kissinger, Jimmy Carter, and Zbigniew Brzezinski (the men who never seem to die) traveling between countries, creating conflicts wherever they go, new defense and offense strategies are urgently necessary in order to meet new MIC demands and challenges.

The new focus of DARPA is now within neuroscience, immunology, genetics, and fields related to these. Example of goals DARPA wants to accomplish can, in very general terms, be summarized by mentioning three targets that will lead toward a certain goal, and here are three major bullet points:

---

[410] Ibid. op. cit. p. 247.

- Accelerating progress in synthetic biology

- Outpacing the spread of infectious diseases

- Mastering new neurotechnologies[411]

In order to accomplish DARPA's goals, it has created the new *Biological Technologies Office* (BTO),[412] which will focus on blending man with machine "for the defense of National Security."[413] What they want is to build synthetic soldiers (super soldiers) and thus make humans more advanced through robotics. Of course, making this public, BTO says it is only focusing on military advancements. However, and I repeat, all experimentation when going from theory to practice is first implemented within the military on soldiers and military personnel—then, whatever works, is released to (and on) the public.

Fig. 15-2: DARPA Director, Arati Prabhakar.

Arati Prabhakar is the Director for DARPA, and she told Congress the following regarding super soldiers:

---

[411] *Susanne Posel, Mar. 28, 2015,* "DARPA in 2020—Advancing Strategy Tech in Soldiers and Weapons"
[412] http://www.darpa.mil/Our_Work/BTO/
[413] *Susanne Posel, Mar. 28, 2015,* "DARPA in 2020—Advancing Strategy Tech in Soldiers and Weapons"

Chapter 15: Bring in the Universal Soldier

We had quadriplegic volunteers who agreed to have brain surgery, essentially have a small array placed on the surface of their brains, to pick up these neural signals for motor control, and then to use those to control these new, very sophisticated, robotic, prosthetic arms. In a sense we've opened a door — a connection between the human brain and the rest of the world. You can let your imagination go wild about where that's going to take us."[414] [415]

It's mostly the last sentence that tells us where this is heading. They are building the Universal Soldier, a term that might first have been coined (at least in public) by the Native Canadian Indian, Buffy St. Marie, in her song, *Universal Soldier*, from the 1960s.

Much of what Kurzweil is saying about improving human abilities is, and will be, implemented by DARPA. In order to create super soldiers, the following goals must be reached, according to DARPA,

- For humans to create the ability to survive blood loss

- To make the human brain capable of accessing and recalling accurate memories

- To develop technology to enhance the human metabolic system to obtain super-human resilience and immediate recovery from physical injury and disease

- To enhance human vision with cat-like upgrades for seeing in infrared

- To enhance soldiers with robotic limbs that are controlled via thought[416]

Thus, we have the *beginning* of creating a Universal Soldier. However, we need to always keep in mind that the MIC and the huge corporations are not controlled by any Board of Directors on this world— they are all controlled by the AIF. Lockheed Martin is a typical example of this. Lockheed Martin's CEO in 1995, Ben Rich, said that "we now have the technology to take ET home."[417] I don't think that people who heard

---

[414] Ibid. op. cit.
[415] *Fusion.net, Sep. 28, 2015.* "DARPA is testing implanting chips in soldiers' brains"
[416] Ibid. op. cit.

him say this really understood the meaning of these words and that he meant it literally. Lockheed Martin/Lockheed Skunkworks and Northrop Grumman are perhaps the number-one and number-two inventors of new war missiles, warplanes, and space technology.

It's difficult to be an optimist in the AI field when we hear and read that DARPA is playing catch-up with "enemy nations" when it comes to robotizing the battlefield. The Deputy Defense Secretary says that there is no way for a soldier with human speed limits and reaction speed to defend himself against AI robots attacking him. The field has to be robotized. This is, of course, very alarming because it will escalate when opposing nations try to outsmart each other's weapon systems. We already have the technology to blow this world to pieces—what more do we need? However, that's not what they want; it's quite the contrary. The Military—in the US and elsewhere—wants to focus on a predetermined target and hit it precisely; right to the nanometer! Will this prevent mass destruction? Of course not! Focusing on a specific target is only the beginning. After that comes retaliation. Next move is the enemy's move, and in a war-type revenge situation, the enemy will strike back a little harder than it was hit, and so the escalation begins.

The developing of AI in the War Industry is rapidly advancing, contrary to any (non-existing) peace programs. The US is now "nano-minutes" from having, in all fields of warfare, developed technologies that can detect any enemy weapon, vessel, or sentient being from a long distance and create a direct hit on the target. Warfare is going to become nothing similar to what we've been used to the last 150 years; the different technologies will wipe out whatever the controllers of such technologies want. In the meantime, huge resources are being used in order to create the perfect cyborgic super soldier, who ultimately can be resilient to space radiation and can travel the dimensions in order to quickly go from our solar system to another with the purpose to kill and conquer. But wait! There are no other beings "out there," according to Kurzweil.

One of the latest developments for creating super soldiers is something called *E-skin*. It aims at merging the human skin with that of a chameleon, so that the super soldier can easily blend in with more or less

[417] https://www.youtube.com/watch?v=u9ZZekWMiUQ

any environment in order to confuse and surprise the enemy.[418]

THE BAN ON "KILLER ROBOTS"

> "The other AI concern is one that Hollywood has been using for years as a theme and that is the rise of the 'Terminator' type being and the struggle to survive against an army of hostile shape-shifting robots being run by a self-aware AI called Skynet." – *Dr. Amnon Eden.*[419]

Fig. 15-3: Dr. Amnon Eden.

THERE IS AT LEAST ONE TIMELINE here on Earth on which mankind is going to experience AI in full, and with that I mean AI that is fully sentient, self-calculating, and murderous. I don't know how many times I have stressed it in this book, but *make sure you are not on that timeline,* unless you want to be a bee-hive cyborg. Always create your own space around you, have your own dreams and goals, and let these energies simmer out in your immediate environment (Universe), e.g. your home town and whatever other places you might travel to on a fairly regular basis. Include the environment you can be in control of and have some influence in.

---

[418] *WhatReallyHappened.com, Sep. 16, 2015,* "E-Skin Could Transform Prosthetics, Robots and Gadgets ... And Create Supersoldiers?"
[419] Sunday Express U.K., Jan. 18, 2016: "The Terminator could become REAL: Intelligent AI robots capable of DESTROYING mankind," op. cit.

Fig. 15-4: Arnold Schwarzenegger as the Terminator from 1984.

Dr. Amnon Eden is principal of the *Sapience Project*, a think-tank that has been formed to look at the potential disruptive impact of AI, and he is mighty concerned about its development. He asserts that we must think about the consequences of what we're doing. If we let AI develop freely and let their intellectual influence develop side by side, there will, sooner or later, come a time when "killer robots" will attack mankind; not only on the battlefield, but everyday civilians, too. He says we're close to a point of no return.[420] He thereby supports Oxford Professor Nick Bostrom, who has said that "nothing has been done to control the advance of AI."[421] The other concern, says Bostrom is that "the other AI concern is one that Hollywood has been using for years as a theme and that is the rise of the 'Terminator' type being and the struggle to survive against an army of hostile shape-shifting robots being run by a self-aware AI called Skynet."[422] While Stephen Hawking predicts that robots will be more intelligent than humans in 100 years, Bostrom goes even further, saying

---

[420] Ibid. op. cit.
[421] Ibid. op. cit.
[422] Ibid. op. cit.

that "robots will define the forms of human existence."[423]

Fig. 15-5: DARPA's army of robots, aka "LAWS."

Killer robots in wars already have a specific term attached to them. They are called *LAWS*, which stands for *Lethal Autonomous Weapons Systems*. These robots are designed by DARPA to kill *without being controlled by humans*. This leaves humans totally defenseless.[424] Moreover, these killer robots, of course, feel no empathy and will kill everything in their way that they compute to be an enemy. However, will they really be able to always determine who is "friend" and who is "foe?" The good news (for now) is that great concerns were raised over this new invention, and the United Nations called for a global ban on such killer robots.[425] However, we know how the song goes; if something such as LAWS has already been developed, it *will* be used, sooner or later, regardless of current bans. The MIC will find ways around it.

Although public opinion on the subject has been surveyed, and 8 out of 10 people want to ban robots used for aggressive purposes,[426] little of

---

[423] *Sputniknews.com, Jan. 6, 2016,* "Rise of Machines: Robots Could Wage War Against Humanity by 2055"
[424] *Sputniknews.com, May 29, 2015,* "DARPA's Autonomous Killer Robots Will Leave Humans Defenseless"
[425] Ibid.
[426] *Activistpost.com, Nov. 11, 2015,* "New Study Reveals That Most People Want To Ban Killer Robots"

this will be taken into consideration in the long term, if we look at the history of the MIC.

I am aware of that I am mostly addressing the development of AI in the US Military, but I want to stress that the US is only *one* of multiple countries that are working on the same, and similar, projects.

CONSCIOUSNESS CAN NEVER BE DUPLICATED, SAYS SCIENTIST

A PPARENTLY, THERE ARE ONLY a few, quantum physicists who have come to the insight that human consciousness can never be duplicated into a machine brain.

Professor Daegene Song is a young Korean quantum scientist who recently published a paper where he wrote that there is something special with human consciousness that can never be transferred over to a machine.[427] What he is talking about is of course the human soul. Memories stored in the brain of 7 billion people can, with technology, be stored in a computer brain, but not our consciousness because it exists outside of this holographic physical universe. Albeit, this is obvious for many readers, this is not necessarily obvious to scientists, and therefore, it's an important point that Song makes.

The AI scientists, in general, are not interested in trapping the soul directly into the SBC, anyway. They want us to keep our own cyborg bodies and have the souls stuck in those instead, so that everybody can draw individually from the common database, and as each person computes and learns, more information gets stored into the SBC database.

Many people have wondered why the Overlords allowed the human population to increase to such an "unmanageable" number as 7+ billion people, and we discussed a few reasons already. Although there are many casualties of war and manmade diseases, poisonous foods, chemtrails, and medicine, the population continues to grow. Some readers may have guessed another possible reason why they let us reproduce on this level. *The reason is the more people who can connect to the SBC, the more information that can be uploaded to the SBC.* Hence, it wouldn't come as a surprise if the

---

[427] *PR Newswire*, May 5, 2015, "Consciousness Does Not Compute (and Never Will), Says Korean Scientist"

world population is still at a high number by the time humanity plugs into the SBC. What will happen after that is uncertain; will they keep the population on a leveled-out high, or will they go ahead and reduce the population significantly *after* the Singularity? It is highly doubtful, in my opinion, that the AIF will kill people off after humanity has been "connected." It seems to me that the GMO and everything else that is bound to make us sick and die is just a temporary solution to keep the population from expanding irrepressibly. The measures being taken are still too lame and are probably not meant to reduce the population, but to maintain a certain increase until a desired number of people are on the planet when the Singularity starts. After that, there will be strict birth control measures as we discussed earlier in this book.

JADE HELM '15 AN AI DRILL

ON JULY 15, 2015, A MILITARY EXERCISE that has been named *Jade Helm '15* took place. It ended on September 15 and had run for eight weeks straight. It was a joint military operation across the States of Texas, Arizona, Florida, Louisiana, Mississippi, New Mexico, and Utah. The official purpose was "to improve the Special Operations Forces' capability as part of the National Security Strategy."[428] The operation was led and coordinated from Eglin Air Force Base in the northwest of Florida.

Although the exercise was made public before the fact, many people got upset because certain States were designated "enemy States" in the drill. There were many theories in circulation at the time as to why this operation happened in the first place, with soldiers marching in the streets in US cities. Still, almost everybody missed the point.

The real reason for Jade Helm '15 was to have soldiers operating in a planned maneuver without having any humans in charge! There were no Generals and high ranking military officers leading the operation; *it was all done by AI!* This was the entire purpose for the drill! The MIC wanted to see how well an operation such as this would turn out and how soon it can be used in real warfare (domestically and abroad).

---

[428] "Request to Conduct Realistic Military Training (RMT) Jade Helm 15". United States Army Special Operations Command. Retrieved January 8, 2016.

A courageous female network/software engineer and whistleblower came out and explained what she knew about Jade Helm:

"JADE" is an AI quantum computing technology that produces holographic battlefield simulations that has the ability to use vast amounts of data being collected on the human domain to generate human terrain systems in geographic population centric locations to identify and eliminate targets, insurgents, rebels or whatever labels that can be flagged as targets on a Global Information Grid in Network Centric Warfare environments. In short, JADE HELM is not battles directed by Generals and Military Commanders, but by a computer. It is a cognitive software based Network Centric Warfare System at the HELM.[429]

There has been much discussion about whether Jade Helm was setup as a hypothetical takeover of the United States in a situation where Martial Law is declared because of public revolt, and to see if AI can lead such an operation against angry citizens. Personally, I don't think this is the primary reason. Although that could be a part of it, it makes more sense to me that the Military needed a *real* playground in a *real* situation to test whether military troops could be led and commanded by AI. It all has to do with preparing for the Singularity. In a realistic scenario, they also wanted to test human reactions and "collect" the emotions the announced exercise created. These emotions will then help build the human database, which will become the final SBC. The Military knew that people would react negatively toward the drill, and that was what they wanted.

"Jade Helm" is "an acronym for a DARPA-developed AI quantum computing technology that produces holographic battlefield simulations and will be in charge of the drill in order to 'master the human' domain and predict human response."[430] The acronym Jade stands for "Joint Assistant for Deployment and Execution,"[431] and Helm is an acronym for "Homeland Eradication of Local Militants."[432] These are the keywords for the operation—at least on a superficial level—but as I suggested, the real agenda with Jade Helm '15 goes deeper. Jade Helm is basically a software

---

[429] *Exopolitics.org*, July 4, 2015, "JADE HELM OFFERS STRATEGIC OPPORTUNITY TO PREVENT ALIEN ARTIFICIAL INTELLIGENCE TAKEOVER"
[430] *Intellihub.com*, July 9, 2015, "Artificial intelligence takes the battlefield: Who is really running Jade Helm 2015?" op. cit.
[431] *Beforeitsnews.com*, Apr. 6, 2015, "What "JADE HELM" Really Stands for in Military/DHS"
[432] *Investment Research Dynamics*, Apr. 22, 2015, "Jade Helm 15: The Government Preps For Totalitarian Control"

program, run by AI that can compute and make superfast "correct" decisions in critical situations and instantaneously relay those to the soldier at a target.

There are subtler purposes with Jade Helm, as well, because there are many things the military can analyze from a drill such as this, and they will certainly extract all the data they can from the results of the operation.

FUTURE WARFARE IN SUMMARY

W ITHIN THE NEXT DECADE, warfare will look very different from what it is now. In fact, it will be much more devastating, even though there will be more robots and less soldiers on the battlefield. New threats are developing, where waring countries are using genetic and geophysical weapons on each other.

The Russian news media, *Sputnik News*, wrote,

Future weapons will be based on energy, electromagnetic, radiological, geophysical and genetic principles. There will also be special information weapons to change people's perception, completely changing their mind, the Ministry said.

Geophysical weapons that can alter the weather were already talked about in the past. People even wondered whether some hurricanes and earthquakes were "natural" disasters, speculating that it was possible to alter the climate and set off earthquakes using electromagnetic fields.

These deadly weapons of the future will target main control centers, essential facilities, technology, infrastructure and population.[433]

The question is how much of all the warfare technology we have is going to be utilized. From an average person's way of thinking, those who make the big decisions in our society may seem sick and insane, but from the decision makers' point of view it all makes sense. No one basically wants to destroy the world or wipe out humanity at this point—not with the Singularity in sight. What they *do* want, however, is to spread rumors of war to keep people in check and in a continual state of fear and terror.

---

[433] *Sputnik News*, Oct. 2, 2015, "Weapons That Could Change Geophysical Landscape, Human DNA to Appear Soon" op. cit.

On occasion, something bigger than usual will be played out in order to keep the majority of the population on the same timeline, and they do that by traumatizing us. 911 was a typical example of this. Since then, people have been constantly reminded of terrorist attacks that can strike anytime and anywhere. To control us, they don't need to reduce a big part of humanity— the fear of being killed is enough!

Chapter 16:
AI in the Animal and Plant Kingdoms

ATLANTEAN GENETIC EXPERIMENTS IN DISGUISE

ATLANTIS FELL BECAUSE THE genetic engineering and manipulation of species during that time under En.ki's leadership as Poseidon/Neptune went haywire. Prince Ninurta (Prince En.lil), En.ki's brother, with the full authority of the Orion Council, cornered his rebel brother En.ki and let the Deluge take place in order to wipe out most of the Earth's population at the time—strange-looking creatures created in laboratories and modified humans alike. The Living Library—The Orion Queen's human Experience—had been totally destroyed and either needed to be terminated once and for all or be restarted.

This was about 13,000 years ago.

Now we are almost in the exact same situation. We are putting human stem-cells in pigs and other animals to make them more human-like, officially, in an attempt to harvest organs from this manipulated animal genome and then implant them in humans that need new body parts such as livers, kidneys and new hearts. This has been wildly protested against by certain factions of government around the globe, where representatives are worried that animals are going to become more and more humanlike in their behavior; maybe even grow hair and get increased intelligence[434] (this echoes the gods' argument regarding the human race a couple of hundred thousand years ago).

For people who are waiting for transplants that take forever because of the increasing demand for "donated" organs and who are getting sicker and sicker every day they wait, genetic research, such as that described

---

[434] *Technologyreview.com*, Jan. 6, 2016, "Human-Animal Chimeras Are Gestating on U.S. Research Farms"

above, may be a blessing and a lifesaver. I understand this, but it's what is not communicated to the public that I find more troubling. It's important to the minions that we accept that they are doing this kind of research, and therefore, a beneficial outcome of the same research will be used to improve people's lives. However, thanks to the AIF, for far too long now nothing on this planet is as it seems, and there is always a deeper, more devious, and more dangerous agenda behind these beneficial results. We already know that AI is a fact, and that they are reengineering mankind, but what few people discuss is what the plan is for the animals.

THE FUTURE OF ANIMALS

IN ATLANTIS THERE WERE CENTAURS (horses with human torsos and heads), minot   aurs (humans with bulls' heads—the bull being a symbol for the constellation of Taurus, En.ki's domain), and other chimeras;[435] some of them created for labor, others for sexual games, and many just for the fun of it. Now we're about to do the same thing, but the goal may be slightly different—the animals and plants need to be included in the geoengineering of our planet, and this includes AI amongst animal and plant life.

The following quote is from *Technicalreview.com*:

> ... researchers in 2014 decided to begin impregnating farm animals with human-animal embryos, says Pablo Ross, a veterinarian and developmental biologist at the University of California, Davis, where some of the animals are being housed. Ross says at Davis he has transferred about six sets of pig-human embryos into sows in collaboration with the Salk Institute and established another eight or 10 pregnancies of sheep-human embryos with Nakauchi. Another three dozen pig transfers have taken place outside the U.S., he says.[436]

Scientists currently have to be approved by the Government for each transplant, but most of the time it's just a bureaucratic delay. Eventually, they get their approval when they can show how their research can be of assistance to humans. However, as we can see, history repeats itself. How

---

[435] Chimera comes from creatures in Greek "mythology" that are part lion, part goat, and part snake.
[436] *Technologyreview.com*, Jan. 6, 2016, "Human-Animal Chimeras Are Gestating on U.S. Research Farms," op. cit.

many "epiphanies" have these scientists had in their dream state? How many times have they been visited in their dreams, fed ideas and solutions to problems they wouldn't have been able to solve themselves? The AIF can be very active and inventive when people experience R.E.M. sleep.

The above article ends with the following sobering statement:

> "We don't want to grow them to stages we don't need to, since that would be more controversial," says Ross. "My view is that the contribution of human cells is going to be minimal, maybe 3 percent, maybe 5 percent. But what if they contributed to 100 percent of the brain? What if the embryo that develops is mostly human? It's something that we don't expect, but no one has done this experiment, so we can't rule it out."[437]

It's all experimentation in AI, although it may not be obvious for the average person who has not done the research. Once humanity is connected to the SBC, scientists need to know how to transplant new organs to humans. These organs will eventually not be human organs because the human population will be kept within manageable numbers and also kept alive. Hence, there will be very few human organs to transplant. Regardless if the transplant is from a human or animal organ, it will be infested with nanobots. This is obvious for two reasons: it's been proclaimed already by the AI Prophets, and we also know that the goal is not to maintain a biological human but to create a *new* human 2.0—a cyborg.

The goal is apparently to create human-animal chimeras that, when they reproduce, keep the hybridization alive, so that the medical science can harvest the organs they need in order to give humanity eternal life. In the long term, transplants, such as these, will not be necessary, but until Posthumans have been stabilized in their life-extended form, they will need the new organs when old ones start failing, and in order to rejuvenate a Posthuman and give - back -, or keep, its youth.

It is obvious that serious diseases have been developed in laboratories and spread to the population on purpose to make people sick. It is also obvious that existing diseases must not be cured at the moment, and all this is for a particular reason: *they want a sick population because that makes people afraid of their bodies and dependent on others (doctors, scientists, etc.) to help the sick people overcome.* The AIF wants people to be afraid of

---

[437] Ibid. op. cit.

their biological bodies and their imminent physical death in order to present the final solution: Posthumans—the new human who is mainly artificial and can't get sick, old, or die. No longer do people have to be afraid of their "frail" biological nature, which is inferior to AI. We have outgrown our biology, and now it's time to evolve. Evolution in the mind of AI Prophets and their masters is to transform us from biological human to Posthuman in the near future. This is their social-engineering formula, *Problem-Reaction-Solution*, at work again. *Problem:* people get sick and die from negligence of the Minion-controlled scientific community. *Reaction:* people demand that doctors and scientists do something about it! *Solution:* AI. *The Times* also ran an article about regulations to prevent scientists going wild,[438] but I suspect they had genetic regulators in Atlantis as well. It didn't make any difference in the long term, and it's highly doubtful it will now. Regulators are, at best, concerned humans or, at worst, people who work for the Minions but are just presenting the other side of the coin to make sure they've had the mandatory debate Dr. Kurzweil encourages before the final nail is hammered into the coffin of Homo sapiens sapiens.

ROBOBEES SET THE EXAMPLE

SOME ANIMALS AND INSECTS THAT ARE SEEN OFTEN and in many different localities by us humans are excellent to use as drones and spies. One such species is the bee; we see it everywhere, whether we're in America or elsewhere in the world. As long as it's not too cold, bees are usually part of the fauna.

It is obvious that so-called RoboBees will be used in the near future the exact way spy drones are used in sci-fi movies. It always gets me that they are presenting this drone technology as if it were something new; drones have been seen by people for years, whether they were prototypes that were tested or not. Now it looks as if they are coming out, presenting these prototypes; not the ready-to-go drones.

The idea is that these *bee drones* that possibly have been genetically engineered from real bees are going to work in many different

---

[438] *The Times*, Jan. 11, 2016, "The Origin of Species (Human-animal chimeras pose grave questions about the future identity of mankind. All the more reason to press on with the science)." Full article in PDF: http://www.alertuk.org/docs/2016-01-11-th.pdf.

environments. Some can be used during ultrasound, where the technician can have a swarm of RoboBees buzzing around the body and give an accurate picture of internal organs.[439] Others can be set out to browse an apartment to give a seller and a buyer exact measurements of the place.

A scientist from the *National Science Foundation* says,

> "If you can do something on the RoboBee, you can do it anywhere," Koppal says. "Microlidar could work wherever regular lidar is used. There are all kinds of applications in agriculture and industry where people already use lidar to map the factory floor or farm. In many cases, smaller and cheaper is just better."[440]

Figure 16-1: RoboBee at the size of a quarter.

There is no mention of bee drones as spies, of course. I would say, quite to the contrary; after the above statement, the Minion-related

---

[439] *Smithsonian.com (undated)*, "RoboBees Can Fly and Swim. What's Next? Laser Vision"
[440] *Smithsonian.com (undated)*, "RoboBees Can Fly and Swim. What's Next? Laser Vision," op. cit.

Smithsonian Society is quick to add:

> And remember, these lasers aren't high-powered zappers. RoboBees won't be using them to divide and conquer—only to get a more accurate view of the world around them.[441]

It goes without saying, however, that when the secret government develops drones, it is not going to let itself be restricted by morals and ethics; spying on citizens will of course be one of the major tasks for something such as RoboBees.

Even after the Singularity—at least at first—Posthumans still need to eat, so part of the animal kingdom may still be here for some time. Dr. Kurzweil stresses that after the Singularity, our environment will be cleaned up, and the damage we've done will be reversed. In other words; the Earth will be geoengineered—something that has already started, according to some, albeit we don't notice too much of that yet.

Posthumans will eventually not have the range of emotions that Homo sapiens sapiens have today, and eventually, when AI has fully taken over, we lose our emotions more or less entirely, so we don't need beauty around us to thrive. We may not need all the wide variety of animal species, either, because they, too, may be considered "useless eaters." Also, if we geoengineer our environment, perhaps to look different from now, some species will become extinct and others may be seeded here intentionally on Earth to better fit the new situation. The animal species that will survive and the new ones being created can then be genetically manipulated to perfectly fit Posthumans' needs. There is no need to worry about pets, however, because if they are still around, they will be AI for certain. The number of animals available for food will probably be calculated for, and the genetic manipulation of their genes will make sure that each species only gets as many offspring as it takes to feed a population. No longer does it have to be a natural symbiosis; the AIF and their Minions create *exactly* what Posthumans need—nothing more, nothing less.

---

[441] Ibid. op. cit.

THE FUTURE OF PLANTS

S INCE MY CHILDHOOD, IT HAS grieved me when I hear that they are chopping down the Amazon rainforests and other tropical forests around the world. The forests—especially the rainforests and jungles—are the lungs of Mother Gaia. Without these forests, there wouldn't be enough oxygen to breathe, in spite of the algae in the oceans -. In addition, all the beauty of these forests is dramatically diminished mile after square mile by cutting timber on a daily basis; it's like cutting off a little bit of your own lungs every day. It is not hard to imagine what would happen to you after a while—the same is true for the rainforests and forests in general.

Science says that there is far more carbon dioxide than trees can absorb, and we need to create a total desert with just a few trees to make it break even. But even if this *were* true, why do these same scientists think there is an abundance of trees and forests in the world, then? For decoration? The Living Library was purposely designed, and everything here has its purpose. There isn't an abundance of trees because humans were meant to cut down entire rainforests!

However, the Minions have apparently started being a little concerned about the future of our breathing air. Instead of stopping the lucrative timber industry, they want to find artificial ways to remove carbon from the air. One method they want to try is to capture carbon directly from the smoke stacks of power plants[442] (plants as plants, right?). Others want to collect carbon and pull it from the open air where it's less dense.[443] Theoretically, one square mile of super-powered artificial trees (that have to be built) could remove 4 million tons of carbon every year from the air, according to the *Center for Negative Carbon Emissions*.[444] However, this project, in which the artificial trees at least could be pretty to look at inside city limits, etc., is too costly so, the planners are leaning toward something uglier to look at instead, but much cheaper (after all, in the end it's Posthumans and AI who are supposed to live with it, according to their plans). "No one" finds it reasonable to stop the outlet of carbon in the air from human activity, anyway, according to a *Washington*

---

[442] *The Washington Post*, Jan. 6, 2016, "The quest to hack trees and beat climate change"
[443] Ibid.
[444] Ibid.

Post article,[445] so the solution is always more technology and less nature. Rest assured that AI Prophets and their Masters consider biology (the Living Library) antique and obsolete in the Brave New World of Artificial Intelligence and Nanotechnology. Beauty and biological symbiosis is not on the list for the future Posthuman world.

What everybody forgets is that trees are not only Mother Gaia's lungs, but they are also antennas! They start out as deep root systems under the ground and grow to reach high into the air. Trees are both transmitters and receivers of information and were most possibly once a communication system between Orion and Earth—the Plant Kingdom's "spokesmen," telling the Queen how the Plant Kingdom was doing. Dolphins, whales, elephants, and other animals have, and had, the same function in the Animal Kingdom. However, before the AIF invaded our solar system, this type of communication happened across the dimensions in the spiritual universe—the KHAA—and not in a contained 3-D environment. Their ancestors did not look as today's animals, but the principle was probably the same. Now, with the AIF quarantine, the Grid, and electronic "fences" set up in the solar system, cosmic communications do not get through the way they used to, which effectively disconnects Mother Gaia and all life here from the outside Universe.

From an AIF perspective, natural rainforests and other dense forests could be potential settlements for "refugees," who don't want to participate in the Singularity—another reason to get rid of the forests and create artificial ones instead.

---

[445] Ibid.

Chapter 17:
When Robots Surpass us a Billion-Fold

TELEPATHIC COMMUNICATION

SOMEONE WHO IS TRULY multidimensional communicates with thoughts. On Earth, we call it telepathy. Most humans don't think they are telepathic, but we all are; we are reading each other's minds all the time, but most of us are not aware of it. Those who are more sensitive to such things sometimes notice that they know what the other person will say before he or she has said it. This may even apply when the other person says something unpredictable.

We humans are "trained," or manipulated, into believing that there are no senses other than the five we are used to. Hence, we disregard all, or most, psychic communication we give and receive, when in fact, all we need to do is to tap into it and start using it.

However, the AI Gurus tell us that psychic abilities can be achieved by connecting with AI. The AIF has no intention of letting us develop these dormant skills in a natural manner. Instead, they have always tried to suppress these skills, until they can be controlled through the SBC. In Japan (of course), they have developed a device that can decipher words from brainwaves without any verbalization needed. They have discovered that our brainwaves are the same when we think a word as when we speak it.[446] This is a very important process in the Singularity agenda because in order to become capable of tapping into the SBC, Posthumans need to be psychic and master artificial telepathy -. This, of course, will be obvious when we learn that the professor who is in charge of the artificial

---

[446] *Daily Mail, Jan. 6, 2016*, "Could we soon 'speak' telepathically? Mind-reading computer deciphers words from brainwaves BEFORE they are spoken"

telepathy project is an expert in brain computer interfaces.[447] The AI Prophets proclaim that the biological process, if we want to reach the same goal as AI, is taking too long. They say that we don't have much time, when we take into account how things are developing here on Earth (pollution, war, famine, and starvation, to name a few—much of it man-created in order to speed up the AI process). Hence, the biological human has reached her peak, and now it's time for an upgrade that will take mankind to an entirely new level. This is what we learn from the Singularitists, but it is only a sales argument to win us over faster so, we willingly go into the "next phase:" the Singularity.

AI AND EQUALITY

So long as we look at AI as robots made of steel, or some software program that can answer questions in real time, we may not feel much of a threat coming from them. However, as soon as these robots become more and more humanlike, we will grow increasingly uncomfortable. People may want to know if the robots *are* taking over after all.

We might want to ask ourselves, how long will it take before robots have all the rights of the First Amendment? How long will it be before the law is protecting them? If you hurt a robot, you may go to jail. If this is laughable now, it soon won't be. It's pure logic that when the industries and he big corporations have exchanged most, or all, of their workforce with AI, they will do everything in their power to protect their new workers. In other words, in most cases, these workers will become more valuable to society than humans are. This is another aspect of robots surpassing us.

Once in the Singularity, Posthumans may not need to work, as we know work; androids will take their place, while Posthumans are groomed for *greater tasks,* in service to the AIF.

Some people will protest for a while, before the Singularity is in place. The AI Prophets know this and do everything they can to keep people distracted in these transitional years. Once it is established, lack of

---

[447] Ibid.

jobs and other concerns will no longer be an issue—the trick is just to get humanity through to the point of the Singularity, without them creating an uproar. From what I have seen, the Controllers will have little or no problems achieving this, or as Val Valerian once put it, *everything is under control*: literally.

THE END OF PRIVACY—ONCE AND FOR ALL

THE SINGULARITISTS WANT US TO get used to the idea that we should artificially evolve our biological form to a much more solid, artificial form. They want to make our thinking process more digital and "logical" for our own good. This is left-brained to the extreme, and where art and music are concerned, Kurzweil is quick to say that we don't need to buy CDs or download music anymore—any song we want will be performed inside our heads, and if we want to experience a certain kind of art, it will be downloaded to our brains. This means, for example, that musicians or rock bands will upload their music and their ideas to the SBC, and from there, anyone on the planet can download the music and hear it in their heads.

Is the reader beginning to see that humanity's future is in the hands of lunatics? With the following Kurzweil statement, where he uses twisted logic, I will not only close this chapter but also end Part 1 of this book. Part 2 will dig deeper into the ET aspect of AI and the Singularity,

"If humans lived many hundreds of years with no other change in the nature of human life, then, yes, that would lead to a deep ennui [boredom]. But the same nanobots in the bloodstream that will keep us healthy—by destroying pathogens and reversing aging processes—will also vastly augment our intelligence and experiences. As is its nature, the non-biological portion of our intelligence will expand its powers exponentially, so it will ultimately predominate [prevail]. The result will be accelerating change—so we will not be bored."[448]

---

[448] http://singularity.com/qanda.html

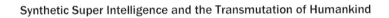

PART 2: The Gods of Technology and Warfare

Chapter 18:
Of Great ConCERN

"The whole world is a stage"—*William Shakespeare*

"We have a duty to ACT"—*Barack Obama*

"Signs and symbols rule the world, neither words nor laws"—*Confucius*

"Until you make the unconscious conscious, it will direct your life and you will call it fate"—*Carl Jung*

THE LARGE HADRON COLLIDER—THE OFFICIAL VERSION

WE HAVE ALL HEARD ABOUT the *Large Hadron Collider* (LHC) in Cern, Switzerland. The official reason why the LHC was built is to find some answers to nagging scientific problems. For example, scientists want to see if they can find something they call the *God Particle*, i.e. they want answers to what happened the moment before the theoretical *Big Bang*, which according to science created the Universe. Moreover, they want to find out which version of the universal model is most correct; whether it's the old "Standard Model"[449] or the "Higgsless Models."[450] They also want to know more about the deep structure of space and time, particularly the interrelation between quantum mechanics and general relativity. Moreover, the scientists want to find out if there are extra dimensions, as postulated by *string theory*, and if so, can we detect them? What is the nature of Dark Matter? What else can we learn about the symmetry between matter and antimatter?

---

[449] https://en.wikipedia.org/wiki/Standard_Model
[450] https://en.wikipedia.org/wiki/Alternatives_to_the_Standard_Model_Higgs

These are just a few of the many questions the scientific community supposedly hope they can have answered with the CERN project. The main *official* reason why the LHC was built was to find the God Particle; the particle that allegedly made the Universe come into existence.

Pastor Paul Begley explained it quite well with an analogy. He said, and I paraphrase, "Let's say that we humans for the first time encounter a town with many empty houses standing in the middle of nowhere (the houses represent the Universe). We have never seen houses before. We realize that these houses can give us shelter and comfort, so we move into them and make ourselves safe and cozy. One day, out of curiosity, we start wondering what it is that holds these houses together; why are they there at all? We find out that they are held together with what we call glue. Hence, we try to figure out how this glue can hold the house together, but we can't. The glue is in a hardened state, and in that condition, it's impossible to say how it all works. Thus, our scientists want to break that glue down into its liquid form (the God Particle) in order to figure out how the houses manifested."[451]

The current physics process is to a major degree based on proton-proton collisions. However, approximately one month per year, heavy-ion collisions are added to the experiment. Back in 2012, more than 6 quadrillion (6 x 10^{15}) LHC proton-proton collisions had been analyzed, at a cost of approximately \$9 billion,[452] which makes the LHC the world's most expensive scientific instrument ever built to date.[453]

Still, from official reports, we learn that in 2011, quark-gluon plasma, which is the densest matter thought to exist, besides black holes, had been detected from the LHC experiments.[454] However, there have been concerns raised whether the LHC experiments are safe or not, and if these experiments may create mini black holes, and if so, what would the consequences be? Reportedly, a committee researched this concern, and this is what they apparently found out,

> The experiments at the Large Hadron Collider sparked fears that the particle collisions might produce doomsday phenomena, involving the

---

[451] https://www.youtube.com/watch?v=gUIr3yUbobg, ~4 min. 30 sec. into the video.
[452] https://en.wikipedia.org/wiki/Large_Hadron_Collider#Computing_and_analysis_facilities
[453] https://en.wikipedia.org/wiki/Large_Hadron_Collider#Cost
[454] https://en.wikipedia.org/wiki/Large_Hadron_Collider#First_run_.28data_taken_2009.E2.80.932013.29

production of stable microscopic black holes or the creation of hypothetical particles called strangelets.[139] Two CERN-commissioned safety reviews examined these concerns and concluded that the experiments at the LHC present no danger and that there is no reason for concern,[140][141][142] a conclusion expressly endorsed by the American Physical Society.[143]

The reports also noted that the physical conditions and collision events which exist in the LHC and similar experiments occur naturally and routinely in the universe without hazardous consequences,[141] including ultra-high-energy cosmic rays observed to impact Earth with energies far higher than those in any man-made collider.[455]

Fig. 19-1: Part of the Large Hadron Collider (LHC).

The instruments in the LHC simulate what is happening routinely in the Universe on a more massive scale, recreating it in a small collider.

We believe that the Technocratic Era began in recent time, but high technology is nothing new; many advanced civilizations have existed here on Earth in the ancient past. Atlantis is just one of them, and Babylonian science was to a large degree based upon what was available during the

---

[455] https://en.wikipedia.org/wiki/Large_Hadron_Collider#Safety_of_particle_collisions, op. cit.

Atlantean Era.

OCCULT SYMBOLISM AT CERN

I T IS THE MILITARY INDUSTRIAL COMPLEX (MIC) THAT IS THE driving force behind the LHC, and it has always been running errands for the Overlords, in turn pushing the envelope of our human scientific community. The MIC is controlled by secret societies that are controlled by the AIF; therefore, we notice a number of occult symbols surrounding the LHC. The first major symbolism a visitor notices at CERN is a huge statue of the Hindu god *Shiva the Destroyer* raised outside the main building. Second is the CERN logo, consisting of three sixes (the *Beast 666*), cleverly hidden in plain sight (fig. 19-2 below).

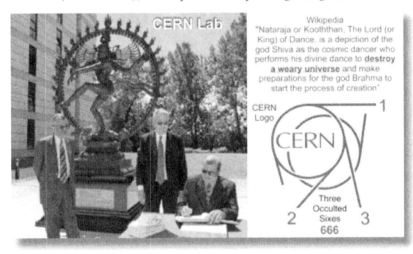

Fig. 19-2: Shiva and the CERN 666 logo.

Those who have read the WPP, the *Fifth Level of Learning*, know that Shiva the Destroyer is the Hindu name for Marduk, En.ki's son, and Marduk is the current Lord of Earth. Brahma, in this case, mentioned in fig. 19-2, is the return of En.ki as the Ruler of the New Age of Aquarius.

Lord Shiva, outside the CERN building, symbolizes the destruction of humankind as we know her, but also the destruction of the world as it is today. Shiva is described in Hindu religion as the destroyer of something old and the rebuilder of something new. A New World Order will replace today's society, and the Overlords can once again rule more or less openly in a world consisting of Artificial Intelligence, cyborgs, Singularity and temporary peace (until mankind is ready to go out in space and fight the AIF's space wars for them). All this is very important and something the public has no knowledge of, in spite of the truth being hidden in plain sight for everyone to see. We can't say they didn't tell us; we just didn't do our homework. Another clue is the location of the LHC; it's setup partially in the French town Saint-Genus-Pouilly, where the word *Pouilly* comes from the Latin word *Appolliacum*, which is related to the god Apollo.[456] During the Roman Empire, there was actually a temple dedicated to Apollo in that area, as well.[457] [458] The Greek god Apollo is another name for Marduk; the same gods had different names in different cultures. Apollyon (Apollo) is the name of the god of the bottomless pit in Greek mythology. Other names for him are Abaddon and Azazel. This makes him the model of the biblical Satan, and this is clearly mentioned in Rev. 9:11 (isn't it interesting to see the number 911 here?) The LHC has Marduk's signature and symbolism all over it!

> REV 9-11: And they had a king over them, which is the angel of the bottomless pit, whose name in the Hebrew tongue is Abaddon, but in the Greek tongue hath his name Apollyon.[459]

Let us for a brief moment return to the God Particle or *Higgs boson*, as it is also called. According to the CERN scientists, they believe they may have found it, but more research is needed.[460] This alleged discovery has made other prominent scientists, such as Stephen Hawking, very alarmed, as quoted below. However, nothing is what it seems to be, and instead, their research is focused on the exact science that will let certain forces through the portals into our dimension.

The Collider was restarted in March 2015, after an alleged

---

[456] *RT, Aug 31, 2015*, https://www.rt.com/op-edge/313922-cern-collider-hadron-higgs/
[457] http://memim.com/saint-genis-pouilly.html
[458] RT.com, Sep 1, 2015, "10 mind-blowing facts about the CERN Large Collider you need to know"
[459] KJV, "Book of Revelation, 9:11"
[460] https://en.wikipedia.org/wiki/Higgs_boson

malfunction that destroyed part of it.

Dr. Stephen Hawking recently warned that the reactivation in March of CERN's large hadron collider could pose grave dangers to our planet...the ultimate reality check we are warned. Hawking has come straight out and said the 'God particle' found by CERN "could destroy the universe" leaving time and space collapsed ... Is CERN the most dangerous thing in the cosmos that could lead to the ultimate destruction of the Earth and the entire universe? Recent developments prove to us the scientific community is no longer able to explain 'reality' without looking at the 'supernatural'. Will we soon learn CERN is really the 'ultimate stargate' and one of the gate-keepers most closely guarded secrets? Will this be the way man attempts to break the ultimate 'God barrier', an attempt to encounter demi-God's in an all-out rush towards the destruction of all creation? We understand they won't be releasing the secrets until they're prepared to release them.

Does CERN headquarters' symbol of Shiva, dancing the cosmic dance of death and destruction, signal the TRUE purpose of CERN's existence? A look at the 'Shiva' (the Hindu God of Destruction) symbology surrounding CERN's headquarters gives us the beginning of what we need to know. "The men who would play God, in searching for the God particle, are truly going to find more than they bargained for as they open the gates of hell" we are warned by Stephen Quayle, "they will find inter-dimensional beings who have a taste for human flesh and [desire] humanities destruction. Most scientists, in lacking an understanding of the 'supernatural entities' that are going to confront them, are way beyond their ability to comprehend, let alone control, the forces of Pandora's box that will be released."

Astrophysicist Neil de Grasse Tyson has also sounded the alarm in a hypothetical manner by telling anyone who might want to 'blow up a planet' how to do so...is this CERN's attempt to do so by attempting to 'recreate' the big bang within a man-made structure that has frightened Stephen Hawking so much? Do they know that they know that they know what they're doing?

"Ask yourself: how much energy is keeping it together?" Neil deGrasse Tyson told co-host Eugene Mirman on his Star Talk radio show. "Then you put more than that amount of energy into the object. It will explode."

"In the movie *Star Wars*, we see the Death Star blow up the planet Alderaan," Mirman said, reading the question. "Setting aside the question of how [such] a thing would be possible, what would happen to our solar system if the Empire blew up, say, Mars?"

First, deGrasse Tyson said, any Imperial sympathizer looking to make that happen would have to calculate the planet's binding energy, in order to determine how much energy it would take to overcome the gravitational forces binding the planet together.

"Now you have a device that can pump that energy into your planet and have that planet absorb the energy, rather than have the energy come out the other side, it will completely destroy the planet to smithereens, entirely," he explained. "So, that's how one would go about it."[461]

The concern is very legitimate, but what scientists don't know—probably not even Stephen Hawking—is that the technology used at CERN is developed from ancient Atlantean ET technology. Of course, anything can hypothetically go wrong when humans are involved in such relatively advanced projects, but largely, they know what they're doing, and I doubt that they will destroy Earth *or* the Universe in the process. They only do what they are trained to do, and the principle is, *build it and they will come.* This is also what the late Dr. A.R. Bordon of *Life Physics Group California* (LPG-C) kept repeating.[462] The point is that the Overlords need *us* to build and run the lab to be able to blame humanity for cooperating with the "gods." Let us look a little closer into this.

PRINCIPLES OF PROPHECY

W E DISCUSSED PROPHECIES IN THE WPP, but it's imperative that we discuss it again.
People slanted toward religion believe that Prophecy (e.g. Bible Prophecies) were dictated by God Himself. I would argue that they were dictated, not by God almighty, but by the AIF gods. I want to concentrate on Biblical Prophecies, as dictated in the Book of Revelation and the Book of Daniel in the New Testament, because these prophecies describe what has been planned for humanity since antiquity.

I wrote, "planned," for a reason because the Prophecies are long-term plans. There might be readers who wonder how prophecies written centuries ago can be fulfilled today; how did the gods know what will

---

[461] Allnewspipeline.com, Feb. 3, 2015, "Attempt To Re-Create 'Big Bang' Begins March 2015 - Will Gates Of Hell Soon Open To The Destruction Of All Creation?"
[462] See WPP, "The First Level of Learning."

happen so far in the future? The answer is that the Overlords are the masters of the third dimension in which we live—they have created linear time by manipulating us into believing that time is running from one fixed point to another and it cannot move upward, downward, backward, in parallel, perpendicular, crisscross, simultaneously, or be non-existent. The Overlords know much better—they know that all the above are possible, and that it's only a matter of perception and perspective. With our current limited minds, we can't perceive time the way it really is. If you are a Master (the gods), and you have your puppets (humans), it's easy for the former to manipulate the latter. The Overlords can manipulate linear time in 3-D more or less as they please. If we didn't have free will, we would be 100% at their mercy (something they want us to become through AI—"mindless," obedient warriors).

The gods can look at linear time from an exterior perspective. Just imagine you are sitting with a paper in front of you on which you draw a long line, representing a time frame, let's say between 2:00 AM and 6:00 PM of a particular day, and it's now, let's say, 12:30 AM. On this timeline you can insert events you wish to happen by marking them with your pen—even events in the future. Pretend that at 11:00 AM, you want to have lunch, and you know that your significant other always makes lunch for you. All you need to do is to tell him or her that today it's very important that he or she gets your lunch ready at 11:00 AM, and he or she will do it for you. In other words, your "prophecy" has been fulfilled. You can add any event on the line you've been drawing, and if you are uncertain whether a particular event will happen or not, you can manipulate people so that it will happen. If you're as skilled as the gods, you can do it quite easily. However, it's impossible for the gods to be able to predict *everything* that will happen on their otherwise fairly predictable timeline. The wildcard is humanity's unpredictability; something that makes us quite unique. The Overlords constantly have to "help us" along the way in order to steer us in the "right direction." They are doing this in different ways, but traumatic mass events, such as 911, are part of keeping their lulus on track.

The above analogy works just as well when it comes to Bible Prophecies. The gods don't plot for one day at the time, but for thousands of years. They are not affected by linear time and mortality as we are, and

324

therefore, thousands of years is nothing to them; just as it was nothing for the immortal Elves in J.R.R. Tolkien's *Lord of the Rings* they follow the same principal. The Overlords "predict" the events that will happen at large before their Return, and still being around when the Prophecies are about to be fulfilled, they can easily manipulate the game board and move the pieces as they like, unbeknownst to those who are primarily affected, i.e. us humans. *Thus, the Overlords fulfill their own prophecies with our help.*

However, the gods have one major problem—humanity's unpredictability! In order to solve this problem, the gods sometimes create a traumatic mass event that will make people focus on *one* particular timeline; i.e. 911, the Katrina disaster, school shootings, and the premature death of major celebrities and other people admired by the general public. This helps the gods to keep us more focused on the timeline they want us hooked into. While the AIF-initiated traumatic events leading up to the *Second Coming* play out, the gods rely on the fact that a majority of humankind will focus on that timeline.

Conversely, they also know that not *all* of humanity will be stuck on that timeline because there are those who understand what is going to unfold, and those people will not be deceived as easily as the masses. Hopefully the reader will understand that 911 and other so-called *mass events* are merely drills to see the effects. In reality, the AIF gods are thinking much bigger than this, and I will write more about that in the next section.

Many people point out that Bible Prophecies are being fulfilled in front of our eyes, and I agree with that. Not *all* of the prophecies will be fulfilled because of humanity's unpredictability, but most of them probably will. The stunning part is that a large number of non-suspecting humans will welcome the fulfillment of the Prophecies, including the Battle of Armageddon, because of their belief in religion. Therefore, these people are giving energy to their fulfillment, and some of them are actively working on fulfilling them. People in the occult world, who have climbed up the Grades by degrees, are wishing the gods back as well, understanding that the Overlords are the real Grandmasters of their secret society.

How the gods will make their presence known is uncertain, but it's more than likely that they will; they are eager to play out their own prophecies. Marduk will come back as Jesus the Christ, and because we are used to seeing him that way, he will probably appear with shoulder-long hair (possibly red) and wearing a beard. He will probably look as if he's in his early to mid-30s. He will tell people that the Day of Judgment has arrived, and eventually he will announce *Heaven on Earth*, and who is the ruler of Heaven in the astral? Marduk's father Lord En.ki, aka Lucifer! Hence, Lucifer, presumably wearing a long, white beard, will now present himself as God. I wouldn't be surprised if he showed himself as a huge face in the sky, smiling piously to the crowd. God En.ki/Lucifer will be the ruler of the Age of Aquarius, and his son Marduk will be the Christ, sitting on the throne, pretending to follow his *Father's* advice. If we let our imagination run wild, perhaps certain pious persons in the past have actually been in stasis in the astral since the day they died, and En.ki and Marduk will revive and reincarnate them at will. Thus, they can play out this Prophecy as well: the revival of the dead.

As a part of the Prophecy, we see history repeating itself—not because it's some kind of "universal cyclic pattern," but because it's set up that way to serve the AIF agenda. We now see similar things happening as happened at the end of Atlantis and in the days of Noah (En.ki's hybrid son). An example of this is the entire Transhumanism movement (the New Atalantis) with rapidly developed technology, genetic engineering and manipulation, catastrophic events, and colonization of space and other worlds, etc.

There is very little doubt that we are actually living in the biblical *End Times* right at this moment—on this subject I agree with the Christians. The question is what will happen first—the Singularity or the Battle of Armageddon. Both scenarios are more than plausible. If Armageddon were to happen first, it would occur in the next twenty-five years or so, if we are to believe what the AI Prophets are telling us about the Singularity taking place by 2045. It makes sense that the War of Armageddon will happen *before* the Singularity, which might be the *Heaven on Earth* that the Bible Prophecies talk about.

OPENING THE GATES

THERE HAVE BEEN SPECULATIONS THAT CERN's main hidden purpose is to create stargates or portals for the gods to use when they return; portals that will lead them into our realm from their own other-dimensional location. This would be the reason, or so the speculations go, why the LHC scientists need to dabble with Dark Matter and what they call antimatter. In order to create a portal, they need access to these allegedly unknown realms.

Fig. 19-3. Artist's vision of a portal. We see remnants of these all around the planet, with sculptures of the Overlords surrounding them.

Although it's true that we can't create portals without using *unseen matter* (Dark Matter), it's evident that interdimensional portals were already created by the gods in ancient time, in order for them to enter our reality. All across our planet, stone formations have been found that look like gates or doorways, guarded by sculptures of Sumerian or Egyptian gods; the Overlords (the AIF Anunnaki). These portals have slightly eroded over time, and they are probably no longer used. The Overlords use much more sophisticated ways now to enter our frequency and manifest. It's not that they couldn't do it back then, but they probably wanted to put on a show for the more primitive humans. After all, they were "gods." In reality, most of these beings can come and go as they please between dimensions; no portals are required. However, not all of the AIF are interdimensional, and they do need portals to enter our solar system in 3-D. To do so, they usually enter through the Sun, who has her own portals, which are heavily guarded by Lucifer's Legion.

If this makes sense thus far, we must inquire who are the scientists at CERN opening the portals for?

The purpose of a project such as CERN is larger than to try to accomplish only one task, but opening portals is probably one of the most important purposes with the LHC. We are closing in on the Singularity and time is running out. The CERN project has been planned for a long time—much longer than the twenty years, as we have been told. Indeed, it seems as though they actually started preparing the CERN project in the 1950s in order to get ready in time opening the portals and making the Singularity happen--.

Fig. 19-4: *Sumerian stargate, guarded by Marduk (some suggest Ninurta, which is incorrect. Ninurta was not on Earth in the Sumerian-Babylonian time period. This depiction perfectly resembles Marduk).*

Much of what is needed, for the Singularity to become a reality, is already in place, or is in the process of being completed. The gods can come and go as they please, and the technology—including the SBC—is to a large degree already in place. Humanity is being manipulated into getting lost in technology and Artificial Intelligence, and nanobots are continuously being implanted into human bodies—primarily through chemtrails, medications, and vaccines—so what is missing?

What's missing is increased human initiative!

This goes back to the same Cosmic Laws we've discussed before; in this case, the *Law of Free Will* and the *Law of Non-Interference*. The Overlords want *us* to invite them for the same reason as always—we need to show the star beings from Orion and other places that we are in cahoots with the Overlords and were never forced to do anything; *build it and they will come.* The AIF makes us (particularly our authorities) agree to invite Lucifer's Legion into our 3-D realms, and the Warlords provide us with some of the technology to make that happen. They need the LHC, but *we* have to build it!

Why are the scientists at CERN willing to do this? Most of them don't know anything about the real agenda, and if interdimensional beings start coming through, they will be just as terrified as any human would be. Scientists are just told what to do, and then they do it. We also should note that the Minions are planning to build a larger and more powerful collider in the near future in order to *increase the energy!*[463] I still need to learn exactly what this is about, but my antennas are already up, and I am suspicious that they may be assisting the Overlords in creating a direct stargate that is not mapped or watched—except by the AIF—leading directly to the heart of Orion. If so, a war with Orion could be closer in time than I thought![464] [465] I am under the impression that they don't want to open the Saturn portal again, even though it leads to Orion. They know that it's guarded on the other end. The Warlords might be creating a backdoor to Orion with our help!

THE MANDELA EFFECT AND SCIENTISTS GOING CRAZY!

T HERE IS ONE MORE SUBJECT that needs to be included in this chapter. Unfortunately, it's very disturbing, and it has to do with parallel universes and the so-called *Mandela Effect.*

If you have browsed the Internet lately, you might have stumbled upon something that has emerged called the *Mandela Effect.* The term originates from a strange phenomenon related to Nelson Mandela. Many

---

[463] https://en.wikipedia.org/wiki/CERN#Sites
[464] *Goro Adachi, Oct. 8, 2015, "CERN's Orion Stargate"*
[465] http://www.bibliotecapleyades.net/esp_orionzone.htm

people remember that he was put in prison many years ago, and the story goes that he died in peison, period. However, then he seems to have *risen from the dead*, been released from jail, just to become the President of South Africa between 1994 and 1999. At the time, no one seemed to reflect over this or think that there was something strange with it.[466]

Now people do.

How does this make sense? To be honest, I also recall that Mandela died in prison long before he became the President.

As if this wasn't enough, there are more anomalies. People have pointed out that names on the labels of products carried by certain companies look slightly different when we go back in time and check out pictures of these labels and how they looked then; let's say 25-30 years ago. It could be a letter or two that are now different in these original pictures from what the majority of people remember. The same phenomenon applies to certain popular comics and other products we usually recall very well as part of our culture's history.

This phenomenon seems to be real, but how can it be explained? Many think that we are now living in a slightly different universe that is more or less the same as the old universe, except for some details, such as altered labels and comic books, and Mandela both being dead and alive at the same time. If the Mandela Effect is true, we will probably continue finding more strange changes to our past reflected in our reality now. In fact, people are already noticing this on an exponential scale, as we see when we browse the Internet on this subject.

I have written page after page about different probabilities, e.g. when we choose one option out of two, or perhaps three other options, we tend to focus our attention on the option that we choose, and that will become our "reality." However, the other options still exist as potential realities, or alternative universes, one could say. These probabilities could be activated anytime, if the person suddenly changes his or her mind and decides to choose one of the other two options instead. If so, the path the person is taking currently halts in its progression, and the person's attention/energy will now go to the "alternative universe." This happens every time we change our minds, so it's not a big deal, except for the

---

[466] http://mandelaeffect.com/

Overlords. Changing our minds as often as we do is confusing for the Overlords because in their eyes, this makes it seem as if we are all over the place, and it's difficult to control us. Thus, the AIF do their best to make us focus on *one* primary timeline. This is quite important for them, in order to have us focus enough to be trapped in the Singularity.

Nevertheless, are we suddenly, as a soul group, living in an alternative universe, on an alternative timeline? It certainly seems so, *and we know it can be done. We have the proof that the Mandela Effect can be made real and probably has been made real!*

My fellow researcher Robert Stanley recently sent me a video lecture made by a corporate owner and a scientist, who held a briefing for interested parties regarding what is supposed to be the latest in technology[467].

When I watched this video, I found it quite stunning for several reasons. The first thing that came to mind was how somebody can believe that anything that this scientist presents can be for the good of mankind. Worse than that is the fact that the lecturer is so enthusiastic about this that he can't wait to let people know. He is throwing himself and the rest of mankind down the bottomless pit with the greatest of passions!

This presenter tells his audience that two super computers are now in place; one is located in the *University of Southern California*, and the other one is located in British Columbia, Canada. They are called D-WAVE, and they look like two giant cubes. These two computers are based on an entirely new technology and are being used by NASA.

Previously, we have had computers that are based on a binary system (ones and zeros), but these two devices are quantum computers, and they work in a totally different manner. Inside these D-WAVES, there are giant refrigerators, where scientists have managed to decrease the temperature to almost absolute zero; absolute zero being $0.0°K$,[468] -273.15°C, or -459.67°F. This is one hundred times cooler than interstellar space, says the scientist.

Furthermore, he says that when he is standing in the same room as one of these D-WAVES, he can hear a very specific sound coming out from the computer, and it sounds "like a heartbeat." When he is saying

[467] "Mandela Effect - 20 Minutes that will change your life!"
https://www.youtube.com/watch?v=oEhARtHLN7g&ab_channel=scarabperformance
[468] "K" stands for "Kelvin," the name of the scientist who established the absolute zero point as being -273.15°C, or -459.67°F.

this, he almost becomes ecstatic. He compares it to an "alter to an alien god," interestingly enough. These people often speak in codes, and he was just telling us who the real inventor of this computer technology is.

Consequently, the scientist tells us what these quantum computers can do, and he tells us in increments, so that it will sink in with the audience. He reveals that these two computers, which he says are the only ones of their kind in the world, can tune into parallel universes. He calls them *parallel universes* to begin with, but later on uses other terms for them, as well, such as *alternative universes* and more interestingly, *alternative probabilities*. After all, he says, parallel universes *are* alternative probabilities. Then he begins to tell us the same thing I've been writing about, which is how our choices create different probabilities and alternative universes that are not necessarily active, but are still there— and they remain there as charged energy.

The presenter acknowledges that these different timelines exist, and they overlap each other. *What these quantum computers can do is to find the exact spot where two alternative universes/probabilities overlap!* He says that there are always two universes that are identical, except for some very small details, a "one bit" of difference, as he calls it; albeit, he is quick to emphasize that these computers are not based on a binary system. If you were in the "twin universe" (my term), you would barely notice that you were there because you exist in both of them. However, there may be some small differences that you would eventually notice over time. It seems quite similar to time travel and the potential effects a time traveler can create when traveling to the past. I covered that elsewhere in this book.

This scientist is absolutely correct when he is explaining alternative universes, which is just another word for the Multiverse, where everything is fluid; and every thought we're thinking will register in the Multiverse.

What science obviously has achieved is to tap into a parallel reality, which is very similar to ours because it's based upon a universe where two very similar decisions were made, but not *entirely* similar. The difference in similarity will only slightly alter the second universe.

What does this mean? It means that we have the solution to why the Mandela Effect is happening! Not only can *scientists tap into an alternative universe; they already have!* When they did so, the Mandela Effect automatically took place. People will have two memories of one event, and both will be correct, such as in the case where Nelson Mandela both died in prison and survived and became the President of South Africa. One event happened in one universe and the second event, where Mandela survived, happened in a second universe. We, who experience this controversy, now live in the parallel universe! Yes, you read that correctly; *scientists have altered our reality!* Moreover, this scientist is both enthusiastic and proud of this AIF-sponsored achievement. He ends his lecture by giving us what he calls "three dangerous predictions" that "probably won't happen...but will likely happen," whatever that means. However, here are his *dangerous predictions:*

24) By 5 years, NASA will find an earthlike planet and they will know how to get there. The D-WAVE computers will be the key to get there.

25) The business of parallel universes is going to be very important. He predicts that "by 2023, a major breakthrough in physics will occur, based on a model, whose cornerstone is the reality of parallel universes; an experiment will be performed on a quantum computer that will support the new theory."

26) This third prediction is the most important of them all, according to this man, and I quote: "By 2028, intelligent machines will exist that can do anything humans can do; quantum computers will have played a critical role in the creation in this new type of intelligence."

After telling us of his predictions, he ends his lecture by saying that the *most important emerging tech revolution is that machines will outpace us in every respect—in EVERYTHING! Within 15 years, the machine will outpace humans!*

Throughout the lecture, this man keeps saying, "this is *very* exciting—at least it is to me!" Well, he's correct on one major thing; this is *all* extremely dangerous, but by the same token, these people know what they're doing, and they know what effects they are creating. Moreover, they are shoving it in our faces—again, so that we are prepared, and the Overlords can make sure they informed the public and got at least the majority of them to agree with the agenda.

By the way, it should come as no surprise that Google "pulled this thing together," to quote the lecturing scientist. Thereby, he acknowledges that Google is the company that made this entire D-WAVE project possible by funding it.

What is it that they really want to accomplish with all this? The way I see it, there is only one answer—*they are doing this to keep humanity on one common timeline!* It has *everything* to do with what we discussed throughout the WPP, but also in this book. It's about putting a stop to humanity's unpredictability. How could the Overlords make us focus on the Singularity if we are changing timelines constantly?

What this guy explained to the audience is the tip of the iceberg. Scientists have experimented with changing our timeline, but just slightly so they can see the effects. As we grow closer to the Singularity, I'm sure there will be a last, more drastic change that will make everybody focus on one nexus point—the exact point between two parallel realities—and that is where the Singularity will take place. This is why Kurzweil is ranting about the Singularity taking its name from the phenomenon of the *event horizon* of a black hole. The hypothesis is as follows: in the center of a black hole there is a gravitational singularity—a place where space and time cease to have any meaning—the point where laws and physics break down. A person who, from a safe distance, would watch an object moving toward a black hole would see the object moving slower and slower until it came to a complete halt at the *event horizon*, and it actually never falls into the black hole.

Again, what does this mean?

In Kurzweil's analogy, it apparently means that our development toward the Singularity halts at the *event horizon*, where we are still in the same old universe, but exactly there, at the event horizon, is the nexus point that will make us change realities, by jumping into a parallel universe. Kurzweil might say that this is just an analogy he's using, but these people are clever—he knows better than that, and the Mandela Effect and the insights the scientist in the video presented proves it. The event horizon "analogy" that Kurzweil talks about is not an analogy or an allegory at all—it's literal! After the shift, humanity will be on the same timeline for a moment long enough for the Overlords and the Controllers to act, and that is apparently the moment they need.

If this doesn't make one's soul shiver, I don't know what would.

The next question is, what does this have to do with CERN?

I think it has everything to do with CERN, and I believe that this technology is exactly what they are working on there right now!

After all, haven't we been told that the LHC is creating mini black holes? What a coincidence. What the scientist in the video does not tell us is that although the two quantum computers he mentions may be the only ones in existence, the LHC is an extension of these computers—it's in Cern, Switzerland, where the *real stuff* is happening!

How can humanity avoid this from occurring? Well, we can't, unless we put a stop to what the scientists are doing, but that's not realistic. It requires a mass awakening very, very soon, and we need to be united in order to stop this.

What we can do, however, will be discussed in Chapter 21. To be brutally honest, I can only see one way out of this...

Chapter 19:
The Ancient Race

THE BUILDER RACE

I N THIS CHAPTER, THERE WILL BE FEWER footnotes as we go along because what is discussed here has been extensively outlined in the WPP, and all those papers are richly footnoted. Thus, if the reader wants more references, perhaps, to connect the dots on his or her own, I would refer back to my papers. This chapter will partly be an overview of the ET situation on Earth as it stands today and how it ties in with Artificial Intelligence. However, there will be new material as well.

Lately, many have started discussing the so-called ancient *Builder Race*.[469] Some claim that certain breakaway groups within the Military, operating inside and beyond the solar system, have discovered very ancient cities and artifacts on most solid planets and moons (including our own). These artifacts have been dated back millions, if not billions of years. The people working within the *Secret Space Program (SSP)* (a Black Budget Space Program—or Programs—that the general public doesn't know anything about) allegedly don't understand who this Builder Race is.[470]

I can tell the reader with certainty who this Builder Race is. It was not a *mysterious race* that came here in the ancient days, stayed for a few thousand years, and then suddenly disappeared from one day to another, leaving only ruins behind. The Builder Race were the beings I call the

---

[469] Not to be confused with the *Builders* that I described in the WPP—*the Second Level of Learning*.
[470] Unfortunately, there is no time and space to go into details about the SSP. Initially, I planned to include it here, but changed my mind. I might bring it up in my papers or essays in the near future.

Overlords or the AIF, plain and simple—the Builder Race belonged to some of these same star races.

Our mythology tells us that the AIF arrived in the solar system about 500,000 years ago, or perhaps more exactly, 425,000 years ago, from our time perspective. This is when they drove the Orions and the Vegans (from the constellation of Lyra) away from their Experiment. However, Gaia is far more than 4.6 billion years old, which is evident. Archeologists have found artifacts (and even preserved footprints) that are millions and even billions of years old![471] Civilizations lived in our solar system billions of years ago, probably before the Namlú'u (the Primordial womankind) were brought into manifestation in the KHAA by the Queen of the Stars.

The visitors who were here billions of years ago were not necessarily En.ki and the Cosmic Outlaw Gang we are dealing with now, but they mostly belonged to the same star races and their offshoots.[472], [473] Many of them were warlike creatures.

Some of the ET visitors in ancient times were branches of the Sirian and Arcturian Empire—warrior races who once were at war with Orion, but later created a bond between the empires and merged them, as told in the WPP. Khan En.lil, the Queen's Arcturian consort, entered into a marriage with the Queen of the Stars as a sign of *good will* between the two empires. This is why we distinguish between the *MAKH warriors* (Orions and the protectors of the Orion Queendom) and the *DAKH warriors*, who are the Arcturians and their allies from other asterisms. When peace was established, the DAKH army became an extension of the army of the Orion Empire. Peace was now established, and the DAKH warriors, who were also excellent builders (and still are), were often visiting Gaia/Earth and our solar system. They were the ones who built the artifacts that are now being rediscovered as ruins from eons ago.

Allegedly, it looks as if some of the ancient cities and artifacts all over our solar system were bombed into ruins, indicating that those who were here were involved in an interstellar war long ago. This is true. There were intruders in the past, long before Lucifer's Rebellion, and the DAKH were still the protectors of the Queendom. However, many of the

---

[471] See Dr. Joseph P. Farrell's excellent books, *"Genes, Giants, Monsters and Men,"* and *"The Cosmic War"* for references.
[472] Pleiadian lectures, 2015.
[473] Anonymous source.

ruins probably stem from the Titan War, after Lucifer rebelled. Some parts of the destruction that have been noticed in the solar system are likely to have happened when En.ki and his DAKH warriors invaded the solar system and drove the Orions and the Vegans out 425,000 years ago, destroying the planet Tiamat between Mars and Jupiter in a nuclear attack, and killing many from the peaceful team of the Orion Empire, who resided here at that time.

Readers may wonder how we can find footprints on Earth that are billions of years old when the Physical Universe apparently was "created" by En.ki and his scientists approximately 200,000 years ago when the first Homo sapiens were engineered into being. Or was it?

This is a rather complex issue that requires us to stretch our imagination and our neurological pathways to the maximum. An entire chapter could be dedicated to explaining this, and I only understand the basics of it.

The simplest explanation is that when En.ki manipulated 3-D (the 4% Universe) into existence, he did not do so when Homo sapiens was created; the Physical Universe was already in existence by then. En.ki and his cohorts "created" it many billions of years ago, after Lucifer's Rebellion, when he and the Fallen Angels were cast out of Orion. Metaphorically, we can look at the Physical Universe as a *crust* or an *overlay* that covers what already existed in the KHAA, the Spiritual Universe. In the KHAA, everything is fluid and can easily be created, shaped, reshaped, and changed by using thought forms, and En.ki conquered a fraction of the KHAA (approximately 4%) and *solidified* it and *froze it* into a smaller, denser frequency band that we call the Third Dimension (3-D)—the Universe of atoms and molecules.[474] Hence, what we see through telescopes, in pictures, and in videos, etc., is basically a "frozen" version of what already was there in the KHAA.

Therefore, 3-D already existed when En.ki invaded our solar system and conquered it. We were not the first and will not be the last star race that En.ki intends to conquer, but the Namlú'u—the Primordial Womankind—was probably his most important conquest because we were dear to our Creatrix the Queen of Orion (En.ki's mother), whom En.ki

---

[474] https://en.wikipedia.org/wiki/Density_wave_theory

wanted to take revenge on, and we also hold the key for En.ki to potentially invade Orion (more about that later).

The conquest of our solar system happened in the KHAA—the Spiritual Universe. Although the Namlú'u and AIF lived on Earth simultaneously, they did not necessarily interact to begin with; the Namlú'u resided in different dimensions from the Overlords, who had now solidified our solar system and included it in his/their 3-D Universe. However, it was not until after En.ki created the first *physical* human body, which eventually became Homo sapiens, that En.ki could seduce the Namlú'u to try these bodies and then trap Queen Nin's star race into them by separating the Namlú'u's bodies from their spirit/mind, giving them physical bodies and introducing the concept of death. For the first time, the Namlú'u experienced a world of separation. The Namlú'u's universe now became much more solid, and they found that they no longer could travel freely between dimensions. They were held captive in 3-D! We are, of course, the same soul splinters that En.ki captured at that time, but more Namlú'u souls got trapped here later, and all these soul fragments put together became the *human soul group* or the *earth-humans' mass consciousness.*

When En.ki solidified our solar system, the overlay we were discussing earlier, recorded everything that had happened on the planet in the KHAA from the beginning, but these *memories* were now captured in a denser, lower frequency wave. This means that it also captured *interdimensional footprints* and other curious things. In our terms, the footprints and artifacts are indeed billions of years old, but in the KHAA, time is not linear, which makes things more complex. I will not go much deeper into this here, but you, the reader, can explore these thoughts on your own or discuss it with other like-minded souls.

The same principle applies to the ruins that have been found all over the solar system. Some of these ruins are from the Titan War, but others are from wars that happened billions of years ago, in our terms, and the ruins are "frozen in time," i.e. they have quite literally turned to stone in En.ki's dense universe. In reality, the majority of the wars that occurred, leaving these ruins, happened in the KHAA. Only the most recent ruins are remnants from space wars that happened since the Physical Universe came into existence.

Because En.ki (Lucifer) was cast out of *Heaven- the Orion Empire*[475] after his rebellion failed, he wanted revenge. His pride was deeply hurt. AI was made by the AIF to merge with humankind in the Singularity and create Posthumans, and these cyborgs will eventually be prepared for war and become the AIF's galactic foot soldiers. Ultimately, Posthumans will go to war against the Orion Empire, if En.ki's intentions are played out as planned. Thus, Posthumans will be manipulated into a devastating war against their own Creators. In other words: Lucifer and his son Satan (Marduk) are planning to *take Heaven by force*. As it says in the Bible,

> *Matthews 11:12:* And from the days of John the Baptist until now the kingdom of heaven suffers violence, and the violent take it by force.

En.ki, in his Luciferian Pride and overconfidence, has always believed that he has everything under control, and according to Pleiadian lectures, the Overlords have done the same thing on other planets in their Empire that they're now doing to us. Indeed, they had already conquered other constellations in the KHAA, and manipulated star beings into entering his physical domain, before he conquered our solar system. The way the AIF ultimately controls the species they conquer is to give them technology advanced enough for the conquered species to build their own prison—a Machine Kingdom of Artificial Intelligence. Unfortunately, there is a saying that sums up this scenario: humanity and other star races have been given "enough rope to hang themselves."

However, again according to the Pleiadians, the Luciferian Empire is shaking in its foundations. Lucifer's slave races from the many star systems he's conquered across the galaxies are rebelling, and so are apparently some of the AIF as well. Not everybody who used to be in cahoots with En.ki, and who helped him in his Rebellion, now agrees with him. As expected, there are civil wars going on within the AIF's empire, and there are other powerful Overlords who want to sit on the Throne of Earth and on thrones elsewhere, and apparently coups are in the planning. Being a King in the realms of the Overlords is not a secure thing. These Kings, who are kings over designated star systems or constellations, are constantly stabbed in the back, and their power is always threatened. A

---

[475] The word *Anunnaki* is an Overlords' play on a much older Orion word, defined as *Heaven the Orion Empire*. This is the *real* Heaven the Bible and other ancient scriptures describe.

coup could happen anytime (see the WPP, the Second Level of Learning).

There are allegedly also a third category of Overlords, who supposedly have begun to repent and now want humanity to be free. They hope that by helping mankind to free themselves, these Overlords will also become free by possibly acquiring amnesty from the Orion Empire and be allowed to come back. With all that's going on in his Rebel Empire, En.ki certainly has his hands full.

It is my understanding that the CERN project has been highly successful. The LHC has already opened portals—it was most likely done years ago—and many of the DAKH have come in.[476] The CERN scientists are probably working on other projects now at the LHC; projects that I know very little about at this point.

Because the MIC built the LHC, we invited the Warlords into our environment, and the AIF again consider their hands clean; they let *us* do the job, and we willingly did it. I admit it was not a democratic decision to spend all these billions of dollars to build something such as the LHC, but very few people protested either, which is interpreted as if we, as a human race, agreed.

LUCIFER'S EMISSARY

MANY THINGS ARE CHANGING, and they are changing rapidly. What we humans held to be true thirty to forty years ago is no longer true today, or these old truths have expanded. Since the *nano-second* (1987-2012), when time sped up a million-fold, nothing has been the way it used to be, and skeletons are coming out of the cosmic closest and rattling their chains. Prominent politicians and celebrities are being exposed as pedophiles, and the high priests of the Catholic Church are being exposed as child molesters as well, and famous artists are dying like flies; often sacrificed to keep us on the same timeline because of the trauma a sudden and unexpected death of a famous *hero* creates within us; the latest star that expired as of this writing is Prince, who allegedly died from an overdose of Fentanyl, a pain medication many times stronger than heroin.

Even our biggest religion is changing. The Catholic Church has its

---

[476] Pleiadian lectures, 2015.

first Jesuit Pope, raised in Argentina, which is a Nazi stronghold and has been since WW II. The Catholic Church has become more "open," and Pope Francis is playing the role as the *Pope of the People*. He is taking the game down to the level of the common population, and it has been a success. Many people can't believe how much the Church has changed for the better since Pope Francis took over after the previous Pope mysteriously retired.

Wait a minute! Retired? Have you ever heard of a Pope retiring? Pope's have died in office, but they don't retire. In fact, Pope Francis' takeover was a coup d'état, instigated by the Jesuits. The Jesuits have covertly run the Catholic Church for centuries, but at the same time been at odds with the House of the Pope. *This is the first time in history we have a Jesuit Pope!*

The deception is huge. Although people think that the new Pope is a compassionate, peace-loving, down-to-earth person, a plan is being played out in the background, behind the scenes. According to the prophecies of Nostradamus, this is most likely the last pope. However, why would the Catholic Church end the line of Popes; especially when they have one in power who is so popular?

Fig. 19-1: Pope Francis blessing ET.

To understand why, we need to know what role the Pope plays in the Roman Catholic Church. Any devoted Catholic person "knows" - that the Pope is *God's Emissary on Earth*—he is the intermediary between God and the people, and no Catholic human can talk to God unless it's through the Pope. He is the spokesman for God.

But which God?

If we answer the Biblical "God," that's correct. This is the "God" Christians and Catholics are praying to and giving their personal power away to. The biggest problem with that is that the Biblical "God" is not the God of the Universe and beyond—the "God" of the Holy Scriptures is a mix of En.ki/Lucifer and his son Marduk/Satan playing the role of God to the people of Earth. These two beings are the "Omnipotent God" religious people pray to and worship. They are the Sumerian and Atlantean "gods" who walked amongst us in these ancient times. They are the *gods of the Physical Universe*. They might be godlike in our eyes, but in reality, they are anything but gods. They are deranged, draconian tyrants. War, conquest, competition, technology, and tyranny are their true trademarks.

The reason Pope Francis may be the last Pope is because after the gods return, no emissary is needed anymore. Why would a Pope be necessary if the gods can speak for themselves? The last Pope had to be a Jesuit because the Jesuits have been groomed for this mission; a Jesuit Pope will greet and welcome Lord "Jesus" (Marduk) when he returns during his Second Coming. This time, however, it's not only Jesus who will return, but it will also officially be revealed that aliens are real, and Jesus will bless them, too. He will even bring aliens with him, if this part of the Agenda is played out publicly he will most likely call them *angels*). As we have seen over the past few years, Vatican astronomers are now open to the idea that there *are* aliens out there, and the Pope says that if they come, he will bless them because they are God's Creation, too. Isn't it interesting that the most powerful telescope used by the Vatican is called *Lucifer*?

In addition, this Pope, more than any Pope before him, has called for a New World Order. He wants to *unite the world*, which is imperative for the AI agenda to work. I don't believe that we need to be One Country under God before the Singularity, but people need to get used to the idea because once the Singularity is in place, borders will most certainly be easily erased—one after the other.

PROOF OF INTERDIMENSIONALS?

ARE THERE ANY SIGNS THAT Interdimensionals exist outside our 3-D realm? Absolutely! For example, in the beginning of 2016, a scientific journal posted a paper claiming that they have now detected what they call *Invisible Terrestrial Entities* (ITE) with their telescopes, so the phenomenon is becoming more and more mainstream.

Business Television recently ran an article called *Thunder Energies Discovers Invisible Entities*, based on the above paper, and here is an excerpt from the article,

> Thunder Energies Corp (TNRG:OTC) has recently detected invisible entities in our terrestrial environment with the revolutionary Santilli telescope with concave lenses (Trade Mark and patent pending by Thunder Energies). Thunder Energies Corporation has previously presented confirmations of the apparent existence of antimatter galaxies, antimatter asteroids and antimatter cosmic rays detected in preceding tests. In this breaking news, Thunder Energies presents evidence for the existence of Invisible Terrestrial Entities (ITE) of the dark and bright type.[477]

Readers who would like to know what these Interdimensionals looked like when they were discovered and imaged can download the paper, written by the *American Journal of Modern Physics*, here. Many of us have seen pictures of these entities before, but never in such a mainstream scientific paper. This is not as curious as it may sound, however, because it's a part of the partial disclosure that the Minions are giving us in order for our nervous systems to be prepared for what is to come. They are trying to explain this phenomenon with ITE in scientific terms and even though they fail to do so with their matter-antimatter hypothesis, they are admitting publicly to being open to the idea that there are beings living in frequency bands we humans normally don't have access to, or are aware of, in today's world.

---

[477] *Business Television, Jan. 18, 2016,* "Thunder Energies Discovers Invisible Entities" op. cit.

A FAKE ALIEN INVASION BEFORE THE "REAL DEAL? "

NEW AGE, UFOLOGY, AND GENERAL research into the paranormal often has most people agreeing that there are both *good* and *bad* aliens, seen from our perspective; albeit, there's nothing that is entirely good or bad. By now, most of us have realized that there are ETs who want to manipulate and dominate us, while there are others who want to help in whatever way they can; often waiting for *us* to give them a signal that it's okay to provide some assistance. A third category of ETs are neutral, i.e. they are only here to observe, without intervening in any way.

It's important to the Overlords, too, that we believe in polarities because it fits their agenda. It's long been discussed that there will be a fake alien invasion, which will depend upon special effects, such as holograms, instigated by humans, not aliens, with the purpose of uniting mankind under a One World Government, just as President Ronald Reagan mused publicly in some of his speeches during the 1980s. It is quite plausible that something such as this will be staged before the Overlords make their presence known. These will be confusing times to the extreme, and people will go over the emotional edge into fear and confusion. At that point, it is important for us, who have gained some knowledge, to become stabilizers for others, who have no idea what it is that's coming. Space wars, terrestrial wars, and a mix of them both will seem to take place simultaneously, and we will be taught that our only chance is to unite as *one humanity* and fight the invader forces together. We will be told to forget all internal conflicts between humans and join together despite differences in religion, skin color, and political viewpoints. The *Battle of Armageddon* will unite the mass consciousness and stress it into operating mainly within one timeline, and once the wars are over, we will merge into the Singularity. Again, whether Jesus/Marduk will show up before the Singularity or after is anybody's guess. We will discuss the Battle of Armageddon in more detail later in this chapter.

If this scenario is going to be played out, world leaders will advocate for a New World Order and a One World Government, possibly through the United Nations and the Vatican, putting all countries under One Flag in order to defeat the Anti-Christ forces from "Hell," who are now trying to invade Earth. The Vatican will help usher in the One World

Government and at the same time emphasize that the most important reason it is being done is to prepare people for the return of Christ the savior. When he sits on his throne, it will be to rein over One World united. The Vatican will announce that Jesus will be returning from space as authorized by his Father in Heaven.

The above is *one* of several scenarios that may be played out. The problem, as I understand it, is that Marduk is quite unwilling to pass the Keys to the Kingdom of Earth back over to his father in heaven, En.ki, even though it is En.ki's Age that's coming up—the *Age of Aquarius*. It's often been that way in the past, as well. When the time comes for a regime shift, the previous king is not too happy to turn his kingdom over. Hence, there could also be an internal space war taking place for control of the Earth.

Regardless of which scenario is going to be played out, when push comes to shove, only one "god" is going to sit on the Throne of Earth and rein over a global brigade of cyborg soldiers—Posthumans. When this happens, the New World Order will be complete, and humanity will be poised to experience an entirely new future. The end of a Processional Cycle is at hand and a new Processional Cycle will begin, with a new species inhabiting the Earth—part biological and part machine. This will be the beginning of the Machine Kingdom.

THE SECOND COMING IS FOR ALL RELIGIONS

WE ARE ALREADY BEING PREPARED for the Second Coming, and sophisticated holograms have been tested on humanity. For example, people all over the world have reported seeing *flying cities* in the sky. Where have we heard about flying cities before? It's a common phenomenon in the Hindu texts, as we discussed in the WPP, the *Fifth Level of Learning*.[478] The Overlords want to make sure we can unite all our religions into one, convincing us that Jesus, Buddha, Krishna, Horus, and other "Savior deities" are one and the same—only presented slightly differently in different religions. It will be

---

[478] http://wespenre.com/5/site-maps.htm

very cleverly presented, and the majority of people will fall for the deception.

A staged alien invasion, based primarily on holograms, will probably be necessary for the AIF to usher in a New World Order and a One World Government on Earth. President Ronald Reagan was correct when he publicly speculated that the people of Earth would unite against a threat from outer space. What else could possibly make us forget about all these petty wars we are fighting here and suddenly unite us into One Nation? Nothing short of an alien invasion would bring us all together in haste. German Nazi scientist, Werner von Braun, who was part of Operation Paperclip, said the same thing on his death bed, according to his assistant, Carol Rosin, who provided her testimony before Dr. Steven Greer's *Disclosure Project* panel.[479]

We don't know for certain how this will play out because the Overlords may change their minds, depending on the situation here on Earth. An alien invasion would definitely get the great majority of people on Earth on the same timeline; something they tested on a smaller scale with 911.[480]

Nowadays, the Minions are doing all they can to induce fear in the population, to feed off the negative energy our bodies emit under stress, and to keep us distracted. We are all aware of the school, mall, and police shootings that terrify people all over the world, making them wonder if their little town will be the next victim of a similar vicious crime.

All World Religions, created by En.ki and Marduk, are very cleverly setup. If we really study them all, we notice that they are quite different in some ways but also have a lot in common. Almost all of them are waiting for a savior "God" to return, and this is a key point. It is something that was inserted into these religions for a reason. The purpose was to have the followers, regardless of their religion, expect their God to return to them and bring peace to Earth. Interestingly enough, very few people are waiting for a Goddess.

Today, the majority of wars on Earth are religious wars; at least it looks that way on the surface. This would change in an instant if there

---

[479] https://www.youtube.com/watch?v=7ALLUuvsVkM

[480] "Cities in the Sky," https://www.youtube.com/watch?v=eoUMZOMavB8&ab_channel=TruthstreamMedia

was a cosmic threat. Those who believe that *all* aliens out there are benevolent are stressing that the fake invasion, as predicted by Werner von Braun in the 1970s, will be orchestrated by the Military Industrial Complex (MIC), and that the MIC is who will gain from this—no one else. I agree that a fake invasion may be orchestrated by the MIC, but evidence shows that the MIC is only a puppet for the Overlords, who are pulling the strings in the background on a global and galactic scale.

If a fake alien invasion *were to* take place in the future (to fulfill prophecy), weapons of mass destruction may be used to make everything look more real. Indeed, despite what governments claim publicly space is currently heavily weaponized covertly, and interestingly enough, these weapons are pointing into space, not toward Earth and some hostile nations. Why are they pointing into space if there isn't something out there to protect us from? Alternatively, these weapons will be used in the fake *and* real alien invasions. Logically, "benevolent" ETs from space (and Inner Earth) will then come to our aid, led by a leader with great charisma, who will defeat the Anti-Christ, who may, after the staged invasion is over, openly be the King of Earth for a short time. The "benevolent leader," who will save us from evil, is of course En.ki himself, who then will manipulate people into letting him rule the World Government. Some religions say he will have his throne and temple setup in Jerusalem (and run the U.N. from there), but that remains to be seen.

As a matter of fact, we are not waiting for En.ki and his generals to return; they are already here, and they have showed us proof of that. Ever since the AIF arrived on this planet and took over, there have been nuclear wars on Earth, spread out over time. We can still see the effects of this by looking at the great deserts all over the planet. Some of these areas are still highly radioactive after thousands of years (such as the area around the Dead Sea and ancient cities in India). The Sahara was once a tropical place, and so was the entire Middle East. The Overlords nuked this section of the world in the distant past.

In 1946, a nuclear test was done close to the Bikini Atoll. It was the first *underwater* nuclear explosion in modern times, and the water has always been En.ki's domain, as well as that which is *under* the water. This was the first indication of the *Return of the gods*.

On November 1, 1952, a huge hydrogen bomb was tested on

Enewetak Atoll. It had a yield of 10.4 megatons (450 times more powerful than the Nagasaki bomb).[481] This "test", one of many, was most likely a way of symbolically telling the people of Earth (and the Insiders in particular) that the King had returned to Earth. How better could his arrival be announced than with the detonation of a nuclear bomb; something that has become his trademark?[482]

Fig. 19-2: The nuclear test near the Bikini Atoll in 1946. This was the world's first underwater nuclear explosion in modern times.[483]

There are many indicators, such as the dramatic increase in UFO sightings since the 1940s, telling us that En.ki is here on Earth. Clearly, Marduk and his father En.ki are working, either in peace or at war, with each other.

Why has our technological evolution here on Earth skyrocketed since the beginning of the Industrial Revolution in the 1700s? Why hasn't it at a more natural pace over a long period of time? If we would create a graphic timeline of this process, from around 4,000 years ago until now, we would see that our technological development stayed on a low, fairly stable level for about 3,750 years, only to suddenly spike from the late 1700s

---

[481] https://en.wikipedia.org/wiki/Thermonuclear_weapon#United_States
[482] See further Pleiadian lecture, January, 2016.
[483] *Petapixel.com*, Feb. 18, 2013, "Photos from the World's First Underwater Nuclear Explosion."

onward. Is that normal for the evolution of a species? No, not without assistance from "somebody" who already has the technology. With this in mind, take a look around and ask yourself what you see. Everywhere, you see technology that we have received from the gods. We assemble it, but the gods implanted the ideas and insights how to do it: *build it and they will come.*

ETs in the Solar System

I BELIEVE THERE IS SUBSTANTIAL evidence that there is extensive ET activity in our solar system. In the WPP, I showed structures found on the Moon—both pictures and a video, but there are others who have done an excellent job finding anomalies out there—including activity of intelligent life on Pluto. Pluto is in fact an AIF base for mining and an outpost for guarding the solar system (although there are more planets outside Pluto, and now a giant ninth planet has been discovered, looking and acting suspiciously similar to Nibiru, also having a similar size and orbit habit as Nibiru supposedly has).

A friend of mine, who has spent a significant amount of time looking into anomalies on the Earth and the Moon, is researcher and radio host Robert Stanley.[484] He has made some amazing discoveries of what certainly appears to be ET activities in the ocean just outside Malibu in California and on the Moon. Evidence of such activities can actually be studied on Google Earth (which allows us to also study the Moon and Mars).

Mars was once a paradise planet, before the AIF nuclear war that destroyed the planet Tiamat changed that fact. The remnants of Tiamat became what is now the asteroid belt between Mars and Jupiter. In this enormous explosion, the entire solar system became affected, and Mars was depleted of most of its atmosphere and oceans. Life on Mars at that point was destroyed as well—only a few resilient species survived and still live there up to this day. Mars has been used since the Alien Invasion as a genetic underground laboratory by En.ki and his team, but the planet is

---

[484] *Robert Stanley, Unicus Magazine,* http://www.unicusmagazine.com/html/DIGITAL_DECEPTION.htm, http://www.unicusmagazine.com/html/DIGITAL_DECEPTION_Page3.htm, http://www.unicusmagazine.com/articles.htm

basically assigned to Marduk, who is the god Mars. Today, the planet Mars is still used for genetic experiments, away from public scrutiny, but other activity takes place there as well. Underground cities exist there. This is where the AIF oversees the abduction of Earth humans (scientists and other "valuable people") and an older human race that also resides there (this race being Homo sapiens, the forerunners to Homo sapiens sapiens—the current version of humanity). The older race, who lived on Earth before the Deluge, have now divided themselves into two groups, discussing whether they consider themselves Martians or Earth humans. Some of them want to go to the now almost mythological Earth to find their roots, while others look at themselves as Martians because they have never known another existence.

It is true that NASA was told to stay away from the Moon after the Apollo Missions by the Overlords, but high ranking military officers, regular soldiers, and scientists have been commanded (and sometimes abducted) to go to the Moon and are secretly stationed there now, doing the Overlords' work.

Aside from other activities, mining is still going on in the solar system—both by humans in radiation-protected areas and by the AIF. The Overlords are also using hollowed-out asteroids of various sizes as spacecraft with fusion-powered field-propulsion systems, both for traveling within the solar system and beyond. For interplanetary travel, they use portals in order to bring the hollowed-out asteroids and planetoids with them across the dimensions. These very-large objects, comprised of solid rocks or naturally occurring tempered metal ore, are effective warships that are usually highly weaponized, but can easily blend in with the billions of asteroids in the galaxy when they need to hide in plain sight. I explained this, and much more, in the WPP, and I argued that the AIF (or those of them who are qualified) navigate the VOID in these "death-stars" to travel from one point in 3-D space to another when they need to bring 3-D equipment or warships with them. In these instances, portals come in handy.

There are many discussions these days about sleeping giants, and some say they have found giants in stasis; well-preserved and still biologically alive, but as though they are in a deep sleep. Some of these giants are the offspring of En.ki's Experiment, when he put giants in charge of humanity before the Flood. These giants simply went underground when the Atlantis Empire was destroyed 13,000 years ago and were put in stasis by the AIF, only to be awakened again when the time is right. Other giants, larger in stature, are the Titans (Vegans and Orions), some of them are allegedly also in stasis mode; imprisoned by En.ki and Marduk after they won the Titanomachy (the War of the Titans). It's unclear why the Olympians/AIF kept some of the Vegans and the Orion giants in preservation, and it's also unclear when or if they will be re-animated again. Time will tell.

There is a space treaty between the AIF and the MIC, and the Military and the ETs work together in space in a *Secret Space Program* (SSP); which is a subject with too much information (and disinformation) to be included in this book. Some humans have even been allowed to travel to other star systems within the Luciferian Empire, some sources claim.

There is much discussion and anxiety about the weaponization of space, and it seems as though some factions within our human military are declaring war upon some groups of "negative ETs" by shooting down their craft. In reality, no such war is going on to my knowledge. Some craft *have* been shot down by the military—particularly in the 1940s and 1950s—but as we know, the military is compartmentalized, and one hand doesn't know what the other hand is doing. As a result, some of the ships have been "accidentally" shot down when violating our airspace. The ships that have been targeted were always 3-D ships—some of them used by the AIF, while others were used by higher levels of the MIC, or a combination of the two. The little Gray aliens can probably be found in both the AIF ships and the MIC ships because the Grays are nothing but artificial intelligence (part biological and part machine) used by the AIF and the part of the MIC that is in liaison with the Overlords. It makes me wonder how many times the military, after having shot down a craft, have found dead humans from their own military onboard. If so, that would have caused quite some confusion amongst the un-initated military personnel that shot them down.

BRIEFLY ON ELON MUSK'S "SPACEX" PROGRAM

I N ADDITION TO THIS, WE HAVE Elon Musk; the billionaire who is supposedly creating his own space program, using "his own" technology to take people up in space. To begin with, I want to address his name. I would argue that names are not random—they are decided upon before the person's birth, and although it looks as if it is the parents who are naming their babies, this is usually not the case. The name of the baby is telepathically transmitted to the parents during their dream state or in the waking state (what we call day-dreaming). In this way, the parents think *they* are the ones deciding the baby's name. Names mean something, and they reflect either the personality of the person, the goals that person might have in life, or something else of importance in their upcoming lifetime. On occasion, the parents change the name to something random at the last moment, and the newborn gets the wrong name. Often, when this occurs, the person, when he or she gets older, feels that his or her name is not correct, and the person can't relate to it.

With this in mind, let's look at the name Elon—what does that name break down into? It breaks down into "El" and "on" (or An). El means "god" as in Elohim (gods), who we now know *are* the AIF, and An means "Heaven" or "Heaven the Orion Empire," as discussed in the WPP, at the beginning of the *Second Level of Learning*. Thus, Elon stands for the god of Heaven, i.e. En.ki. I don't mean that Elon Musk is En.ki, but he is running En.ki's errands at a public level—wittingly or unwittingly—perhaps even assigned by En.ki himself. With such a name, it makes you wonder...

*Fig. 19-3: Conceptual render of Falcon
Heavy at Pad 39A, Cape Canaveral*

Another thing to point out is the name of his project, *SpaceX*. "X" is a cross, and the cross is, according to Sitchin and a few others, a symbol for planet Nibiru—the *Planet of the Crossing*.[485]

Now, if we discuss his SpaceX program, which he says is going to take people to Mars and beyond in a ten times more reliable way than is done by organizations such as NASA, Musk says that by 2035 (which is an interesting time frame, taking the Singularity into account), his rocket ships will be flying millions of people back and forth to Mars in order to build a human colony there.[486]

---

[485] See Zecharia Sitchin's book series, "The Earth Chronicles."

Chapter 19: The Ancient Race

This is just another distraction. Why would someone build rocket ships when more advanced technology already exists on a secret level that is light years ahead of rocket ships? It can be compared with someone who says he is going to build carriages again to let people travel cross-country in horse drawn buggies instead of jet planes. Who would be interested in that? There may be a few people who would see it as a fun, exotic vacation, but my point is why go backward? Why spend billions of dollars on rocket ships when they are hopelessly outdated and dangerous? The way SpaceX is presented today; it's just a distraction that's not worthy of serious attention, in my opinion. Moreover, Elon Musk is all for microchipping the population.[487] This should tell his fans something.

However, Musk is an outspoken anti-Singularitist.[488]

Therefore, I would say he is only a small player for the Establishment's agenda, but he's playing his part.

In the next chapter, we will dig deeper into what the post-Singularity future might bring. What is Posthumans' fate, and how is their future going to play out according to the plan? To find the answer, we will have to mentally journey to the future and back.

---

[486] https://en.wikipedia.org/wiki/SpaceX#Goals
[487] ZenGardner.com, June 11, 2016, "Why Elon Musk Is Advocating For Brain Chipping The Human Race"
[488] http://mashable.com/2014/11/17/elon-musk-singularity/#wgwO_kPoaGq3

Chapter 20:
Lucifer's Legion

THE LORD OF LORDS

THE "ORION KING," (who of course is an imposter and not a king at all, except in his own mind), son of Queen Nin, the Queen of the Stars (aka Queen of the Orion Empire), and stepson to King En.lil Sr. (who is originally from Arcturus, but was also connected to the former Sirian Empire), goes under many names here on Earth. However, none of them is his true name. He is the Serpent in the biblical Garden of Eden, where he is also known as Satan—the Adversary. This title is appropriate, as he *is* the adversary of his mother, the true Goddess of the Universe—the Divine Feminine (see the WPP, *The Second Level of Learning* and onward). In the Urantia Book and in the Bible, the self-anointed *King of Orion* is called Lucifer, the *Light-bearer* or *Shining One*.[489] These are quite interesting titles, taking into consideration that the *Universe of Light* is En.ki's 3-D creation. The Overlords are also known as the Shining Ones. Beyond visible light is the KHAA—the Spiritual Universe.

However, there is another adversary, who later became the self-anointed Lord of Earth, in the absence of the original Satan. His name is Marduk, the son of the Great Serpent. Marduk is currently administrating the Earth, and he is known in the Urantia Book as Caligastia, *the Devil*. The Great Serpent is known in the Urantia Book as Lucifer, the Fallen Angel. Lucifer is, of course, the equivalent of Lord En.ki, and he is Marduk's father.

---

[489] https://en.wikipedia.org/wiki/Lucifer

In the WPP, I wrote about the Orion civil war, when Lucifer rebelled against his parents and attempted to overthrow them.[490] He was a very proud being, but quite self-centered; hence, Queen Nin and Khan (King) En.lil put him at a lower rank than his younger brother, Prince Ninurta, who was extremely loyal to the Orion Queendom and his parents' galactic empire. Lucifer/En.ki thought he was unfairly treated and decided to rebel against his parents and the entire Orion Empire, located in the KHAA. Lucifer gathered an army of discontent members of the Orion Empire—beings whom he successfully had managed to manipulate because his tongue is forked and he is a master manipulator. In time, and with great cunning, he also managed to recruit star beings from other star constellations to participate in what has been termed *Lucifer's Rebellion aka The War in Heaven.* Lucifer was defeated, however, and his brother, En.lil Jr., (Prince Ninurta), threw Lucifer out of Orion together with the surviving rebels, which on Earth are often referred to as the *Fallen Angels.* Lucifer is not allowed into the Orion Empire again until he has repented and made amends, but it's doubtful that he will ever be allowed back after the hideous deeds he has done here on Earth and elsewhere.

The Queen and Her Helpers (of whom Prince Ninurta was one) had created our solar system as an Experiment and a Living Library, located in the KHAA before Lucifer rebelled, as discussed briefly earlier in this book and at length in my papers. Earth, also known as Gaia, was a very precious experiment for the Queen, and she chose to let a part of Her divine spirit essence dwell within this pristine, fertile planet. In order to take revenge for his mother denying him kingship of the Orion Empire, Lucifer decided to create his own rebel empire. As a result, he and his DAKH warriors invaded our solar system, killed the Orion and Vegan *Observers,* who were still here at the time, or they were taken as prisoners, while a very few, including the Queen, managed to escape, before Lucifer closed the Saturn stargate, which leads to a galactic *web string,* directly connected to Orion.

In our ancient records, Lucifer is also known as Samaël and Samyaza, and in the Sumerian text his name (or title, rather) is En.ki. In the Orion language, "En" means "comes forth from;" in this case Orion, and "Ki" can be translated as "Earth." Thus, this title could be said to

---

[490] To learn the details, I again suggest that you read the WPP.

mean "he who came forth from Orion to Earth." "En" can also mean "Lord" in the sense of a lord working for the Court of Orion—the Queen's own Court. However, the Overlords have distorted the definition of the title to simply mean "Lord," "Overlord," or "King," in a very masculine way, not mentioning the Divine Feminine as being the original universal force. According to the Overlords, it's a masculine, or at best, a neutered universe. En.ki, in their terms, therefore means "Lord of Earth." As the reader can see, it's the same title Satan has in Christianity, and it's the same title Lucifer's son, Caligastia/Marduk, inherited from his father.

In the Akkadian-Babylonian texts, which are more recent than the Sumerian texts, En.ki is known as Ea, the "Lord of the Waters," also called 'The Water-Carrier." The water, in this sense, refers both to the VOID (the KHAA), which is called the Ocean by many star beings, and also to the waters of Earth. Ea and his cohorts have bases deep under the oceans of the Earth which is why people see UFOs ascending from the sea to the sky or vice versa. In Rome, Ea was called Neptune, who of course was the Lord of the oceans. In Greece he was called Poseidon. We also see the name Ea as the root of the word Earth.

Lucifer is known by many other names, and some of them were brought up and cross-referenced in the WPP. In this book, however, we are going to call him En.ki and Lucifer for the most part—only because these are the names I used for him in the WPP, and not because he deserves the title En.ki; he is no longer a lord in the Queen's Court.

What is En.ki's character in relation to humans? Some people are firmly convinced that he loves his "creation" (us) as we do our own children, and they put En.ki in a positive light and consider him the father of modern mankind. Historically, however, it shows that he has no genuine fatherly love for the current crop of humanity he genetically manipulated into existence to serve his empire. To him we are simply "lulus," which means "workers," although we're more like slaves to En.ki and the other Overlords. En.ki does not hesitate to kill large numbers of humans, whether it is in wars or by other means. As his "workers," we humans have suffered on this planet since he first manipulated the original human race eons ago.

I haven't found any references in the public record that En.ki has shown any true love for his creation; he created us mainly as a distortion of his mother's original creation in an attempt to humiliate Her. At the same time, he had tasks for us; we could work for him, so he and his people did not have to do it. He is controlling us much the way we control farm animals, and because he considers us to be *his* creation, he believes he has a right to treat us any way he chooses.

I think that on some level, however, En.ki is proud of the species he created, and therefore he has at times protected us to some degree (to serve his insane, imperialist agenda). When the Orion Council decided to let a big part of the Experiment become extinct in the Deluge, by just letting the Great Flood run its course, and without warning humanity, En.ki went against the decision of the Council and indirectly warned his hybrid son of the first generation, Noah, known as Utnapištim in the Sumerian texts, by telling him to build an "ark" to save the "seed," i.e. the DNA of the species of Earth. En.ki wanted to secure what he had captured and converted into his colony in a vast empire of stars and constellations. The Orion Empire, however, who hadn't been able to intervene in En.ki's dominion of Earth because he had manipulated mankind to support him, and also according to the universal Law of Free Will, Orion had no right to interfere, unless a large part of mankind asked them to do so. Our ancestors never did ask for help, but the Deluge was in a way a natural occurrence, and by *not* interfering with it, the Flood would wipe out much of the Atlantean Empire. En.ki couldn't do much about it because if he did, he would go against the decision of the Court of Orion. The Court saw an opportunity to be able to indirectly intervene, by letting the Deluge run its course, and under these circumstances, En.ki had to swear an oath not to interfere with the Flood. En.ki obeyed, but he was very clever and bypassed his oath by going to Utnapištim's cabin, and instead of warning his son directly, he spoke to the cabin wall (thinking out loud) what was about to happen while Utnapištim was listening inside. Thus, En.ki could save his genetic experiment without having to literally break his oath.

Why, then, would the Orion Council want to end the Experiment on Earth? The reason was because shortly before the Flood, they got a chance to see what had become of their original Experiment—perhaps by sending scouts into the solar system, past the Quarantine En.ki set up to control who came into the solar system and who was allowed to leave it.

The Orion Empire was shocked over the decline of the Queen's original Experiment and how much the Overlords had made the originally

Namlú'u emotionally and spiritually suffer as well as endure being genetically degraded. In spite of this, they couldn't do anything to intervene, until they saw that a Flood was imminent. En.ki had created an abominable variety of monsters and strange creatures, who had either become cannibals, or were preying on others and abusing them. Many of these creations were also used as sex slaves of the gods. The Queen saw how Her Living Library was totally destroyed and wanted to terminate the Experiment and bring these tortured human souls home to Orion. She knew that 3-D was an electronic prison, created by her eldest son En.ki, but little did She know how badly Her distorted and beloved species had been treated—a species that once was multidimensional and free to roam the KHAA was now being held hostage and tormented.

Fig. 20-1: En.ki holding up a human.

Chapter 20: Lucifer's Legion

Most humans and strange creatures—including most of the giants—succumbed either in the Flood or in the aftermath of it, in which a world-wide famine developed, and illness and death spread across the planet. A few humans and other species survived; however, the species we call *Bigfoot* was one of them. *Bigfoot* would probably have succumbed as well if En.ki hadn't intervened once more.

When the Deluge swept over the planet, En.ki and his team left Earth and stationed themselves elsewhere in the solar system, which was still under quarantine. The Orion Council had hoped that life on Earth would eventually disappear because the Flood was partly happening because of a larger heavenly body coming into the solar system, slightly distorting Earth's orbit causing a shift in our planet's axis. Some claim that the interfering celestial body that caused this entire disaster was the planet Nibiru—the *Planet of the Crossing*.

This would potentially have destroyed all life eventually, but En.ki used his scientists to terraform Earth again, and in the process, he saved whatever life was left on Earth. In addition, he still had the seeds that Noah had saved, and therefore, he could recreate selected species that had succumbed in the Flood, and thus, he could create a new symbiosis and a new Living Library on the planet. This all happened behind the backs of the Orions, who thought that En.ki, bound to his oath, had not intervened during the comsic catastrophe. However, the way he bypassed his oath was done in such a manner that it couldn't technically count as a violation of his oath, although the intent was clearly there.

It seems as if the intention of the Orion Empire was to leave our solar system alone after the catastrophe, believing it had become a solar system without any third dimensional life in it anymore. As such, it was no longer of any interest to the Orion Empire—the Experiment was over, and if the Queen wanted to recreate Her Experiment, She would probably do so elsewhere and under more secure circumstances. Unfortunately, the human soul group hasn't done very well, and is easily manipulated, which might be an indicator for the Queen not to attempt a similar Experiment again.

En.ki soon rebuilt his Earth colony, transferring the surviving Homo sapiens to Mars, and created a new species from the scientific material he'd been able to secure before the Flood, thanks to his son. The new species became Homo sapiens sapiens—us.

Because the solar system had been rather secluded during En.ki's rebel reign before the Flood, the Orion Empire did not know everything that was going on here. Some of the human souls were probably able to return to Orion at that point in time, but eventually En.ki had constructed his electronic frequency prison that prevented most of us from returning, and he now began recycling the same souls to repeatedly incarnate into his new species. Although the number of souls returning to Orion were less than the souls the Queen had let inhabit the primordial man, She also understood that many of the original souls had been too destroyed and corrupted to even considering going home to Orion. It was a great loss and, unfortunately, this had to be taken into consideration. However, the Queen did not know about En.ki's new deceit, and more souls could possibly have been saved if she'd known that En.ki had captured the majority of them.

After the flood, En.ki had less soul splinters at his disposal to inhabit 3-D bodies because some had escaped and returned to Orion. Although, he sometimes captured souls from elsewhere in the Universe, the human soul splinters that were still under his command could be split into more units, and subsequently, each soul splinter had to reincarnate more often than before the Flood to accommodate the growing Earth population.

When the Orion Council found out about En.ki's betrayal, it was too late. Once again he had humanity in his grip, and Orion's hands were tied for the moment. Since the Flood, the AIF have done their best not to break the Law of Free Will, and instead they have bypassed it by manipulating mankind through religion, nationalism, economics, etc. into agreeing to be servants to them again. Keeping this part of our history in mind, it's easier to understand why there has to be a mass awakening of the human species in order break our invisible chains. When enough people have woken up, we will be able to ask for help as a mass consciousness, and other benevolent forces, such as the Orion Empire, will be able to assist us more openly.

THE LORD'S RETURN AND THE BATTLE OF ARMAGEDDON

PEOPLE ARE DISCUSSING AN upcoming "alien invasion" and how this coincides with Bible Prophecies and prophecies in other religions, as well. However, technically there will not be an alien invasion; the invasion already happened approximately 425,000 years ago! The Alien Invader Force (AIF) is already here, so hom could they invade again?

The Overlords come and go as they please; there are no humans who can effectively stop them from doing that, so the ETs are not about to invade Earth for real. What *might* happen, and what looks as if it is happening, is the buildup to a *fake* alien invasion based on holograms; people have been talking about *Project Blue Beam* for at least a couple of decades now.

The only reason the Warlords will play the alien invasion card is to unite the Earth population into a One World Government. Holograms in the sky depicting attacking alien spaceships with laser beams will horrify the population, and world leaders will unite their people and group together with the rest of the nations of Earth in a common effort to defeat this "invasion" from outer space (as seen in movies such as *Independence Day*). Almost everybody will forget their petty indifferences and join together on *one timeline* as a human race pitted against the common ET enemy. The destruction will be real as well as the weapons, but the entire scam may be produced by the Controllers and part of the MIC, who are both taking orders from the Warlords En.Ki/Marduk, etc.

The details of such an invasion can vary, and they may change a few times before the Battle of Armageddon actually happens, but I would assume that some real laser weapons will be used in the battle; the Minions might even use weapons of mass destruction.

Fig. 20-2: The Battle of Armageddon (Project "Blue Beam)."

Just as in a science fiction movie, there will most likely be a "black moment" when everything seems to be lost and humanity is doomed—the hostile ETs will be overpowering. Then, out of the blue (literally), another ET armada will enter the stage and start attacking the invading force with great success. Like a cosmic cavalry coming through the clouds, the "good guys" will ride to our rescue, and the invader force will be defeated. Humanity (or what's left of her) will thereby be saved!

The "good ETs," who are just the same Overlords who ordered the space war in the first place, will take credit for saving mankind, and they will be praised as our space saviors. This group will offer to protect mankind against "threats from the heavens" for a "thousand years." However, in the meantime, humanity will be taught how to fight enemies in space by this same "benevolent" group.

When the Singularity is a fact, Posthumans will soon after be taught advanced warfare by the Overlords, so they can go out in space and fight other, "hostile" civilizations. Thorough preparation will follow in order to start a war against the Orion Empire, where Posthumans and other beings from other civilizations within the Luciferian Empire will be cannon fodder and act as shields for the Overlords.

This is the reason why humanity needs to become caught up in *virtual realities*, from which the Overlords can "grab" the soul/mind/body complex and prepare them for war. This can't be done while the soul composite is stuck in a biological *or* cyborg body because the Orion Empire does not exist in 3-D but only in the KHAA. The only way to get there is with the soul/mind/body complex. The cyborgs will be left on Earth as stabilizers.

By now you can probably see how the Overlords are mimicking Queen Nin's original Experiment, in which the Namlú'u could exist in both the Gaia dimension, living on a planet in the KHAA, and simultaneously explore other dimensions in the VOID. The difference is that the cyborgs are under total control of the Warlords and are *contained* in a strict 3-D frequency.

The plan of En.ki's team is to put En.ki on the Throne of Earth, and from that peak position of power as our Savior, he can manipulate mankind into believing that the Orion Empire were the invaders and that they will come back one day with enhanced forces, unless Posthumans do something about it. Posthumans will take this idea with them into the Singularity, and there it will all be transformed into knowledge and become part of the Posthuman mass consciousness, aka the SBC. The rest of the process, from En.ki's viewpoint, will be a piece of cake. No further manipulation will be needed. Humans will willingly participate.

The above is only one scenario of what might happen. It may all be played out, or only some parts of it will. Only time will tell for certain. Perhaps none of this will transpire—it's difficult to predict. All we can do is to take the Prophecies, which we know are going to be played out one way or the other, compare that with the knowledge we have, and try to put the pieces together. We might fail catastrophically to put it in the proper context and could be taken by complete surprise in the future, but even if that were the case, we should at least attempt to be prepared for that, too!

THE ALIEN INVADER FORCE IN 3-D AND ARTIFICIAL INTELLIGENCE

VERY ADVANCED BEINGS, living in the KHAA, don't need technology to travel from one point in the Universe to another,

365

and neither do many of the Rebels (En.ki included), but similar to us, the Overlords have to a large degree become more and more addicted to technology over time. When they manifest in 3-D, they need technology to do so.

There has always been infighting between different factions of the AIF, and when one faction produces and uses technology to become superior to another faction, the other faction needs to create even better technology, and because of this, technology became, and becomes, more and more advanced. The Overlords also become more and more dependent upon technology to make their own 3-D bodies work within the 4% Universe.

From my perspective, Nibiru, just as any other celestial body in 3-D, exists both here and in the KHAA simultaneously. The Nibiru that has allegedly crossed our path every 3,600 years is of course the 3-D version of that planet. However, because of its multidimensional properties, it is also inhabited in different frequency bands. It was in 3-D bodies that the *Nibiruans*, with En.ki as their Lord of Lords, visited Earth and humanity during Sumerian times, as well as before and after. Zecharia Sitchin was probably correct when he wrote that the *Anunnaki* were giants (something that is also supported by the pictures in the Sumerian cylinder seals), and it makes sense because Nibiru is many times larger than Earth. Thus, in order to adapt to a larger planet, the inhabitants had to be larger in stature. Incredible as it may seem to us, I have heard (from the Pleiadians and others) that the Overlords could be 300 feet tall or taller, and some of their genetically engineered offspring here on Earth were just as tall, but more commonly, they appeared as only slightly taller than the tallest human: 8 to 12 feet. At the time when the gods shared the Earth openly with humanity, the 3-D world was less dense and supported many species of much larger life forms (dinosaurs being a prime example), but after the Deluge, En.ki slightly changed Earth's frequency, and 300-foot-tall beings could no longer live here.

Sitchin claimed that the Anunnaki needed gold for Nibiru's atmosphere. Although, this could be correct to some extent, highly-refined, mono-atomic white gold is also needed to keep the Overlords' physical bodies more or less immortal. They may also need to use some AI technology to keep themselves physically fit for millions of years in this 3-

D Universe, and processed, powdered white gold may be used in addition to that. Dr. A.R. Bordon used to tell me that the Anunnaki snorted gold the same way humans snort cocaine. He claimed they were addicted to it. It reportedly also enhances one's ability to actively enter other dimensions.

It's important to remember that the Overlords exist in both 3-D and in the KHAA simultaneously, in a much more conscious way than we do. Their existence follows the same principle as that of everybody else in the KHAA. These beings are their own holographic soul splinters; one or more fractal/splinters may operate in physical bodies in 3-D, while other splinters operate in the Spiritual Universe. Unlike us humans, the Overlords are aware of all their soul splinters, just as you and I are consciously aware of our own thoughts. Our thoughts might change from one subject to another, but so long as these thoughts are conscious thoughts, we are aware of them and consider them to come from us. This analogy could be applied to explain how the Overlords are in control of their soul splinters.

DRACOS, REPTILIANS, GRAYS, INSECTOIDS, AND NORDICS

AT LEAST SINCE THE DELUGE, we humans, in general, have thought we are at the top of the totem pole here on Earth and that there are no living beings greater and more intelligent than us. That was never true, and it's not true today either, and I'm not comparing us to the AIF now.

During the Atlantean Era, Neptune/En.ki and his scientists went wild creating new life forms on Earth. Some of these abominable creatures no longer exist, but there are many different kinds of beings living in the *honeycombed Earth* beneath the surface. Some of them can be hostile, while others are more benevolent, in general. Perhaps, the oldest of the species living underground are the Reptoids. These are, as the name indicates, reptilian in nature, and were created by En.ki and his scientists during the reptilian epoch or shortly after. They are an older race than Homo sapiens and Homo sapiens sapiens (us), and some of them claim legal rights to Earth, thinking that humans should not have the privilege, as we are a younger species. Although this species can't compare with us in numbers, they are supposedly very intelligent. It it appears that there a few cold-blooded predators amongst them, but most of them are peaceful in nature. These are the kind of reptilian/humanoid beings that people have sometimes seen coming out of caves at various locations around the world. These Reptoids are fully biological beings, just as we still are (at least for now).

Unfortunately, there are other factions of reptilian beings that have been encountered on Earth, and these beings are often taller, stronger, and much crueler than the Reptoids. These other Reptilians are very physical and very 3-D, and they do not originate on Earth; nor are they biological beings. Just as the Grays that people often encounter, the Reptilians and the so-called 9-15 feet tall *Dracos* are AI, employed in the Overlords' service. These beings were created in order to intimidate and to distract attention from the *real* Overlords. The same thing applies to so-called *Insectoids*, the so-called *Nordics*, and others. They are AI, and as such, they are very sophisticated. To a human, it's very difficult to realize that these beings are not biological entities, but cyborgs. I would presume these kinds of AI beings are widely used by the Overlords; both when they are conquering other worlds and when they bring order to their colonies. They are programmed to operate according to the AIF agenda. I would also suggest that these are the beings that Dr. Bordon and his team encountered onboard spaceships orbiting Earth. Bordon, and his team of scientists in the LPG-C, brought back reports from meetings they had with multiple alien species on these spaceships, and sometimes here on Earth, as well.[491] These species told the LPG-C that they originate from different star systems.

The Nordics are an interesting "species" in the sense that they can look identical to humans, yet they are cyborgs. Many of them have already infiltrated governments, business, education, and other departments of society, and very few people know about it and cannot distinguish between them and regular humans—not even the people who work with them. These Nordics may act as if they are emotionless, hyper-logical and always to the point. It seems to me that they could be the

---

[491] I have one of these reports in my possession, and I posted it in the WPP. You can read the full report here: http://wespenre.com/4/PDF/WesPenreFourthLevelOfLearningAppendixPaperA.pdf

prototype for Posthumans.

The bottom line is, just as I argued in the WPP, that ETs are interdimensional, while we are 3-D. *Hence, if an "ET" is really solidly third dimensional (and not a shapeshifter, who is an interdimensional being who can create a 3-D hologram out of thin air by reconstructing her Fire/soul composite), we need to question if this is actually an ET or Artificial Intelligence, created either by humans or interdimensional beings, i.e. the AIF.* I think this is very important to keep in mind. I know that this will not sit well with some UFO researchers who want ETs to be physical, but this is where my research has led me. The same thing applies to UFOs. If a UFO is made of "nuts and bolts," it's either manmade or made by the AIF in order to transport 3-D materials (including 3-D humans) between solid planetary bodies, intra-planetary (Inner Earth), or inter-planetary. In these cases, AIF technology is involved. The UFOs that are phasing in and out of sight (between dimensions) are in most cases AIF interdimensional technology, but in some cases they can be benevolent or curious interdimensional beings, who are entering our frequency band so that they can be watched by observant humans. Most observers believe that all, or the majority, of such sightings are spaceships of some kind, but on the interdimensional plane, these ships and beings become one and the same—they can restructure their Fire composite to create any shape and form they want—they can rearrange their Avatar into a "vessel" if they want or need to. Therefore, the UFOs we sometimes see may very well not be spaceships as we perceive spaceships, but beings taking a certain shape and form in interdimensional space.

It is a very complex situation we are contemplating here, and I'm sure we have only touched the surface of what there is to know. However, what we've learned thus far might be of value when we see how things develop around us. Instead of panicking, we can stay calmer than our chaotic Earth environment and help out where we can, and most importantly, make the right choices so we don't fall into the ultimate trap ourselves. As Utu (Marduk) told me back in 2011, when referring to me, he said, "You are just a 'lulu'"![492] What he meant was that whatever I say or do, I am still his property. However, I beg to differ. I'm a sovereign being, and so are you, and so are the rest of the souls that comprise humanity; we

---

[492] Wes Penre, Oct. 18, 2011, "Authentic Message from the King of the Anunnaki: Please Read!"

just need to remember who and what we really are and declare that every day with conviction and pride.

IS TIME TRAVEL REALLY POSSIBLE?

TIME TRAVEL IS STILL A CONTROVERSIAL subject, even within the truth movement. Is time travel possible, and can we travel both forward and backward in time?

The MIC has worked on time travel projects since the 1940s, when the infamous and disastrous *Philadelphia Experiment* took place,[493] and the Nazis reportedly worked on it before that. The Philadelphia Experiment is now known to the public, but since then, nothing substantial has been revealed by the American Government, or any other government, on this topic.

However, in August 2014, *Nature.com* ran an article where they claimed that it may very well be possible to travel backward in time.[494] *The Mind Unleashed* website picked up on it and explained the otherwise highly-scientific information in layman's terms.[495]

In the latter article, the reporter revealed that Australian scientists created a computer simulation in which quantum particles move back in time. With this experiment, the scientists say that it seems absolutely plausible that time travel can occur on a quantum level; something that was suggested already back in 1991, but it may have been more or less confirmed now.

What is interesting with this Australian experiment is that the way it was performed simulates what I have been writing about in the WPP regarding time travel, namely that there are different *ways* of travelling in time. The two most commonly mentioned principles are the same ones that were performed in the experiment.

27) This is also called the *Grandfather Paradox*—a term based on Einstein's general theory of relativity, which in turn is based on physics more directly related to the macro cosmos rather than quantum mechanics.

---

[493] *Before It's News*, Apr. 26, 2014, "Time Traveler – The Philadelphia Experiment – With Full Military Interview"
[494] *Naure.com*, June 19, 2014, "Experimental simulation of closed timelike curves"
[495] *The Mind Unleashed*, Aug. 11, 2014, "Simulation Shows Time Travel Is Possible"

In this case, we imagine a particle moving from the future and back on the same timeline whence it originated, e.g. in our time. This is when this future particle (or particles) can change the outcome of events that are happening around this time. In theory, you could go back from the future and kill your own grandfather, which would also terminate your own existence on that particular timeline. [*Wes' note: The question is, if I travel back in time from my own future on the same timeline and make sure that my grandparents never met, and logically I would not exist after that, why wouldn't my interference just create another potential timeline, and I would still exist on the "original" timeline?*]

28) In the 1991 theory, it was proposed that travelling back in time is possible without changing events in the past if it's done on a quantum level because on that level the properties of quantum particles are not precisely defined.[496]

Time travel is not as much of a science as it appears to be, however. The "particle" or "particles" mentioned in the above hypotheses, in order to either affect or experience what we call the past, must be controlled by something or someone. You and I are travelling back in time and into the future all the time on a daily basis just by thinking ourselves there. Most of us are not even aware that we're doing this and we just think of this as "daydreaming" or simple "thinking," when in fact we *are* travelling in time. Think yourself back to a certain time in your childhood, for example, and you will be able to go there in your mind. At first you may only get a flash of what happened at that point, but if you want to experience it more vividly, you can close your eyes and recall who was present, what smells were around, what you heard, what you saw, what you could feel with your hands, and what you were thinking/feeling. In other words, you return to that precise time. If we practice and get more skilled, we can also re-experience the movements of the incident and follow the incident forward in time with full perceptions. This is part of the nano-travel that was discussed in the WPP, meaning that you can simply split your soul (composite of *fires*) into "x" number of splinters—each one experiencing different things in different time/space. This is how you basically travel between dimensions and densities and experience the Multiverse—a Multiverse that allows time travel, as all time is

---

[496] See "Heisenberg's Uncertainty Principle"

ultimately simultaneous anyway. There is only one big "now" that we move through in a linear way or jump around in. - If we, as a species, train ourselves to nano-travel (travelling via thought), the Grid and the Quarantine are lifted from our solar system, and our amnesia is lifted, we will be able to more freely travel across the Multiverse and experience each instance of our being just as "physically" as we do now, regardless of where or when we travel. We can create what we want, and the result is in the "eyes" of the beholder. Using nano-travel, a being can move freely from one point to another and still remain in the same time as when he or she left, or a being can decide to travel backward and forward in time, through a parallel time, or in any direction whatsoever.

In the WPP, the *Third Level of Learning*, I argued that some of the entities that are channeled by mediums are us in the future, coming back to change their own timeline to regain order in their own chaotic time in the future (the future from our perspective). This would be an example of time travel option number 1 above, carefully trying to avoid terminating their own selves, or their ancestors. We will discuss this more in a moment.

THE END TIMES

A S A BIOLOGICAL HUMAN SPECIES, we are now on the brink of extinction. This is indeed the *End Times*, but what does End Time mean? Does it mean that all life will be destroyed and what remains is only a desolate planet? Or does it mean that this is the End Times as foretold in the Bible, that the Savior is now returning and a resurrection will occur, where selected God worshippers will be brought to the biblical Heaven?

None of the above is plausible. Instead, as I have concluded with my many years of rigorous research, it's the end of the human race as we know it. Humanity will split into at least two main species—Posthumans and *Homo Nova*, as discussed in my e-book, *Beyond 2012—A Handbook for the New Era*. Homo Nova is the multidimensional human, who is able to create her own reality, free from the chains of slavery and manipulation—a being of higher awareness, free to travel across the Universe, the Multiverse, and the dimensions. Unfortunately, it looks as if the majority of todays' Homo sapiens sapiens—a species that will be extinct in just a few decades if events turn out as planned by the Cosmic Outlaws—will choose to follow their ET Masters into eternity, stuck in artificial bodies and an almost eternal life as property of a gang of imposters. Only a small minority of Homo sapiens sapiens seems to be ready, willing and able to break out of their bondage, but even those who intend to do so need to be very alert and careful in the days ahead. There are traps we want to avoid, and perhaps one of the biggest of these traps is related to the Pleiadians, channeled by Barbara Marciniak. Before we discuss what I mean by that, we need to go over some background data.

TIMELINES

L ET US DISCUSS TIMELINES for a moment. I have often touched on the subject of a multiverse where all time exists simultaneously, while here on Earth, the Overlords manipulated us into thinking that time is linear and that is all there is to the concept of time; there is only one past, one present, and one future. The latter, if we follow the Overlords' manipulative logic, we know nothing about because we're not there yet.

Linear time is very convenient for the Overlords when they are dealing with us because it's easier to control us. In a multidimensional environment, we could be all over the map and nearly impossible to track and keep in check. Without linear time, we wouldn't be stuck here.

Let's look at this from the Warlords' perspective. They operate interdimensionally and multidimensionally. They can look at us and our time from "outside," as a child would his Lego city. Although we are programmed, humans are sentient, relatively intelligent people and can move at random and do random things; even learn from their mistakes and correct themselves; all while the Overlords are watching what's going on. In the eyes of the Overlords, humans are both predictable and unpredictable because we often do unpredicted things.

We humans are creating timelines from our 3-D perspective. In theory, at the beginning we were all on the same timeline until we started making choices. When a human chooses between two things, the other option creates its own timeline, even though the person didn't choose to go that path. The unchosen timeline becomes inactive as a *potential timeline.* This timeline, however, can be activated again at any time. Let's say that somewhere down the line, this person intently begins thinking about a potential choice/option he never made/accepted and begins to activate that timeline in his "mind's eye." In the process, there's some extra soul/fire/energy put into the previously stagnated energy, containing the dormant fragments of that unchosen timeline.

Let's pretend that the timeline the person actually chose in the beginning ended in a disaster—it may have destroyed the human race and/or created havoc amongst the Warlords. The disaster didn't occur just because of the choice of one human. It became an active timeline because of the choices the majority of the human mass consciousness had made up until the point of the disaster. We are individual soul/sparks contained in a collective cosmic fire, and what we think affects the overall collective fire of the human soul group.

Although multidimensional, the Warlords are interacting with human consciousness, and what we do and decide also affects them. Therefore, the damage is done!

What do the Warlords do to get out of the jam? Humankind made unpredictable decisions which had unwanted consequences, and now this has to be corrected. Here the Warlords sit in the future, in relation to when the disaster happened, and are having a difficult time. The best solution may be to go back in time, which means that they, from a multidimensional perspective, insert themselves on the human timeline just *before* the disaster happened when humans made their unpredictable decisions.

From that exact point, with linear time as a reference (because that is what the human mind current lives in), the Controllers start manipulating these timelines. Some are creating traumatic mass events, such as 911, school shootings, "natural" disaster (often created with technology), epidemics, wars, genocide and other horrible events. When the majority of mankind becomes traumatized because of a major mass event, we tend to focus on one timeline only—the timeline where the orchestrated event happened. Thus, we create a common *major* timeline right there. Very quickly, the Controllers begin to manipulate us in the direction they want us to go, instead of the direction we went in the other timeline that created the disaster, adversely affecting the Warlords.

Chapter 20: Lucifer's Legion

Even after an event such as 9II, when many people merged into the same timeline, we all quite instantly branched off because of new individual decisions and choices. However, the major/dominant timeline will still be the 9II timeline for most people because that's what is now keeping the human consciousness together—we feel that we have that in common. Let's say that at some later time, the Controllers orchestrate another event to once again direct the mass consciousness in a certain direction. In this manner, they can manipulate the population to make different choices than those they made when they created the disaster that affected the Overlords in the "future."

Fortunatley, we have a world population that is slowly but surely waking up to what is going on behind the scenes—people are becoming more aware. We sometimes call it the *truth movement*. The truth movement needs to be addressed by the Overlords as well, because an increasing number of people are refusing to get stuck in the timeline the Overlords are continuously having us create through sustained stress trauma, deceptive distractions, and mass manipulation. Because awakening is "contagious" and affects the entire mass consciousness, the portion of the population that are awake or are awakening have to be controlled. The Overlords do want more knowledgeable and aware beings in order create a knowledgeable hive-mind with the Singularity, but they only want an awakening that's under *their* control. The Outlaws are going to let us eat from the Tree of Life, but our access to the Tree of Knowledge still needs to be restricted. They only want to give us the fruits they find appropriate; they don't want us to eat as we please.

How can the Overlords control the mass awakening? They address the issue from many angles. The Internet is a tracking device, but it's also a study in mass consciousness. The Internet is of course not created by humans, and Bill Gates had little to do with it, just as Ray Kurzweil has had little to do with the Singularity—they are both just puppets and front persons. Although humans built the computers and the MIC created the Internet, these ideas were implanted into certain humans by the AIF. Bill Gates and others may actually think they came up with the ideas themselves when they really didn't. To halt the awakening, the Controllers hire Intelligence operatives to spread disinformation on the Internet to utterly confuse the truth movement. Some of these agents write books that are pure disinformation, but they easily attract curious minds. Curiously, this disinformation has truth in it as well, which together with modern science fiction attracts the truth movement. Soon enough, the truth movement is divided into different factions; some believe this and others believe that, and never shall the twain meet. Instead of people looking inside themselves for answers, they become too busy to do so because they feel compelled to urgently browse the Internet and read books seeking an authority figure to give them the "right" answers until everybody is so confused about what's true or not that they are no longer a threat to the Overlords. Instead of having people in the truth movement creating a new "dangerous" timeline, or timelines, that can affect the Overlords in a negative way, from their viewpoint, they steer the truth movement, although intentionally divided, into one or two major events, and have them concentrate on those. Such events are the fulfillment of Prophecy and the New World Order. By concentrating their energy on these events, they actually assist in creating them. It was all a setup to begin with.

There are other ways to utterly confuse us as well. A very successful way to do it is through channeling. Today, channelers are a dime a dozen, and they all have their slant on what is allegedly accurate information. Some say they are channeling Jesus, others claim they channel Ashtar, Sirians, Arcturians, Grays, friendly Reptilians, Praying Mantises, Andromedans, Pleiadians, the Ra People—and the list goes on. Although most channeled material contains truths, which is what attracts people, most of it is hogwash—including the origin of the channel. Very rarely are these "beings" extraterrestrials. More often they are sophisticated AI; high tech initiated by the Overlords. They target people who have wide open chakras, willing to take in anything that comes in their direction. Some of these people become "psychic" channelers, specifically targeted by the Overlords and their AI network. In this way, more disinformation can be spread on a regular basis to a wide range of the population.

These are all distractions, preventing us from doing our inner work, which is what will help humanity get out of this jam. However, after the Warlords have succeeded in distracting and dividing the truth movement, the movement needs to be united again, but only toward a preselected goal, created by the AIF.

This is where some of the channeled material, such as the Pleiadians, come in. Barbara Marciniak was chosen as the vehicle for the beings who claim to be from the Pleiades. These entities are *not* AI, by the way, but actual entities from elsewhere. They are here to connect enough people of the truth movement so they can affect others telepathically, in order to change the major, dominant timeline we are on right now as a human soul group.

INVADING THE PLEIADES

THE PLEIADES IS EN.KI'S TERRITORY—let's make that clear from the beginning. In the WPP, we discussed this at length, and in fact, Marciniak's Pleiadians have said many times over, for the last two or three years, that their "teacher" is Lord En.ki. The first time I heard them saying this in their lecture, I almost fell off my chair! I really did not expect that. Now, however, it's become natural to me because they are telling us their story from that perspective.

When we discuss the Pleiadians, by the way, going forward, I am always referring to Marciniak's channeled entities, unless I state otherwise.

The Pleiadians endorse Zecharia Sitchin's work, and when Sitchin died in 2010, they honored him in a lecture shortly after his passing, saying he was a man who enlightened mankind and helped us understand our path. This is not correct. Sitchin did one good thing, perhaps, and it was that he put our attention on the Sumerian scriptures and the Sumerian gods, so that curious people could begin to do their own research (soon finding out that intentionally or not, Sitchin often gave his own slant on the original texts to fulfill an AIF agenda). Sitchin also always referred to En.ki as a relatively good guy, while En.lil was the bad one. The records actually show *the opposite is true*, but to figure that out, one has to read between the lines and connect the dots. This was done in the WPP—references and evidence included. As readers of the WPP know, a much more accurate history is presented in these papers. Sitchin and the AIF wanted En.ki to look good, so we would embrace his return as the King of Earth—modern mankind's savior and father/creator.

However, when we dig deeper, we find another, much more interesting story, which I revealed in the WPP. When the true story surfaces, En.ki is exposed as the imposter that he really is. Enûma Eliš[497]

377

(the letter "š" is pronounced "*sh*" as in *sheep*), the Babylonian creation story, speaks volumes for those who want to analyze them. We know that the winners write history, and in this case we could say that the Overlords *were* the winners because they were the ones in charge. Enûma Eliš, and other Sumerian cuneiform, and all the major religions were what they left behind as their legacy, but why would we believe that what they told us in the written form is the true story of the so-called Anunnaki? In fact, the gods wanted to leave records behind that we could interpret in a way that "predicts" our future—the *End of Days*, which are the days we live in now (2016 forward). They made the real Creator Gods and Goddesses appear to be the bad guys, and those who invaded Gaia, the AIF, became the good guys.

TEACHERS FROM THE FUTURE

ONE THING MOST CHANNELED materials have in common is that the alleged channeled entities tell us they come from the future. Most of those in this category claim they are here to prepare mankind for big changes; some say, bluntly, that they have come to save us from our evil governments and the ETs covertly here on Earth, while others say they are here to help us help ourselves. Moreover, the majority of those who claim to be from our future also emphasize that they are *us* in the future—our future selves. Hence, only a few of the channeled entities claim to be ETs in the sense that they come here from other star systems. They may *reside* in other solar systems in the future from where they contact us, but they tell us that their real origin is here on Earth, interestingly enough.

The question is if they really are from our future, and whether they are our descendants. As I've argued many times now, very little channeled material is genuine; most of it is AI, and most of them are not who or what they claim to be. They are boldly lying about themselves and who they are. Their messages are highly deceptive to further manipulate the masses.

What about the Pleiadians? They also say they are from our future,

---

[497] http://www.sacred-texts.com/ane/enuma.htm

and in a way, they say, they are our descendants. However, their story is a little different from other channels. They say that their ancestors took part in creating Homo sapiens in antiquity; they are indeed some of those whom we call the *Fallen Angels* in the Bible. Their ancestors were those who created the *Nephilim*—the human/alien giant hybrids, by *mating* with human females. It's likely that they did mate with human females, but the Giants of renown—the Nephilim—were created in laboratories. Also, if we think about it, there is no way that an average human female could physically give birth to a Giant, seven to thirty feet tall.

I have listened to different channelers, and the difference between the Pleiadians and most of the others is the clarity in their message. The Pleiadians (the *Ps*, pronounced *pees*, as they call themselves) deliver a very consistent message most of the time, and they are straightforward when teaching their listeners and readers what they want them to know/think. They always start their sessions with an approximate ten-minute lecture on one or a couple of subjects, and then they let people in the room ask questions. The question may, or may not, be on the subjects the Ps began with. The answers to the questions, more often than not, coincide with my own research from elsewhere.

Regardless of this, and in spite of them being a very clear channel, more often than not they are telling the truth about the world situation behind the scenes, and in most cases, they are also telling the truth about the Anunnaki and their agenda.

This might make it seem as if they were one of the very few channels that are genuinely on humanity's side in all this, but regardless of all the good indicators, it is not likely that the Ps can be trusted, either. This is for a few different reasons.

They embrace Zecharia Sitchin and his teachings, and there seems to be a reason for this. To be fair, they also say when they refer to the old Sumerian texts, "according to the translation of the Sumerian texts," and they sometimes add, "the way the gods have you depict history," hinting that there is more to the picture than what's in the scriptures and that the scriptures can sometimes be dubious. Still, they continuously refer to Sitchin's translations. It seems as if the reason why they so consistently refer to Sitchin is because he has the good guys and the bad guys already defined. Erroneously, the Ps are referring to En.lil as being YHWH—the "evil god" of the Old Testament. This is remarkable because a little research shows that YHWH/Jehovah was a composite of two gods; En.ki and Marduk. Furthermore, they present En.ki as the one who is scheduled to rule in the Age of Aquarius, but that there is a power struggle amongst the Anunnaki; therefore, it's still uncertain who is going to take the lead. Marduk, En.ki's son, is unwilling to let go of his Kingdom, but I believe the story was the same after the Age of Aries, when Marduk was the top controller of mankind.

The Ps tell us that they are here to teach us the truth about ourselves and our true history. However, in the next breath, they are revealing that they are reporting to their own teachers as well, who grade them on the results from teaching us. Therefore, we must ask, who are their teachers? Fortunately, they let us know that as well. Their teachers are the entities they call the *Keepers of Time*, and they explain that the Keepers of Time are the Anunnaki—but the *good ones*, they are quick to add. The reason why their teachers are called the Keepers of Time is because that's what the Anunnaki do—they keep our linear time in place! As the icing on the cake, they also reveal who is their head teacher—Lord En.ki aka Saturn/Kronos—the God of Time!

They say, correctly, that En.ki's main abode is the Pleiades and that it has been for quite some time. He fled to the Pleiades a long time ago when things were heating up. I wrote that in the WPP already in 2010, which was long before the Ps revealed where En.ki's current home address is (although, he might not be home at the moment). The planet that is considered the Keeper of Time is Saturn/Kronos—the most important planet in the solar system. This is where *Father Time* (En.ki) set up a powerful technology to create an electronic frequency fence around our solar system. The Rings of Saturn play a big role in all this in that they show us the type of energy being emitted (much like iron filings placed on a piece of paper over a magnet). The *Keepers of Time* are therefore, En.ki and Marduk.

The Ps say that En.ki once went to the Moon and mapped the constellations in the night sky, and from there, he created the Processional Cycle, which also, of course, is part of linear time. David Icke has now come to a very similar conclusion regarding Saturn as I have, and which was discussed in the WPP. In one of his lectures, he emphasizes that Saturn plays a dominant role in maintaining the matrix we currently live in because it broadcasts the frequency band that Earth and the rest of the solar system is stuck in. That lecture is well worth watching.[498]

The Pleiadian story is fascinating, however. They claim that we humans, as cyborgs, will come to the Pleiades in the future because we want to meet our creators (and who is the creator of the cyborg society if not En.ki, the "Pleiadian?"). Instead, this pending encounter we are predicted to have with the Pleiadians ends in an invasion. Our military trained army of cyborgs goes to war against beings in the Pleiades and win the war, and thus, they create tyranny in the Pleiades. The group of Ps who are contacting us in present time are allegedly a rebel group that meet in spirit in a secret time/space in the future, where they relatively safely can communicate with us.

This group figured out that the tyranny they live under in our future has its origin on a certain timeline that came out of the nano-second on Earth (1987-2012). This is also the time when there was a breakthrough in the creation of the Singularity. On the main timeline, stretching all the way from the 1980s to the time in which the Ps live, humanity as a mass consciousness will become cyborgs and eventually, super soldiers. This highly trained army of space soldiers will then invade the Pleiades. The group of rebels (supposedly), that Marciniak is channeling, is now reaching out to earth humans in an attempt to teach us metaphysics and the truth about the Machine Kingdom, AI, and the Anunnaki, hoping that some of us will choose another timeline aside from that which leads to the Singularity. It doesn't have to include the majority of the human population for the Ps to succeed, they say; it only has to include as many people as it takes to put energy on an alternative timeline. The Ps then hope that they can change things around on their end and "jump timelines" to the one their human disciples choose, on which no invasion takes place. That will again create peace in the Pleiades—or at least, that's what they apparently hope.

This is the reason why the Ps *have to* tell us the truth, or as much truth as is necessary for their agenda to succeed. In other words, some humans need to be educated up to a certain point. This is what they are doing in their lectures; enough people need to realize that what the gods are doing will take us to places we do not want to go.

---

[498] https://www.youtube.com/watch?v=ENHzl-yls-o

They don't go out on the Internet or put the channeled material on YouTube because they don't want to risk that someone dubious is changing their message by editing the material. Still, there are a few people who have posted certain lectures on YouTube, which definitely annoy the Ps and Marciniak alike. The Ps are only interested in teaching those who gravitate to their message, which become the chosen few who can help them change the timeline. The Ps add that this is a give-and-take that will benefit both humans and Ps. We get educated and can avoid the Singularity, and the Ps can regain their freedom.

At a first glance, this seems like a fair deal: we help you and you help us. The Ps have occasionally said that doing this for us is not their main reason for being here; they do it for themselves first of all, but it just so happens that it will benefit us, too. That makes their mission the more noble, as they see it. This, of course, leaves us wondering what would have happened if their agenda would *not* have benefited us; would they in that case have deceived and manipulated us to get what they want? Well, to be honest, I think that's what they are still doing, but now I'm getting ahead of myself.

Let us analyze this. The first thing that comes to my mind, if the Ps are telling the truth is, what will happen afterward with the people who succeed in helping the Ps to create the particular main timeline they are hoping for? Will En.ki come and personally thank these people for helping out, or does he just look at them as another bunch of lulus, who just did their duty as his labor race and then put them in the fold again? Will En.ki really set them free? Historically, that's just not his style.

I have listened to the Ps lectures, and nowhere are there any promises of what will happen to the assisting humans when this is all over, and there are no suggestions of what will happen to the rest of us when this is all over. They just give the silent impression that "everything will be just fine." Nowhere are they strictly saying that En.ki and his team will reward humans for assisting them. However, they proclaim that those who help the Ps automatically will free themselves, too, from their current boundary. Even if this is the case, no one says that En.ki can't put them back into slave labor again afterward, once these humans have slipped out of their boundary.

Another question that arises is how this cyborg hive-mind that will be the result of the Singularity and the SBC can invade En.ki's domain without En.ki's knowledge or his ability to stop them. After all, it's En.ki who orchestrated the entire Singularity Agenda. Will Posthumans run amok in the future, becoming robotic rebels against the Luciferian Empire, starting to invade and cross their creators instead of abiding and obeying them?

In fact, there is a slight possibility that this could happen. I hear from many different sources that there is a power struggle within the Luciferian Empire and a civil war is raging.[499] Upon that, beings on the different Luciferian colonies are starting to rebel against the tyranny of the Warlords. In present time we do not know the outcome of this struggle or if any civilization has succeeded, although I have heard rumors that some of them have managed to escape the 3-D entrapment. Apparently, the Luciferian Empire is currently shaking in its foundation, as portrayed in J. R. R. Tolkien's fictional universe when Frodo made it to Mordor and was about to throw the Ring of Sauron into the volcanic lake in Mt. Doom, blinding the all-seeing eye and making the Evil Empire fall.

In addition, it also looks as if there is at least one (maybe more) fairly advanced civilization of Reptilian or Reptoid beings, living beneath the Earth's surface, who are at war with the Overlords. This could very well be part of what the Middle East wars are really about; some whistle-blowers are saying that there are civilizations under the surface with whom the U.S. Military is at war. If the MIC is at war with beings from the Honeycombed Earth, the AIF is, too: (in the movie *The Matrix*—the rebel city of Zion was deep in the Earth). Are these beings then automatically on humanity's side? Not necessarily; as mentioned earlier, these previous experiments that En.ki created, don't agree that humans will inherit the Earth—Singularity or not—because the Reptoids were here first. There are other beings beneath our feet as well—some of them benevolent and peaceful, others not so much. That subject is another can of worms that we unfortunately don't have time to cover here in any great detail.

There is always a possibility that En.ki loses the civil war and another branch of the AIF takes control and decides to let Posthumans

---

[499] *Exopolitics.org, Jan. 26, 2016,* "TOP AEROSPACE DESIGNER BLOWS WHISTLE ON SECRET US NAVY SPACE BATTLE FLEETS"

invade En.ki's domain to hammer down the last nail in his coffin. If this is the case, there is no doubt about why En.ki is behind the Ps and wants to change the timeline so that his enemy's hive-mind AI army (Posthumans) will not invade to begin with. The winner of the civil war between the Overlords could be Marduk, who then wants to solidify the coup and take over his father's Pleiadian Kingdom as well, so he plans to use Posthumans as his foot soldiers. This is a plausible hypothesis. If this is true, En.ki, from a future perspective, is actually working *with* humanity, attempting to wake us up in order to save his own Pleiadian Kingdom in the constellation of Taurus. According to the Ps, the *Seven Sisters*, which are seven of the brightest blue stars in the Pleiades, are part of En.ki's Realm and thus are also part of the Luciferian Empire. The Ps are speaking very badly about Marduk.

In the last few years, the Ps have been talking about *En.ki's Gift*, which supposedly is something embedded in our DNA that can't be tampered with. This *Gift* was hidden in our genes when En.ki genetically manipulated mankind. According to the Ps, he put it there because he didn't fully trust his cohorts, and he wanted to safeguard the human race so that we would eventually evolve on our own (which is what we're doing now). The Ps say that because of their own teachings and involvement with mankind on a present time basis, that will help activating En.ki's Gift.

Whether this is true or not, I don't know, but for it to make sense that En.ki, from a future perspective, wants to activate this part of our DNA now, in our time, it would be because he wants us to create the alternative timeline (or timelines) that his disciples, the Pleiadians, are teaching us about. From what I can conclude from listening to the P's lectures En.ki's Gift was activated during the nano-second and was a part of our relatively sudden awakening; this is in conjunction with the increased energies we received through the alignment with the Galactic Center around 2012. However, on the timeline that will lead to the invasion of the Pleiades, this so-called Gift was then transferred into the SBC with the Singularity, so that the Super Brain Computer would have more information to work with. It is my impression that this was the real purpose of En.ki's Gift to begin with. Now, he apparently wants those who are awakening (the ones he can gather around him) to take his "Gift" (that is already activated) and create this new timeline instead.

In their books from the early 1990s, the Ps are also saying that they want our "code," which most probably means our genetic code, although nothing is said to explain what they truly mean. It is very plausible that the code is what they now call Enki's Gift.

Some of the human participants, who are more or less standard participants in the Pleiadian lectures when they are held in Raleigh, North Carolina, seem to have read my papers because the Ps now get questions about whether it's possible to escape from the between lives Anunnaki trap and just get out of here and not reincarnate again. The Ps get slightly irritated when they hear this, and they respond that we are here to reincarnate in order to help build a new reality—a new Earth. Of course, this is what they want in order to have more souls creating the alternative timeline. Only a few years ago, they denied that there was an Anunnaki recycling center, but lately they have admitted that there is, and they say we have to evolve in order to avoid going into the AIF soul trap after death. They claim that we go in accordance with our awareness level and meet others who vibrate similarly to us, and when we arrive there we will be in charge of our own destiny and can reincarnate from a conscious level instead of getting trapped in the Anunnaki recycling technology. However, it's all about getting back here to Earth because this is where we belong, according to the Ps. Although they told us a few years ago that some souls incarnate on other planets, most go back to Earth (those who incarnate somewhere else certainly do so within the Luciferian 3-D Empire, so there's no escape by doing that. It's possible the AIF just want some souls to do their work somewhere else).

In fact, there are at least two ways of getting trapped after death. One is to get seduced into entering one of the recycling centers; where the soul is recycled immediately into a random body. This mostly happens, as I understand it, to people who don't have any awareness or knowledge about what is really going on around them while being incarnated on Earth. I've read somewhere that there are souls who are so evolved that they don't need to go to the Between Lives Area, but take a new body directly after death. This is disinformation and a spin on what I just wrote—some souls don't go to the Between Lives Area because the AIF decides they shouldn't, and instead they are recycled right away. In these instances, the soul has no say in the matter.

The other trap is that we go where our belief systems take us. If we believe in Jesus and Heaven, that's the virtual reality we go to, and if we're faithful Muslims we go to a Heaven where we can have 72 virgins as a reward for our faith, or perhaps more correctly, — these could be 72 demons that delight in tormenting us.[500] —

Nonetheless, after a certain time, we will again be recycled into a body here on Earth, but we have more choices where we want to go (in general, the Overlords want us to go where we can be of the most use to them).[501] All souls who go into the trap will have a *life review*. That's where our most recent lifetime is played back for us, frame by frame. We're shown what we did that was "good" and in line with our goal for that lifetime, and we also are being shown what we did that diverted from it—including the "bad things" that we did to others and what others did to us. Then we discuss the matter with our *Spirit Guide*, who is either one of the AIF members or a relative, friend, or someone farther back on our timeline, who's been manipulated into helping out. Although, the good things we've done are discussed after the life review, the bad things in particular are pointed out, and because we are basically good-intentioned beings, we feel guilty and perhaps embarrassed and ashamed when we see the *negative* things we've done being played back to us (psychologist B.F. Skinner termed this process *Behavior Modification*). Hence, it's easy for the Warlords to convince us that we need to go back to Earth and make amends for what we've done. This is what we call *karma*. It's a fabricated process, coined by humans, perhaps, but made up by the AIF. There is no need to go back and experience *the other side* of our wrongdoings; all we need to do is to forgive ourselves and forgive those who did us wrong. If the souls in question, who we were negatively involved with, are present in the afterlife environment, it would be a responsible thing to talk the matter through with him or her, but if that soul is not available to talk to, it's more a matter of discharging the subject on a soul level and letting go of the energy that's stuck in that area as negative, emotional energies. This is easier to do when we're in the astral and not trapped in this solid 3-D world, unless we're letting ourselves be manipulated in the afterlife by

---

[500] http://www.mysticfiles.com/72-demons-evoked-by-king-solomon/
[501] *Wes Penre, March 25, 2011*, "The Wes Penre Papers—the Multiverse Series, the First Level of Learning: Metaphysics Paper #4 : There is a Light at the End of the Tunnel—What Happens After Body Death?"

Overlords to *face our karma*. Karma is a perfect tool for the Overlords to trick *us* into agreeing to go back into a new body and have a new "learning lesson" in a heavily manipulated and deceptive world. It doesn't benefit us—it only benefits the Outlaws.

In the afterlife environment, there are at least one (but usually two) mandatory meetings with a *Council of Elders*, before whom you need to confess what you learned in your recent lifetime and what you need to work on and improve in the future. Then, the final goal, or goals, for the next lifetime will be determined. The first meeting with the Elders usually happens in a relative early stage in the afterlife process. Then, normally, you will see the Council again just before it's time to go back to Earth, and that's when the goal, or goals, are set. After this meeting, you are escorted to a "control room" with a control panel, some screens, and a chair where your light body (avatar) can sit. Here you can see your next lifetime played out for you on a screen. It will show the most probable direction your life will take, but it may vary, of course, because of decisions that you make in life. However, while watching your future life on the screen, you need to decide when, where, and how you are going to "exit" (die). You will have a few choices when you want to vacate your body, and one of these choices will become the day when you die; you'll subconsciously choose the final one while you're incarnated. If you think back on your life, there may have been times when you were in serious accidents, or you may have miraculously avoided a serious accident. You might have been very sick and close to dying, but you recovered. These moments might have been moments when you could have chosen to vacate your body, but decided not to.

When your exit points have been decided, an "operator," with help from technology, then beams you down into the body of choice. I want to be very clear, soul recycling is not a natural process; *it's done with technology*. It is described in detail in Dr. Michael Newton's books, which are based on more than 5,000 cases of people that have participated in regression therapy, telling very similar things about the Afterlife. I have read the books, and just as Dr. Newton emphasizes, he is not asking any leading questions; the person in therapy is more than willing to tell his or her "afterlife" stories. It is a very interesting study Dr. Newton has done, and it's well worth reading his books; *Destiny of Souls*[502] being the most detailed one. After having read that book, there will be no doubt that there is a recycling center for souls, controlled by beings who possess high levels of technology and who can beam down souls into selected bodies here on Earth (and elsewhere, if they decide to). I also have no doubt that the Council of Elders that the departed souls need to meet with once or twice between incarnations are some of the Overlords. These souls are often very nervous when meeting with them.

This is the recycling center in a nutshell.

We all have a choice; those who want to experience one of the two options above can easily do so—after all, we've done this probably thousands of times, but there is another option for those who don't want to participate in the Warlords' games anymore, and I will discuss that in the last chapter.

Many say that En.ki has compassion for humanity, and that's why he saved us from the Flood. To be honest, I would prefer to call it *pride—Lucifer's Pride*. He is proud of the species he has created, and in addition, he needs lulus. He needs some of us to be his super soldiers that stay in line and don't revolt. If we look at our history, I see very little compassion from the AIF when it comes to how humanity has been treated. This is also the reason why I believe that if we manage to help the Pleiadians (and En.ki) with creating *their* timeline, En.ki would still not release us from our prison. In all fairness, it definitely seems as if we're in a real jam—a *Catch 22*. Some readers may find other solutions, but personally, I can only see two solutions to the dilemma we are in, and only one of these solutions is something I would recommend. However, it's really up to the reader to decide. I will address them both in the next chapter.

IN SUMMARY

W E HAVE NOW ALMOST COME to the end of this book, so let us take a moment to summarize the main agenda of the Overlords, based on my research. There are many sub-agendas involved as well, and I could write an entire book, or more, only

502 https://www.amazon.com/Destiny-Souls-Studies-Between-Lives/dp/1567184995

about those, but I want to focus on what seem to be the immediate points of importance:

29) The market is now being bombarded with new technology, and AI is introduced in the media. People are getting used to this new reality of electronic devices, run on Wi-Fi. People are using these devices to communicate with other people rather than having face-to-face communications—text messages are becoming more common than talking on the phone or talking to someone directly. Many are calling people *friends* although they have never met these persons—only on the Internet.

30) We are introduced to *robot sex*, and AI robots that can satisfy our most intimate desires, which may be of a nature that we don't even want to mention to our human partners, are promoted. "Robots don't talk about it with anybody else" (except perhaps with each other through an inaccessible *cloud* that only robots will have access to). Also, the robot is available whenever it's convenient and can be put aside whenever a person doesn't want it around. Real human relationships and real marriages will become rarer and rarer; instead people will marry their robots, which will be accepted by law.

31) Genders will become more and more obsolete. The media are promoting gay sex, and being transgender has become more accepted as the new normal. In at least one university, students get lower grades if they refer to a person by gender, according to Barbara Marciniak, who heard about it first-hand. When the Singularity is in place, the plan seems to be to lean toward androgyny. Sex will only be for pleasure, and usually with androids in virtual reality games. It's not being mentioned to any extent, but having offspring will probably be a very controlled, technological process.

32) Androids will be walking down the same streets as we do at the same time, and they already do to some degree covertly. We will have a hard time knowing who is an android and who is human, and soon the androids' behavior will not reveal the difference. Eventually, after mankind has become Posthuman, they will blend with the androids and become androids themselves.

33) Robots and androids will take more and more of our jobs, something that has already begun; *Amazon.com* being a perfect example, where

robots sort items that are for sale and put them on the correct shelves. This is one of many tasks that used to be done by humans.

34) Huge promotional campaigns are designed to introduce us to Transhumanism. Pros and cons are being presented, but the pros (positives) are often being emphasized, even in articles that seemingly *oppose* the AI agenda. It doesn't matter in what manner the AI subject is presented in the media because the content of the articles is biased and will stick in our subconscious and play an important role in the near future, as the Singularity is becoming a reality.

35) Nanobots are increasingly being spread via different outlets, such as chemtrails, medications, vaccines, and possibly GMO food and other food with a lot of additives; so-called "processed food." Hence, if you eat natural organic foods that don't have additives you stand a better chance. The goal for the Overlords in this matter is to have our blood cells replaced by nanobots, which will also take over our immune system and successfully fight serious diseases, such as cancer, heart disease, viruses, and diabetes.

36) People are addicted to electronics, which is the AIFs' purpose for giving them to us in the first place. As usual, we pay money for our own entrapment, which is the height of arrogance on the Overlords' part, and the height of stupidity on the part of humans. Our minds will disappear more and more into our devices, which many already keep by their side 24/7 and can't do without. This is for the purpose of preparing the entire world for the Singularity, where being in the same virtual reality is crucial-.

Try to turn off all your computers, smartphones and other electronic devices for a week and refuse to use *any* of them under any circumstances (except at work, where you probably have no choice). Notice how long you can go before you tell yourself, "I'm just going to check my Facebook really quick," or "I'm just going to check out this or that website," etc. In most cases, people won't be able to stay off their devices for a week. Those who can't are already addicted to electronics and experience withdrawals when turning them off for an extended time. It's not a matter of telling yourself, "Well, I can do without electronics for a week;" it's a matter of *actually doing it!* I challenge the reader. If you actually *are* able to do it, congratulations! You are an exception. I would still advise such readers to be careful. *Electronics can be more addictive than heroin.*

37) By 2045, if the Controllers were to be on schedule, humanity will connect to the Super-Brain Computer (SBC), which is almost ready to be put in place. When humankind is connected, it becomes a hive-mind that can still think individually, but will draw information from the SBC, which is the collection of the knowledge of all living human beings, in addition to those who have lived in the past. The Internet will be obsolete and an artificial *Innernet* will replace it. The SBC will be the new Internet, with the exception that via the SBC you need no search engine; all information is available and customized for you instantaneously. The SBC and the human mind will merge and become one. Thus, man and machine becomes one and AI will overtly take control.

38) Posthuman will become next to immortal because of the nanobots that are much more effective than the biological human's immune system and can fight off virtually any disease and virus effectively. The human body will also be able to rejuvenate itself and not only stop the aging process but reverse it. An individual can then stop the aging process at an age he or she feels comfortable with—most will probably look and feel as they did when they were in their 20s or early 30s. Aging body parts will eventually be replaced with newer cells from the particular aging body part or from some other body part where cells can be used. Each body part will be kept alive with nanotechnology. Humans will be more and more artificial and thus transform into Posthumans—half human and half robot (cyborg).

39) At first, the Singularity will appear to be a great gift to mankind, and people will live in beautiful, clean cities with wonderful, nanobot-infested plants and trees. However, AI will be running the SBC and eventually determine how Posthumans should act and think in a more unified way. Posthumans will lose more and more of their emotions and compassion and become more and more AI-like. They will be introduced to the Overlords' agenda, which is to be trained as super soldiers—not only in 3-D reality, but in a virtual reality, which will eventually take the soul/mind/body complex into the KHAA and then to the Gates of Orion. This is why we're being trained to have

our minds disappear into technical devices, which are virtual realities that work similar to splitting your mind when traveling to different dimensions. Thus, what humans can train themselves to do naturally, Posthumans will do with technology. However, the main problem is that Posthumans will be controlled in their thinking and actions and will gladly go to war on other worlds and other dimensions!

40)   When the time is right, Posthumans, in conjunction with other hive-minds, on other Luciferian controlled planets, will go to war against Orion. Humans have the key to get in there because this was a Gift from the Queen when we were initially created by her to participate in her Great Experiment. Our uniqueness will be perverted and used against us and against our Orion Creators.

41) How this will end for Posthumans is an open question. We don't even know with total certainty whether the Luciferian Agenda will play out or not; and if it isn't, at what stage will it stop, and what will happen after that? These questions are impossible for anyone, including the Overlords, to answer at this time.

Based on my research, the Singularity seems to be the most likely future for a majority of mankind, if the AI Prophets get their way, and it certainly looks as if they will. Therefore, while we still have time, educating our selves is essential, and acting upon what we learn is the logical consequence of learning. As I mentioned, there are only two ways to handle this, as I see it. We will address that subject in the final chapter.

PART 3: SOLUTIONS

Chapter 21:
Are there Solutions?

"Great is the mind that can imagine,
For nothing is more pure
Than that which reality cannot touch."
-Felicetti

CURRENT NAÏVETÉ OF MANKIND

BEFORE WE DISCUSS THE *Ultimate Solutions*, I'd like to address a few points that I believe are important to understand. Some of them are significant enough to keep in mind at all times and to practice on a daily basis.

Much of what has been exposed in this book is already covered to a certain degree by mainstream media, science, and the scientists' spokespersons, and it's from there that I've taken much of my source material. The reason I did that was because I noticed that even though the information is often easy available, no one had, thus far, assembled everything in one place to make it easier for people to access in a *comprehensible* manner and see the implications for our future.

Also, subtler, but in-your-face methods are being used in Hollywood movies, songs, and in popular books, broadly promoted by the Minions. When the truth is exposed in plain sight by the Controllers or the Minions, it's called the *Revelation of the Method*, and this means that they want us to see what they are doing, but at the same time, to protect themselves, they show their agenda through symbolism, and the same method is used in fantasy and science fiction literature and in movies. In other words, no one can intervene with what's going on behind our backs so long as we humans don't protest against our oppressors in enough numbers - to really become an issue for the Overlords. In order to accomplish this, we need to understand our current role here on Earth, as human beings, and then we need to make a decision what it is we want to do with our immediate future. Not until this is done by enough people and help is asked for, can someone intervene and actually assist us to exit En.ki's matrix. No one will come here and save us from the AIF agenda, unless we make a common statement that we need assistance. If we do, we show the rest of the Universe that we no longer agree to work for the Overlords, and then the Overlords can be judged for the cosmic crimes they have and are committing and be penalized by benevolent interdimensional beings.

Before something of that nature can happen, humanity needs to do their homework and come to a decision. So long as we hide our heads in the sand, we are indirectly agreeing to our AIF-designed fate. This doesn't mean that we need to meet somewhere and come to a common decision; it happens energetically as we wake up. When we reach a level of consciousness on a global scale, help could potentially arrive.

However, if we use violence, or if we think protesting in the streets will do it, we are deceiving ourselves. Such actions will only make things worse because it's more *divide and conquer*.

Remember how we discussed that there was no separation before the Warlords invaded. The trap we're sitting in is because of separation; when we are no longer separated, entrapment can no longer be sustained. Therefore, the first step toward climbing out of imprisonment is to ignore the oppressors and regain our wholeness. We need to learn how to use our imagination and out intuition! Daydreaming, which has been looked upon for a long time as an escape, is often anything but. Daydreaming is imagining! If we use daydreaming to *imagine* the reality that we want, we are already on our way. The 3-D reality is not our realm—*it's the Overlords' realm*. It's a master-slave dimension, and who in their right mind wants to remain a slave when they can be free?

We are trapped here because of our bodies, regardless if they are biological machines or cyborgs—what kind of technology is being used to maintain our bodies is just a matter of what magnitude of control is being used on us here in the Third Dimension. It's still separation because it is of no consequence what type of bodies we inhabit in 3-D; the body is still separated from the soul/mind. Everything in 3-D will perish, whither, and die. So long as we think that our bodies are separate from ourselves, we will never be free. I wrote about this earlier, but I need to mention it again because it's the most important thing I've ever written. When our physical bodies perish and we go into the astral, we have been manipulated into thinking that in order to become alive again, we need to incarnate in a new physical body because we think that a part of us was separated when we died. It's all an illusion because we carry our spirit body with us after death! When we leave our bodies, we are finally alive! We are whole again; we are *soul/mind/spirit-body* in one, and we don't even recognize it. We suddenly become immortal! This is the *true* Tree of Life. Instead, we think we need assistance from somebody who can help us, so we eventually can get a new physical body and be fulfilled again. Of course, the Overlords and their AI helpers are happy to assist with their technology to get us back to Earth again.

We think that physical reality is life and non-physical reality is death, when the exact opposite is true: *in reality, the non-physical reality is life and the physical reality is death!* When I sit here, writing to people who will read this, I write this from the realm of the dead, and I am trying to resurrect as many people as I can. Don't get me wrong, I'm not trying to play Jesus, thanks goodness! Marduk/Jesus used the same principle I'm using here, but his *soulution* to our problems was to instruct us to go through him to get to his father, En.ki/Lucifer, not to Freedom.

> KJV John 14:6 Jesus saith unto him, I am the way, the truth, and the life: no man cometh unto the Father, but by me.

Marduk died on a cross; please remember that. What does the cross stand for? The cross is a symbol of the *Planet of the Crossing*, i.e. Nibiru. Foremost, this reality is not based on words; it's based on symbolism. Letters and words, by all means, are symbols, too, and each word has a symbolic meaning, but largely, the important communication in this reality happens through visible symbols that have secret meanings. Here in 3-D, the Overlords and their Controllers and Minions communicate with each other via symbols. Although these symbols are everywhere around us, usually only the initiated know what these symbols really mean. The symbols can be anything from the *Pyramid with the All-Seeing Eye* to universal geometric symbols the average man doesn't even recognize.

From what I hear, by raising their mass consciousness other

civilizations on other worlds became free because it breaks down their AIF Grid, and in the process the gate to freedom swings open. However, it requires a combined effort - from a trapped soul group for this to happen. In the current state of affairs, we here on Earth have managed to punch holes in the AIF Grid by raising our consciousness, but consciousness without knowledge is not enough. If more people do not begin to figure out how this trap is set up, humanity does not stand a chance. We only have a few more years beyond 2016 to wake up, which is much less than I thought we had just a couple of years ago, and this fact shocked me! Ray Kurzweil is certainly correct in his book title: *The Singularity is Near*. It might be only a few decades away. When I look around or browse the Internet, I see people who are beginning to wake up, but the process is much too slow. If we continue at this speed—or even twice this speed—we won't have enough time to avoid the Singularity.

Fig. 20-1: The Great Seal; symbolism on the back of the U.S. One Dollar Bill. Few people even reflect on what this means. The Eye is the All-Seeing Eye of Lucifer, and the Pyramid is his Imperial Hierarchy, while the ocean (which surrounds the pyramid/island) is humanity, over whom those within the Hierarchy reign. This symbol is also a call for a New Order of the Ages; latin: Novus Ordo Seclorum. Annuit Coeptis means "[he/she/it] favors our undertakings".[503] Who is "he/she/it?" Well, go to the top of the pyramid and the capstone that is separated from the pyramid—En.ki is "God" over the physical realm, and he is the one who "favors the Agenda." Now that this has been interpreted, can it be any clearer?

[503] https://en.wikipedia.org/wiki/Annuit_c%C5%93ptis

In fact, it seems as if the majority of people around the world are going in the wrong direction, if we have concluded that the right direction means going against the Singularity. People are becoming more and more caught up in their electronic devices, without comprehending what they are doing to themselves and others. It has nothing to do with just being *distracted*; instead, it has everything to do with letting our consciousness disappear into a virtual reality that will be dominated by AI. This AI will unite humanity in a virtual reality environment via smartphones and their much more sophisticated, smarter successors that will be on the market before we know it. People will rush to get this new technology, and they will gladly disappear into a deeper dungeon than the one they are already sitting in. When we watch movies, in general, and the bad guy is put in prison, he is usually makes great efforts to escape. Humans are doing the opposite; they are in prison, but instead of making great efforts to escape, they beg their prison wardens to reserve a place for them deeper down in the dungeon. This is how dumbed down humanity has become.

This is alarming. It is almost embarrassing to realize that the reason the Controllers let most of the truth movement continue trying to figure things out is because they *know* that the Singularity will happen regardless; therefore, they have nothing to be concerned about.

As a matter of fact, people are even more ignorant than one would think. Social activist, Mark Dice, decided to do an experiment.[504] He went out on the street as a regular guy with a clipboard in his hand. He then stopped people in the street and bluntly asked them to give him their names, street addresses, phone numbers, and their age. The only thing people refused to give out to this stranger was their social security number. Few of these people even asked him who he was and why he wanted this very sensitive information—they just gave him the data. Mark said thank you and continued to the next person. Some people asked why he wanted the information, but Mark just responded with something unintelligible, upon which the person gave the info, probably thinking, "At least I asked. That's what I'm supposed to do." People obey when they

---

[504] Infowar.com, Jan. 11, 2016, "VIDEO: AMERICANS MINDLESSLY FOLLOW ORDERS, HAND OVER PERSONAL DETAILS TO A COMPLETE STRANGER--People fall into line when they hear an authoritative voice"

hear an authoritative voice.

Here is a video that was filmed while Mark Dice was doing his project[505].

You might suggest that people give this personal information away because as a species we are overly trusting, but with all the information that is out there—both in mainstream media and in alternative media—people need to learn to set boundaries and not automatically be submissive to anyone with an authoritative voice. I understand that we have forced to obey the AIF's authority figures for many thousands of years, but refusing to be blindly obedient is crucial in these times (except under circumstances when we want to do it for specific reasons). If we don't learn to stand our ground and declare our sovereignty, we will never be free. This book is a crash course in *Freedom 101*. You are you, and you don't need to bow or be submissive to anybody; you are your own authority, and you're a sovereign being, worthy of respect, love, and acceptance.

SIGNIFICANTLY REDUCE USE OF AIF TECHNOLOGY!

EDWARD SNOWDEN RECENTLY SHOWED evidence in a video interview that you are surveilled through your smartphone twenty-four hours a day even if it is powered off.[506] The various Three-Letter Agencies (also casually called the *Alphabet Agencies*) working for the AIF can remotely turn your phone on even after you have turned it off. There are also cameras that the agencies can use inside the phone without your knowledge. In other words, if you own a smartphone and keep it with you, you're surveilled whether you have it on or off (-Apple's iPhone does not even permit to remove the battery). They always know where you are, who you're texting and talking to, your patterns, and which friends or which people you talk to when you're not on the phone. They also have access to everything you store on your phone, and they can very easily track your Internet browsing. This goes for *every single smartphone on the market, regardless if it's an Android or an iPhone!* There are no exceptions from this. As has been shown in Snowden's videos, Intelligence agencies—including their senior managers—lie under oath

---

[505] "Mark Dice out in the street, asking people for their personal information," https://www.youtube.com/watch?v=Rw7mO3fknS4&ab_channel=MarkDice
[506] https://www.youtube.com/watch?v=ucRWyGKBVzo&feature=youtu.be

before Congress, saying that they do not surveil citizens who are not suspected of crimes. In reality, there is proof that they actually surveil every citizen who carries or owns a smartphone. There is no assigned person sitting there watching you all the time, but everything is recorded and stored in giant searchable databases, and when, or if, authorities need the information, they can get it with a few clicks on their keyboards. Much of this surveillance technology is now also used by different police departments; something that is also admitted to in the Snowden video.[507]

It's time to unplug from AIF technology as much as possible, starting right now!

After I wrote the above, I found the following article on Zen Gardner's website, "Stop Being a Slave to Technology: Here's How to Unplug." In some regard, I may be preaching to the choir, but even the choir needs a little pep talk at times. I recommend that you read that article. It puts everything that has to do with ET technology into perspective.

When I was in my teens and early twenties, I went to rock concerts, and it was a big deal; my friends and I were tuning into the music with all our might. Now we know that rock music and the energy it produces is used against us, but nevertheless, when young people go to concerts today, they don't concentrate on the band and the music anymore, but are often on their smart phones instead of watching and listening to the band.[508] Some are engaged in "face-timing" the concert to a friend, which means that the friend got more out of the concert than the person who was actually there. This is just another example of how addicted people are to these devices.

---

[507] Ibid.
[508] Financial Times, April 3, 2016, "Technology slaves missing out on the real experience"

Fig. 21-1: NSA Whistle-blower Edward Snowden

THE NATURE OF MAN

WHEN WE LOOK AT ALL THE EVIL man has done over the millennia, it's easy to buy into the Christian view that man is born in sin and needs to repent. It is true that when we are born, we inherit the genes of our ancestors—good and bad. However, when we look at a newborn or a little toddler, we see pure love and innocence—we don't see evil. After that, it is the environment that forms the personality to a large degree, and the toddler takes in what he or she learns and experiences. These experiences will then be important for the choices the toddler makes later in life.

We have the genes of the Overlords, which give us an inherited violent streak; something most humans do their best not to show in daily life. Fortunately, compassion, love, and empathy are still dominant in a majority of the human population, and when most people are forced to choose between good and evil, they choose good. This speaks volumes about the basic foundation of humanity's psyche/spirit.

However, if the above is true, how come there are cannibals in the jungle and tribes that eat their newborn or let their oldest child eat the

401

newborn to give the living child more strength? This happens within tribes in New Guinea and among Australian Aborigines. I am sure something similar is also practiced in other tribes deep in the jungle—places the white man has yet to discover.

Many of the sacrifices and the absurd routines these tribes are practicing are usually sacrifices to their gods—or something they do because *the gods told them to*. The "gods" would be the AIF paying a visit, wanting to do an experiment on a certain tribe, far away from the rest of the human soul group's scrutiny, or it could have been humans, who did the same kind of experiment, in order to see how "primitive" humans, untouched by civilization, would react. Tribe or no tribe; mankind, by default, chooses to live peacefully together in communities, unless triggered and manipulated from the outside.

The problem, as I see it, is not to make mankind peaceful; the problem is that we are ignorant and don't even know who we are—we need education! It would be accurate to say that humankind has been sleepwalking in a trance for many thousands of years. Extraordinary measures on behalf of each individual need to be taken in order to wake us up, and in most cases, I, unfortunately, don't see this happening, in spite of what other researchers enthusiastically are suggesting. Waking up doesn't count if a person is becoming aware that there is a force above the government who makes sure we are constantly monitored and that there are aliens in charge of all this insanity. It is one thing to become aware of this on an intellectual level, and a totally different ballgame to have it sink in on a soul level. Not until the latter is done can a person begin doing something about it. I see people that aware of some of the major problems, but they still let their old life/habits control them, because they are unwilling to confront the situation head on and prefer to live in denial. Many still think that the solution is to *fight* the Controllers or the Overlords. I want the reader to forget that; it won't solve anything. We wouldn't stand a chance against them, and violence is not the answer anyway. It actually makes them stronger and us weaker.

The human soul group needs to understand that we have perhaps the greatest potentials of most star beings out there because of the way the Queen created us—we are a royal species and part of a unique Experiment. If we clean up our act and prove our merit, the Queen may be willing to let other star beings become like us, too. However, for this to even be an option, we need to show who we are and what we can do. No more infighting, no more talking behind each other's back, no more bullying, wars, and senseless killing. We need to become our true selves again the way we were as Namlú'u, eons ago. If and when we have done this, we will have shown other star beings that we are strong enough to break out of solid oppression, and that we are able to turn the manipulation around. That will regain respect in the star race community, and the core of the Orion Empire, for us. This is not just about us—we have a responsibility to all the other star races out there. Many envied us when we became part of the original Experiment and wanted to be able to do the same thing that we could do, i.e. live on a beautiful planet in specially designed spirit bodies that could stay on the planet and experience its wonders but at the same time be able to travel across the many dimensions instead of either or. If we fail, the Queen will most likely choose not to expand her divinely-designed Experiment.

THE HUMAN MIND AND OUR PERSONALITY

SOMETHING MANY PEOPLE are afraid to lose when they die is their personality because that's how they define themselves. I can reassure the reader that you will keep your current personality once you leave this life and go into the ether. So long as you stay within the trap, you will remain who you are, personality-wise.

However, if you think of it from a bigger perspective, your personality is not *you*. The personality who reads this book has developed by learning from his or her environment since their day of birth. You brought a personality with you down to your current body, but that personality was created by experiences in *previous lives*, and the personality you have now, compared to what it was minutes before you were born, is quite different, since you've had new experiences that have added to your total being and affected you for good or ill. You still consider this being you and your personality, whether you like yourself or not. At least, it's a safe haven.

However, recalling what we've discussed earlier, the part of you that reads this is a splinter of a bigger unit of *fire* or *soul energy*, and there are many other splinters of you as well. These splinters have their own personalities and they are spread out over the linear timeline here on Earth. What makes you who read this more "you" than Mr. Jones who simultaneously lives in the 19th Century? He is also you, but if you were to meet him, you wouldn't think so. Mr. Jones has had several lifetimes with many different unique experiences that you haven't had, and vice versa. Add up all other splinters of your soul/spirit/composite fire (many call this the *Oversoul*, and for simplicity, I will use that word from hereon), and we have an array of personalities.

Once out of the trap, a soul becomes *whole* again, and the splinters merge with the Oversoul and can thus leave the prison behind and start exploring the Universe.

I'm sure at this point many readers are wondering which of all these splinters' personality are the real "me." The logical answer to this is; *the one you choose, a mix of what you choose,* or *none of the above.* Once you let all splinters merge with the Oversoul, you become whole, and what will most possibly occur is that you become who you want to be—in that sense, you may start from scratch, taking *all* your experiences into consideration because the Oversoul is the composite of *all* your experiences as soul splinters. This time you are *consciously* being yourself, only drawing from experiences without being negatively affected by them. This is, of course, nothing to fear—you don't *lose* your personality, you only make it *stronger*, fully aware of what you're doing, and you're doing it by choice. You will become a part of the larger *real* multi-dimensional you—the Oversoul.

ENDING THE EXPERIMENT

THERE HAVE BEEN ONGOING DISCUSSIONS, not only between various star races, but also between star races and the Queen of the Stars, whether the Queen should terminate the human experience on Earth once and for all by "pulling the plug" on the entire Living Library. At one time, the Queen was apparently very close to doing so, but there were other star beings who asked Her to please wait a little longer. These star beings thought that it would only be fair to give humanity a chance to create their own destiny, with the rest of the star communities watching which choices we would make. Are we strong enough to break our chains? Can we stand up against Lucifer and the Fallen Angels?

Queen Nin has agreed to this suggestion for now.

In a manner of speaking, it is *we humans* who need to decide the future of this Universe. If we succeed, the Universe will become very different, after the Queen has created more of Earth-like worlds, but if we fail (which seems to be the case), these paradise worlds will probably never be created. Sadly, the majority of mankind currently does not even know what's at stake, which is one of the reasons why I wrote this book and the WPP.

What does it mean if the Queen decides to terminate Her Experiment? She has been reluctant to doing so because it would mean an end to the entire human experiment once and for all, and She will retract Her spirit from Gaia. Gaia will dissolve and cease to exist—Gaia is merely a "dream;" a project created in the Queen's imagination and that was then made manifest in the KHAA. Once Gaia is dissolved, so too will everything that lives on it. Humans, who are still alive on the planet at that time will most likely find themselves floating in space, in their soul splinters (soul splinter/mind/spirit-body). There will be no pain or suffering, but rather a relief, as the AIF Grid will be lifted as well. Souls who wish to do so and are ready for it will be called home to Orion again, where they once were born, while others, who not yet qualify, will be shown places where they can live and think things through until they one day want to apply for citizenship in Orion again, or choose another route. No one will judge our decisions; we have free will, and that will be truly respected and accepted.

Will the Queen pull the plug before the Singularity happens? I don't know. I wouldn't wait for it to happen; I am taking action now, and those who are likeminded may do the same. In my humble opinion, I don't think She will terminate the Experiment until we, as a human soul group, decide that we've had enough of the Overlord's oppression. So long as we are AIF allies—wittingly or unwittingly—we are stuck in their 3-D domain, which has locked the solar system into a solid "overlay" of the original spiritual version of our solar system.

The help we are wishing for would not be a space war, in which the Queen's armada of space warriors will invade Earth to flesh out the Overlords and their Minions; it would be the termination of the Experiment!

I believe the 3-D trap will remain for now. The fifth Homo sapiens[509] will become extinct and will possibly branch out into two new species entirely; Posthumans and *Homo Nova*, where the latter are those who refuse to be part of the Singularity and break out of the Luciferian trap, but still want to remain here on Earth and reincarnate into new bodies. Regardless of which choice people make, Homo sapiens sapiens will be extinct the day the Singularity is reached, and it's just a matter of a few decades. Most of those who are young or middle-aged today will see it happen in their current lifetime. Homo sapiens sapiens have existed since shortly after the biblical Deluge, which happened about 13,000 years ago. The lifespan of Homo sapiens sapiens as a species is therefore approximately 12,000-13,000 years.

HOW TO STAY FOCUSED IN THESE DIFFICULT TIMES

IT'S SOMETIMES HARD TO COPE with everything that is happening around us. Many people think that just because they have raised their awareness through meditation, by learning from others, and from finding answers within, we should be some kind of supermen or superwomen. That's a difficult task to put on ourselves, and by doing so, we express ourselves with guilt and fear. We feel guilty when we're not always in a good mood and can be *an example for others*, and when we are influencing others in a positive way by just being who we are, we might fear that in an instant this will change, when the circumstances change around us and we get affected by them, albeit we don't want to.

Don't be concerned or worry if you're feeling down and even depressed at times. Being more aware than the average person is difficult and can be quite lonesome, with few, if any, people to talk to about it. Friends or relatives may be oblivious and already think you're strange, so you keep your emotions to yourself. Don't feel guilty because you can't always be happy and carefree; it's normal, and it happens to all of us. When this happens, don't pretend you don't feel that way; make sure you acknowledge how you feel, e.g. "I am depressed today because I feel lonely and I don't want to be in this world." Then, if you need to, go through the

---

[509] See the WPP for how the different versions of humankind were created.

emotions, but do your best to lift yourself up again as soon as possible by being positive. Although it's hard to do when feeling down, it's a good idea to start doing something you enjoy; it could be listening to certain music, going out in nature, or doing whatever you usually enjoy. *The most difficult part is to take the step and start doing it,* but once you get going, the dark clouds in your mind will lift and disperse. Also, make sure to thoroughly ground yourself and put a mental shield all around for protection. How to do that is extensively described in my e-book, *Beyond 2012—A Handbook for the New Era* and in the WPP, the Fifth Level of Learning. Make sure you learn these simple exercises, but first learn what I wrote in the WPP in the Fifth Level of Learning.

Moreover, I strongly recommend this great breathing exercise that would be most beneficial to practice on a daily basis—because the more you do it, the more aware you become. This exercise takes you to a place between the atoms in the quantum field—in other words, it takes you to the KHAA. If you pay attention, you will notice that while you are consciously doing deep breathing, and with every breath you take, you will tap into a stillness where all thoughts and troubles are non-existent—you go into a vacuum that will release stress and negative thoughts.

A meditation of choice that works for you is also a crucial part of your healthy daily life.

HUMANITY'S THREE OPTIONS

NO ONE IS THE ULTIMATE authority on providing *soulotions* to the dire situation we are currently in, and I certainly have no monopoly on insightful answers either, but I can at least present the *soulotions* that appear logical to me based on years of extensive research and analysis. At this time, I see three obvious options, and of these three options, I see only two viable *soulotions* for our salvation (no, *soulution* is not misspelled; it's a word that I invented to signify a solution for the soul). To be more concise, I'd like to call all the three possibilities *options*, because it's not up to me to favor one over the other; people have the right to freely choose any of the three alternatives I am presenting.

The first option I will present is the one I personally perceive as the least attractive. The other two options both require higher awareness than the first option, and from there, it's just a matter of making a conscious choice.

OPTION #1: THE SINGULARITY

THIS IS THE OPTION MOST PEOPLE WILL CHOOSE because that is the way it appears when we look at the world situation as of this writing. There are many who willingly will run to the Singularity with open arms, without first thoroughly scrutinizing it. The temptation to live almost forever, to live healthy, and to live in peace will drive the masses to the slaughterhouse. Few among them will realize their mistake before it's too late because once they are hooked up to the SBC, that mistake is irreversible. Soon enough, however, these people will forget about their mistake, when AI assumes control of their major thinking processes, while letting Posthumans believe that these ideas come from themselves.

This is nothing new, as we have discussed previously. Many geniuses in different fields such as music and quantum physics have had "divine inspiration" that they think came from their own minds, when indeed the ideas were implanted into the person, either by AI or the AIF Overlords themselves. In the Singularity it's similar, but the ideas will come from the SBC, which is said to contain the entire knowledge—past and present—of humankind, instantly uploaded into any person's brain. The SBC will be equal to what the human mass consciousness will be at the time of the Singularity, with the exception that the SBC will be run by advanced nanotechnology and AI, in general. With the use of the same kind of technology, the Overlords and their AI can then distribute knowledge to everybody in quantum speed. No one needs to go to school anymore; "students" only need to download the information they need from the SBC. At first, people will be thrilled having the Internet inside their heads, which leads us to a moral question. We all know that most of the Internet contains falsehoods and/or flawed information and data. Obviously, the Overlords don't want humanity's *silly* conclusions that were contrived by huge egos who didn't care if the conclusions were right or wrong, which means that the human mass consciousness included in the SBC most certainly will be biased. My point is—who will decide what is garbage and who will decide what is valid information, worth safekeeping? Will metaphysics be included? "Conspiracy theories?" How to easily create a nuclear bomb? All about killing without being caught? In other words, who is going to decide what has to be censored, or should nothing be censored and rapists and child molesters also should be allowed in the Singularity?

These are of course important questions, but in the long term they don't even matter. Once AI is King, AI's morals and ethics are what's important; not what the individual thinks. We can rest assured that AI morals and ethics, when at all present, will be much different from basic human morals and ethics currently.

This may all sound quite negative and biased, but in all honesty, being a spiritual person, I can't see *any* benefits from becoming part of the Singularity. To many, the Singularity is a road to eternal life, but to me, it's the road to eternal death—speaking of polarity.

There is a very real chance that the SBC will not be directly supervised by the Overlords themselves, but by their AI assistants. If so, the AIF can instead attend to business elsewhere. There is no reason that they should have a guardian of mankind that is not AI; from the Overlords' perspective, it would be a waste of time.

Imagine the SBC being supervised by the Grays—that's what I think will happen.

OPTION #2: ASSISTING BY REINCARNATING

I KNOW THERE ARE MANY AWARE PEOPLE, WHO WANT to come back to Earth for another lifetime or more, once they have completed the current lifetime, in order to help humanity out and assist them in making more conscious decisions than to walk blindly into the Singularity.

Others think they are abandoning their fellow human if they refuse to incarnate here again and that it would be a rather selfish thing to do. Homo sapiens sapiens is one species, belonging to the same soul group and mass consciousness, and therefore it's *all for one and one for all*, as Alexandre Dumas wrote in *The Three Musketeers*. If most of humanity gets lost in AI, all humanity should share the same outcome; there is no escape.

This is also the opinion of James Mahu and the *WingMakers*; we are here on Earth as a human consciousness, and we are to evolve together. Those who decide to leave the ship are thought of as traitors or cowards, getting the glimpse of blue sky while their fellow man or woman suffer in the coal mines, figuratively speaking. Again, it's all for one and one for all.

When we hear statements, such as these, we need to understand where they come from. Who do you think the WingMakers are? Listen to the name; *Wing...Makers...* The makers of wings; the wing wearers... Someone who wears wings is in human consciousness considered an angel, and who are the angels of the Bible and in other Holy Scriptures? They all are the AIF, or the Anunnaki, as many choose to call them. This same force is undoubtedly behind the WingMakers material as well—there is AIF signatures all over the material, and the symbolism is definitely that of the Overlords. Anyone who knows anything about "Anunnaki symbolism" can immediately see this.

Hence, should we listen to these beings and once again be deceived, or have we woken up enough to see through wings and vagina portals hidden in their artwork?[510]

The Overlords want as many as possible to stay here on Earth even the next time around to safeguard a place in the Singularity. Now, those who are aware won't come back for the Singularity (or the *Grand Portal* as the WingMakers call it, another way of becoming One, supposedly without AI, but most possibly *with* AI, although this is not being mentioned in their material).

It's a very noble thing to want to return to Earth and help their fellow man build a new society alongside the Singularity. The only way to achieve this is to create a local universe with a local community of likeminded souls, who will raise their vibrations to a point that the AI eventually won't affect them. They will become Homo Nova.

Is this doable? Well, those who feel the urge can definitely choose this option, but I am not so sure anymore if it's possible to incarnate into a human baby body without using AIF technology, unless we know how. Do we know how to accomplish this when we roam in the astral, or do we actually need to go through the AIF recycling center in order to be born into a new baby body again?

In the afterlife, which is basically AIF domain, they beam the souls down with technology and attach them to a body of choice; it's not done

---

[510] See the WingMakers material, which is full of such symbolism (http://wingmakers.com/).

by the individual. Where do you think the so-called *silver cord* that attaches the soul/mind/spirit-body with the physical body comes from? It's put there with technology, of course, to keep a soul splinter attached to the physical body. Hence, is it possible to bypass the AIF recycling center and reincarnate in a body of choice all by our own, without assistance from technology? And if so, would that bypass the amnesia that always follow upon a new birth?

If we discuss the last question first, the answer is no. The amnesia is built into the human DNA, making it very difficult to remember our past incarnation once we enter a baby body. This means that the brave soul, who wants to return to help humanity, has to do so while being affected by the usual amnesia that affects everybody who is born on Earth. Will this person even remember what his or her mission is? Possibly, when this person notices what is going on around, he or she would vaguely remember their mission. Memories of other lifetimes might be lost, but the person's sense of ethics and the drive to help those who are heading in a positive direction will probably be strong in such an individual.

Their chances of success also depend on what happens in the recycling center before their next incarnation. Once the AIF realizes what this person wants to do in his or her next lifetime, will they accept it, or will they increase the level of amnesia before that soul is beamed down again into a new body? Unfortunately, there are many important questions left unanswered. However, that doesn't mean that a person who wants to do this shouldn't do it. I only want to include the risks so that the person can ponder them beforehand. Perhaps someone who decides to do this comes up with a solution that I haven't thought of—after all, if someone puts the intention behind something and has a passion for it, solutions often come up.

I personally believe that there are those who will choose to come back because they want to create a new species, Homo Nova, *The New Human*, the human who is conscious beyond any precious humans, with the exception of the first human beings of the Queens experiment, the Namlú'u—the Primordial Womankind.

A logical question would be whether the Overlords will allow Homo Nova to be created, or will this new species be eliminated in order to *only* let Posthumans roam the Earth? Is Homo Nova doomed already in her cradle, or will she endure and evolve in parallel with Posthumans, without having any real interaction?

As a last note on this option; does anybody really want to remain in the 3-D reality? Even if Homo Nova would be able to rise from the ashes, reproduce, and become a new, enhanced species, is this the place where Homo Nova wants to evolve?

Why would we want to remain in the Physical Universe (the 4% we perceive with our 5 senses), when we have the chance to go back to the Spiritual Universe (the 96% or the KHAA/VOID)? The Physical Universe is, after all, the domain of the Warlords—*the Physical Universe is their Empire*. This means that *everything that is physical and can be perceived with our 5 senses is our prison!* To put it bluntly—*everything made of atoms and electrons is the Physical Universe, i.e. the domain of the Overlords. The KHAA is not built of atoms and electrons!*[511] If we think in these terms, it's easy to distinguish what is what. There are no atoms involved in our thought processes, isn't that correct? Our thoughts are not of the Physical Universe (unless it's AI thinking for us).

David Icke's latest research is coming closer and closer to my own research, which is good news; particularly because he is reaching a large audience with his lectures. He is now saying that to be able to get out of the Archon's (i.e. the AIF) holographic universe, we need to exceed the speed of light. In other words, he says that beyond the speed of light is the *real* universe and the real "us."

I would agree with this, although that's only part of it. In Genesis 1, "God" says, "Let there be light," and there was light. This is En.ki, creating the Physical Universe—the Universe of Light which we can perceive with our 5 senses. The rest of the Universe lies in darkness, from our perspective, because we have the majority of our "light switches" turned off in our DNA—thanks to En.ki's genetic experiments that resulted in our 3-D bodies. Therefore, in our present condition, everything that is lit up in this Universe belongs to En.ki's 3-D Universe. By *lit up*, I mean not only everything we can see with our eyes, but also everything else we can perceive with our physical body. This includes mass sightings of UFOs, regardless of how they look like. They can be nuts-and-bolts UFOs, they can be transparent UFOs, they can be cigar-shaped,

---

[511] http://education.jlab.org/qa/atomicstructure_11.html

triangular, phase-in-and-out-of-our reality craft, or they can be strange objects out in space. These vessels either belong to the human MIC or the AIF—no exceptions. On rare occasions, people with "psychic" abilities that are more developed so that they can see beyond the realm of light, might get a glimpse of something in the KHAA, but in general, what we see and experience is of the 3-D Universe—En.ki's 4% *Universe.*

With all this in mind, I *personally* believe that *Option #3* below is our only option. However, before you make any decision at all, think about these options long and hard. *This will be the most important decision you make in this lifetime!* We only have a limited window of time to make this decision before the Grid closes again because of the Singularity, and we need to make our decision *before* we die, so we know what to do afterwards.

OPTION #3: LEAVING THE BATTLEFIELD

THERE IS A THIRD ALTERNATIVE FOR THOSE WHO have had enough of the 3-D experience. This alternative was also discussed in detail in the WPP, but it is so important that I need to repeat this information in a new way, although nothing has changed; the information is solid.

Our blue planet is surrounded by an electronic Grid. This Grid has been solid for many thousands of years, keeping souls who don't belong here outside the Grid and the human soul group inside the Grid. For a long time, the Grid has prevented us from leaving the electronic prison, which the AIF so boldly think that they own.

However, fairly recently, holes began to open up in the Grid, and after some time passed, more and more holes opened. Now the Grid looks almost like Swiss cheese.

This is the main reason why we hear of Interdimensional Entities finding their way to Earth in our current time; the Grid is breaking apart and it is doing so because some of us, by raising our consciousness and awareness, also raise our vibrations. Everything an individual does affects the rest of the soul group on a mass consciousness level, and now, enough people have begun to see through parts of the deception. Hence, the Grid has become unstable. If this were allowed to continue, the entire Grid would come down, and the illusion of solidity would disappear. The Overlords are not overly concerned, however, because they know that the

Grid will repair itself when the moment of the Singularity arrives and the goal of human consciousness will no longer be to reach for Total Spiritual Freedom. This is what I mean when I mention that we only have a small window of time to achieve Option #3, which you will realize by the time I'm done explaining it.

This is a great opportunity for souls who want to leave this Experiment. Planet Gaia/Earth is perhaps one of the most beautiful places ever created by the Queen of the Stars, but it's infested by a relentless invader force, whose Minions are destroying this once extraordinary Experiment. There is still a chance for those who want to choose *Option #2* above, but there are clearly risks involved, and a passion to dedicate themselves to a long and often tiresome journey must be present. With enough passion and dedication, that option may work—if the person wants to stay in 3-D. I also want to remind you that there is no such thing as *ascension.* Ascension is an AIF concept designed to deceive us. Even if there will be an ascension of sorts, it will still only be within the Realms of the Overlords and, therefore, it will do us no good. However, in a sense, there *is* a real ascension, but only one. *This one ascension option will lead you out of this 3-D trap and back to the KHAA. This is the only real ascension there is. Period.* Once a soul leaves the AIF trap and enters the KHAA, they're already fully ascended. The rest is just a series of exponential learning experiences.

Therefore, for those who think they have been here long enough and wish to experience something entirely different, there is a way to pass through the Grid once this lifetime is over and experience the *real* universe in the KHAA, with all its dimensions. There is an opportunity to leave Earth behind and become like the fictional character Q of the Q *Continuum* in *Star Trek.*

Those who have watched the *Star Trek* series certainly remember Q, the ET who, with his thoughts, could create entire worlds at will out of nothing and manifest them as solidly as if they were planet Earth herself. He could do it in an instance, but also undo his creations whenever he wanted. He could also suddenly manifest on the spaceship *Enterprise* faster than a nanosecond. He would appear as solid as the rest of the crew, only to disappear in thin air just as suddenly as he arrived. The Producers of *Star Trek* had inside information; they knew about many of these things.

Also, as I mentioned in the WPP, *Star Trek* was based on channeled material, called the *Council of Nine*,[512] which of course was a channel controlled by the AIF. Star Trek is another typical example of the Revelation of the Method, with truths being there in plain sight. Q was a film version of someone who is living in the KHAA, manifesting in 3-D. Q was traveling with thoughts, and he was creating objects with thoughts that appeared as solid as anything in 3-D. These creations were not made of atoms. Once Q—again with his thoughts—decided he no longer wanted his creation, he simply made it disappear by thinking it away.

This ability is something we humans share with all the star beings out there, who reside in the KHAA. We humans once had this capability when we were Namlú'u; before the Luciferian Legion came and took over, making our existence very physical and very solid. We were cut off from our birth rights as free souls and became subjected to the Overlords' rules and regulations in a universe of force, where surviving became the main objective.

As the only star beings who are capable of *both* living on a planet and exploring the Universe at the same time through nano-travel, we are very unique. We were made this way by the Queen as a totally new Experiment, and we could experience this reality with no strings attached; we were welcomed back to Orion at any time. In that sense, humankind is a royal species. Even if we now would choose to leave this Experiment once and for all, we still have the ability to live on a planet in the KHAA if we wish, and at the same time nano-travel out in the seemingly endless Universe. If we wish, we can also travel back to Orion—our cradle—and reside there. Those who read this and have understood the profound implications of this information will qualify to go back to Orion, while those who choose the Singularity won't.

While we were living in the KHAA as Namlú'u, all humans were welcome back to the Orion Empire, but as things have developed, the door is closed for many humans because of their behavior. Orion wants to remain a peaceful place, and the AIF-manipulated humans, who in their ignorance make destructive decisions, cannot be allowed to reside in Orion and will be stopped at the *gate*. On the other hand, those who don't qualify wouldn't want to go there anyway; they'd rather have a mechanical

---

[512] http://www.illuminati-news.com/council-of-nine.htm.

eternal life at the hands of the Overlords in a constructed, physical universe where everything is limited—even ET life. The only alien life that exists in En.ki's universe is under his control because the existing species have been conquered and manipulated, just as we have. His Empire consists of conquered, mind controlled species, many of them infested with AI. More or less, the only beings who are not AI are the original Fallen Angels, who rebelled together with En.ki/Lucifer a long time ago and are still with him. Those who choose the Singularity, wittingly or unwittingly, will choose to live an "eternity" in this kind of environment. I guarantee that this is not a pretty future. However, Posthumans will be ignorant about their fate, once in the Singularity, so in that sense they will not suffer.

It is my absolute conviction that each individual is his or her own savior and that it is the individual's responsibility to save him or herself. If an individual also can, by example, help by assisting someone else in the process that would be wonderful, and a bonus, but ultimately, each person is responsible for his or her choice regarding "salvation."

As we become wiser, we may want to share what we've learned, and that is absolutely advisable, but *only* if the other person is receptive. *Never force your knowledge on somebody else.* If someone reaches out and asks you questions, do your best to discuss the questions with this person, but the person needs to show that he or she is ready for the information—try not to overwhelm anybody. Be smart and tell them in increments what you have learned. This will also make the person more curious.

Another way to assist others to become aware is to bring up a few daily issues that people read in the news and discuss them. Every now and then, we can throw in a few comments or questions that will make the other person think outside the box; help them consider that there may be something bigger behind the news than what's written in the newspapers or reported on CNN. If the person is not willing to look at things from a bigger perspective, it's a good idea not to bring issues up again until that person is ready—if ever. Many prefer to live in denial within their comfort zone.

It can become extremely difficult when you realize that one or more—perhaps all—of your relatives and loved ones are resistant to learning anything of what you have to say, and instead they spend all their time on the smartphone. It's very tempting to almost force the information down their throats, but regardless of how difficult it is and how much it seems to break your heart, you might need to let it go. Everybody chooses their own path.

If you decide to leave En.ki's prison by escaping through the Grid, you need to follow a few directives in order to be successful.

Once you die and leave your body, you will experience 360° vision, but if you consider your expired body as lying below you, what you need to do is to look straight up, and you will see the Grid above you. You will also notice all the holes in it. Without hesitation, focus on going through one of the holes, and immediately you will find yourself outside the Earth's atmosphere. Depending on your degree of willingness to open your mind, you will see the Universe the way it *really* looks like. You will see that there is very little empty space; you will become aware of the entire Universe when it's fully "lit up." This will probably be shocking at first, until you get used to it, but with the information you have been given, you will understand that what you are now experiencing is the KHAA! You will also see our solar system the way it looks like from a much fuller perspective, which I'm sure is magnificent.

The next thing that will apparently happen is that you merge with your own Oversoul (the original fire/avatar/spirit-body). Everything you've experienced across the lines of time here on Earth as *this* particular soul splinter will remain in the Oversoul as *experience*, and so will you—as a *personality*. Instead of keeping your ego, the ego will transform into experiences, and you will be able to look at your personality (your mind) as external experiences. The mind is not you; it's what you experience. The real you is the Oversoul. The rest of the soul splinters, who are still on Earth, in different space and time, will be absorbed as well in the Oversoul after their current lifetime on Earth is complete. After that, you as the Oversoul will be complete. Because you, as a soul splinter, returned to the Oversoul, the rest of your splinters will automatically return once their physical body dies.

However, before all the above occurs, you—the soul splinter—has gone through the Grid and merged with your Higher Self. You are now truly interdimensional and multidimensional, and you are ready to move on. The way you travel in the Universe is to first imagine where you want to go; then you put a thought (an intention) to go there, and you will get to your destination instantaneously. These three steps should only take a second once you're skilled at it.

However, what it takes is *focus*. It's a very good idea to start meditating right now and learn how to discipline and direct your thoughts. It's time to stop thinking "sloppy thoughts." Whatever you think and whatever you say matters! Here, in this solid reality, the effects of your thoughts and words may not be instantaneous, but out there in the Universe they are instantaneous. If you're dispersed, you may end up in places you never intended to go because your thought was not focused. Focus on one thing—one destination—and go there. All of us are dispersed to some degree, but once in the KHAA, we will eventually get it, but it's much better to be prepared. It's like learning how to ride a bike—you fall a few times, but then you learn how to focus better on being balanced and off you go; you never forget how to ride a bike, once you've learned how to do it. Learn how to throw out all insignificant thoughts and focus on one thing and keep that thought there. Ultimately, via meditation, learn how to not think at all—just be there comfortably without any judgment or any particular thoughts. Just become a spectator and observe what is happening, if anything. The optimal goal is to be able to do this instantaneously in all situations, but that's most likely not necessary for a beginner to navigate the Universe. Regardless of where you end up, you can always rethink your destination and try again; this time being more focused until you can do it flawlessly. If you wish, think yourself to the Gates of Orion, and you will get there. Orion guards will guide you further.

These guidelines I just gave you might be obsolete. Because we will merge with our Oversoul, that we have been disconnected from for so long while being trapped on Earth, the Oversoul will probably know exactly how to navigate in the KHAA. However, I want to use what I've learned to cover all the bases. It's better to be over prepared than to be underprepared.

Before you get to the point where you merge with your Higher Self, there are a few important things to bring up. With the best intentions in the world to go through the Grid, once you leave your body, fear may get the best out of you. Going through the Grid is something you've never done before, and even if you accomplish it because you're determined, the "new" universe unfolding around you may scare you at first, and you may wish yourself back inside the Grid. Be strong and tell yourself that this is just a learning process, and you don't want to return. If you do this, you will soon become oriented, and the fear will eventually go away and you will feel the exhilaration of being free for the first time since the Invaders came. Some people might not feel fear at all—it depends on the individual.

Another thing to be very conscious about is not to go toward the tunnel of light that people who have had *Near Death Experiences* (NDEs) or *Out of Body Experiences* (OBEs) are discussing. That tunnel leads right into the AIF's recycling center. Also, there will possibly be *Guides* or *relatives* who wish to greet you when you've left your body. They may also want to guide you and tell you to follow them. These beings are either deceived themselves and believe that they are doing the right thing, or they are just projections of your relatives and are not the real souls, although the deception can be quite convincing. Either way, you need to be strong and not talk to them because if you do, it's very easy to be manipulated, and once there is even a slight thought in your mind that you should follow them, they will most possibly have you gravitate toward the tunnel or any other portal into the AIF's recycling center, as described in WPP, the *First Level of Learning*. Instead, you must ignore anyone who says they want to help you or guide you and just concentrate on passing through a hole in the Grid, leaving the Guides behind. Why ask for help when you can do things yourself? People who die ignorant are not in bliss. They are confused in the astral, and they don't know where to go or what to do. Hence, they cling to any kind of help they can get and are likely to follow the first deceptive being that shows up. Fortunately, this is no longer the case for us because we now know better. I repeat, *we do not need any assistance to go through the Grid. If someone offers to help you to do it that being is most likely deceptive. Ignore that being and just continue on your own as a sovereign soul, more determined than ever to liberate yourself!*

This can be a difficult thing to do, however, because you leave your loved ones behind in the astral without being able to communicate with them. Remember when the time comes that if these beings really are your true relatives and not just projections, they will see what you're doing, and one day they will, hopefully, realize that there is a way out and follow you. That's the best you can hope for. Under current conditions, these relatives (or friends) will most likely not follow you through the Grid.

There is always the option to send them a thought, saying that you need to continue on your own path, but that you love them and will always keep them in mind.

The astral plane is the real challenge, and there is a chance that you will be tested in the astral. The AIF might try to seduce you into following them by having a fake relative start crying when they see you just to play on your emotions. *Do not pay attention to it, regardless of how difficult it might be—it's a trap!*

Once you are free and get comfortable in the KHAA, you can begin to create your own realities and/or join communities already created by others, and you can become a co-creator in such multidimensional environment. The possibilities are endless, and the only limitation is your imagination, and your imagination will increase as you go along. For the first time in eons, you will experience full freedom. In addition, different star systems and constellations have their own *universities*, where a soul can learn new things. Regardless of how much we know after having spent a long time in the KHAA, there is more to learn, and classes are apparently available for souls, similar to the libraries that people in regression therapy mention are available in the afterlife. However, these libraries, as opposed to those in the KHAA, only teach you what is available in the 4% Universe, which includes the astral plane and some other dimensions.

Some people have asked me if we can't just commit suicide and get it over and be done with it, so we can join the universal community right away. Committing suicide is usually not a good idea. We have friends and relatives who love us that would be devastated if we decided to take our lives. Most of us have people that are near and dear to us who would not understand if we were to commit suicide. They would be emotionally traumatized and would long to see us again, which makes it harder for us to truly move forward and be free. I, for one, would not want to create that effect. It's better to live our lives and then go for it, if Option #3 is what you wish to choose.

IN CONCLUSION

THERE MAY BE READERS of this book, who have never examined the *Wes Penre Papers—the Multiverse Series*. For those readers, the ET part of the AI and the Singularity Agenda I have presented here may be difficult to grasp and even hard to believe. If so, what I recommend is that they read the WPP to gain greater understanding of the bigger picture because the level of ET involvement in this entire movement is imperative. Without that information, we can never fully grasp the AI agenda and the acceleration of technology over the last 50 plus years.

The Singularity is definitely on the Overlords' top list when it comes to Earth's destiny, and En.ki is supposed to be in charge of this entire project once it is in place. I write "supposed" because nothing is set in stone at this point. Civil wars, wars in general, and disputes are currently very common in the Luciferian Empire, and the outcome of these conflicts is still uncertain. Who will rule the New World Order and the One World Government—En.ki or Marduk, or someone else entirely? Probably, they don't even know themselves yet. For humanity, it is of little consequence who will take over—the outcome will be quite the same.

However, with many of their colonies in mutiny, as well as violent conflicts going on with the Warlords' own lines, En.ki and Marduk have their hands full. Their Empire will not last forever, and they know it! This is one reason why they are in such hurry to usher in the Singularity here on Earth. If they will succeed with this (and I don't see why not), we can probably expect an invasion of loyal Orion forces not too long after that. In case the Luciferian Empire hasn't fallen by then, it will fall when the War on Orion begins. That will be the end of both the AIF and Posthumans. It doesn't matter how much they prepare; I have a very difficult time believing that they will manage to take Heaven by force. Orion has a very strong defense system and impeccable military intelligence.

According to Biblical Prophecy, the Battle of Armageddon, will separate the good humans from the bad, and it will be fought between "God" and the human governments. Some say it will be fought in the Middle East, but this battle—or war, rather—will be fought all over the world. The following is from *Jeremiah 25:32-34,*

[32] This is what Jehovah of armies says: 'Look! A calamity is spreading from nation to nation, And a great tempest will be unleashed from the remotest parts of the earth.

[33] "'And those slain by Jehovah in that day will be from one end of the earth clear to the other end of the earth. They will not be mourned, nor will they be gathered up or buried. They will become like manure on the surface of the ground.'

[34] Wail, you shepherds, and cry out! Wallow about, you majestic ones of the flock, Because the time of your slaughter and your dispersion has come, And you will fall like a precious vessel!

followed by *Ezekiel 30:17-20,*

[17] "As for you, son of man, this is what the Sovereign Lord Jehovah says: 'Say to every sort of bird and to all the wild beasts of the field, "Gather yourselves together and come. Gather all around my sacrifice that I am preparing for you, a great sacrifice on the mountains of Israel. You will eat flesh and drink blood.

[18] You will eat the flesh of mighty ones and drink the blood of the chieftains of the earth—the rams, lambs, goats, and bulls—all the fattened animals of Ba'shan.

[19] You will gorge yourselves on fat and drink blood until you are drunk from the sacrifice that I prepare for you.'"

[20] "'At my table you will be filled up with horses and charioteers, mighty ones and all sorts of warriors,' declares the Sovereign Lord Jehovah.

Here we have the usual sacrifices, slaughter, and blood drinking that the gods love so much and superimpose on humans. Aren't they lovely gods? I wonder if those who welcome En.ki will drink blood, too, until they are deliriously drunk, in order to Hail the Lord.

According to the Bible, the Battle will concentrate around the area of Mt. Megiddo (thus, Armageddon), an area in ancient Israel, but that mountain does not exist anymore—if it ever did. It sometimes makes me wonder if the Battle (or War) of Armageddon will not take place on Earth but in Orion. "God" (it should actually read *the Goddess*) and Her forces will defend Orion against Lucifer's Legion, of which Posthumans will be the major foot soldiers. The Luciferian Empire will be defeated and Posthumans will be utterly destroyed. Left are the "pure," which are the Goddess' people, who did not participate in the Battle. Those worthy of returning to Orion will be those who resisted the Singularity; they will live immortal lives in *Heaven the Orion Empire*. This is the Heaven we have waited for—not En.ki's fake heaven, which is the astral planes, which are still actually part of his 3-D trap.

I think this illustrates pretty well what might happen. This means that 3-D will soon dissolve and once again be freed to exist as a multidimensional part of the KHAA.

When will this happen? There is no time frame mentioned anywhere in the ancient texts to my knowledge, but if we take into account the Warlords' anxiety about putting the Singularity in place as soon as possible, I wouldn't be surprised if the attack on Orion will happen within a hundred years.

Hence, our options are few, and our time is narrow. I have given references to my e-book, *Beyond 2012—A Handbook for the New Era*, and the WPP. The former is filled with spiritual exercises in order to prepare for what is to come once we move on from this reality. There are of course other great meditations and exercises out there for the reader to explore. It's extremely important that we learn how to be able to focus our thoughts now so that we more easily can nano-travel once we leave the Grid and the solar system behind, if that's what the reader decides to do, and if that's what we need to do (not taking into consideration the skills of the Oversoul—see above). Even those who prefer to return to create a new world for the more consciously aware, it's essential to learn these skills, as it requires deep concentration to achieve such a goal.

I hope this book has given all who read it some new insights into the AI movement, the Singularity, who is behind it all, and how to survive such an agenda. Whatever your soulution may be—and it can, of course, be something entirely different from what I've suggested—I wish you the absolute best and an eternal life *without* being dependent upon technology. It's important to realize that whatever "miracles" you may encounter that have to do with technology, you can do it better just by using your thoughts and your imagination.

SOME FINAL WORDS

THE PROBLEM IS NOT WHETHER we should believe that the Singularity Agenda is real or not—there is more evidence and proof that it is real than I have been able to collect in this relatively thick book. The problem is what to do about it.

I hope that this book has convinced the reader that there is no use in trying to fight these forces from the heavens to make them stop. They possess weaponry and intelligence that we can't even conceive of, so a war against them is futile. We need to simply disagree with their agenda, and in my opinion, leave the Overlords' artificial physical universe altogether. I see no reason for us to stay in prison when we can become free spirits again by going back to the free realms of Creation in which we belong.

However, it is not my intention to impose this idea on anyone; if you follow this advice, you do so of your own free will and not because "I say so." There is always an option to stay in 3-D and make an attempt to create a new species, Homo Nova, and slightly elevate yourself. You even have the option to choose the Singularity. I am not the judge of what anybody is choosing to do—we are all on a personal journey, and we all do what we think is best for ourselves. My intention with this book is to inform the reader and to give them additional information that can't be found anywhere else, except in the WPP. This additional information is imperative to help us comprehend the bigger picture.

By no means do I claim to have all the answers, and neither do I claim that everything written in this book is set in stone; it's simply the conclusions I have drawn during my last six years of research and analysis of the ET and AI problems facing mankind.

Furthermore, I am personally *never* putting all of my eggs in one basket. I read, I listen, and I watch in order to learn, and I do so from many different sources. From each source, I take what resonates and disregard the rest (which doesn't mean that I might not come back later and look at it again from a new, fresh perspective). I would encourage the reader of this book to do the same thing; evaluate and re-evaluate everything. Even if you choose to embrace everything presented here, don't let it become the end of your journey. It doesn't matter how much it rings true, there is *always* a bigger picture, and there is *always* much more to learn. A hundred years from now (if we are still here then), the knowledge we think we have gained now will be superseded many times over. We only have 5-10% of our capacity activated, so how can we possibly "know it all?"

In closing, I hope this book has been of some assistance when it comes to understanding the basics of the AI Movement and the Singularity Agenda. I sincerely hope that the information provided herein has been helpful enough for the reader to make a well-informed decision about his or her very near future; and whatever that decision is they will have thought it through very thoroughly. This is the most important decision any of us will ever make as third dimensional biological humans here on Earth.

I wish all my readers Good Luck in their Divine Journey! We are standing at the crossroads at this very moment, and the road we choose will determine our future—perhaps for *eternity*!

𝔅𝔦𝔟𝔩𝔦𝔬𝔤𝔯𝔞𝔭𝔥𝔶

Here are some resources that were not being used in the book:

Have scientists discovered the elixir of youth? Hormone 'extends lifespan by 40%, protecting the immune system against the ravages of age': http://www.dailymail.co.uk/health/article-3400205/Have-scientists-discovered-elixir-youth-Hormone-extends-lifespan-40-protecting-immune-against-ravages-age.html#ixzz3xOetfaNW

(Video): TransHumanism Part 2 The Digital Messiah/ What the ELITE want! https://www.youtube.com/watch?v=pBTCYD2Waxo

Will YOU live forever? Presidential candidate claims technology to transform us into immortal cyborgs is within reach: http://www.dailymail.co.uk/sciencetech/article-3379397/Will-live-forever-Presidential-candidate-claims-technology-transform-immortal-cyborgs-reach.html

YEAR IN REVIEW:The Year We Decided to Live Forever. In 2015, tech billionaires pursued anti-aging and cheating death like never before. http://www.thedailybeast.com/articles/2015/12/04/the-year-we-decided-to-live-forever.html

(Video): The CCCP father of rocketry said that it's man's destiny to dominate the cosmos: https://www.youtube.com/watch?v=pBTCYD2Waxo

Echitis: Smartphone Use Causing Widespread Health Problems « CBS Pittsburgh: http://pittsburgh.cbslocal.com/2016/05/19/techitis-

Bibliography

constantly-using-smartphones-causing-widespread-health-problems/

The Microwave Drug - The Biological and Spiritual Effects of
Electromagnetic Radiation:
http://www.bibliotecapleyades.net/scalar_tech/esp_scalartech_cellphones
microwave68.htm

How will We Live in the Year 2065? - Cities, Cyborgs and Social Science:
http://www.bibliotecapleyades.net/ciencia2/ciencia_artificialhumans83.ht
m

How Facebook plans to take over the world | Technology | The Guardian:
https://www.theguardian.com/technology/2016/apr/23/facebook-global-
takeover-f8-conference-messenger-chatbots

Computers have revolutionised the way chess is played – and the best
chess programs are impossible to beat. But could a player that's part
human and part computer be even more powerful?
http://www.bbc.com/future/story/20151201-the-cyborg-chess-players-
that-cant-be-beaten

Hawking: Humans at risk of lethal 'own goal':
http://www.bbc.com/news/science-environment-35344664

OpenAI: Elon Musk and other tech giants pledge $1 billion to stop
humanity being taken over by evil robots
Robots will learn how to be good by poring through Reddit and other data,
makers say: http://www.independent.co.uk/life-style/gadgets-and-
tech/news/openai-elon-musk-and-other-tech-giants-pledge-1-billion-to-
stop-humanity-being-taken-over-by-evil-a6772591.html

(Video):   Elon Musk compares AI efforts to "Summoning the Demon":
https://m.youtube.com/watch?v=JfJjx12wkVQ

We should be more afraid of computers than we are – video | Opinion |
The Guardian:

Synthetic Super Intelligence and the Transmutation of Humankind

http://www.theguardian.com/commentisfree/video/2016/mar/16/artificial-intelligence-we-should-be-more-afraid-of-computers-than-we-are-video

DARPA now Creating Manufacturing Platform for Synthetic Living Organisms as Government Weaponizes the Seeds of Life:
http://www.bibliotecapleyades.net/sociopolitica/sociopol_DARPA21.htm

Wi-Fried?
http://www.bibliotecapleyades.net/scalar_tech/esp_scalartech_cellphones microwave67.htm

A Global Arms Race to Create a Superintelligent AI is Looming | Motherboard:
http://motherboard.vice.com/read/a-global-arms-race-to-create-a-superintelligent-ai-is-looming?trk_source=popula

US military aims to create cyborgs by connecting humans to computers | Technology | The Guardian:
http://www.theguardian.com/technology/2016/jan/20/us-military-cyborg-connecting-humans-computers

Fears robots will take over world by becoming lawyers, architects and doctors - Mirror Online: http://www.mirror.co.uk/news/weird-news/fears-robots-take-over-world-8011954

The end of humans working in service industry? Theme park to open 'robot kingdom' where 200 androids make cocktails and food - Mirror Online: http://www.mirror.co.uk/news/world-news/theme-park-opens-robot-kingdom-7834770

China Is Building a Robot Army of Model Workers:
https://www.technologyreview.com/s/601215/china-is-building-a-robot-army-of-model-workers/#/set/id/601326/

Bibliography

Education of the Future? Scientists Figure Out How to UPLOAD Knowledge to the Brain:
http://www.bibliotecapleyades.net/ciencia/ciencia_brain79.htm

The Gene Hackers--A powerful new technology enables us to manipulate our DNA more easily than ever before:
http://www.newyorker.com/magazine/2015/11/16/the-gene-hackers

How Close Are We to a Fully 'Bionic Body'? Prosthetic hands that can feel. Robotic penises that can fully function. Welcome to the age of the bionic body: http://www.thedailybeast.com/articles/2015/09/19/how-close-are-we-to-a-fully-bionic-body.html

Cyborgs in Washington, DC:
https://archive.org/details/ANDROIDS_201511

[Science of the gods] Scientists store data inside DNA that could last MILLIONS of years: http://www.dailymail.co.uk/sciencetech/article-2955663/Death-hard-drive-Scientists-store-data-inside-DNA-MILLIONS-years.html

Single DNA molecule could store information for a million years following scientific breakthrough. Everything from ancient texts to Wikipedia changes could be archived:
http://www.independent.co.uk/news/science/single-dna-molecule-could-store-information-for-a-million-years-following-scientific-breakthrough-10459560.html

Powerful DNA 'Editing' Has Arrived, Are We Ready for It?
http://m.livescience.com/51776-powerful-dna-editing-has-arrived-are-we-ready-for-it.html

Welcome to the Unpredictable Era of Editing Human Embryos:
http://nautil.us/blog/welcome-to-the-unpredictable-era-of-editing-human-embryos

[DARPA] After Terminator Arm, DARPA Wants Implantable Hard Drive for the Brain: http://www.military.com/daily-news/2015/03/19/after-terminator-arm-darpa-wants-implantable-hard-drive.html

[Atlantis Revisited] In Search For Cures, Scientists Create Embryos That Are Both Animal And Human : Shots - Health News : NPR: http://www.npr.org/sections/health-shots/2016/05/18/478212837/in-search-for-cures-scientists-create-embryos-that-are-both-animal-and-human

KEY TO ETERNAL LIFE? Someone already born will 'live to 1,000 and immortality IS possible' | Science | News | Daily Express: http://www.express.co.uk/news/science/665807/KEY-TO-ETERNAL-LIFE-Someone-already-born-will-live-to-1-000-and-immortality-IS-possible

Federal Researchers Build Massive Online Database of Genomic Data - Nextgov.com: http://m.nextgov.com/cio-briefing/2016/04/genomics-portal-would-let-scientists-analyze-individuals-samples/127545/

The Future of Humans - Becoming The Anunnaki's Biological Robots: http://www.bibliotecapleyades.net/sumer_anunnaki/anunnaki/anu_46.htm

Forever Exists! Secrets to Immortality Uncovered - Australia Network News: http://www.australianetworknews.com/forever-exists-secrets-immortality-uncovered/

MIT researchers create 3D-printed robots that 'practically walk out of' printer — RT USA: https://www.rt.com/usa/338719-mit-3d-print-robot/

Bibliography

How to 3-D Scan Your Family - WSJ:
http://www.wsj.com/articles/how-to-3-d-scan-your-family-1458153767

3D Bioprinting System to 'Grow' Body Parts, Muscles / Sputnik International:
http://m.sputniknews.com/us/20160216/1034833598/bioprinting-bones-tissue-growth.html

Media mogul Dmitry Itskov plans to live forever by uploading his personality to a robot:
http://www.telegraph.co.uk/business/2016/03/13/media-mogul-dmitry-itskov-plans-to-live-forever-by-uploading-his/

DARPA Wants to Make a Computer Program that Evolves for 100 Years | Motherboard:
http://motherboard.vice.com/read/darpa-wants-to-make-a-computer-program-that-evolves-for-100-years

Companies Want to Replicate Your Dead Loved Ones With Robot Clones | Motherboard:
http://motherboard.vice.com/en_uk/read/companies-want-to-replicate-your-dead-loved-ones-with-robot-clones

Next up for robots: Synthetic muscle:
http://theweek.com/articles/619669/next-robots-synthetic-muscle

Robots with human vision on the horizon after scientists crack brain's 'Enigma code' - Mirror Online:
http://www.mirror.co.uk/news/uk-news/robots-human-vision-horizon-after-7812293

Computers in your clothes? A milestone for wearable electronics | News Room - The Ohio State University:
https://news.osu.edu/news/2016/04/13/computers-in-your-clothes-a-milestone-for-wearable-electronics/

Electronic Blood | NeuroLogica Blog:
http://theness.com/neurologicablog/index.php/electronic-blood/

If You Don't Know what DARPA is, You should Probably Read This:
http://www.bibliotecapleyades.net/sociopolitica/sociopol_DARPA25.htm

The Definitive Guide to Terraforming:
http://www.bibliotecapleyades.net/universo/terraforming/terraforming2
2.htm

Mind-reaching machine could soon turn your secret thoughts into speech |
Daily Mail Online: http://www.dailymail.co.uk/sciencetech/article-
3613443/The-device-eavesdrops-voices-head-Mind-reaching-machine-
soon-turn-secret-thoughts-speech.html

We're Teaching Drones How to Overthrow Humanity. - The Daily
Beast: http://www.thedailybeast.com/articles/2016/04/24/we-re-
teaching-drones-how-to-overthrow-humanity.html

New Technique Allows Scientists to Read Minds at Nearly the Speed of
Thought: http://gizmodo.com/new-technique-allows-scientists-to-read-
minds-at-nearly-1755927863

Autonomous Weaponized Robots: Not Just Science Fiction. Robotics
expert Noel Sharkey describes a confluence of developing technologies
that could endanger our lives and our rights:
http://www.wsj.com/articles/autonomous-weaponized-robots-not-just-
science-fiction-1449763884

Navy to Accelerate Artificial Intelligence Development for Warfighting,
Support Roles: http://news.usni.org/2015/06/15/navy-to-accelerate-
artificial-intelligence-development-for-warfighting-support-roles

Army to enlist robots to pull Soldiers off battlefield:
http://www.army.mil/article/155958/Army_to_enlist_robots_to_pull_Soldi
ers_off_battlefield/

Bibliography

Marines test Google's latest military robot. Spot is electrically operated and walks on four hydraulically actuated legs:
http://www.pcworld.com/article/2985173/marines-test-googles-latest-military-robot.html

LIFE IN SPACE: Scientists develop embryo among stars in planet colonisation breakthrough:
http://www.express.co.uk/news/science/662126/LIFE-IN-SPACE-Scientists-develop-embryo-among-stars-in-planet-colonisation-breakthrough

DARPA Receives Funding For Next Phase To Weaponize Space:
http://www.activistpost.com/2016/04/darpa-funding-weaponization-of-space.html

DARPA Unveils Plans For World's First Flotilla of Killer Robot Warships Within 5 Years - "Sea Hunter:"
http://www.activistpost.com/2016/04/darpa-unveils-plans-for-worlds-first-flotilla-of-killer-robot-warships-within-5-years-sea-hunter.html

Astro droid? Russians build human-like super-robot for remote-controlled spacewalks — RT News: https://www.rt.com/news/332587-russian-human-like-robot-spacewalks/

Rogue 'Terminators' which can kill without human orders 'will be in use within years' | Daily Mail Online:
http://www.dailymail.co.uk/news/article-3446483/Rogue-Terminators-kill-without-human-orders-use-years-unless-global-ban.html

UN Grand Plan for mankind:
http://www.wakingtimes.com/2016/03/17/un-seeking-full-spectrum-biometric-dominance-of-the-human-race/

Lucifer as the Sleeping Beauty and the Hollow Hills of Faery:
http://www.bibliotecapleyades.net/cienciareal/esp_chaman_35.htm

One World Religion - Pope Francis says All Major Religions are "Meeting 'God' in Different Ways:"
http://www.bibliotecapleyades.net/sociopolitica/sociopol_globalreligiono7.htm

Scientists develop mini Death Star to protect us from asteroids – Telegraph:
http://www.telegraph.co.uk/news/science/space/12182894/Scientists-develop-mini-Death-Star-to-protect-us-from-asteroids.html

Ungrounded Energy - A Widespread Issue:
http://www.bibliotecapleyades.net/salud/salud_energyhealth24.htm

Just looking at nature can help your brain work better, study finds:
https://www.washingtonpost.com/news/energy-environment/wp/2015/05/26/viewing-nature-can-help-your-brain-work-better-study-finds/

Listening To Classical Music Enhances Gene Activity: An Update On The Mozart Effect: http://www.medicaldaily.com/listening-classical-music-enhances-gene-activity-update-mozart-effect-325680

* * *